Financial Planning For High Net Worth Individuals

BEARDBOOKS

Financial Planning For High Net Worth Individuals

Richard H. Mayer & Donald R. Levy

EXECUTIVE SERIES

2004 Edition

ISBN: 1-58798-232-3

To my wonderful wife, Virginia—Dick

To my wonderful wife, May—Don

Foreword

I know Richard Mayer, and he is a dynamic expert on planning for the affluent. I am happy to see that he is joining the group of authors who contribute to the knowledge of cutting-edge techniques in this area. The group that he has assembled, with the assistance of attorney Donald R. Levy, is testimony to his objective to provide a balanced treatment of these ideas without blanket endorsement of any single approach. In general, this book should be an effective answer to the pessimist. Subsequent editions of this book are expected to continue to bring the latest techniques and opportunities to the reader's attention.

Lawrence Kudlow

Preface

In these uncertain economic times, today's high net worth investors are looking for new ways to preserve and enhance their wealth and are willing to spend top dollar for the best ideas. The trouble is that uncovering those ideas—and weighing their merits—takes time and resources. Access to expert advisers with insights to share is limited, at best. *Planning for the Affluent* provides that access. This book is a comprehensive, authoritative guide to the art and science of wealth management written from the real-world perspectives of many of the most respected practitioners in the field.

Whether a certified public accountant, estate planning attorney, money manager, financial planning professional, or bank trust officer, the reader will find exclusive, highly useful insights and portfolio diversification tools that will help distinguish his or her services from those of other advisers. The vast majority of the ideas presented in this book are original, proven methods not replicated in any other single source, and they are ready to be implemented right away.

Planning for the Affluent is not intended to be a page-turner; it is a source book that wealth management advisers can turn to when looking for in-depth answers. This book endeavors to make a complex subject more understandable without oversimplification. Each chapter is a thoughtful and thorough treatise on an important concept. The reader looking for a new approach will find it first by reviewing the basics that the chapter authors have set forth. The reader looking for an informed opinion and/or who needs to rethink an idea will find that the table of contents and index point to the areas where issues can be, and often are, restudied. As a further aid to the reader, the chapters are grouped into three parts:

1. General Principles;
2. Major Applications; and
3. Special Techniques.

A reader interested in life insurance approaches, for example, may want to begin with General Principles, to review and consider the new Nobel Prize-winning behavioral economics theory that helps diminish downside risk and reduce fiduciary liability. The reader may then continue to Major Applications, which includes, among others, chapters on the creation of a new insurance company as an investment and the art of hedge fund investing. Special Techniques will introduce the art of private annuities and the use of education plans.

Throughout, *Planning for the Affluent* emphasizes issues of interest to multimillionaire investors and their advisers. It will also interest investors who are on the fast track and can thus hope and even expect to achieve greater wealth; this book will help them to maximize their financial planning opportunities.

In general, *Planning for the Affluent* is an effective answer to the pessimist. It is both optimistic and realistic. The world offers many great opportunities that should not be lost sight of in spite of short-run difficulties and obstacles that sometimes interrupt a solid, long-term plan. This book is full of new ideas and the latest techniques for applying long-standing methods. This book will assist advisers in developing new approaches and better techniques to benefit their clients. In doing so, advisers will benefit themselves by differentiating their services and capturing the attention of gatekeepers. Innovative strategies and proven methods will open doors and each idea or technique will pay for itself many times over.

Planning for the Affluent is a desktop reference book for every serious wealth management adviser. Subsequent editions are expected to continue to bring the latest techniques to the reader's attention.

Richard H. Mayer

Donald R. Levy

About the Authors

Richard H. Mayer, CLU, Registered Investment Advisor, is chairman and chief executive officer of Executive Compensation Systems, Inc. and Divitiae LLC of Savannah, Georgia and Old Greenwich, Connecticut. He has more than 40 years of experience in the insurance industry, much of which has been devoted to executive compensation planning in corporate markets. He is recognized as a pioneer in the implementation of variable insurance products and the use of employer and employee grantor trusts and funding arrangements for employer sponsored pension programs. He has designed and implemented executive compensation plans for numerous Fortune 500 companies and has been a member of a number of professional trade associations including the AALU, Million Dollar Round Table, the International Forum, and Top of the Table.

Donald R. Levy, JD, MBA, is an attorney and benefits consultant. A graduate of Harvard College and Harvard Law School, he received an MBA in accounting from New York University. Mr. Levy has more than 40 years of experience as a pension administrator and tax planner. He practiced law with Wall Street firms and served as Vice President and Employee Benefit Consultant to Johnson & Higgins, as Vice President-Human Resources and Director of Employee Benefits at United States Tobacco Company (now UST, Inc.), as Senior Consultant at William M. Mercer, Inc., and as Senior Technical Consultant at Prentice Hall where he authored the *Pension Handbook*. Mr. Levy is co-author of the *IRA Answer Book*, *Quick Reference to IRAs* and *State-by-State Guide to Managed Care Law*, and is co-editor of the *403(b) Answer Book*, published by Aspen Publishers. He has taught at the University of Connecticut, has served as panelist for the Practicing Law Institute, and has lectured before various professional groups.

David D. Avasthi is a consultant for U.S. and European corporations and insurers in traditional as well as cutting-edge product design and risk management. His insurance career has spanned over two decades in various senior management positions with insurance companies including AIG, CIGNA, and more recently with Munich Re/American Re where he was Group Vice President for Innovative Business Solutions and Strategic Applications in Princeton, New Jersey and Munich, Germany. Mr. Avasthi has also had experience as a risk management consultant for corporations and insurance companies as an employee and resource for insurance brokers including Aon in New York and MBD Reinsurance Brokers in Brussels, Belgium. He was also the founder and chief executive officer of a successful managing general agent, which finally became part of the international credit insurer, COFACE, Paris. Mr. Avasthi holds an MBA from the Bernard M. Baruch Graduate School of Business.

Thomas J. Boczar, Esq., CFA, is the Director of Marketing/Financial Institutions for Twenty-First Securities Corporation, where he markets and assists in structuring innovative arbitrage, risk management, and hedged investment strategies to professional investors. His clients include a number of prominent banks, trust companies, investment advisers, brokerage firms, family offices, accounting firms, and other financial institutions. Mr. Boczar began his career as a tax accountant with Touche Ross. Later, he was a lawyer specializing in corporate finance and M&A with Mudge Ross Guthrie Alexander and Ferdon and at Cahill Gordon & Reindel. Mr. Boczar has authored numerous articles on stock concentration risk management and other applications of financial derivatives and has been a featured speaker at numerous conferences. He has also taught courses on tax planning for investors using equity derivatives and other financial instruments. Mr. Boczar holds a JD, an MBA, a Masters in Professional Accounting and a BS in Finance, and has completed post-graduate coursework in Financial Engineering. Mr. Boczar is currently pursuing an LL.M. in Taxation from New York University School of Law. He is admitted to the bar in both New York and Connecticut. Mr. Boczar is also a Chartered Financial Analyst and is a member of the Education Task Force of the Private Wealth Management Committee of the New York Society of Security Analysts.

Michael Burns is a Partner and Deputy Team Leader of the Insurance Team within Appleby Spurling & Kempe's corporate/commercial department. Mr. Burns practices in the area of insurance, specializing in all aspects of insurance with an emphasis on rent-a-captives, life and annuity products, segregated accounts products, securitisation and risk and capital markets transformation structures, and associated insurance structures and products. He is also the Team Leader of the Segregated Accounts Products and Financial Structures Inter-disciplinary Practice Team and is responsible for all aspects of the development, promotion, and delivery of segregated accounts products to the firm's clients. Mr. Burns joined Appleby Spurling & Kempe as an Associate in June 1992. He became a Partner in April 1998.

Prior to his tenure with the firm he worked for eight years in Canada, where he gained significant experience in the banking industry, as a law clerk to the Justices of the Federal Court of Canada, and as a lawyer with the leading Canadian law firm of McCarthy Tétrault. Mr. Burns holds a BA from Mount Alison University, Canada, an LL.B. and an MBA from Dalhousie University, Canada, and a Master of Law from the University of Cambridge, England. He has been a Fellow of the Institute of Canadian Bankers since 1982 and a member of the Bermuda Bar since January 1993. Mr. Burns is a member of the International Bar Association, the Law Society of Upper Canada and the Law Society of England and Wales. He has been a speaker at various international venues including the IBC Life & Annuities Forum, the International Captives Congress, and the World Captive Forum. Mr. Burns has written various articles on topics such as life and annuity products, rent-a-captives, segregated cells, and the role of Bermuda in the offshore world and is a periodic contributor to various publications including *Global Reinsurance* magazine, *Offshore Investment*, *Bermuda Insurance Update*, and *Derivatives Report*.

Craig R. Campbell is a principal of Tribeca Strategic Advisors, LLC, a tax and business planning firm for high net worth individuals; a principal of Tribeca Capital Management, LLC, a Registered Investment Advisor (RIA) based in Phoenix, Arizona; and a shareholder of Huish Campbell, P.C., a Phoenix, Arizona law firm practicing in the areas of tax law, business law, and estate planning. Mr. Campbell has conducted seminars for various legal, accounting, investment, and insurance professionals in the Phoenix area. Mr. Campbell graduated *magna cum laude* from Arizona State University with a BS in accountancy and was awarded the Arthur Andersen Outstanding Junior Award. He received numerous awards for accounting and business students. Mr. Campbell graduated from the College of Law at Arizona State University.

Christopher Carosa, CTFA, MBA, is President of Carosa, Stanton & DePaolo Asset Management, LLC, an SEC-registered investment adviser specializing in providing exclusive private investment counsel to individual trustees and fiduciaries who desire highly personalized portfolio management and who choose to emphasize a conservative long-term investment philosophy. The firm is a leader in using techniques derived from the new Nobel Prize-winning behavioral economics theory to help diminish downside risk and reduce fiduciary liability. Mr. Carosa also serves as President and Chairman of the Board of the Bullfinch Family of No-Load Mutual Funds, which includes the Western New York Series—the only mutual fund that invests primarily in companies with a significant economic presence in western New York (see www.bullfinchfund.com). Mr. Carosa is a Certified Trust and Financial Analyst. He received his undergraduate degree in Physics and Astronomy from Yale University and his MBA from the Simon School. A former host of The Western New York Investment Report on WWKB-AM, he is a respected speaker and has written numerous pieces pertaining to investing, including the book *Due Diligence: The Individual Trustee's Guide to Selecting and Monitoring a Professional Investment Adviser* (see www.carosastantonanddepaolo.com for details). Mr. Carosa has prepared articles based on his extensive and unique research in the area of behavioral economics and is currently researching a book tentatively titled *A Road Mistaken: How to Profit by Avoiding the Seven Deadly Sins of Professional Money Managers*. He is the President of the Upstate New York Chapter of the Financial Planning Association.

Robert N. Gordon is President of Twenty-First Securities Corporation, which he founded in 1983. Before founding Twenty-First Securities, Mr. Gordon was the partner in charge of risk and tax arbitrage at Oppenheimer & Company. Prior to that, he worked at Laidlaw, Adams & Peck, where he became a regional manager and senior vice president. He has been in the brokerage business since 1976. Since 1991, Mr. Gordon has served as an adjunct professor at the New York University Graduate School of Business, teaching a course on applications of arbitrage theories. He has been involved with the Securities Industry Institute at the Wharton School since 1979, starting as a student, becoming a lecturer in 1983, and serving as chairman in 1994 and 1995. Mr. Gordon is also active in the Securities Industry Association, having served as an SIA director, as treasurer, as chairman of the Tax Policy Committee, and chairman of the New York District. He is a member of the Wall Street Tax Association. He is also on the boards of the Securities Industry Foundation for Economic Education and the Adler Planetarium in Chicago. Mr. Gordon is the co-author of *Wall Street Secrets for Tax-Efficient Investing*, which he wrote with Jan Rosen. He has also written several articles on arbitrage and hedging strategies, including a monthly column for *On Wall Street* magazine. He serves on the editorial advisory boards of *Derivatives Report, The Journal of Taxation and Investments,* and *The Journal of Wealth Management.* In addition, Mr. Gordon is a frequent lecturer, with engagements that include numerous for-profit seminars groups as well as annual speeches on derivatives at the SEC's International Institute for Securities Market Development and regularly lectures on the taxation of derivatives for the International Association of Financial Engineers.

Jay A. Harvey, CLU, ChFC, AEP, was Executive Vice President of Advisors Resource Group, Inc., in charge of all phases of private placement variable universal life insurance and high net worth financed insurance premiums. Mr. Harvey worked jointly with Mark. P. Silverfarb, CEO of Advisors Resource Group, in training its national sales representative and outside related professionals in advanced uses of investment grade and death benefit oriented life insurance products; he advised national law firms, accounting firms, trust departments, and money managers on the use, design, and implementation of these products. In 2002, Mr. Harvey advised three major insurers on the redesign of their private placement products for both onshore and offshore versions and conducted seminars for the estate and tax partners of major law firms all over the country. Mr. Harvey was a frequent speaker and lecturer, having given several hundred lectures and seminars throughout his career. He received his BA from the University of Pennsylvania and his MA from Teachers College, Columbia University, and earned the designations of Chartered Life Underwriter and Chartered Financial Consultant from The American College in Bryn Mawr, Pennsylvania.

Edward Higgins was President of Higgins Advisory Group, a Darien, Connecticut-based firm established in 1980 to serve as a family office for a select group of clients seeking to centralize the management of their personal financial affairs. Corporations that provide this service to their key executives as a company-paid or -sponsored fringe benefit have also retained the firm. Higgins Advisory Group is a co-general partner of Bayberry-West Partners, L.P., an investment partnership that permits its clients to invest in a diversified portfolio of private hedge funds and managed accounts, most of which are either closed to new investors or that have minimum investment investors. Mr. Higgins was a graduate of Lafayette College and Georgetown Law School and had taken advanced courses in taxation at Georgetown and international law at the Parker School of Columbia University.

Karl N. Huish is a principal of Tribeca Strategic Advisors, LLC, a tax and business planning firm for high net worth individuals; a principal of Tribeca

Capital Management, LLC, a Registered Investment Advisor (RIA) based in Phoenix, Arizona; and a shareholder of Huish Campbell, P.C., a Phoenix, Arizona law firm practicing in the areas of tax law, business law, and estate planning. Mr. Huish is a licensed attorney and a member of the State Bar of Arizona. He is a CERTIFIED FINANCIAL PLANNER™ practitioner (CFP™ practitioner), and has held the NASD Series 7 and other securities licenses. Mr. Huish is a frequent lecturer on a variety of advanced tax and financial topics. He received his BA in economics from Brigham Young University, with highest honors, and his JD from the University of Chicago, with honors. He was the recipient of the John M. Olin Student Fellowship in Law & Economics at the University of Chicago Law School.

Barclay T. Leib is principal and founder of Sand Spring Advisors LLC, a Morristown, New Jersey-based financial advisory and alternative asset management firm. A 1981 Wilson Scholar graduate of Princeton University's Woodrow Wilson School of International and Public Affairs, Mr. Leib has worked in the global capital markets for over 21 years. He began his career at J.P. Morgan where he ran Commodity and Foreign Exchange Derivatives Trading until the end of 1986. In 1987 he accepted a position as First Vice President and head of the Proprietary Trading and Arbitrage Group within Paine Webber's Fixed Income Department. In 1989, he moved to J. Aron Goldman Sachs where he was a senior member of their global currency and commodity option trading teams until the end of 1992. Mr. Leib shifted primarily to strategy and hedge fund sales work between 1993 and 1998, working first as a Vice President in Foreign Exchange Options Trading at Barclays Bank and then later at Societe Generale in a similar capacity. Throughout his years on bank trading floors, Mr. Leib worked extensively with derivatives, systematized trading models, and technical trading methodologies. Before founding Sand Spring Advisors in late 1999, Mr. Leib became a full-time market analyst and financial writer for the Princeton Economic Institute. He has also written on financial markets on a freelance basis for *Derivatives Strategy* magazine, *Plan Sponsor* magazine, Hegeworld.com, PrudentBear.com, SafeHaven.com, Bloomberg, *Financial Executive* magazine, and *Treasury & Risk Management* magazine.

Charles C. Morgan is President, Nonqualified Benefit Funding, with Prudential Financial. Mr. Morgan joined Prudential as an Assistant General Counsel of the Law Department Tax Section in January 1976 where he was responsible for the tax and ERISA issues pertaining to pensions, life and health insurance, and insurance products. He moved to Group Operations in the spring of 1987 as a consultant on life and health benefit issues. Prior to joining Prudential, Mr. Morgan was affiliated with Massachusetts Mutual Life Insurance Company in Springfield, Massachusetts, and the Law Offices of Cornelius, Collins, Higgins and White in Nashville, Tennessee. Mr. Morgan has prepared benefits-related congressional testimony for Prudential and has testified on behalf of both Prudential and various insurance industry associations at numerous IRS hearings. He has written numerous articles on medical benefits and life insurance product issues and is a frequent speaker and panelist on retiree medical funding and other life and health plan topics. Mr. Morgan received his JD from the Vanderbilt University School of Law and his MBA from Pepperdine University. He received a BA from Wesleyan University. Mr. Morgan holds a professional designation as Chartered Life Underwriter as well as the Advanced Pension Certificate. He is licensed as an Investment Company and Variable Contracts Products Principal and an Investment Company and Variable Contracts Products Representative. Mr. Morgan is licensed to practice law in Massachusetts, New Jersey, and Texas.

Michael M. O'Mara is founder and senior office of both O'Mara Financial, Inc. and Elm Street Partners, Inc. Founded in 1984, O'Mara Financial was initially an investment-banking firm dedicated to real estate and continues to operate a small portfolio of apartment communities. O'Mara Financial grew to become an investment firm specializing in investment analysis and research for a variety of clients including individuals, pension plans, and trusts. Founded in 1993, Elm Street Partners is the general partner of three hedge fund of fund partnerships for private investors and is dedicated to providing investment services for institutions and high net worth individuals. Prior to founding O'Mara Financial, Mr. O'Mara was a member of small marketing management team within the Boston corporate office of John Hancock. While with Hancock, he served as a member of the financial services acquisition committee. Registered as a general securities representative with the NASD, he is also a member of the National Futures Association and a registered Commodity Pool Operator (CPO) with the Commodity Futures Trading Commission. He is a graduate of the University of Arkansas.

David L. Smith, CLTC, spent five years as a U.S. Naval Officer before entering the insurance industry in 1964. During his career, he served as Vice President of Sales for two New England Life Insurance Companies and Vice

President of Financial Services for an international insurance brokerage firm. In the mid-1990s he anticipated that long-term care insurance would play an increasingly important role in financial planning and protecting assets of older Americans. In 1999 he opened his office in Centerbrook, Connecticut dedicated to long-term care issues. Mr. Smith is a graduate of Bates College.

Martha S. Staniford is a member of Sontag Advisory LLC, a registered investment advisory firm providing wealth management, financial and estate planning, asset allocation, and investment management services to individuals, families, and related parties. Ms. Staniford was previously responsible for overseeing and directing the development of CIBC Oppenheimer's Wealth Management Alliance (WMA) program. The WMA program was designed to provide a full complement of products and services for high net worth individuals, families, and family offices. She was also responsible for business development involving CIBC Oppenheimer's nonresident alien and international private client businesses. Before joining CIBC Oppenheimer, Ms. Staniford was a Managing Director at Bankers Trust Company and BT AlexBrown. She was responsible for the high net worth brokerage operation and the Latin American Private Banking Division within Bankers Trust's private bank as well as part of the Capital Markets Group and Investment Banking Division. She has also worked at Chase Bank, Rohm & Haas Company, and GTE Corportion.

Albert Swanke is an independent consultant to the insurance and related financial services industries. He has over 35 years of experience as a financial executive and venture capitalist. He has conceived, developed, and managed new businesses and handled mergers, acquisitions, and restructurings. Since early 2001, Mr. Swanke has been affiliated with Gill & Roeser, a New York-based financial adviser and reinsurance intermediary, where he is a Senior Vice President. He was an active participant in their successful conception, development, and funding of Olympus Re, a new Bermuda reinsurance company, in late 2001. Mr. Swanke served as Managing Director of The Firemark Group, Inc. from 1992 to 1997, with responsibility for private equity and investment banking, where he was instrumental in capitalizing two private equity insurance funds with more than $65 million. From 1987 to 1992, Mr. Swanke was a Principal of Insurance Venture Partners, a firm specializing in investment advisory services, venture capital, and strategic consulting, which he helped found in 1984. Prior to

1987, he served in financial management positions at American International Group, American Express Bank, and INA (CIGNA). He earned a BA degree from Yale University and an MBA from Columbia University.

Graham R. Taylor is a leading partner in the law firm of Altheimer & Gray's San Francisco office and is well known in the Australian-U.S. business, venture capital, and financial communities. Mr. Taylor is a director of the Australian-American Chamber of Commerce (San Francisco) and Chairman of the San Francisco-Sydney Sister City Committee. He has successfully represented many U.S. and Australian companies doing business across the Pacific, from start-ups to public companies. Mr. Taylor received LL.B and B. Commerce degrees from the University of New South Wales, Australia in 1975 and his LL.M. from Yale Law School in 1978. He is a member of the Australian, New York, and California Bars.

Pamela Woodburn, CFP, STI, TEP, is Senior Manager, Global Wealth Strategies with Royal Bank of Canada Private Banking, NYC. Based in California, she oversees the development and implementation of customized international wealth management solutions for high net worth clients in the South Western United States. These customized solutions encompass estate planning, minimization of tax and asset preservation, while utilizing international trusts, foundations, and companies. Canadian-born, Ms. Woodburn studied business administration and marketing at the British Columbia Institute of Technology in Vancouver between 1982 and 1984. She successfully completed the Canadian Securities Course, and joined the financial industry in 1988. Later, she received her Life & Disability Insurance License and subsequently obtained her Certified Financial Planner (CFP) and Specialist of the Trust Institute (STI) designations. Ms. Woodburn's experience has included brokerage, insurance, financial counseling, domestic trusts, and estate planning. During more than a decade of service with RBC Financial Group, she has received numerous awards, including the Bank's prestigious Leo Award. Ms. Woodburn is a member of the Canadian Association of Financial Planners, the Society of Trust & Estate Practitioners, and the International Tax Planning Association.

Kenneth A. Ziskin maintains a boutique "Family Wealthy Strategy" practice from his Los Angeles office. His practice emphasizes legal representation of individuals and families in connection with wealth strategies planning and implementation. Mr. Ziskin holds an "AV"® rating from Martindale-

Hubbell, which signifies that his "legal abilities are of the very highest standard" and his "professional ethics and conduct are above question." Mr. Ziskin was one of the first estate planning experts to become a Fellow of the Esperti Peterson Institute for planning for high net worth individuals and families. He served as an Adjunct Professor at the University of Southern California Law Center from 1991 to 1994 and has served two terms as a member of the Financial Institutions Committee of the State Bar of California and on numerous advisory committees and task forces set up by bank regulatory agencies. He is a member of the task force that rewrote the California Financial Code in the late 1970s and the author of several articles on financial, tax, and securities law matters and has also been active as a lecturer to professional groups. Mr. Ziskin has testified as an expert in Federal Court, and has been designated as an expert in several state court matters. He appeared regularly on The Business Channel (KWHY-TV 22) from 1996 through 1999 to discuss "Beyond the Living Trust" estate planning strategies. Mr. Ziskin received his JD from the University of Southern California Law Center in 1972, where he was Executive Editor of the Southern California Law Review and a member of the Order of the Coif national honor society.

Acknowledgments

I appreciate this opportunity to mention a few of my friends who have directly or indirectly helped me in the preparation of this book. First and foremost I would like to thank each of the chapter authors who have written the book and deserve most of the credit. Additionally, I could not have succeeded in this project without the support of the following people: Patrick J. Paladino, for his critical financial analysis; Michael M. O'Mara, CPO, for his insight into the hedge fund world; Theresa M. Burns, CFA, for illustrating and formatting the arcane subject of hedge funds; Dean H. Hamilton, CLU, for his expertise on the proper structure and pricing of private placement variable universal life insurance; Robert Eastham, for his knowledge of the administration of offshore life insurance companies; Hugh T. McCormick, JD, for consulting on many legal issues pertaining to offshore transactions; Robert D. Colvin, JD, and Karl J. Feitelberg, CLU, ChFC, leading authorities to the very wealthy with expertise on purchasing insurance offshore and domestically; Andy Carstensen, for his many kind introductions to those individuals who could answer troublesome questions; Albert H. Swanke, Jr., for his unparalleled patience and skill on capitalizing an offshore insurance company; Michael Barrett Watson, for being one of those that could help answer those troublesome questions; my old friend Owen R. Stryker, for his in-depth knowledge of the offshore market; John A. Kulak, for his tireless effort to explain the cash management process for hedge funds; Daniel Fitzgerald, FSA, MAAA, EA, for being the first to explain to me the proper structure of investing in an offshore insurance company; Donald D. Cameron, CLU, who taught me how to do things right offshore and wrote "Rules for the Road," an invaluable brief on the subject; Edward P. Jaeger, an old friend who introduced me to many of the leading life brokers in America; Vincent J. Marold and Bucky Isaacson, who introduced me to the sophisticated capital markets for funding; Michael Simoff, for his endless discussions on investment strategies; Stanley M. Karp, a sophisticated investor who believed in the project and its ultimate success; Nicholas L. Ihasz, who early on explained the possibility of hedge funds; John M. Pagli, for the many important introductions to the hedge fund industry; Michael Boyd, who helped me get started in the hedge fund world and was forever patient; Eric D. Jacobs, a tireless supporter of our effort to build an offshore entity; John K. Hillman, CPA, a friend and counselor and probably the most knowledgable authority on private placement life insurance in the United States; Colin C. James, life insurance company CEO, who patiently let me work through the myriad of detail; Andeas Barten, who always maintained a positive attitude even through our many iterations; David C. Erdos, JD, for listening to the endless complications and drawing the relevant documents; John Fulvio, CPA, for his early advice on the complex accounting issues; Ward Hinkle, JD, for his creative thinking and in-depth analytical skill; Craig Campbell, JD, LLM, for instantly recognizing the offshore potential; Jeffrey S. Bortnick, JD, one of the foremost attorneys in the United States on the inner workings of offshore companies; William Fong, CPA, for his attention to important detail and keeping us out of trouble; Stanley Dickson, JD, for his continued interest and confidence through thick and thin; and finally, Linda H. Van Gorden, Director of Administration for my firm, for assuming many responsibilities while I focused on this book.

Richard H. Mayer

Summary of Contents

Contents

PART 1. GENERAL PRINCIPLES

Part 1. General Principles

CHAPTER 1

Introduction to Wealth Management

Richard H. Mayer and Donald R. Levy

Synopsis

This chapter introduces some of the aspects of wealth management that are explored in later chapters and describes the substantial changes that have occurred in the field in recent years.

§ 1.1 Wealth Management Planning Issues

To be considered in financial planning for the affluent are a number of key issues.

The authors of this chapter wish to thank Martha Staniford, the author of chapter 11, for her suggestions in their preparation of this chapter.

§ 1.1[a] Multigenerational Planning

An important aspect of multigenerational planning is the implementation of broad objectives once those objectives are set. For example, once the tax aspects of generation skipping are mastered by the client under the tutelage of his or her adviser, the details of what to do are next on the agenda. Should trusts be established? Are dynasty IRAs (individual retirement arrangements) a good idea for this client situation? Should real estate or fund investments be utilized? How about jumbo amounts of life insurance? Should the second-to-die approach be utilized if appropriate?

§ 1.1[b] Establishing a Life Insurance Company

There is ample opportunity for the ultra-high net worth investor to establish a life insurance company within the Treasury regulations and within what is believed to be the spirit of those regulations. By the time this book is published, the Internal Revenue Service (IRS) will have undoubtedly issued a notice or some other type of pronouncement on this subject.

Because of rumblings in the Treasury Department and attacks by some members of Congress on hedge fund life insurance wraps, on reinsurance schemes, and regarding interpretation of Internal Revenue Code (IRC) Section 817, it is important to make a distinction between the formation of a properly functioning life insurance company and the recent establishment of certain offshore companies. Most of the concern is focused on three issues: (1) investor control, (2) assumption of risk, and (3) adequate generation of new life insurance premium. These points are addressed in chapter 5.

§ 1.1[c] Hedge Fund Investing

Hedge fund investing is something every wealthy individual may want to consider. The role of commodity trading advisers in a diversified portfolio needs to be understood, as must the advisability and necessity of diversification that protects the investor without creating a mediocre return. Of course, nothing can be guaranteed and good results need to be maximized. Critical to success are using statistics and other tools, selecting a well-qualified investment or hedge fund manager, and avoiding common mistakes.

Hedge funds have a variety of flexible trading styles. They can match long exposures with short positions that are equally strong and can retain the flexibility to move into such other asset classes as foreign exchange and commodities. Alternative hedge fund styles, which are described in chapter 7, include long only, dedicated short, short biased, long-short diversified, long-short small capitalization, long-short large capitalization, long-short global, long-short country specific, long-short sector specific, regulation derivative equity oriented, value driven—market and sector neutral, statistical arbitrage driven—market and sector neutral, convertible bond arbitrage, options arbitrage, event-driven opportunistic, merger arbitrage, fixed-income arbitrage, mortgage-backed arbitrage, multi-arbitrage, and mutual fund market timing.

§ 1.1[d] Life Insurance

Life Insurance for the super-affluent may sometimes be arranged with negotiated individual rates; and through a family limited liability company it may be possible to insure both parents with no gift tax issues, since the new entity owns 100 percent of the insurance proceeds.

There is no vehicle that can achieve tax efficiency under U.S. tax law as well as an insurance product. Insurance products can also be utilized successfully in an offshore context. The details of the offshore life insurance company's growing role in wealth preservation, including the opportunities and advantages a life insurance company can provide and step-by-step guidelines for forming one, are explained in chapters 4 and 5.

Life insurance is fine in many cases but presupposes that the proposed insured is in good health or at least insurable with a rating. When insurability is a problem, attention may immediately go to annuities, with the possible aid of group term insurance to manage the risk of early death.

§ 1.1[e] Succession Planning

Succession planning has traditionally been a concern for the individual entrepreneur related to his or her closely owned business. Will children continue in its management? How will the equities be balanced between descendants who will be participants and those who have other interests or are not capable of handling the same level of responsibility?

One strategy is to create a master plan that may not be spelled out as such but may instead be quietly implemented by the client and his or her advisers. The master plan will include retirement strategies and a time line for filling nonfamily, key person positions needed to keep the business profitable. Emergency plans will also be necessary. These too may not be totally spelled out but will be understood by the key players.

Essential to the success of the succession will be the financial planning process to see (1) that necessary cash is likely to be available at each stage; and (2) that investment opportunities are maximized so that the family can achieve long-term family objectives and self-insure against any unexpected dilemmas or disappointments.

§ 1.1[f] Executive Benefits

A broad array of deferred compensation and executive retirement plans are available to the affluent individual and his or her family. (See chapter 12.) The possibilities are there whether the wealthy individual is an executive of a major public company, a closely held corporation, or an entity created just by the family. The rules in this area are well established and allow nonqualified benefits that would clearly be discriminatory if immediate tax deductions were the objective.

§ 1.1[g] Offshore Arrangements

Offshore products are not for everyone, but for certain investors they are just the right fit. Chapters 4 and 5 provide insights into the typical motivations for offshore investing, outlining benefits and dangers and describing some of the attractive offshore products available to investors.

Offshore trusts are a way to maximize investment return and gain fair and appropriate tax advantages. They often make sense, but there are control and jurisdictional issues to consider. These issues can be especially intricate when there are multijurisdictional families involved.

One of the advantages of going offshore is the privacy that some foreign jurisdictions provide. In the United States many facets of an investor's background can be learned from both public and private records, but in offshore jurisdictions there may be laws preventing the disclosure of confidential information and imposing criminal penalties for their violation.

On the other hand, a disadvantage of going offshore might be the need to have a local trustee resident and active in the host country. This trustee might not be insulated from a local political crisis, and that might delay important trust business or even put trust assets at risk. Another concern might be the unpredictability of law changes, or expropriations affecting the liquidity of an investment in ways that are less predictable in a foreign jurisdiction than they are in the United States.

Tax policies are in a state of flux as a result of possibly extreme and unreasonable applications tried by some investors and frowned on by some government regulators. Before entering into these arrangements it is necessary to be wary of what may lie down the road and to consider current policy trends and the political climate.

§ 1.1[h] Traps for the Unwary

Inherent in planning for the affluent is preserving wealth for future generations to the extent permitted by the laws of descent and without terrible tax consequences. This part of the financial plan needs to be reviewed constantly, and particularly when acts of God change the playing field. In appropriate situations family foundations should be planned, especially when immediate cash flow needs can be met easily. In addition, when corporate employment is in the picture, it is necessary to avoid golden parachutes that can be unnecessarily costly in a tax sense. Finally, there is the trap for the unwary in generation-skipping limitations. It is sometimes easily avoided but needs to be anticipated.

§ 1.2 Cutting-Edge Investment Products

Planning for the affluent interfaces with many cutting-edge investment products. Because they are cutting edge, the list of these investments may keep changing. Some products will lose favor and new ones will be developed, some of them really being modifications of those now existing. At the moment the following approaches are prominent and are fully described in the appropriate chapters of this book:

- Hedging and monetization strategies (see chapter 7)
- Fund of funds (see chapter 7)
- Offshore products (see chapters 4 and 5)
- Derivative tools: options, swaps, and forwards (including annuity wraps, deferred variable life insurance, and equity swaps) (see chapter 12)
- Exchange funds (see chapter 7)
- Private placement variable universal life insurance (PPVUL) (see chapter 12)

The Treasury Department and Congress are taking an increasingly critical look at PPVUL policies. By the time this book is published, the Treasury Department may have issued a notice regarding PPVUL and Congress may have proposed legislation. It is imperative that the investment underlying a PPVUL contract not be the same as any investment available to the public outside the PPVUL contract. The investment must be cloned or otherwise identified as a distinct asset and separate from any other. The intent of the investment cannot be solely to gain tax advantages.

Under current law withdrawals from a PPVUL are tax free up to basis (equal to the amount of total premium paid in). Funds extracted above basis are taxed at ordinary rates. If the excess funds are obtained by loan, they are considered tax free.

> **Caution.** If funds are borrowed and the PPVUL contract is subsequently terminated, except by death, full recourse of the loan portion will be taxed at ordinary rates.

If borrowing occurs, sufficient assets must remain in the PPVUL contract and sufficient investment yield has to be generated to keep the PPVUL policy in force; otherwise, potentially adverse tax consequence can occur. The tax efficiency of a life insurance policy will not accommodate investment losses, either short or long term, against outside income.

Notwithstanding these important caveats, the cutting-edge products listed above are often useful in carrying out various strategies and techniques in the following areas:

- Asset protection
- Tax planning
- Estate and financial planning
- Investments
- Trusts
- Insurance
- Private annuities
- Investment banking
- Long-term care planning

Private annuities are intended to remove the property transferred from the estate of the transferor for tax purposes. The annuity is often paid at least partially from the transferred property. This may straddle the line between a valid annuity and a retained life estate and could result not only in unintended estate taxes but also in unintended income tax consequences.

§ 1.3 Wealth Management Revolution

A revolution has occurred in the need for and methods of modern wealth accumulation and preservation. Conservative, rigid trustees have been supplanted by a vast and varied group of financial planning institutions; and as a source of investments, the "nifty fifty" have been replaced by an enormous array of alternatives. These alternatives have diluted the supremacy of a few blue-chip stocks and bonds, which must now compete with other investment opportunities that are screened for the wealthy by members of the expanded financial planning industry.

Indeed, the roles and responsibilities of the trustee in wealth preservation have become international. The international trustee must account for the original cost or value of each investment, cash receipts, and cash disbursements, as well as values at the end of each accounting period. It also remains imperative that the trustee be given the powers necessary to be flexible and even opportunistic about investment opportunities and to respond properly to changes in the family situation and the world economy.

Today's need for more wealth management services has been caused not just by an increase in the number of wealthy families. It is the direct result of the aging of this population and its increased life expectancy. The need is compounded by the greater life expectancy of the expected heirs and descendants of wealthy individuals. Business growth has, with some interruption, spawned this rise in average wealth, as has the growth of corporate compensation paid to senior executives; reflected in the long-term growth of the stock market, these increases have stayed ahead of the rate of inflation and have been stimulated in recent years by steadier and more modest inflationary pressures. Still, the possibility of value swings has put a premium on diversification to protect investors against the risk of forced liquidation at inappropriate times. Various patterns of diversification are needed so that flexibility is retained. At the same time wealthy individuals must avoid overdiversifying so that growth does not become mediocre.

Part of the change in investment management has been the result of the vast increase in the information available to investors and the timeliness of information; Wall Street is not the sole source of this information. Timely financial information comes from sources all over the country and around the world. Opinions are diverse and readily reported, and clients are better informed and prepared for discussion with their advisers. Even after consolidations, there remain many choices among large, medium-sized, and small purveyors of wealth management services. Wealthy individuals more frequently use several sources, even while using just one or two gatekeepers.

The growing number of young investors and young advisers, whose youth may belie their extensive education and experience, has broadened the scope and diligence of wealth management advisers. This has led to many new ideas concerning diversification and protection against volatility. The younger blood has influenced more experienced advisers to challenge established methods that may no longer be appropriate. Decisions on how long to hold onto a sputtering investment and when to take advantage of an investment opportunity due to an asset's sluggishness need constant review, and it is becoming increasingly apparent that the value of property of all kinds is less and less predictable.

Strategy has become more important. Alternative strategies may include fund of funds, art and other collectibles, real estate, hedge funds, private equity, futures, and indexes. When these alternative strategies become of interest, they need not be immediately added to a portfolio.

Not only are investment alternatives more numerous; there are also many more particular ways to implement each investment alternative. Academically sponsored and supported think tanks have added their input to the knowledge mix and lively debates have resulted. The increasing complexity of planning for the affluent has been matched by the increasing competition among financial planners, which is based on the blending of many ideas and the development of challenging new ideas and their adoption or rejection by different members of the enlarged wealth management community.

The increase in competition has caused volatility in managers, as well as in the investments they recommend. The pressure to produce short-term results sometimes affects the strategies and tactics of these individuals; this may not be of long-run benefit. Using a consultant to recommend and manage the managers is an alternative that is not always financially warranted even for affluent families or individuals, and it does not necessarily increase the likelihood of better results. One solution is for family members to become better informed and to establish guidelines on how policy is to be determined for the family's financial managers and how it is to be reviewed. Good communication can be critical and can be achieved without having the managers become yes-men and -women for their clients. Objectivity in the advice given is absolutely critical. Although everyone wants to see good performance, it can be equally important to encourage creative solutions to special problems and to judge over an acceptable period (not too short) whether the results are better than they would have been if previous policies had continued to be followed.

In the post-modern portfolio theory era, during which many investors have from time to time blamed their managers for results they considered less than satisfactory, the question naturally arises, how can clients and their consultants best manage the managers? How long should managers be given to produce the desired results? How should it be determined whether results are sufficiently satisfactory to justify a continuation of service in the interest of allowing for a decent longer-term result? What criteria should be used to monitor the performance of investment advisers or managers, after selecting them based on such criteria in the first place?

A manager's ability to maximize performance is not the only criterion to consider. The main purpose of the portfolio, in the eyes of the client, may be to fund the college education of a particular beneficiary, a comfortable retirement for another, or a charitable endeavor. Minimizing taxes may be a secondary objective. The client's goals always need to be taken into account in selecting a manager.

Maximizing return is usually a major goal, but the level of risk in relation to the objective must also be given considerable weight. Another consideration is whether to emphasize income rather than total return. For the affluent, total return is often considered the right approach but liquidity is always important as well.

Furthermore, chasing performance that is never quite achieved may drown a good portfolio with costly turnover. There needs to be an appropriate balance between constantly reviewed multiple objectives.

It is just such a balance that is presented in the following chapters.

CHAPTER 2

How to Select and Monitor a Professional Money Manager in the Era of Behavioral Economics

Christopher Carosa

Synopsis

This chapter is adapted and updated, and portions are excerpted from *Due Diligence: The Individual Trustee's Guide to Selecting and Monitoring a Professional Investment Adviser,* ©1999 by Christopher Carosa, CTFA, published by ARDMAN Regional, Ltd., to which the reader should refer for more information on this subject.

Nothing attests to the failure of modern portfolio theory more than the current dissatisfaction with—and resultant high turnover of—the money managers hired by today's affluent investors. Why is modern portfolio theory to blame for investor frustration? How can today's affluent investors find greater contentment with their money managers? How can an affluent investor best determine whether a money manager's service level has dropped to a point of concern? What questions must an affluent investor answer to monitor a money manager successfully? How long should an affluent investor give a money manager before firing him or her? Why should performance results be the last thing looked at?

Although a single chapter may not offer sufficient space to answer these questions properly, it can introduce some leading-edge concepts. This chapter answers some of the most critical investment questions affluent investors might ask by summarizing a process affluent investors can use to select and monitor a professional money manager in the era of behavioral economics.

§ 2.1 Matching an Investment Goal to an Investment Philosophy

The first and most important step toward achieving success in long-term investing is to identify the purpose of the investment portfolio the investor has the duty to oversee. As part of this step, the affluent investor should have documented the specific goals and dreams of each portfolio beneficiary (including, perhaps, his or her own), cataloged a target date for reaching each goal, determined the portfolio's goal-oriented target (GOT), which represents the minimum required investment return, and set in place a strategy to address liquidity requirements. With the help of a tax accountant and an attorney, the affluent investor should also have considered the income needs of the beneficiaries, tax consequences, legal and regulatory concerns, and any other unique needs and circumstances.

After establishing an inventory of present and future beneficiary needs ("lifetime dreams"), the affluent investor can complete the next phase of the investment process. Each lifetime dream needs to be placed within a category describing a generic investment goal. Over time the investment goal associated with each lifetime dream will shift from one category to another. The necessity of this shift will become apparent when the categories are described.

The affluent investor will be under great pressure to use the traditional categories of investment goals, which the financial industry has unfortunately embraced as creed. The affluent investor must therefore show great fortitude in avoiding the use of these traditional goals, and should not even concede their use as shorthand descriptions of what affluent investors really intend.

The traditional investment goals have been defined as

1. Safety of capital;
2. Growth of capital; and
3. Income generation.

For decades, investors have been taught—rightfully so—that these goals conflict with one another. In other words, the more emphasis the investor places on one goal, the less likely he or she will achieve the other two goals. All these goals, in practice and in theory, fail to account for inflation. In addition, there is a mountain of evidence suggesting that total return investments produce consistently higher returns for long-term investors than do income-generating investments. A set of practical investment goals will better serve the affluent investor. These practical investment goals can be defined as

1. Wealth accumulation;
2. Wealth preservation; and
3. Wealth distribution.

These investment goals help the affluent investor concentrate on the pragmatic matters of investment management. By using this practical terminology, the investor directly relates goal attainment to an investment strategy. More important, these goals work together rather than conflict with one another.

How these practical investment goals coalesce can be seen through the example of a ten-year $100,000 lump-sum college tuition payment. This lifetime goal begins with a wealth accumulation goal, moves to a wealth preservation goal, and ends with a wealth distribution goal. The specific investments associated with a lifetime goal will change as the investment goal changes. For example, the college tuition lifetime goal might initially require an equity portfolio, then a short-term bond portfolio, and then a money market portfolio.

Unfortunately, split-interest trusts emphasize the traditional investment goals rather than the practical investment goals. This results in codifying the split-interest conflict within the body of the trust document. *Split-interest conflict* refers to trusts that identify two or more different beneficiaries, each with a different (and conflicting) interest in the trust; hence, split-interest, which is a problem trust attorneys strive to avoid. Today's trust lawyers are mindful of this conflict and try to mitigate it to the extent possible. Eliminating the conflict may not be possible in some types of trusts.

§ 2.1[a] Eliminate the Obvious

The failure to determine a tangible goal is the greatest deterrent to successful investing. Many different kinds of investment styles and philosophies can yield successful results. When a portfolio lacks a real-life direction, however, the naive investor easily falls into the trap of chasing performance or other common investing mistakes. After all, the naive investor has no measure other than that of performance. He or she does not see the portfolio as a college education, a comfortable retirement, or a charitable endeavor. Without these discernible milestones as a guide, the naive investor has no better method for gauging success than investment performance. The sophisticated investor, however, has defined a tangible milestone and assigned a proper investment goal. As a consequence, the sophisticated investor is prepared to focus his or her energies exclusively on the one true task—helping the beneficiary achieve the defined lifetime dream. (For split-interest trusts this may be an oversimplification. By documenting the conflicting needs and goals of the current beneficiary and the remainder beneficiary, the affluent investor is better prepared to construct an investment policy that treats each party as fairly as possible under the circumstances.)

With the substantive purpose defined, the affluent investor moves to the next step—identifying the appropriate investment philosophy. The aggregation of all goals defines the overall investment strategy. Within this overall investment strategy, each goal may have a specific investment philosophy assigned to it. The affluent investor needs to decide which philosophy to employ before he or she can go any further.

Many goals permit or even require multiple investment philosophies. Most goals also preclude a few investment philosophies. This becomes most obvious when a goal's target date moves closer. Still, there are many investment philosophies that are appropriate for goals of any duration.

For example, the ten-year lump-sum college tuition payment shows how multiple philosophies operate. In the first five years, the goal has a long-term duration and the investor may select a GOT of an average investment return of 12 percent per year. In the last five years, the goal has a short-term duration with a GOT of an average investment return of perhaps only 3 percent.

While in the long term phase of the goal, the portfolio has a wealth accumulation investment goal for which an average return of 12 percent per year has been projected. In a typical investment environment, this aggressive projection immediately precludes investment in most types of bonds. (Obviously, when government interest rates exceed 12 percent as they did in the early 1980s, bonds may become a perfectly acceptable investment in this situation.) The 12 percent projection generally also eliminates a portfolio constructed solely of income-oriented equities. Even so, the affluent investor can examine portfolios invested exclusively in junk bonds, growth stocks, or value stocks, as well as mixed portfolios, to name but a few options.

While in the short-term phase of the goal, the portfolio has a wealth preservation investment goal and a wealth distribution investment goal. A smaller average return of 3 percent per year is targeted and the investments selected must minimize or even eliminate capital risk but must do better than inflation (assume 3 percent inflation). The affluent investor would therefore generally avoid equity-oriented and long-term bond portfolios and focus instead on money market reserves or bonds maturing within five years (depending on the interest rate environment).

By going through this process, the affluent investor eliminates the most obviously inappropriate investment philosophies, but still must choose from numerous alternatives. Indeed, theoretically, there are as many alternatives as there are money managers and mutual funds.

One investment philosophy may be obviously inappropriate for the affluent investor. Many financial firms offer tax-advantaged products (e.g., variable annuities) or invest in tax-advantaged securities (e.g., municipal bonds). These products and securities may or may not be appropriate for a taxable portfolio, depending on the investor's tax bracket and the potential for changes in the prevailing tax rates. More important, it is very difficult to justify placing any tax-advantaged product or security in a nontaxable portfolio, such as an individual retirement arrangement (IRA), a 401(k) plan, a 403(b) plan, or any other employee benefit retirement plan. As a general rule, investors should be especially wary and do lots of research before investing in a tax-advantaged product or security.

§ 2.1[b] Avoid the Seven Deadly Sins

Affluent investors are often conservative long-term investors because (1) their investment portfolios have a time horizon exceeding five years and (2) they want to act with prudence with regard to the nature of their investments. The affluent investor can meet these two needs by eliminating all investment philosophies that commit any one of the seven deadly sins of professional money managers.

Describing these sins in great detail is beyond the scope of this chapter. Some of them may seem obvious; others may require investigation into the underlying academic theory. The following summary of the seven deadly sins of professional money managers will help the affluent investor know what to avoid:

1. *Income obsession.* Professional money managers often unknowingly hurt the long-term interests of investors by unduly emphasizing income-oriented securities at the expense of total investment return. Over the long term, total return investments tend to achieve higher rates of return than income-oriented investments. Investment data for the 60 years ending in 1995 show the Standard & Poor's (S&P) 500 had a long-term average return of 10.5 percent while long-term corporate bonds had an average annual return of only 5.7 percent.[1]

   To avoid this sin, the investment philosophy must recognize the practical investment goals. The affluent investor must avoid the traditional goal of income generation because it no longer applies. Income-oriented philosophies cannot be tolerated unless they deliberately take total investment return into consideration. By focusing on total return, the affluent investor should increase the likelihood of meeting the chosen investment goal and, in turn, attaining the particular lifetime dream.

2. *Mistaken risk.* Professional money managers have faith in risk management even though no statistically valid definition of risk exists. The investment industry, piggybacking on academia, tries to define risk in terms of volatility (the variability of investment return). This practice often results in the use of risk-adjusted measurements that have come to represent an industry-accepted excuse for underperformance. In fact, volatility weighs above-average performance (a good thing) the same as it weighs below-average performance (a bad thing). This practice begs the question, is some risk good risk while other risk is bad risk?

   To avoid this sin, the affluent investor must choose an investment philosophy that fully recognizes that most forms of risk management represent a siren song for the long-term investor. The investment philosophy should use industry standard benchmarks like the S&P 500 (or Wilshire 5000) and the Consumer Price Index (CPI) to explain the risk associated with that philosophy. Most important, the investor should avoid investment philosophies that contain complex statistics such as those used in regression analysis, unless they focus exclusively on semi-variance (or downside risk). The affluent investor should remember that industry standard risk measurements can lead to false or damaging investment decisions. The conservative long-term investor cannot be led astray by attempts to measure short-term volatility.

3. *Bond insecurity.* The investment industry and academic theory have long held that bonds reduce the volatility of a portfolio. In fact, since the 1970s the bond market has been just as volatile as the stock market and long-term returns on equities have outpaced those of bonds. (For the 20 years ending in 1995, the average annual return of long-term government bonds was 10.45 percent versus 14.59 percent for the S&P 500.[2]) Furthermore, stocks and bonds tended to move in opposite directions 30 years ago, but today they generally move in the same direction.

   To avoid this sin, the affluent investor must choose investment philosophies that rarely, if ever, invest in long-term bonds. By avoiding long-term bonds, conservative long-term investors increase the probability of meeting their GOT. Stocks have exhibited more favorable long-term growth results than have bonds. Unfortunately, many trust documents restrict beneficiaries to investment income. These trust documents leave individual trustees with little or no option but to place fixed-income securities in the portfolio. Those who act as individual trustees for these types of trusts cannot avoid this sin but should understand the effect the trust document has on investment policy and the future growth of the trust. These individual trustees should be prepared to document why fixed-income securities must be included in the trust portfolio and why the inclusion of these securities will likely impede asset growth over the long term.

4. *Diversification.* Overdiversification, as well as underdiversification, can damage long-term investment returns. Nothing dramatizes this more than investors who purchase as few as two or three different mutual funds for the sake of diversification. These investors almost guarantee that they will consistently underperform the market because they end up owning a de facto index fund while paying a higher management fee than they would have if they had just purchased an index fund. Any investment philosophy under consideration by the affluent investor must take measures to ensure that portfolios do not suffer from overdiversification. Affluent investors will find this strategy benefits their portfolios because overdiversification increases portfolio trading costs and makes it more difficult to meet the GOT.

5. *Asset misallocation.* Very few professional money managers will admit that asset allocation is nothing more than a fancy name for market timing and guarantees nothing. It seems as if a cottage industry of consultants has emerged as a result of the investment industry's addiction to asset allocation. The industry likes it because it yields impressive graphs and colorful charts investors can easily understand. In reality, the theory behind asset allocation is neither predictive nor consistent over time.

   To avoid this sin, the affluent investor must avoid investment philosophies that employ the traditional stock-bond-cash asset allocation. In addition, the affluent investor should avoid using seemingly more sophisticated asset allocation models that attempt to concoct an optimized mix of arbitrarily defined large-capitalization, mid-capitalization, small-capitalization, domestic, international, and global equity asset classes. Instead, the conservative long-term investor should choose an investment philosophy that makes allocations primarily across equity sectors through fundamental security analysis. No one can successfully time the market with consistency. Asset allocation means trying to time the market. In the spring of 1975, Nobel-Prize winning finance professor William F. Sharpe showed in an article published by the *Financial Analysts Review,* that while an investor can get better returns by timing the market, that investor would have to correctly predict when to switch into and out of stock 70 percent of the time. More recently (January/February 2001), *Financial Analysts Journal* published a study covering the years 1926–1999. This study updated and confirmed Sharpe's earlier work and further cautioned, "As the holding period increases, the needed accuracy also increases."

Most ominously, several studies warn the biggest risk of market timing involves being out of the market at crucial moments. In his book *Investments, Analysis, and Management, Eighth Edition*, Charles Jones states, "Over a recent 40-year period, investors who missed the 34 best months for stocks would have seen an initial $1,000 investment grow to only $4,492 instead of $86,650." Missing only a few significant days will result in long-term investment performance that trails behind even a bank savings account.

Many affluent investors will find that, in one way or another, trust documents (or their equivalent) may require some form of asset allocation. For example, a trust document may require the investment portfolio to invest in a fixed percentage of stocks and bonds. (So-called balanced portfolios generally invest 50 to 60 percent of portfolio assets in stocks and 40 to 50 percent of portfolio assets in bonds.) Furthermore, trust documents may assign a specific use for investment income; this also requires the trustee to practice some form of asset allocation. When the affluent investor who acts as an individual trustee has no choice in the matter, he or she should document why the portfolio has invested in fixed-income assets and the negative impact these investments may have on the long-term growth of the portfolio.

6. *Modern portfolio theory: no longer modern.* The capital asset pricing model, the Nobel Prize–winning financial theory as used by many investment professionals to help them decide how to invest client assets, is like driving forward by looking in the rearview mirror. Investing is not a science, no matter how many statistical graphs one has. Past results can never guarantee future results. Affluent investors cannot allow themselves to be deluded by academic theory. They must rely solely on practical considerations. Therefore, they must pick an investment philosophy that does not use any of the techniques of or any software that employs the capital asset pricing model. Affluent investors must seek investment philosophies that rely on fundamental analysis to classify qualified securities. No affluent investor or professional money manager can predict the future by analyzing the past.

7. *Arbitrage Pricing Theory: repackaging a failure.* Past results can never guarantee future results, no matter how many rearview mirrors one has. Refining formulas to make them more statistically precise does not add practical value; garbage in still means garbage out. Affluent investors must realize the true problem of Modern Portfolio Theory is not that it needs further refinement, but that it cannot be used to predict the future. The affluent investor should avoid any investment philosophy that tries to translate any academic theory into industry practice. While this is a fascinating intellectual exercise, it offers no guaranteed positive results in helping to reach any designated investment goal. Describing the past in greater detail does not permit one to predict the future.

§ 2.1[c] Incorporate Useful Generic Investment Principles

The National Association of Investors Corporation (NAIC) has developed some very helpful generic investment principles. The affluent investor should reflect on the appropriateness of these principles. In the event these principles have relevance, the affluent investor should ensure that the selected investment philosophy includes these principles in some way.

The NAIC suggests long-term investors follow these three principles:

1. Invest regularly.
2. Reinvest dividends, interest, and capital gains.
3. Make investing a habit by
   - (a) taking full advantage of tax-deferred retirement plans,
   - (b) investing (including money placed in tax-deferred retirement plans) at least 10 percent of gross income, and
   - (c) never removing anything from an investment portfolio unless the money will be used in direct connection with the goal tied to that portfolio.

These principles may not be relevant to or even allowed in certain types of trusts. For example, some affluent investors may not find themselves in a position to invest regularly because their investment portfolio represents an initial lump-sum payment of some sort or because the Internal Revenue Service (IRS) penalizes certain trusts that accumulate investment income rather than distribute it.

Another generic principle bears mention. Affluent investors should regularly monitor the long-term impact of taxes and inflation on the investment portfolio, the investment goal, and the lifetime goal.

By avoiding the most obvious mistakes and incorporating the most useful principles, affluent investors can confidently match each of their goals to an investment philosophy. At this point, the affluent investor will find that he or she may choose from many acceptable investment philosophies and should be satisfied with selecting a fairly general philosophy. The affluent investor will then interview several professional money managers, each of whom will have a bias as to which investment strategy will work best given the investor's chosen investment philosophy. Short of a rigorous academic review of the pros and cons of different investment strategies, the affluent investor can review these pros and cons through the money manager interview process. It is beyond the scope of this chapter to advocate which investment strategy is best.

§ 2.1[d] A Final Word About Risk

As noted above, mistaken risk is one of the seven deadly sins of professional money managers. Some affluent investors, however, may feel the need to incorporate risk or the beneficiary's risk tolerance into choosing an appropriate investment philosophy. Indeed, an attorney may instruct the affluent investor to assess the risk tolerance of the beneficiary as part of the requirements of the prudent investor law. Furthermore, most financial professionals will insist that an investor assess his or her own risk tolerance (and they will eagerly provide a personalized questionnaire just to prove their earnestness). It is to be hoped that by now, the reader can see that investment goals derive from lifetime goals, not from any person's risk tolerance. In the extreme case, should a 25-year-old of low risk tolerance invest his or her IRA in money market funds or certificates of deposit? Of course not. Likewise, an affluent investor (at least one concerned about his or her own liability) would not place a risk-tolerant octogenarian in extremely risky naked options.

How should an affluent investor correctly incorporate risk tolerance into the overall investment process? First and foremost, he or she should never consider risk tolerance ahead of lifetime goals and associated investment goals. Risk tolerance can skew the perceived needs of the beneficiary. The investment goal should always be considered first.

Once the investment goal is established, one can identify several investment philosophies, or methods of reaching that goal. Each method may or may not offer a different level of risk. To the extent the different methods offer different risk levels, one can select a preferred risk level. For example, among other choices, an affluent investor may select from investing exclusively in junk bonds, exclusively in growth stocks, or exclusively in value stocks to attain a 12 percent annual return. An affluent investor with a low risk tolerance would avoid junk bonds and growth stocks and select the value stock philosophy.

Therefore, the affluent investor may incorporate risk tolerances into the investment process without subordinating investment goals to risk tolerances.

§ 2.2 Selecting the Money Manager

Having documented the lifetime dreams of the beneficiaries of the trust, categorized those lifetime dreams into investment goals, and eliminated all improper investment philosophies and concepts, the affluent investor has, in a very general way, matched investment goals to the most suitable investment strategies—before even looking at valid strategies—and is ready to select a money manager. Many people consider this the most enjoyable part of the process. If the investment process were to be likened to the process of buying a car, choosing a money manager would be akin to going to the showroom and test-driving.

The car-buying analogy was chosen with a purpose. How often do car buyers begin looking at cars and test-driving them before doing any homework? Do they know what they will use the car for? Have they researched which cars are most appropriate for that purpose? Do they know all the cars that experts have labeled lemons? Have they asked around and found out what car dealers to avoid? People who fail to make the effort to complete this preliminary work often buy a car on impulse and find themselves disappointed. Picking the wrong professional money manager can be devastating.

§ 2.2[a] The Definition of a Professional Money Manager

As used throughout this chapter, *money manager* refers to two types of entities:

1. Investment advisers registered with the U.S. Securities and Exchange Commission (SEC) under the Investment Advisers Act of 1940 or registered with the equivalent agency of a state; and
2. Mutual funds registered with the SEC under the Investment Company Act of 1940.

There are many investment products available in the marketplace that do not fall within this definition of money manager. For example, investment partnerships are often not registered under the Investment Company Act of 1940 nor necessarily managed by a registered investment adviser. Although these products are usually legitimate, they lack the investor protections afforded by regulated entities. Brokers, insurance agents, and financial planners may also be registered investment advisers but are not considered as such in this chapter because of the many conflicts of interest inherent in selling securities. Finally, this chapter does not discuss banks or trust companies because of their complex regulatory environment. A banking institution may also have conflicts of interest with regard to investing a portfolio.

What are the primary differences between the two entities in the above definition? Registered investment advisers manage individual client portfolios. Each client actually owns the stocks in his or her portfolio. Registered investment advisers generally provide more personalized service than do mutual funds, which pool client assets in one common portfolio. Mutual fund clients own shares of the mutual fund while the mutual fund owns the stocks in the portfolio. Whereas individual portfolios can be managed with specific client tax preferences in mind, all mutual fund shareholders must share the tax liabilities of the mutual fund. Finally, mutual funds usually accept clients with much smaller portfolios than do registered investment advisers.

Which of the two entities should an affluent investor select? Strictly as a rule of thumb, based on the fees charged by money managers, investors with portfolios worth less than $100,000 should limit themselves to mutual funds. Similarly, investors with portfolios worth more than $500,000—with one important exception—should seek the more personalized services of a registered investment adviser. The exception to this rule involves portfolios of employee benefit plans that offer some form of participant choice. Because mutual funds are valued daily and are unitized, they may be more appropriate for these types of portfolios. For investors with portfolios ranging from $100,000 to $500,000, the choice of entity is less obvious. An affluent investor with a portfolio within this range will need, among other things, to factor in the impact of price and personalized service before making a decision with regard to the preferred entity.

§ 2.2[b] The Background Check

After deciding whether to seek a mutual fund or a registered investment adviser, the affluent investor can move on to the background check. First, the affluent investor should generate a list of potential money managers by consulting the telephone book for a list of local money managers and consulting Nielson's Investment Adviser Directory, which sorts money managers by city and state. Furthermore, local business publications often publish a list of local money managers. The affluent investor may also hire an investment consultant to provide a list of money managers.

Once a simple list has been generated, the research phase begins. The investor should try to find out about the money manager without contacting the money manager directly. This accomplishes two purposes: (1) the investor can obtain unbiased information and (2) the investor can avoid being placed on the money manager's prospecting list. The affluent investor should try to gather indirect sources of information from local publications, the Internet, and local attorneys and accountants (unless, of course, these professionals offer investment advice or have any other conflict of interest).

Once the affluent investor generates a list of candidate money managers, he or she should try to identify other people in a similar position who have hired professional money managers. The SEC does not permit registered investment advisers to use client testimonials in advertising. Therefore, the investor must conduct a proactive search for clients willing to provide references.

During the background check, the affluent investor looks for several answers. He or she will want to confirm that the money manager practices an investment philosophy broadly similar to that required by the affluent investor. The affluent investor will want to get some sense that the money manager exhibits an acceptable level of client sensitivity and provides adequate client service. Most important, the background check affords the affluent investor with the opportunity to begin to assess the character of the money manager. After completing the background check, the affluent investor can begin interviewing the money manager candidates.

Investment performance has not been mentioned as part of the background check, not to dismiss investment performance, but for three reasons.

First, it is easy to get reliable performance figures for mutual funds, but it is difficult to get reliable performance figures for individual portfolio management. There are ways to obtain equity performance figures for money managers, but these performance figures do not speak to total portfolio performance. The same money manager may manage two different portfolios in different ways. Unfortunately, performance information on individual money managers can really be obtained only from the money manager, who is the only one in a position to explain how the performance figures relate to the affluent investor's required investment philosophy. Second, a money manager should not be eliminated prematurely (i.e., before the interview). A money manager with poor investment performance can still offer important insights, even if those insights show the affluent investor what not to do. Finally, as is more thoroughly discussed at the end of this chapter, past results do not predict future results.

§ 2.2[c] The Interview Agenda

The affluent investor should have a written agenda for the candidate interviews and a list of questions he or she wants answered. By having an agenda, the affluent investor controls the interview process. Without an agenda, the affluent investor risks being consumed by the candidate's sales presentation. The agenda for each interview, which should take about one hour, consists of these sections, which are discussed below:

- Casual introductions (5 minutes)
- Summary of the affluent investor's needs (15 minutes)
- Brief summary of the money manager's background (5 minutes)
- Review of the money manager's investment philosophy and stock selection process (30 minutes)
- Thank you, good-bye, and review (if any) of follow-up tasks (5 minutes)

Obviously, the interview process might be more difficult, if not impossible, with regard to mutual fund candidates. Still, the affluent investor should try to interview the portfolio manager of the mutual fund candidate. In addition, the affluent investor may want to prepare a list of questions for each section of the agenda. These questions may differ from investor to investor.

§ 2.2[c][1] Casual Introductions. After announcing him- or herself to the receptionist, the investor will probably have a short wait in the lobby if he or she is on time. When the candidate comes to greet the investor, the investor should introduce him- or herself by stating his or her name, position, and the reason for the meeting. The candidate may be allowed the courtesy of a similar introduction. At this point, and before even leaving the lobby, the investor needs to confirm that the individual with whom he or she is speaking will be the individual responsible for choosing the specific investments for the investor's portfolio. If this individual is not the portfolio manager who will be assigned to the investor's account, the investor should abruptly excuse him- or herself by apologizing for the misunderstanding and by rescheduling an interview with the correct person. Alternatively, the investor may wait in the lobby until the actual portfolio manager comes out to greet him or her.

An affluent investor will strictly demand the most personalized service and therefore must avoid speaking with anyone other than the portfolio manager. Some professional money managers place a premium on "asset gathering" rather than personalized portfolio management. These advisers will assign a sales representative to talk to all clients. The portfolio managers talk only to the most important clients. In the worst case, the money manager will not have any portfolio managers and instead will rely on an impersonal committee to make broad investment decisions to be applied to large numbers of clients. The existence of sales representatives or the lack of portfolio managers should signal to the affluent investor that the money manager in question may not offer personalized portfolio management service.

§ 2.2[c][2] Summary of the Investor's Needs. Once the investor has confirmed that the candidate being interviewed will be his or her portfolio manager, the investor will need to spend a significant amount of time discussing the needs of his or her portfolio. In this section of the agenda, the investor will want to introduce the portfolio manager to his or her investment objective and the reasons why he or she has chosen his or her investment philosophy. The investor should not allow the portfolio manager to begin debating the merits of the investor's philosophy over other alternatives. Such debates are never-ending and usually come about because the portfolio manager does not share the investor's philosophy. By the time the investor begins interviewing candidates, he or she should have settled any debates regarding investment philosophy. Beyond intellectual curiosity, a portfolio manager seeking a debate is really trying to make a sales presentation. The affluent investor must view this negatively.

The investor must be sure to tell the portfolio manager the ultimate lifetime dream or dreams associated with the portfolio. The candidate also needs to know whether the portfolio is short term or long term and the GOT. Regarding the target rate of return, professional money managers always try to lower client expectations. This is acceptable, but the investor will need to determine how uncomfortable the candidate becomes when the investor suggests his or her target annual rate of return. An investor should not hire a money manager who is not confident that he or she can achieve the target annual rate of return over time. Finally, the candidate should be told whether the portfolio is taxable or tax exempt and whether the investor expects the portfolio to be invested primarily in common stocks or in money markets and short-term notes. Again, a portfolio manager who tries to sell the investor other asset classes may be inappropriate.

§ 2.2[c][3] Brief Summary of the Candidate's Background. The preceding section of the agenda mentally prepares the candidate to launch into a sales pitch. As a result, many money managers attempt to seize the agenda at this point. It is therefore critical for the investor to stick to his or her agenda. Asking the candidate to provide a *brief* summary can remove any urge within the candidate to begin a sales presentation. It will also give the investor important insight into the candidate's experience, character, and ability to provide personalized service. The affluent investor faces the challenge of completing this section of the agenda in five minutes. Speed helps induce focused answers.

To gauge a candidate's experience, the investor will usually ask how long the candidate has been employed by the firm, how long he or she has been in the industry, and how long he or she has managed other clients with an investment philosophy similar to the investor's. The investor should ask about previous employment, college degrees, and professional certifications. These questions will give the investor a sense of how much intellectual weight the candidate carries. Most important, these questions allow the investor to determine whether the candidate has experience through different market cycles, thus making him or her less likely to panic during a downturn and abandon the investment philosophy.

To gauge a candidate's character, the investor will have to ask some direct questions. Most important, the investor will want to know whether the candidate has ever been convicted of a felony or a misdemeanor or whether the candidate (or his or her firm) has ever been cited for a violation by any regulatory agency. Finding out how late the candidate works helps indicate whether the candidate is a workaholic or is otherwise not well-rounded. Some people might feel this is counterintuitive. These people might say good investment managers are notorious for not being well-rounded. This may be true for a select group of money managers who find themselves regularly appearing on national television, but it is an ad hoc argument to assume only non-well-rounded people make good money managers. In the real world, the affluent investor will probably not be interviewing a jet-setter. More important, since the affluent investor will likely want a long-term relationship with the candidate, it would be wise to avoid someone who might have a tendency to burn out or graduate to national television.

In addition, the investor should try to find out what the candidate does in his or her free time. Ideally, the investor will want to work with someone who has a healthy mix of work, family, and community activities. A person who has a history of serving on community boards would be attractive. The issue of outside activities, including serving as an officer or a director of a professional society, has created much controversy among professionals of all sorts. Some employers want their salaried professionals to spend all their waking hours at work (this increases productivity without increasing costs, since salaried professionals receive the same pay no matter how many hours they work). The affluent investor should look favorably on professional money managers who actively support their community and profession. The lack of such active support can often imply that the money manager cares more about increasing his or her own personal wealth than about helping the community. Affluent investors would be better served by avoiding such selfish characters.

The affluent investor should determine whether there have been any recent ownership changes or whether there are any planned ownership changes. Changes in ownership may invalidate character conclusions reached during the interview.

Gauging the candidate's ability to provide personalized portfolio management service is straightforward. The investor should just find out how many portfolios the candidate manages and how many client relationships he or she has. Another indication of potential service problems comes about by asking how often the candidate is out of the office, either for vacation or for business. The affluent investor will also want to ask how often the candidate both speaks to and meets with clients and about the frequency and content of client reports.

Since personalized service is represented by more than just numbers, the affluent investor should ask a few open-ended questions: How does the money manager provide personalized service? How can funds be withdrawn from a portfolio? What formal process does the candidate undertake to incorporate specific client considerations into portfolio management? Does the candidate rely on investment direction from another person or from a committee?

§ 2.2[c][4] Review of the Money Manager's Investment Philosophy and Stock Selection Process. In this section of the agenda, the affluent investor seeks to hear the candidate justify how the investor's investment philosophy can be used to meet the investor's investment goal and, ultimately, to achieve the lifetime dreams identified earlier. In addition to looking for answers to these questions, the affluent investor should keep an ear out for warning phrases. If the candidate makes any of the following statements, the conservative long-term investor might be better off avoiding that money manager:

1. *"We invest in convertible bonds, long-term bonds, options, futures, currencies, commodities, foreign securities, and initial public offerings,"* or *"we invest in a whole lot more than just exchange-listed securities, over-the-counter securities, and short-term Treasury notes."* Why is this a warning signal? This money manager does not seem to be sure what type of investments he or she should concentrate on. Worse, any of these types of securities does not merit the conservative label. By making this statement—or one like it—the money manager is really saying that he or she prefers to talk investment jargon than to understand the complex needs of an affluent investor. Furthermore, the use of jargon, or a broad array of investment products, betrays this manager as a jack of all trades but master of none.

2. *"We have a long history of producing superior risk-adjusted returns."* Why is this a warning signal? One of the seven deadly sins of professional money managers, mistaken risk, alludes to the folly of trying to define any investment environment in terms of statistics. The affluent investor might want to pay more attention to this money manager's use of statistics. The affluent investor must maintain focus on the portfolio's actual long-term return, not narrowly defined risk-adjusted return or even a more broadly defined, yet arbitrary, market return.

3. *"We seek to reduce volatility by investing in long-term government bonds."* Why is this a warning signal? Bond insecurity, another of the seven deadly sins of professional money managers, points out that long-term government bonds do not reduce volatility. The affluent investor must avoid becoming impatient when confronted with this statement. Once the money manager makes this erroneous statement, the affluent investor will gain nothing by pointing out, for example, that in all of 1994, in the first quarter of 1997, and in the first quarter of 1999, long-term bonds clearly did *not* reduce volatility. This tends to move the manager into a defensive posture and produce a meaningless and potentially time-consuming debate. Rather, the affluent investor would treat himself better by merely noting factually incorrect statements for his or her own use and listening quietly to what the manager says.

4. *"We don't think of ourselves merely as money managers; we see ourselves as risk managers."* Why is this a warning signal? This statement refers to one of the seven deadly sins, mistaken risk. This chapter advocates an investment process that places tangible investment goals ahead of any subjective assessment of risk. The affluent investor who has successfully understood this process immediately understands why he or she needs to hire a money manager, not a risk manager. Indeed, the greatest risk faced by the affluent investor is selecting a money manager who fails to appreciate the needs and the goals of the affluent investor.

5. *"We've incorporated <u>the Nobel Prize–winning Modern Portfolio Theory.</u> [this can also be filled in with arbitrage pricing theory, statistical analytics, and other terms] into our investment process."* Why is this a warning signal? As pointed out above (see § 2.1[b]), the capital asset pricing model, the arbitrage pricing theory, or any other academic theory based on the rational investor cannot really help anybody pick the best investments. They may yield elegant mathematics, but there is no causal relationship between elegance and successful investing. The affluent investor generally appreciates the efforts of academics but realizes the difference between the world of theory and the world of experience. The affluent investor, however, should demand that the candidate explain how behavioral economics is incorporated into the money management discipline.

6. *"We use a proprietary [or industry-accepted—it doesn't matter] portfolio optimization program capable of producing sophisticated analysis in*

easy-to-read color charts and graphs." Why is this a warning signal? As the deadly sin of asset misallocation illustrates, portfolio optimization uses statistical assumptions that have no merit and, in the worse case, is nothing more than a fancy way of saying "market timing." The affluent investor must be especially careful not to fall down the slippery slope of market timing. This requires discipline. Short of spending a lot of time doing personal research, the fastest path to discipline is simply rejecting jargon associated with portfolio optimization, which can always be used to prove a point using past data but can never be used to predict the future investment return of a portfolio.

7. *"We don't have any individual portfolio managers; we ensure consistent investment management through our investment committee."* Why is this a warning signal? An affluent investor wants consistent investment and prefers to deal with the same person over the long haul. A committee structure usually covers up portfolio manager turnover by de-emphasizing the portfolio manager. As in any service business, the ultimate product is the person delivering the service, not the service itself. The affluent investor cannot afford to forget the golden rule of the service industry: Always talk to the person whose name is on the door.

8. *"We are so dedicated and work so late at night that we have cots as well as desks."* This statement portends ominous consequences by admitting classic workaholic behavior. The person making this statement is also saying, "My work is more important than my family, my friends, my community, and my own health. In fact, my work is more important than you." The affluent investor will want to discourage such behavior because it leads to unproductive work habits that may hurt the investor's investment portfolio. The affluent investor must avoid attempts to help the money manager by pointing out a problem, even one as severe as workaholism. Why? First, the affluent investor, unless he or she is a mental health professional, should not offer mental health advice. Second, making such a point will only insult the money manager and lead to an argument.

9. *"We don't have time for community organizations or professional societies. Our clients are our top priority."* Many casual observers see this as a positive statement. As a potential client, one always wants a service provider to say that its clients are its top priority, but this priority could never justify the commission of a crime for the sake of the client. The affluent investor prefers a well-rounded professional money manager.

The money manager who makes this statement is unwilling to give back to his or her community and profession. An affluent investor generally does not want to work with a professional who cares only about making money. The affluent investor will want the professional money manager to volunteer to serve as a director or officer of community and professional nonprofit organizations.

§ 2.2[c][5] Thank you, Good-Bye, and Review of Follow-Up Tasks. In the last section of the agenda, the affluent investor permits the money manager candidate 30 minutes of free-form discussion. When the affluent investor feels he or she has enough information, the interview is over. Before concluding the interview, the investor should review any follow-up tasks and thank the candidate for his or her time.

§ 2.2[d] Why Character Is Important

Ultimately, in selecting a professional money manager, the affluent investor seeks to enter into a fruitful long-term relationship. The ultimate success of the relationships will require trust, understanding, and open communication. Therefore, the affluent investor needs to assess the character of the candidate money manager.

To do this, the affluent investor needs to personalize the selection process and focus on the individual who will ultimately manage the portfolio. The nature of the questions that will need to be answered may make this exercise difficult or impossible to conduct with mutual funds. If possible, these questions should be directed toward the portfolio manager of the mutual fund. For registered investment advisers, these questions should be directed at the person who will be responsible for managing the portfolio and for servicing the affluent investor. (Advisers who have more than one person assigned to these tasks might need to be eliminated from contention. A team of experts makes it more difficult for the affluent investor to know who has ultimate responsibility.)

Below is a list of typical questions that can help the affluent investor determine his or her comfort level with the character of the professional money manager:

1. Would the investor allow a convicted felon to manage his or her portfolio, even if the manager has a performance record that doubles every year?

2. Is the investor confident that the person he or she is dealing with today will be there tomorrow? Has there been stable ownership? Will ownership continue to be stable?
3. Does the person who best knows the investor and his or her needs and goals also make the portfolio management decisions?
4. What formal process does the money manager undertake to incorporate specific client considerations into portfolio management?
5. Is portfolio management compromised, for example, by the use of an investment committee?
6. Is the portfolio manager really taking investment direction from someone else (e.g., an investment committee, an economic policy group, a stock review and selection group, a trust and investment committee)?
7. Is the money manager a well-respected member of the community, as evidenced by roll-up-the-sleeves—as opposed to resume fodder—service on volunteer boards, in local government, and in professional societies?

The answers to these questions can indicate to affluent investors that what they thought was personalized service is really not. An affluent investor must immerse him- or herself in achieving his or her lifetime dream. This requires an effort at personal intimacy. To truly help affluent investors, the professional money managers they select must be able to deliver personal intimacy.

§ 2.2[e] Making the Selection: One or Multiple Money Managers?

After interviewing all the candidate money managers and carefully reviewing the notes of each interview, the affluent investor can select one money manager from the pool of candidates. Very often the affluent investor will believe it is necessary to select multiple money managers. Does the hiring of multiple money managers offer any advantages to the affluent investor? Most professionals readily embrace this notion.

There might be several reasons for this view. The affluent investor may want to have a portfolio segmented into domestic and foreign portions. Rarely can one money manager successfully manage both portions. Generally, a money manager will excel at only one style. In their quest to gather more assets, many money managers may offer different styles (sometimes referring to different styles as different investment objectives), but they are probably only good at one of those styles. The investor must hire a manager for the style for which the manager is best known. If the affluent investor wants multiple investment styles, hiring multiple money managers would be appropriate. For example, each option in a multiple option participant choice employee benefit plan represents a different investment style and most likely will have a different money manager.

Another school of thought holds that investors might be better served by hiring multiple money managers with the same style. The risk of this approach is overdiversification. Rather than hedging their bets by hiring multiple money managers, affluent investors should just avoid hiring money managers about which they have concerns. It is better to hire the one near-perfect money manager than hire three mediocre money managers.

If the affluent investor wants to hire multiple money managers, the aggregate portfolio must be broken into component portfolios for each money manager hired. Since the component portfolios are smaller than the total portfolio, the affluent investor will need to reassess whether a registered investment adviser or a mutual fund would be more appropriate for each component portfolio.

Once the affluent investor makes the general decision of hiring one or multiple money managers, the specific selection or selections can be made. It is a good idea for an attorney to review the investment management agreement. Most investment management agreements will be just fine, and the affluent investor should avoid making any unnecessary changes. Still, legal review will help prevent any truly disadvantageous language.

§ 2.3 Monitoring the Money Manager

The next important task in the investment process is monitoring the money manager.

§ 2.3[a] Revisiting the Investment Goal

Before the investor can even begin to monitor the money manager, he or she must review the reasons for choosing that money manager in the first place. The affluent investor must be prepared to remove a money manager who has done a credible job if the investor's investment goals have changed and must therefore start back at the beginning. The affluent investor must review his or her status to determine whether he or she has substantially the same lifetime dream. Has the lifetime dream changed in any way? If so, then everything else changes and the affluent investor needs to restart the process.

If the lifetime dream remains the same, the affluent investor must determine whether the milestones on the critical path have been met. These milestones can include spending and saving behavior, depletion of or addition to the investment portfolio, and other factors important to moving toward attainment of the lifetime goal. If progress has lagged, the affluent investor must ascertain how far behind schedule it is. The affluent investor must also make an assessment of why progress is off target. Finally, the affluent investor must calculate what can be done to get progress back on track.

After reviewing his or her lifetime dream and the milestones on the critical path, the affluent investor will need to determine whether the chosen investment goal is still appropriate. Over time, the goal associated with a lifetime dream may shift from a long-term investment goal to a short-term investment goal. In some cases, superior investment returns may allow the affluent investor to move from a wealth accumulation goal to a wealth preservation goal. If the investment goal changes, it is likely that the affluent investor will need to change money managers, no matter how well the current money manager has performed.

§ 2.3[b] Revisiting the Money Manager Selection

Having re-evaluated the initial assumptions and determined their continued relevance, the affluent investor can begin reviewing the money manager. This review will be unnecessary if the original investment goal has changed. It is very unlikely that the affluent investor will select the same money manager to handle a portfolio with a different investment objective. The affluent investor monitors the money manager by reviewing the adviser's character, service, and investment results. The character issues are similar to those discussed in the selection process (see § 2.2[b]). After working with the money manager, the affluent investor may want to add a few more character questions such as whether the money manager has ever lied, whether he or she conspicuously consumes, or whether the affluent investor dislikes the money manager.

When reviewing the money manager, the affluent investor must ask if the money manager has provided excellent personal service. This may be the most important question. It is vitally meaningful for the affluent investor to know whether the money manager is reaching any capacity limits before such limits detrimentally impact investment performance.

At this point it may be useful to examine the concept of capacity limits as applied to the manufacturing sector versus the service sector. (The investment advisory business is like any other service business.) One cannot readily apply what works for the manufacturing sector to the service sector. For example, when a manufacturer hits a capacity limit, it just builds a new factory and hires more people. A manufacturer can do this because the primary asset of the firm lies in its ability to transform tangible raw materials through an easily copied mechanical process. The service sector, however, relies on the creative talents of a single person or, at most, two or three people who have grown up together in the business and share the same intellectual history of their mutual business experience. There is no practical solution to increasing the capacity limits of a service firm.

> **Example.** Assume a very creative individual starts a service business. As the service firm becomes more successful, it attracts more clients. Eventually, the service firm reaches the limits of its capacity. The creative entrepreneur can no longer take on additional clients without reducing the service level of existing clients. Unfortunately, rather than accepting fate, the creative person hires a business consultant who persuades him to hire associates and to delegate work to them. The consultant's advice appears to pay off and the service firm continues to grow for another year or so.
>
> Suddenly, the firm stops growing and starts contracting. The creative person, his reputation of success tarnished, cannot explain why. Of course, had he accepted the reality of the service industry, he would have understood that he was not selling widgets but, instead, his own vital creativity. His "product" is his ability to transform his creativity into a favorable end result for his clients through a very personal process.

Failing to provide an adequate level of service may prove a good predictor of a money manager's future shortcomings. If the affluent investor feels the money manager has grown too much to provide the kind of personal service the money manager initially provided, the affluent investor should talk to the money manager before firing him or her. All other things being the same, the affluent investor might be better off giving the money manager measurable targets and a time frame in which to meet them. If the money manager fails to meet these targets within the stated time frame, the affluent investor must fire him or her.

§ 2.3[c] Some Revealing Questions

How can an affluent investor best determine whether the service level has dropped to a point of concern? Certainly, not returning phone calls in a timely fashion or failing to answer written correspondence would qualify as a serious degradation in service. Here, however, the service considered must be the complete package, not just being cordial to the client. The affluent investor will also need to determine the relationship between service and investment results. Below are listed several questions the affluent investor must answer to monitor the money manager:

1. Is the money manager deviating from his or her stated investment philosophy? The affluent investor originally hired the money manager because that money manager had an investment philosophy appropriate to the needs of the affluent investor. If the money manager fails to pursue or deliver that investment philosophy, he or she should be replaced.
2. Does the money manager still understand the nature of the affluent investor's lifetime dream? A money manager who is not sensitive to the lifetime dream of the affluent investor may make a crucial investment error.
3. Is the key investment decision maker still the key investment decision maker? The affluent investor originally selected the money manager because of the key investment decision maker, who is almost always a principal of the firm. The key decision maker may change over time. This could be the result of death, retirement, change of ownership, or even semiretirement or delegation to former subordinates. Any time the original key decision maker removes him- or herself from actively managing the investment portfolio, the affluent investor must begin the money manager interview process again. The affluent investor does not necessarily have to fire the money manager but cannot assume a different person using the same corporate name will provide the type of service originally envisioned.

4. Is there any indication the key investment decision maker has lost competence? Loss of competence can occur in two broad areas:

   a. Executing the stated investment goal; and
   b. Servicing the affluent investor's lifetime dream.

5. Does the money manager consistently and significantly underperform other money managers the investor might choose from? This question should not be confused with the subject of performance. The first key word is *consistently*. The investor should not agonize over annual deviations in performance and must give the money manager three to five years before concluding anything about the consistency of his or her performance. The second key word is *significant*. Just below average is acceptable; the bottom quartile is not. The third key phrase is *other money managers the investor might choose from*. The investor should avoid:

   a. Comparing his or her money manager to one that employs a different investment philosophy, since different investment philosophies perform differently in different investment markets;
   b. Comparing his or her registered investment adviser with something that is not a registered investment adviser, since a registered investment adviser can give the investor a much more personalized level of service than a mutual fund can; and
   c. Comparing his or her money manager to an artificial index, since all indices combine stocks by certain criteria that may not match the criteria important to the investor's investment philosophy. Indices do not include transaction costs or related portfolio (advisory, custodial, or brokerage) expenses. Index portfolios are generally available only through mutual funds, and as stated above, a registered investment adviser should not be compared with a mutual fund.

6. Is the money manager someone with whom the investor still wants to do business? The affluent investor would probably prefer ending a business relationship with a money manager recently convicted of a crime. Other character traits might cause concern. For example, the money manager may not have done anything illegal, but if he or she is developing a reputation for questionable ethics, the affluent investor might want to sever ties. There may be personal reasons for no longer doing business with a money manager: conspicuous consumption, support for ques-

tionable causes, or disdain for participating in worthwhile community activities.

§ 2.4 The Role of Performance Results

To this point, the investment process has been discussed with nary a reference to investment performance. Neophyte investors might question the logic behind this omission. They incorrectly assume that investment performance drives all investment-related decisions. By now, the affluent investor realizes that his or her ultimate purpose must be his or her only guiding vision. From his or her list of lifetime dreams, the affluent investor derives all other considerations, including the generic investment goal, the specific investment philosophy, and the hiring of a professional money manager. Investment performance, to the extent the affluent investor uses it, becomes relevant only in extreme cases and most likely in the monitoring phase of the process. Although a money manager should not be hired based on past investment performance, significantly poor performance can and should justify the removal of a money manager. Very rarely can a money manager provide compensating service to justify risking the long-term objectives of the investment portfolio.

§ 2.4[a] A Common Mistake: Chasing Performance

This chapter has tried to dissuade the affluent investor from chasing performance. The siren song of top performance beckons the inexperienced investor, and like the temptress of the Greek epics, will shipwreck investment portfolios against the rocks of reality. The affluent investor understands why every mutual fund prospectus and every money manager advertisement must include the phrase "past performance is no guarantee of future results."

That last year's winners are rarely this year's winners goes without saying. One needs only to explore the back issues of popular magazines to see this. There are many magazines to pick from to prove this point. Some magazine covers tout "The Top Ten Mutual Funds to Buy" while other magazines take a more reserved approach by merely reporting the top performing funds. For example, *U.S. News & World Report* features a yearly report on the best performing mutual funds. In each annual issue, the magazine lists the top ten funds by investment category. Table 1 shows the top ten aggressive growth funds for 1994, 1995, and 1996.[4]

Table 1. ***U.S. News & World Report*** **"Best" Aggressive Growth Funds**

	1996	*1995*	*1994*
1.	State Street Research Global A	Alger Capital Appreciation	Seligman Communications & Info A
2.	Interactive Investments Technology	Fidelity Select Electronics	Govett Smaller Companies
3.	Warburg Small Company Value	Govett Small Companies A	Alliance Technology A
4.	PBHG Technology & Communication	Smith Barney Special Equities A	Merrill Lynch Technology
5.	Fidelity Select Energy Service	Dean Witter Health Sciences	PBHG Emerging Growth
6.	Fremont U.S. Micro-Cap	TCW/DW Small Cap. Growth	Robertson Stephens Value Plus
7.	G.T. Global Natural Resources A	Fidelity Select Air Trans.	Fidelity Select Health Care
8.	EV Marathon Gold & Natural Resources	Invesco Strategic Health Sciences	Fidelity Select Computers
9.	Rydex OTC	PIC Small Cap. Growth	Fidelity Select Medical
10.	CGM Realty Fund	BT Investment Small Cap	BT Investment Small Cap

During these three years, only one fund ended up on more than one annual list. No 1995 "best" fund repeated as a 1996 "best" fund. This analysis can be repeated with any magazine's annual top ten list and the results would be similar. Clearly, an affluent investor should never assume this year's top performer will be among next year's top performers. History shows such an outcome to be highly unlikely.

Martin S. Fridson explains this phenomenon elegantly using the February 11, 1991, issue of *Barrons* for his example.[5] *Barrons* listed the top ten performing mutual funds for a selected period as shown in Table 2.

Table 2. *Barrons* Top Ten Mutual Funds

	One Year	*Five Years*	*Ten Years*
1.	Fidelity Select: Bio Tech	GT Global Japan	Fidelity Magellan
2.	Fidelity Bond Performance	Financial Portfolios: Health	Merrill Pacific: A
3.	Shearson Currency: Pound	GT Global Pacific	Phoenix: Growth
4.	Financial Portfolios: Health	Nomura Pacific Basin	CGMA Capital Development
5.	Fidelity Select: Health	Merrill Pacific: A	Sequoia Fund
6.	Kemper Global Income	First Investors Global	Fidelity Destiny I
7.	Equity Strategies	Fidelity Destiny II	Quest for Value
8.	Shearson Currency: Deutschmark	Fidelity Select: Food	Japan Fund
9.	Fidelity Deutschmark Performance	Oppenheimer Gold & Specialty Mining	Oppenheimer Target
10.	Scudder Global: International Bond	Japan Fund	Lindner Dividend

Table 2 further complicates decision making based on historic performance. No top ten-year performer finished well enough to make the one-year top performer list. This reveals a critical point. Many investors know it is foolish to look at one-year numbers because different market sectors do well in different years. Yet these investors willingly rank money managers by longer-term numbers under the mistaken idea that "things even out" over time. Table 2 shows that only two funds (both Asian funds) from the ten-year list made the five-year list. Likewise, only one fund (in the health sector) from the five-year list qualified for the one-year list. The data provided in these two tables can lead to only one conclusion: Past results do not guarantee—or even predict—future results.

Chasing performance—that is, creating a portfolio that is always one step behind—leads to higher portfolio turnover. Turnover, in general, makes it easier for the affluent investor to lose focus on the true purpose of the investment portfolio—the predetermined investment goal. This lack of focus increases the chance the affluent investor will not manage the portfolio assets in a manner that will maximize the probability of attaining his or her lifetime dream.

§ 2.4[b] A Rule of Thumb

The affluent investor has a better alternative than succumbing to the marketing pressures of the financial industry. The affluent investor should always be aware of long-term performance and should have some idea how the selected money manager compares to similar money managers. Although affluent investors must research performance, they should never make a decision based solely on performance. (They must be aware, however, that extremely poor performance generally occurs alongside other impeachable offenses.)

When researching investment performance, the affluent investor must become familiar with how performance is calculated. Again, the purpose of this chapter is not to explain or advocate any of the methods available for measuring investment performance. Its purpose is only to implore the affluent investor to collect performance data in a consistent and reliable fashion. Clearly, the least worrisome manner in which to do this is for the affluent investor to calculate performance on his or her own. Yet, many affluent investors have no practical option other than relying on performance figures provided by their money manager. In this case, the affluent investor will need to know how the money manager calculates performance. In looking at firm-wide performance figures, the affluent investor will need to verify that the data include only accounts with an investment philosophy identical to his or her philosophy. Just as important, the affluent investor will need to confirm that all qualifying client assets have been included in that performance figure.

When analyzing investment performance, the investor must remember the objective of the research. The conservative long-term investor should be concerned, for the most part, only with gross underperformance. Consistent gross underperformance will likely cause the investment portfolio to fail to achieve the planned milestones on the critical path. The affluent investor cannot accept such failure. More to the point, average to slightly below average performance can be accepted if the portfolio remains reasonably likely to achieve the intended targets. Here's a simple test: Would the investor have selected the same money manager if his or her performance was slightly less than the average? The answer should be yes if the investor has focused on the character and philosophy of the money manager.

From the long-term perspective, gross underperformance should clearly worry the affluent investor. From the conservative point of view, the affluent investor also needs to be suspicious of gross overperformance. In many cases, short-term gross overperformance need not disturb the affluent investor because it may be due to short-term market sector fluctuations, which happen all the time. The conservative investor needs to investigate the reasons behind longer-term overperformance. Many times such overperformance could be the result of riskier investments, such as initial public offerings, foreign securities, currencies, derivatives, commodities, futures, options, and a myriad of other investment fads. Adequate long-term performance can and should be achieved without these kinds of risky investments.

A rule of thumb for the affluent investor is never to look at past performance when selecting a money manager. Industry advertising practices make this difficult. The affluent investor, in the face of the data assembled here, should understand why it is useless to screen money managers based on past performance. Of course, once an affluent investor begins monitoring the money manager selected, performance results should be one—not the only—basis for measuring that money manager. More important than finding the money manager with the highest performance is finding the money manager whose philosophy most closely meets the investor's needs.

---

1. Ibbotson's Stocks, Bonds, Bills and Inflation 1996 Yearbook.
2. Id.
3. New York: John Wiley & Sons, 2002, p. 304.
4. *U.S. News & World Rep.*, Feb. 6, 1995; Jan. 29, 1996; Feb. 3, 1997.
5. M.S. Fridson, *Investment Illusions—A Savvy Wall Street Pro Explodes Popular Misconceptions About the Markets* (New York: John Wiley & Sons, 1993).

CHAPTER 3

Wealth Preservation: The Roles and Responsibilities of an International Trustee

Pamela S. Woodburn

Synopsis

There is no question that financial security is important to one's peace of mind. An international trust is one of the many sophisticated strategies that may be used to strengthen and enhance that security. In fact, the formation and administration of an international trust or company can offer benefits in a number of situations. It is an avenue well worth exploring for any wealthy person interested in any of the following:

- Preserving one's wealth
- Confidentiality in the management of one's financial affairs
- Solutions unique to one's needs
- Managing assets held in a number of different countries
- Keeping one's estate for the benefit of family members and others
- Distributing one's assets in a timely, cost-efficient manner
- Minimizing or eliminating probate or legal fees applicable to one's estate
- Investing in securities not available in one's home jurisdiction
- Protecting assets from political and economic instability
- Reducing or eliminating capital gains tax, income tax, or inheritance tax
- Earning substantial but perhaps short-term or erratic income, such as royalties or sponsorships
- A close and continuous relationship with those working on one's behalf.

An international trust can help meet any or all of these objectives. To understand how, it is first necessary to understand the concept of a trust. This concept is fundamental to the ability of a trust—domestic or international—to achieve one's estate and tax planning objectives. The principles applicable to international and domestic trusts are the same.

§ 3.1 What Is a Trust?

Trusts date back at least to the Middle Ages. They were used during the Crusades and other foreign campaigns to hold assets during prolonged absences. Over the centuries, the concept of a trust developed in countries using the English common-law system. Trusts do not exist in most civil-law countries, although different legal institutions that fulfill a similar purpose may exist. Generally, courts in civil-law jurisdictions will not recognize a trust relationship.

The following is a definition of a common-law trust:

> A trust is a conscientious obligation, voluntarily undertaken, but enforceable by law when undertaken to hold or administer, or to hold and administer property conscientiously, for the benefit of another person or persons.[1]

A common-law trust arises when a person (known as the settlor or grantor) transfers legal title to property to another person (known as the trustee) for the benefit of identifiable persons (known as beneficiaries). A trust differs from a contract in that the only person who may enforce the trust is the beneficiary, or a court acting in place of the beneficiary; only the parties to a contract may enforce a contract.

To be valid, a trust must have a settlor, a trustee, and identifiable beneficiaries. The beneficiaries may be identified by name, or as members of a class—for example, "my children" or "my grandchildren," which would include children or grandchildren not yet born at the time the trust is created.

These three parties need not be different. It is possible for somebody to settle a trust and be a trustee. This is often the case, for instance, when parents establish a trust during their lifetime for a dependent child. A trust will not fail for want of a trustee, because a court will appoint one.

Although the trustee has legal title to the trust property, a beneficial interest is held by the beneficiaries. When one person acts as both settlor and trustee, he or she cannot also be the sole beneficiary. In other words, a single individual cannot have both a legal and a beneficial interest in the property, or the structure no longer constitutes a trust. The settlor-trustee can, however, be one of a number of named beneficiaries.

It is common practice for a settlor to gift a gold coin or a nominal sum such as $100 (the corpus of a trust) to bring a trust into being. Once that has been done, other assets can be transferred to the trustees over time. Such additions are best documented. The documentation may specify whether the added assets are to be held on the same or different conditions as the assets already in trust. Assets of all kinds can be placed in a trust, including bank accounts, real estate, stocks and bonds, mutual fund units, limited partnership interests, and shares of private businesses.

In summary, for a trust to exist, three elements must be present:

1. Identifiable trust property (the subject matter);
2. Clearly defined terms for the trust (the words); and
3. Identified or identifiable beneficiaries (the objects of the trust).

The relationship between the trustee and the beneficiaries is fiduciary in nature. The trustee holds a position of confidence toward the beneficiaries, and the law imposes an especially high standard of care (fiduciary duty) on the trustee as the dominant party in the relationship. For instance, the trustee is expected to put the interests of the trust and the beneficiaries before the trustee's own interests.

Most trusts are not permitted to operate in perpetuity. Eventually, they end. This can occur in a number of ways:

1. The trust may reach its termination date.
2. There may no longer be trust assets.
3. The trust fund may be divided (carved up) among the beneficiaries on an actuarial basis.

§ 3.1[a] Testamentary versus Inter Vivos Trusts

Two categories of trusts are testamentary trusts and inter vivos trusts.

A *testamentary trust* is a trust created under the terms of a will and operates only following the death of an individual (the testator). Before the testator's death, the terms of the trust can be modified, or the trust can be canceled, simply by having a new will or codicil prepared. Testamentary trusts are funded from the proceeds of the deceased's estate as set out in the terms of the will.

An *inter vivos trust,* as the name suggests, is a trust established while an individual is alive. It comes into effect once the document or deed is executed and the trustee receives the initial trust fund. Although inter vivos trusts are established during the settlor's lifetime, they can continue operating after the settlor dies.

§ 3.1[b] Revocable versus Irrevocable Trusts

Testamentary trusts are, by nature, irrevocable. Although they can be changed anytime before death by changing one's will, once the trust comes into effect it cannot be altered—unless the trust itself provides for variation or the trustee and/or beneficiaries succeed in an application to the competent court to vary the terms of the trust.

Inter vivos trusts, on the other hand, may be revocable or irrevocable. Revocable inter vivos trusts can be terminated by the settlor at any time. This allows the settlor to change his or her mind and take back all, or some, of the assets in the trust. If the trust is irrevocable, the settlor cannot revoke the terms of the trust and has no legal right to control or take back any of the assets of the trust.

In essence, the settlor of an irrevocable trust gives away ownership of the assets transferred into trust. It is this permanent change in ownership that may create tax advantages and estate planning opportunities.

§ 3.2 International Trusts

Three factors come into play in determining a trust's residency:

1. The proper law of the trust;
2. Where the trustees are resident; and
3. Where the trust is administered.

When these are in the settlor's home jurisdiction, the trust is a domestic trust; where they are not, the trust is an international trust.

International trusts are usually, but not exclusively, inter vivos trusts, and they are often discretionary, meaning that the trustee has discretion as to when and how to distribute either capital or income of the trust to the beneficiaries. Different rules and tax laws apply depending on the country in which the trust is resident.

Figure 1 shows a schematic of an international trust.

Figure 1. International Trust

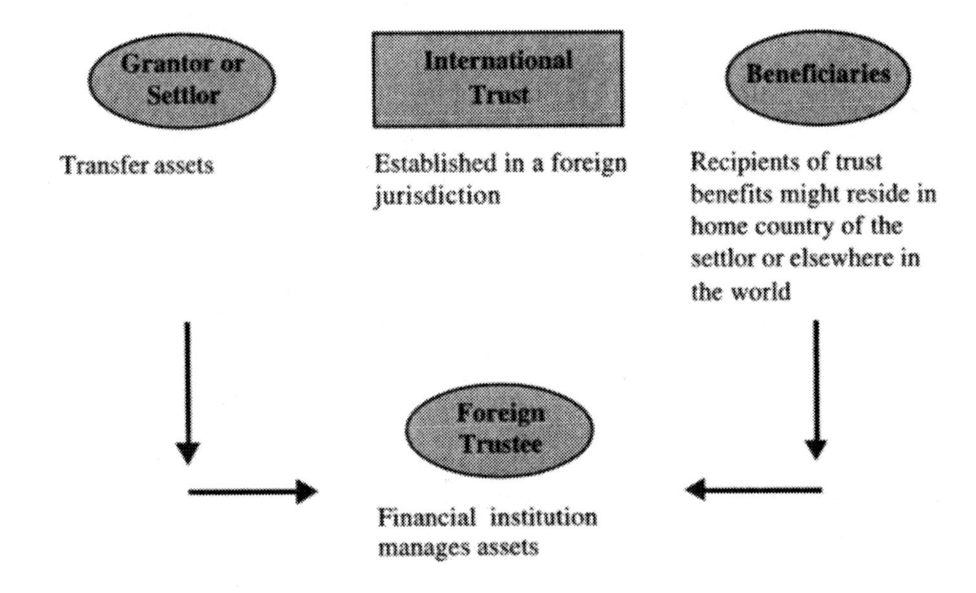

Retaining control may be a settlor's biggest concern when establishing an international trust. Many people would like to enter into a trust structure but are reluctant to cede control. In some instances, they effectively bind the trustee's hands by trying to control the trust during their lifetime—and afterwards, too.

Their concern is understandable. A trust that has been expressly and completely constituted, and with respect to which the settlor has not expressly reserved a power of revocation, cannot be revoked. This can present serious problems when the trust is set up without due care.

> **Example.** A gentleman established an irrevocable international trust in which he placed most of his assets. Neither he nor his wife was named as a beneficiary of the trust. In fact, the trust was worded in such as way that no one in the family could benefit from the trust during the gentleman's lifetime.
>
> Years passed, and the gentleman's business began to fail. He wanted to access some of the funds in the trust to prevent bankruptcy. He asked the trustee for a distribution of capital from the trust to tide him over during this difficult time.
>
> Unfortunately, the trust's terms were clear. Neither he nor his family could benefit from the trust and there was no way, under law, that the trustee could revoke the trust or even encroach on the capital to provide him with an injection of cash.

It is the perceived loss of control that keeps many individuals from establishing a trust structure, no matter how potentially beneficial to themselves and those they wish to benefit. Combined with a well-structured estate plan, however, a trust is an effective way to *take* control.

An effective estate plan will ensure that the settlor's assets pass to the individuals the settlor truly wishes to benefit; that the settlor's assets are not depleted by taxation; that the settlor's assets are protected from litigation; and that the settlor's accumulated wealth will see the settlor through his or her last years whether the settlor is incapacitated or not. At the same time, it is most important to leave sufficient assets outside of a trust structure or have a structure flexible enough to allow access to funds so as not to end up as the gentleman in the example above did.

To feel comfortable with the trust structure, it helps to know what a trustee can and cannot do under law. The trustee, as legal owner of the trust assets, has a duty to ensure that the provisions of the trust are carried out and the beneficiaries' interests protected. The trust deed can provide a mechanism whereby the trustee can be removed and replaced by a new trustee if that is considered appropriate. In jurisdictions that accept the trustee concept in law, the trustee is subject to statutes governing the actions of trustees in addition to the terms of the trust deed. The removal provisions can be used only when a trustee has provided unsatisfactory service or committed a breach of trust.

§ 3.3 The Trust Deed

The key document that an international trustee will follow is the trust agreement or trust deed. The term *agreement* implies a contract. A trust is not a contract, just as a will is not a contract. Therefore, the remainder of this chapter uses the term *trust deed* or *deed,* not the term *trust agreement.*

§ 3.3[a] Provisions of the Trust Deed

The trust deed, a written document, sets out the terms of the trust. It establishes how the settlor intends to work with the trustee on an ongoing basis once legal ownership no longer resides with the settlor. (In the case of a testamentary trust, the terms are contained in the clauses of a will.) The trust deed states what property is transferred to the trustee, the powers and obligations of the trustee, and most important, how and under what circumstances the income and the capital of the trust will be distributed to the beneficiaries.

The trust deed should clearly set out what the settlor wants done and give sufficient power to the trustee to carry out its duties. Generally, the trust deed can expand or override some of the restrictive provisions of the trustee acts, allowing a settlor to establish the terms under which the trust operates, as well as the parameters of the investments that can be made.

The trust deed is an extremely flexible document. It may be drawn up in many different ways to meet the settlor's requirements and concerns. The key provisions in trust deeds deal with how trust assets are to be disposed of and administered and how trustees are to be paid and protected against loss.

The provisions of the trust deed will vary from case to case, but fundamentally, the trust clauses will cover the following areas:

Governance of the trust. Proper law—that is, the law of the jurisdiction of the trust—will govern most matters relating to the trust, including its administration. The trustee, however, can select a different law to govern the trust.

For example, the trust could be a Cayman Islands trust under law, but the administration could be conducted in Guernsey, Channel Islands.

Renunciation by and addition of beneficiaries. Any of the beneficiaries can decide to give up their interest in the trust fund if they want to. The trustee has the power to add new members to the class of beneficiaries.

Exclusion of beneficiaries or other persons. The trustee may have the power to exclude any person, including any beneficiaries, from benefiting under the trust. This power is especially important if a beneficiary is sued by a creditor. During the time of dispute, a prudent trustee will ensure that the beneficiary being challenged cannot benefit from the trust so that the pursuing creditor could not seize the benefit. That beneficiary's interest can be reinstated after the litigation ends.

Appointments of trusts. The trustee may have power at any time to create further trusts for some or all of the beneficiaries. This power can be used, for example, to create a life interest or other fixed interest for particular beneficiaries, or to create subfunds for separate groups of beneficiaries.

Distribution of trust income and capital. The trustee may have discretion to make distributions of capital or income of the trust fund to any of the beneficiaries at any time. In the unlikely event that any part of the trust fund is still held in trust at the expiration of the trust period (generally 80 to 150 years, depending on the jurisdiction), the trustee is to distribute it for the beneficiaries, in shares usually decided by the trustee.

Appointment or application of trust property. The trustee may be empowered to transfer trust property to trustees of other trusts for the benefit of one or more beneficiaries.

Appointment of new or additional trustees. The trustee may have the power to institute a change of trustee; however, this power is often given to a third party named in the trust deed. The settlor can then have greater confidence that an outside party is looking out for the beneficiaries, and if that party is dissatisfied with the trustee chosen, he or she can choose a new one.

Liability of the trustee. The trust may provide protection for the trustee from various liabilities. In particular, the trustee and the trustee's delegates and connected persons are not liable for any depreciation or loss, except in the case of fraud, willful misconduct, or gross negligence (see § 3.8). The trustee may also not be liable for any negligence or fraud of any delegate or agent appointed by the trustee in good faith or in reliance on the advice of or delegation to any investment adviser or manager.

Remuneration. Any corporate trustee may act on its usual terms and conditions, including remuneration. Any trustee who is engaged in any profession, business, or trade may charge his or her usual professional charges for work done in the execution of the trust. Absent specific provision in the trust deed, however, a trustee is not entitled to remuneration. Any trustee or connected person is also permitted to contract or transact with the trustee of any company owned by the trust and to be interested in any such contract or transaction. In such a case, the trustee will not be liable to account for any resultant commission profit or benefit.

Trustees' general powers. The trustee may have very wide powers in administering the trust. Although certain powers are conferred on a trustee by law, a prudent trustee would want to ensure that the following powers are in the trust deed:

- Power of appointment and advancement
- Power to make payments to infants
- Power to ignore interests
- Power to allow beneficiaries to disclaim benefits
- Power to exclude and add beneficiaries
- Power to change proper law
- Power to delegate powers
- Power to appoint trustees
- Powers of investment

  —Power to form companies

  —Power not to interfer with company in which trust is interested

  —Power to employ agents

  —Power to employ investment manager or adviser

  —Power to use nominees and custodians

  —Power to make loans

  —Power to borrow

  —Power to permit occupation of property by beneficiaries

- Power to pay duties and taxes
- Power to sell, lease, and exchange
- Power to appropriate
- Power to engage in trade
- Power to guarantee debts
- Power to effect compromises
- Power to insure trust property
- Power to give indemnities
- Power as to land
- Power as to chattels
- Overriding residuary powers

In general, the trustee has to exercise its powers in the interest of the beneficiaries of the trust. The trustee may also be able to release, restrict, or delegate virtually any of its powers under the trust.

Irrevocability. The settlor of the trust cannot revoke it.

Investment decisions. The trustee has full discretion regarding trust investments. The trustee has the power to acquire property for occupation, use, or enjoyment and to permit persons to use and enjoy property. The trustee is not required to maintain a balance between income and capital nor to diversify trust investments. The trustee may indefinitely retain any property transferred into the trust by the settlor or any member of the settlor's family.

Business holdings. The trustee is not obliged to appoint any representative to the board of any company owned by the trust and has no responsibility to be concerned in the business of such companies. The trustee has various powers in relation to companies owned by the trust, including the power to compromise rights as a shareholder, to convert into companies with unlimited liability, to wind up, dissolve, or liquidate companies, and to exercise voting rights. The trustee may also act as a director or employee of any company owned by the trust and can be paid for doing so. Trust property can in certain circumstances be transferred into a company.

Lending and borrowing. The trustee may lend, let, or hire any money or other property on such terms as the trustee sees fit and without any responsibility for loss or damage to that property. When the recipient of the property is a beneficiary who dies before repaying or returning it, the trustee can waive the right to such repayment or return. Before granting a loan, a trustee must understand the purpose of the loan and whether it will be secured against the trust assets. A trustee can provide for an interest-free loan, although the beneficiary who receives the loan should obtain independent advice to ensure there are no negative implications. The trustee can borrow money for purposes connected with the trust and have discretion to give guarantees and indemnities to or on behalf of any person. The trustee may also create charges over trust property and enter into contracts.

Use of trust property. The trustee can appropriate or allocate particular parts of the trust property to a beneficiary and has the power to make valuations for these and other purposes. The trustee can engage nominees to hold property on the trustee's behalf, engage money managers, and give proxies and powers of attorney to others to act on the trustee's behalf. The trustee has power to give warranties and undertakings, such as on the sale of trust property. The trustee can purchase and deal with annuities and life insurance policies.

Immovable property. The trustee has extensive powers to deal with any immovable property (land or buildings) held in the trust and has no duty to repair or insure such property. Any prudent trustee will, of course, insist that a property agent be appointed to ensure that the property is adequately insured and maintained so as not to become a wasting asset of the trust.

Dealing with minors. When a beneficiary is not an adult or is otherwise legally incapacitated, the trustee may make payments to an appropriate person acting on that beneficiary's behalf.

Recordkeeping. Accounts of the trust have to be kept and may be audited. A prudent corporate trustee will have internal audit procedures to ensure trusts are audited by individuals outside of the jurisdiction of the trust.

Payments out of the trust. The trustee has the power to decide whether to treat money as capital or income and whether any outflows or losses should be paid out of capital or income. The trustee pays any duties, fees, or taxes arising with respect to the trust fund. Expenses and liabilities of the trust are payable out of the trust fund or its income. The trustee can institute and defend against legal proceedings.

Multiple trustees. When there is more than one trustee, they can act by majority. Corporate trustees can act by their duly authorized representatives. Agents can be employed by the trustees to act on their behalf. The trustees can form companies and carry out a trade, either alone or with others.

§ 3.3[b] Importance of a Well-Drafted Trust Deed

The time and effort spent preparing a detailed and explicit trust deed are minimal compared with the problems that can arise when the deed is not properly prepared. The potential for future litigation by beneficiaries is a considerable risk.

> **Example.** Parents decide to disinherit one of their children. To avoid any sort of claim that the child may have on the estate, the parents place much of their estate in trust. The trust assets will not pass under the terms of the will and will not be part of the estate.
>
> There will no doubt be a disgruntled child when the parents die. If the assets in the trust are considerable, that child is likely to seek legal action in hopes of proving that the trust failed, or perhaps was poorly drafted, so that he or she can then lay claim to the estate assets. If it can be proved that there was never a trust, the assets thought to have been transferred to a trust would pass through the parent's estate and the child could win the challenge.

The key thing to remember is that the trust deed should provide the detail necessary to avoid time-consuming and costly court proceedings in the future because the language in the deed seems ambiguous to a beneficiary who is keen to challenge the trust's terms. The settlor may have established the trust with the best of intentions, but often a beneficiary will not see it that way. For this reason, the trust deed should be reviewed carefully with legal counsel.

The number of powers that a settlor will provide the trustee in his or her own deed depends on what the settlor wants to accomplish and who is to benefit from the trust. At first blush, many of the powers may seem unnecessary; however, it is vital to think ahead. Any powers not in the deed may be excluded, depending on the statutory powers granted to trustees in the jurisdiction of the trust. A deed should cover any situations that may arise not only during the settlor's lifetime but also for the lifetimes of the settlor's children or grandchildren or nieces and nephews—the generations the settlor intends to benefit from the creation of the trust. The trustee will be bound by the terms set out in the trust deed. The more flexibility the settlor provides, the easier it will be for the trustee to adapt to changing situations.

A settlor who does not understand the clauses in his or her trust deed should ask an attorney to explain them. The seemingly harmless removal of one clause could perhaps limit a power that the trustee will need in the future; one clause too many might provide a trustee with more discretion than the settlor would like.

To understand how future generations can be affected by the actions of a settlor, one need only look at trusts that were established in the first half of the 20th century. It was then commonplace for a husband to establish a trust for his wife so that she would be taken care of after his death. Women of that era seldom knew how much wealth their husbands had accumulated and knew little if anything about investing. The dutiful husbands of the world therefore placed monies in trust for their wives and often restricted the trustee to investing in only fixed-income instruments to furnish their wives with income.

Typically, the surviving spouse did not have the power to encroach on the capital of the trust. The widow could enjoy the income during her lifetime, but the capital of the trust would go to the children on her death.

Back then, this looked like a wonderful estate plan to many a husband. The wife would be taken care of, the money securely invested, and ultimately the wealth would stay in the bloodline. As time went on, however, the restrictions imposed in these spousal trusts caused problems. As interest rates fell, the income decreased while the cost of living and taxes increased, leaving the widows with a lower standard of living than they had previously enjoyed. There was no way the widow could access the trust capital because the capital was reserved for the remainder beneficiaries, usually the children. Many spouses challenged these trusts because they simply were not providing sustenance. Unfortunately, not all challenges resulted in more income for the widow.

Another problem arose when the widow died and the capital was distributed to the children. Many complained bitterly to their trustee that surely the capital should have been double or triple the size of what they received. If the money had been properly invested, it could have compounded at a rate of 8 or 10 percent annually; however, the trust deed did not allow for the purchase of equities, which would have made such returns possible. What the settlor perceived to be sizable gifts when he created the deed turned out to be only modest, because the trustee lacked the freedom to invest appropriately.

A trust deed can be as flexible or as restrictive as the settlor wishes; however, many quality trustees will not accept trust appointments when the deed to be administered is overly restrictive.

§ 3.4 Choosing a Trustee

The definition of *trust* in the *Gage Canadian Concise Dictionary* is "A firm belief; faith; a confident expectation; the condition of one in whom trust has been placed; rely on; depend on; *adv* trustworthy—that can be trusted."[2]

By transferring assets into a trust a settlor is giving up legal title to those assets and is relying on a person or a corporation to follow the trust. Therefore, it is imperative that the settlor trust the person or corporation chosen as the trustee. Too often, individuals establish trusts without a thorough understanding of the relationship between the settlor and the trustee.

It is paramount that the settlor find an international trustee of the highest quality. Careful consideration must be given to the individual or trust company chosen. Broadly speaking, the characteristics one should seek in a trustee are trustworthiness, sound business judgement, commitment of time to fulfill the duties, impartiality, continuity of service, knowledge of trust and tax law, and experience in trust management and administration.

A high-quality trustee will not accept a trust that has not been properly drafted and, if necessary, vetted by a lawyer in the trustee's jurisdiction to ensure that the trust complies with local laws as well as the corporation's trust policy.

§ 3.4[a] Questions to Ask

Following is a list of questions a settlor should consider asking prospective trustees:

1. *How many trust professionals does the company have internationally?* This question goes to quality of service. What happens when the trust officer goes on vacation? Who is overseeing the administration of the trust then? A settlor may want to consider trustees that offer trust teams so that if one individual is out of the office, the settlor can be confident that another employee who understands the issues will be available.

2. *How many years of experience do the company trust professionals have? What are their professional qualifications?* A settlor should look

for trust professionals from legal or accounting backgrounds or who have a solid trust designation behind them, which is proof of educational accreditation specializing in the subject of trusts.

3. *What kind of experience do the company's trust professionals have with trust litigation?* Trusts are often challenged after the settlor's death by disgruntled beneficiaries. It is important that the trustee understand this and be able to deal effectively with the beneficiaries and the courts (if it goes that far).

4. *How many trusts does the company administer? How long has the company been in the trust business?* These questions go to experience. A trustee with a multitude of trusts all over the world and years of experience is more likely to administer a trust effectively.

5. *Does the company appreciate the home-country implications of the proposed trust arrangements?* Establishing an international trust does not exempt a settlor from the laws of his or her home country. It is important that a trustee understand the legalities of the settlor's home country to ensure that the structure works in the settlor's legal regime as well as in the regime of the international jurisdiction.

6. *Does the company have the resources and knowledge base to keep the trust of continuing use?* In the world of international estate planning, new concepts are being introduced all the time, typically because the laws in the home country change. A trustee should understand the planning and stay on top of changes so that the trust will continue to work from the home country's legal perspective and from the trust jurisdiction's legal perspective.

7. *What are the company's due diligence requirements?* Strict due diligence requirements attract legitimate clients. A trustee that does not ask for a lot of detail may be more interested in earning fees than in helping a settlor accomplish his or her objectives.

8. *What type of trusts does the company administer—complex ones involving real estate or other illiquid assets or simple structures holding only marketable securities?* This queston goes to the quality of the trustee and the level of service a settlor can expect. If the prospective trustee has never administered a trust that holds real estate or private company shares and those are the types of assets the settlor will be placing in the structure, there may be more room for error.

9. *What steps does the trust company take to ensure that confidentiality is respected?* A settlor will want to ensure that the trust officer will not divulge information to certain parties. In fact, confidentiality laws bind many employees and it may be considered a legal offense to provide information to anyone not authorized to receive it.

   For many, confidentiality is a dirty word when it comes to international trusts. Why, they ask, is confidentiality so important? What does that person have to hide? More often than not, the reason for establishing an international trust is legitimate and grows out of the family situation that requires privacy and protection.

   Example. A family establised two international trusts, all of the income of which was to be attributed back to the settlors. There was no tax benefit in doing so; however, their son was a spendthrift and had no real career direction. The parents were concerned that if their son knew their true wealth, he would never seek out a career of any substance and would simply wait for his inheritance. In the eyes of the parents, the only way to avoid this situation was to establish trusts in a foreign jurisdiction.

10. *Does the trustee know what administrative or other actions might taint the trust and its objectives*? It is important that the trustee understand its role and powers.

11. *Who are the company's external auditors?* A settlor should ensure that the trustee will be audited by a reputable external third party, such as a major accounting firm.

12. *What type of internal audit procedures does the company have?* Many high-quality trustees will have large internal audit departments that will complete random audits in the various jurisdictions where they are located.

13. *What accolades or endorsements has the company received?* A settlor should look for a trustee known for quality of service and administration.

14. *What is the company's financial strength?* A settlor should ensure that the trustee has sizable assets so that there is little likelihood that the firm will go bankrupt.

15. *Does the company offer related services, such as in-house investment management, custody, lending, and banking?* This aspect can be extremely important. For example, settlors often use their trusts to provide a guarantee for a loan or line of credit. If the trustee does not have a lending department, it would not be able to provide this ancillary service.

§ 3.4[b] Value for Services

A trustee must consider many factors in establishing how much to charge. They include the following:

1. Is there tax planning involved? If so, is it well-established planning or new, aggressive planning?
2. What is the quality of the advice the client is receiving? Has the client received advice from leading lawyers and accountants?
3. What is the residence of the settlor?
4. What is the nature of the trust assets—artwork, commercial real estate, private company shares, quoted securities, or cash?
5. How diversified will the trust assets be and thus, risk minimized? Will any one investment comprise more than 50 percent of the trust fund?
6. What is the anticipated activity of the trust? Will there be more than ten transactions a month or fewer than three?
7. Who will be the custodian of the assets and thus, risk Minimized? Is the custodian controlled by the same institution as the trustee? If an outside custodian is to be used, what is the quality of that custodian?
8. Did a recognized legal firm prepare the trust deed?

§ 3.5 The Letter of Wishes

A trust deed generally gives the trustee the power to make payments for the "maintenance, education, or benefit" of each beneficiary. It can therefore be useful for the trustee to have guidance as to how the money is to be used and the circumstances under which the trustee should encroach on the capital of the trust and pay it out to a beneficiary. A *letter of wishes* is a document that provides the trustee with insight into the wishes of the settlor and with guidance when the settlor is unavailable to provide feedback. It can have significant influence.

When establishing an international trust, settlors should consider visiting their international trustee to communicate their reasons for establishing the trust and what they deem important for their families or those who are to benefit under the trust should they not be available for consultation in the future. Typically, a trust officer will then make notes to file and prepare a memorandum. In many instances, however, personal interaction is not possible. In such a case, a letter of wishes provides guidance for the trustee.

For example, if the settlor wants a beneficiary to receive monies only for certain items such as education or accommodation, that should be specifically stated in the letter of wishes so that there is no ambiguity. If the settlor wants to ensure that his or her children receive a high-quality education, that should be stated in the letter of wishes. If the settlor does not want the children to receive money for things like a racecar or a trip around the world, these wishes should also be made known to the trustee.

The beauty of a letter of wishes is that it is not a legally binding document. The settlor can amend it at any time to reflect changing circumstances such as marriage, divorce, births, deaths, and so on. It should be reviewed every two to three years, in light of changing circumstances; however, a settlor must be careful not to provide the trustee with a letter of wishes too frequently, or the trust could be challenged. Certain authorities might consider that the settlor has not given up control of the assets and that the mind and the management of the trust are with the settlor.

A letter of wishes is discoverable, as are a trustee's notes to file. A memorandum prepared by a client's attorney and addressed to the trustee may not be.

§ 3.6 Recordkeeping

A trustee must keep accurate accounts concerning the trust property and be ready at all times to explain the administration of the trust to the beneficiaries. That is why a trustee will act only on requests received in writing with signature(s). Requests made over the telephone or email will not be fulfilled unless followed up in writing. Trustees are well aware that they may have to justify their actions at some point in the future.

An international trustee should be prepared to provide a full, detailed trust accounting each year. This will include the following:

- An accounting showing what the original property consisted of and its value at the time the trust was established
- An account of all monies received
- An account of all monies disbursed
- An account of all property remaining on hand and its present value

Principal and income may be dealt with separately, and the accounts must be divided to show receipts or disbursements of both.

Settlors will often request that the beneficiaries not receive trust statements. Under law, however, they have the right to receive statements, and if they are receiving monies from the trust, they will probably want to know about the trust.

If a beneficiary is not receiving any monies (e.g., because he or she is a minor and is not scheduled to begin receiving trust monies until age 25), it is not necessary to provide statements. Once the beneficiary reaches age 25 and begins receiving monies from the trust, however, he or she will no doubt want to see statements—typically, all the statements from the time the trust was created.

A full annual trust accounting is sent annually. Statements can be sent semiannually if required, although there may be an extra charge for this. If an outside investment manager is used to manage the monies of the trust and the trustee is asked to duplicate its records, the trust will also incur extra costs.

§ 3.7 Managing the Trust's Investments

An area of great concern for many settlors is the investment decisions made within the trust structure. Much of today's wealth has been earned by market-savvy individuals who cannot believe that a corporation can manage their money as well as or better than they have. Settlors often want to manage the monies placed in trust themselves or to have those monies managed in the same manner in which they managed their own money.

As noted in § 3.3[a], an international trustee may have the power to employ agents. An investment manager is such an agent. If properly worded, the trust will not be restricted as to how to invest; however, the fundamental fiduciary duty of a trustee is to preserve and increase the assets held in trust for the beneficiaries. Once the trust is established, the trustee is not acting personally for the settlor (who may have been the trustee's original client) but for the trust beneficiaries. It could be considered a breach of trust for a trustee to invest 100 percent of the trust monies in extremely aggressive stocks, because as surely as those stocks can rise, they can fall. A trustee could be sued for what could be seen as investing carelessly without the prudence required to ensure that the trust assets be preserved.

A trustee's duty is to conduct trust business with the care with which a reasonably prudent businessperson would conduct his or her own affairs.

Many argue that a professional corporate trustee owes a higher duty of care than an individual acting as trustee and can be liable for loss caused to a trust by neglecting to exercise the special care and skill that it professed to have. This is not to say that speculative investments are not permitted if the trust deed has authorized them, but it would be foolhardy for a trustee to allow a majority percentage of trust assets to be invested in this manner unless the trustee is specifically required to do so under the trust's terms or the trustee is effectively released from being considered negligent by the beneficiaries. (See § 3.8.)

There is no hard-and-fast rule on how the monies settled into a trust should be invested. Each trust structure is as unique as the clients themselves are. Before the trust is established, it is important that the trustee ascertain how the settlor would like the assets invested. A settlor needs to have basically the same conversation with the trustee that he or she has when shopping for a money manager. The trustee needs to understand the size and type of the assets being placed in the structure; the reporting currency; and the life of the trust. (A trust that is to be wound up in three years would probably be managed very differently than a trust that is to last 100 years.) The trustee will appoint an investment manager, usually after discussions with the settlor.

It is not necessary for the institution that acts as the trustee to act as the investment manager, although using the same institution to act as both trustee and investment manager may make a reduction in the overall fees possible. Regardless of who is chosen as the investment manager, the firm will have to demonstrate to the trustee that it is a solid money manager with experience, adequate resources for investment research, and a proven track record. Typically, the trustee will ask to see an investment proposal so that it can evaluate the suitability of the proposed investments before entering into an investment management agreement with the proposed manager. The settlor may be able to review the proposal and enter into three-way discussions with the trustee and the investment manager to ensure that everyone is clear on the investment parameters. The ultimate decision on appointment of investment managers should, however, rest with the trustee.

Even if an investment manager acts as an agent in investing the trust assets, the trustee retains responsibility and should insist on seeing regular reports and valuations. As part of the monitoring process, the trustee will conduct regular reviews to ensure that the ongoing management of the portfolio is effective and take action when appropriate. An investment manager might be dismissed, for example, if the portfolio's performance has placed it in the fourth quartile for 12 consecutive months.

The assets that one wants to "play with" should be kept outside of a trust structure. If one wants to speculate, one should do it with one's own money and transfer into a trust only the assets that one wants to be preserved for beneficiaries.

§ 3.8 Breach of Trust

Trustees have the following legal obligations:

1. Trustees cannot transfer rights, powers, or obligations to a third party. They must act for themselves.
2. As the owners of the trust property, trustees have an obligation to invest and manage the trust property according to the terms of the trust. They must also be ready to account to the beneficiaries for their management of the trust property.
3. Trustees are personally liable for acts or omissions that adversely affect the trust property or the beneficiaries.
4. Trustees must deal impartially with the beneficiaries.
5. Trustees cannot use the property in any way to benefit themselves. For example, they are prohibited from purchasing property from the trust unless specifically permitted to do so in the trust deed. They are, however, entitled to compensation for their services as provided in the trust documents.

Unfortunately, things do not always run according to plan. Sometimes, trustees do not live up to their obligations. There are six principles that must be considered with respect to a breach of trust:

1. As long as the trustee has acted with honesty and reasonable prudence, the trustee ought not to be compelled to compensate the beneficiary for a loss brought about by the trustee's actions.
2. The courts' objective is to compensate the beneficiary for any loss that has occurred. The courts may insist on a higher standard of care when the trustee is a corporation or an individual who claims to be an expert and receives remuneration for services.
3. The trustee is liable for personal acts and omissions that, subject to the trust's proper law, may extend to those of co-trustees.

4. The express trustee is liable for breach of trust but so is any person considered a trustee by operation of law (where the law will deem a trust to have arisen in order to secure an equitable result).
5. When more than one trustee is in breach, the beneficiary may pursue any or all of the them for compensation.
6. A breach of trust occurs if the trustee enters into legal relationships with third parties that are or will be breaches of its obligation as trustee.

There are generally three categories of breach of trust:

1. Misuse—for example, using the trust property for personal purposes, fraudulently disposing of assets at less than fair market value, or keeping an undisclosed commission.
2. Maladministration—for example, paying unjustifiable expenses or paying debts that are not legally enforceable. If a debt is a moral obligation, it is wise for the trustee to consult the beneficiaries before making payment to ensure that they agree that the payment should be made.
3. Negligence—for example, failing to safeguard assets adequately or failing to pursue assets, by legal action if necessary.

The courts exercise their jurisdiction to remove trustees if interests of the beneficiaries are in jeopardy. In such a case, allowing the trustee to continue may be to the detriment of the beneficiaries.

A trustee has an onerous fiduciary duty to follow the terms set out in the trust deed. It is therefore important for the settlor to allow some flexibility in the trust deed and not to control every little aspect of the trust. The law exists to help ensure that a trustee fulfills its fiduciary duty or suffers serious legal and professional consequences.

§ 3.9 The Role of Protector

Sometimes, despite setting out clear language in a trust deed, fully understanding a trustee's legal duty, and providing direction through a letter of wishes, a settlor still feels uneasy delegating so much power to the trustee. In these situations, appointing a protector may provide the reassurance the settlor needs.

A protector may have the power to appoint a new trustee or new beneficiaries, veto the trustee's decisions, act as arbitrator, or furnish investment advice. The person may be a close friend or relative of the settlor, a business associate, or a corporate body, and is usually located in a legal jurisdiction different from that of the trustee.

Trust professionals often recommend that the protector be given only limited powers. Otherwise, he or she may be interpreted by the courts to be acting as a co-trustee. If the courts can successfully argue that the supposed protector is, in fact, a co-trustee, they could argue that the trust is resident in a jurisdiction other than the one intended. For example, if the protector resides in the United States, it could be argued that the trust is a U.S. trust. In addition, the protector, if seen as a co-trustee, takes on all of the responsibilities of a resident trustee under law.

From a trustee's perspective, having a protector may be helpful if the protector has knowledge of the family's circumstances. The protector can render invaluable assistance to the trustee, particularly with decisions regarding beneficiaries' requests for money. Having a protector can, however, make trust administration more cumbersome and could result in higher fees if the protector must be consulted frequently.

The protector typically does not receive information such as trust statements. Unless the deed specifically requires that the protector receive trust statements, providing such information to the protector would be a breach of trust.

It is important that the settlor trust the person or corporation named as protector to act with the beneficiaries' interests at heart. It is preferable that the protector not be resident in the settlor's home country, especially if the settlor has provided him or her with a number of powers, lest the trust be deemed to be resident in that country rather than resident in the intended jurisdiction. Protectors should not be resident in the United States, the United Kingdom, or Canada, because of these jurisdictions' unattractive tax regimes.

§ 3.10 Creating an International Company

Anytime one is considering creating a trust, one should consider the potential advantages of owning assets through an international company. There are many circumstances under which forming an international company can reduce income tax, inheritance or succession taxes, and capital gains tax. Trusts and company formation services can complement each other or be employed independently.

An international company is often formed, with or without a trust structure, for tax or estate planning purposes or when ownership of an asset cannot be registered directly in a trustee's or owner's name. It may provide shelter for one's property or investment portfolio. There may be taxation advantages, both in the country of investment and the country of residence, and it can add flexibility to one's overall estate plan.

There are times when it is preferable to act anonymously through an international company rather than directly. In addition, in planning an estate, transferring an international company's shares to another party may provide greater flexibility than transferring the assets held by the company itself. An international company may be created for a particular purpose today, but adapted to deal effectively with other types of assets in the future.

The uses of an international company in financial planning are as diverse as individual business and financial interests. Typical applications include the following:

- To hold investments, such as securities or works of art
- To act as a holding company in order to centralize ownership of other companies owned around the world
- To hold real estate
- To own an interest in bloodstock
- To own ships, yachts, and aircraft for private use
- To provide reinsurance opportunities
- To hold copyrights, trademarks, and licenses

If one owned an international company directly, one would be the shareholder; however, the shares of many international companies are owned by international trustees. The fiduciary duty of the trust company hired to administer the company and provide company directors is similar to a trustee's fiduciary duty.

Figure 2 shows a schematic of an international trust with an underlying international company.

Figure 2. International Trust with Underlying International Company

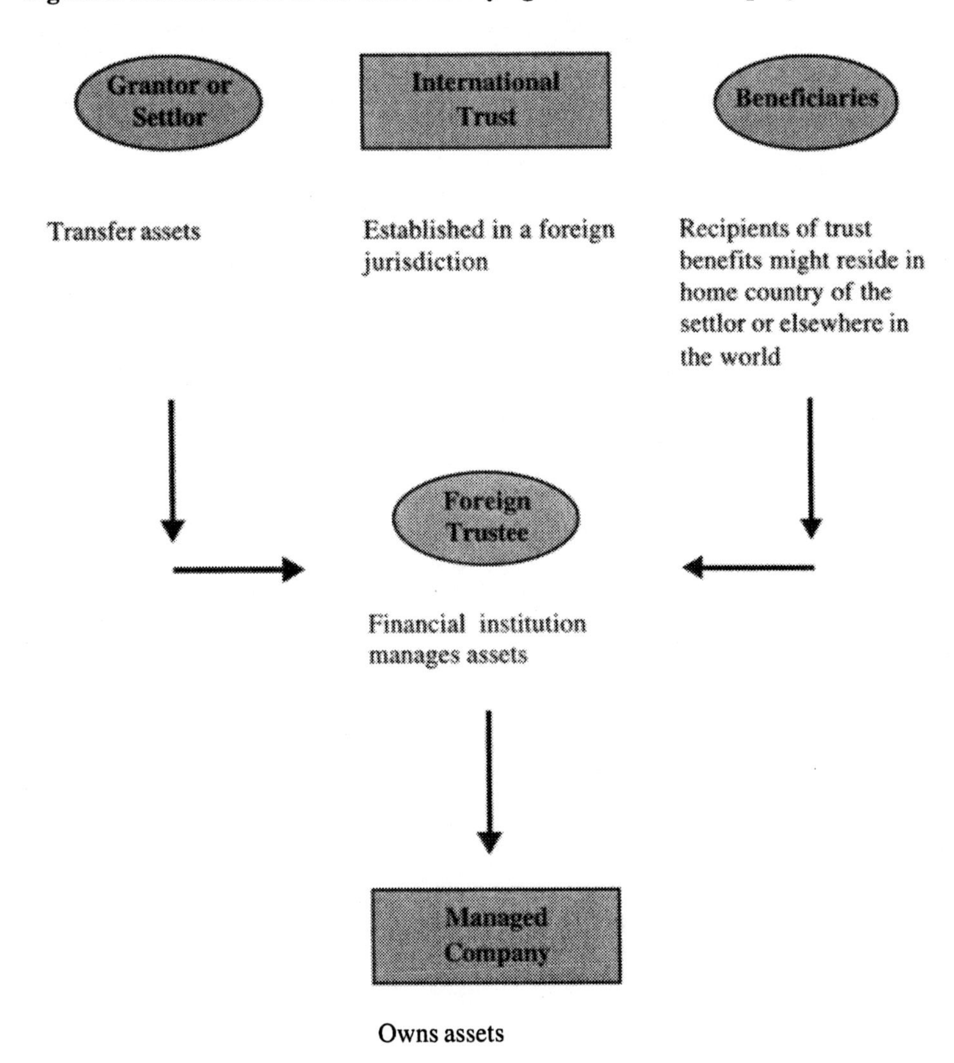

§ 3.11 Due Diligence

Whether one is establishing an international company or an international trust, an international trustee typically will require the following:

- Completion of a client application form, which will provide basic information such as name, address, birthdate, citizenship, and reporting currency

- Certified copies of the passports of the client or of the settlor and the primary beneficiaries, if applicable
- Two letters of reference for the client or the settlor, one banking and one professional
- Trust deed (provided by a lawyer or an accountant)
- Declaration of the source of the funds (e.g., inheritance or sale of a business)
- Fax indemnity form to allow the trustee to receive instructions via fax

Most high-quality international financial centers are countries that have strict laws against receiving the proceeds of crime and therefore will not allow an institution to accept clients whose identity has not been verified or who cannot establish the legitimacy of the funds to be injected. Some of the world's well-known international financial centers are Switzerland, Bermuda, the Cayman Islands, the Bahamas, the Channel Islands, London, and Hong Kong.

§ 3.12 The Need for Professional Advice

The first step to any estate plan is to find a competent professional to offer sound guidance on wealth transfer, wealth preservation, and tax minimization. An international trust offers a multitude of potential benefits to wealthy individuals and their heirs, but an international trust is not an arrangement to be entered into lightly. A trust is not a product. When one creates a trust, one is doing much more than placing one's money in a bank account or investing in a mutual fund.

Once created, an irrevocable trust cannot be changed (except in limited circumstances by a court order or if specific powers are given to the trustee). This makes it imperative that the trust deed or will that is to create a trust at death be properly drafted and accurately reflect the individual's wishes. Since a good trust deed can be very complex, working with an experienced professional, proficient in international estate and tax law, to draw up the trust document is recommended.

Professional assistance is even more important in creating an international trust, which is governed by the laws of the foreign jurisdiction specified in the trust deed. The individual drafting the document must be familiar with the law of that jurisdiction or the deed may not achieve the settlor's objectives.

The draftsperson must also be familiar with the tax laws of the settlor's home country and of the international jurisdiction where the trust is to be located in order to ensure that the two work efficiently together. Most international trusts will be drafted by an adviser chosen in the home jurisdiction; however, an international trustee of high caliber will have the deed presented by the domestic adviser vetted by a lawyer in the trust's jurisdiction to ensure it is in keeping with the laws of that country.

The trust deed must be flexible, yet the language must be clear and the beneficiaries adequately and precisely identified by name or by class. If beneficiaries cannot be identified, the trust will fail for uncertainty. Every reasonably foreseeable eventuality must be addressed.

In selecting a tax or legal adviser, one should carry out one's own due diligence by asking for references, understanding an adviser's practices, knowing an adviser's educational background. Knowing that one has an adviser of high quality can only bring peace of mind.

Once one determines that a properly constructed estate calls for an international trustee, one should apply one's due diligence requirements to this professional as well. If the answers to the questions listed in § 3.4[a] are comprehensive and positive, one can feel confident that one has chosen a trustee of high quality.

---

1. Jenks, *Book of English Law,* p. 379.
2. 2002, pgs. 923 and 924, definitions 1, 2, 5, and 6.

CHAPTER 4

Going Offshore: Tax and Trust Aspects

Graham R. Taylor

Synopsis

Reasons for going offshore for portfolio investments, life insurance, trusts, partnerships, and so on vary depending on a person's domicile and nationality. For example, a Latin American investor will be more concerned about political stability than a U.K. investor. This chapter is written principally from the perspective of a U.S. investor, who is generally more motivated by asset protection concerns than a similarly situated non-U.S. investor, because of the litigious nature of U.S. society. A typical offshore investor will have at least $2 million of investable assets, but individuals with as little as $200,000 to invest also invest offshore, at least in a simple way, such as by investing in international mutual funds.

Going offshore has its risks and rewards. Doing one's homework before proceeding is always necessary. Offshore is not for everyone and the increased costs of being offshore must be justified by quantifiable net benefits;

however, for the adventurous in search of benefits, attributes, and investments not available domestically, going offshore can be the right solution. This chapter discusses some of the reasons U.S. investors seek offshore financial products, some of the dangers of offshore investing, and some attractive offshore products that are available to U.S. investors.

§ 4.1 Privacy

Privacy is a major goal of offshore planning. In the United States, someone who knows where and how to look can discover most things of interest about an investor through a search of public and privately available records. Many offshore jurisdictions, on the other hand, have strict privacy laws designed to protect against frivolous litigation, among other things. For example, in most offshore jurisdictions an employee or officer of a bank may not reveal that someone has an account there nor reveal any details of the account. Criminal penalties are imposed on any bank employee who violates these laws. Therefore, offshore planning can constrain the efforts of foreign government agencies, competitors, or plaintiffs attempting to gather private information, although many offshore jurisdictions have mutual legal assistance treaties with the United States and other nations under which legitimately needed information can be properly sought by foreign judicial agencies. The treaty procedures are rigorous, however, to protect against "fishing expeditions."

Privacy also serves as a barrier against unwarranted or frivolous creditor litigation. Most offshore jurisdictions do not require filing, registration, or disclosure of asset protection trusts. This makes it more difficult for a potential litigant to gather the information necessary to litigate. Strict secrecy laws applicable to trust company employees, officers, lawyers, and accountants also make it difficult for a putative creditor to gather the information needed to formulate a claim. Such information might include information about the existence of the asset protection trust itself, its beneficiaries, the identity of the people controlling or benefitting from it, and the value, type, and location of its assets. This level of confidentiality is important to many who want to protect their life savings.

§ 4.2 Estate Planning

An offshore investment can provide substantial estate planning benefits. The assets from an offshore trust can revert to the settlor on the occurrence of certain events such as the trust settlor's death, or the trust can be irrevocable and only benefit persons other than the settlor.

The value of trust assets is frozen vis-à-vis the trust settlor's estate as soon as there is a completed transfer. In most onshore jurisdictions, property transferred to a trust in which the trust settlor is also a beneficiary can be reached by the trust maker's creditors, to the same extent the settlor is able to receive benefits from the trust. The Internal Revenue Service (IRS) can also consider such a transfer to be incomplete. If, however, an offshore jurisdiction does not permit creditors to reach trust assets, the transfer is complete and will usually be excluded from the trust settlor's estate for U.S. estate tax purposes, although there may be U.S. or other gift tax consequences to the initial transfer.

The estate planning considerations are different if the investor chooses to make use of a private or publicly available annuity. The then present value of an annuity at death will be included in the trust settlor's estate, unless the annuity is structured to terminate at death.

Another general consideration in estate planning is the rule against perpetuities. Most U.S. states permit trusts to continue only for "a life in being, plus 21 years." Offshore trust laws often do not include this rule or they permit trusts to continue for a very long time (so-called dynasty trusts). Jurisdictions that have abolished the rule of perpetuities or allow trusts to continue for a very long time include the Cook Islands, the Turks and Caicos Islands, and St. Vincent and the Grenadines. Offshore jurisdictions sometimes permit 100-year trust accumulation periods, which allow truly multigenerational estate planning structures to be created.

The laws of the jurisdiction of the trust, rather than the laws of the home jurisdiction of the settlor, will govern who is entitled to benefits under the trust. This can be important in avoiding will contests from disgruntled heirs or the strict forced heirship rules that apply in many South American and other civil law countries.

§ 4.3 Access to Non-U.S. Investment Products

Assets in an offshore trust are not necessarily physically located in the jurisdiction where the trust is located. Many trusts are set up in foreign jurisdictions such as the Cayman Islands or the Bahamas while the trusts' assets are located in Switzerland, in England, or even back in the United States. Thus, the trustee may not have physical possession of the assets, but has legal control. From a legal or tax perspective, the assets are considered to be at the original situs of the trust, i.e., the offshore jurisdiction.

Whether the assets are located at the situs of the offshore trust or in another foreign jurisdiction, by going abroad the trust settlor has opened up the opportunity to invest in non-U.S. investment products. An estimated 90 percent of the world's best performing mutual funds are, for securities laws compliance reasons, not available for sale in Canada or the United States. They are available for sale only to qualified offshore individuals, trusts, partnerships, or corporations. Thus, by indirectly investing in foreign investment products using offshore investment companies or trusts, a U.S. investor can obtain more diversification and potentially higher returns on his or her investment portfolio.

Offshore variable annuity programs, for example, provide a wider variety of investment options than U.S. variable annuity contracts. U.S. law imposes strict limitations on the nature of annuity investments and the ability of the contract owner to select them. All investments must be diversified under a strict numerical test and the owner must not possess "investor control." With an offshore annuity, the chosen investment adviser may be the client's independent U.S. investment adviser or another recognized asset management group. Annuity investments must still be diversified if the annuity is a variable annuity, and are normally held in a segregated account. Returns are determined solely by the performance of the investments in the owner's underlying segregated account.

Another advantage of a segregated account is that the annuitant's assets are not included on the issuer's balance sheet and thus are not subject to the other debts of the offshore issuer. Indeed, the laws of some offshore jurisdictions (e.g., the Cayman Islands, Bermuda, Guernsey) guarantee this. A negative factor is the one-time 1 percent U.S. excise tax levied on premiums paid for an annuity contract purchased by a U.S. person from a foreign issuer on the life of a U.S. citizen or resident.[1]

Some offshore jurisdictions place restrictions on the investment funds domiciled within their borders, which need to be investigated before proceeding. Common restrictions include restrictions on investment in illiquid or non-exchange-traded securities; restrictions on the use of options, futures, swaps, and other derivative instruments; restrictions on borrowing; restrictions on investment in other funds; and restrictions on short-term trading. Although offshore investment opens more doors than it closes, potential offshore investors should be aware that some foreign regulators take a more paternalistic view of their role in regulating investment funds than the U.S. Securities and Exchange Commission (SEC) does.

§ 4.4 Higher Yields on Bank Deposits

Strong global securities markets and the higher yields available on foreign debt instruments have attracted U.S. investors who perceive foreign securities as a means to increase investment returns and diversify portfolio risk. Bank deposits in major foreign banks, for example, offer above-market interest rates in part because they are not subject to U.S. deposit insurance assessments, reserve deposit requirements, or high U.S. regulatory costs. Large investors may be more interested in higher yields than in deposit insurance coverage. The coverage, after all, is limited to a relatively small amount per investor per bank ($100,000).

In the early 1990s, continued and strengthened cost-free Federal Deposit Insurance Corporation (FDIC) insurance for investors in foreign banks (and the influence of Canadian, Japanese and European banks that offer investors a wider range of services than their U.S. counterparts) intensified foreign competition for offshore banking business, including dollar-denominated transactions. The FDIC Improvement Act was amended in 1993 to provide that a deposit has to be payable in the United States to qualify for FDIC insurance. Federal regulators interpret this amendment to mean that holders of foreign deposits do not have a preference over other bank creditors; this drastically reduces or eliminates recoveries of foreign deposit holders. With or without such a limitation on foreign deposits, the advantage of higher yields in foreign banks is usually more persuasive to many U.S. investors than the limited insurance the FDIC provides. Moreover, many non-U.S. banks have stronger balance sheets than U.S. banks and are impartially rated by international rating agencies. For example, Rabobank of the Netherlands is a AAA-rated bank.

§ 4.5 Income Tax Planning

The United States requires recognition and current taxation of all gains on property transferred to an offshore trust. This results in a tax that is the same as the tax that would result if the property were sold at fair market value on the day of the transfer. This tax can be avoided if the offshore trust qualifies as a grantor trust. Once an offshore trust loses its grantor trust status, however, U.S. recognition of gains will be required immediately. For example, if the U.S. grantor of a foreign grantor trust dies and the trust continues in existence, the continuing trust will typically become a foreign nongrantor trust for U.S. tax purposes.

An offshore trust designed to protect assets will usually be structured as a grantor trust under the Internal Revenue Code (IRC). A grantor trust is not a separate taxpayer. Instead, any income, loss, deductions, or credits from a grantor trust are reported on the U.S. trust maker's income tax return. The trust settlor may use his or her Social Security number and does not need to obtain a separate U.S. taxpayer identification number for the trust.

In addition, the IRS requires reporting of the creation of a foreign trust within 90 days of its formation. Contributions to the trust of appreciated assets must also be reported. The U.S. beneficiary of an offshore trust must report his or her interest on Form 1040, U.S. Individual Income Tax Return, and must report also distributions that he or she receives from the foreign trust on Form 3520.

One way to save on taxes while preserving some of the advantages of offshore planning is through the use of an offshore annuity. Like U.S. annuities, offshore annuities allow the value of the contract to increase tax free before payments begin; however, offshore annuity issuers are typically untaxed on this "inside buildup," so the payout ratio to the U.S. annuity holder is higher.

§ 4.6 Investment Expertise in Non-U.S. Financial Markets

Although there is no shortage of qualified asset managers and other investment professionals in the United States, no one individual or group is capable of providing investment expertise on a worldwide basis. Thus, U.S. investors who want international exposure are faced with the hurdle of finding qualified and trustworthy money managers for non-U.S. financial markets. Such investors need to investigate the background and track record of the people and institutions with whom they seek to deal and ensure that the planning strategy to be adopted is within the bounds of the legal and tax framework of the offshore jurisdiction and of the investor's home jurisdiction.

When an investor chooses a money manager, the relationship between the two will usually be concluded through a written contract. Investors generally choose to do business with large and respected international institutions. Many banks in offshore jurisdictions have high-quality in-house money managers. There are also qualified specialist investment professionals outside the banking structures, who may provide an even more attractive alternative for the client whose primary goal is enhanced economic return and international diversification. All advisers will have a general fiduciary obligation to the investor, which may, however, be limited or modified in the written agreement. Money managers will also typically operate under fee schedules, based on a percentage of the assets under management and often including additional performance bonuses. The written contract will specify whether the money manager has discretion in making investment decisions for the client or must consult with the client before initiating transactions.

When choosing a money manager, and possibly a separate bank custodian of assets as a further protective measure, it is worthwhile to interview a number of qualified and reputable advisers and custodians. The investor should initially consider asset protection, but should also put a lot of time into finding advisers with whom he or she is comfortable on a personal level and who are accessible and responsive.

§ 4.7 Political Risks

Political stability, economic stability, and civil stability are difficult elements to evaluate, but they should be accorded great weight when determining offshore situs. Unlike an offshore corporation, which may be able to transact international business without any ongoing contact with the host jurisdiction, an offshore foundation or trust will typically have a manager or trustee and perhaps other professionals resident and active in the host country. A local political crisis can cause irreparable delay for urgent business and put assets at risk. Offshore investors also face the risk that the local government will change its laws and expropriate or make illiquid the offshore investment.

It is worthwhile to ensure that the local offshore professionals (e.g., lawyers, accountants, bankers) are honest and ethical. A thorough investigation of the people with whom business is to be done may reveal past illegal or unethical behavior. International accountants, law firms, and bankers can often help with referrals. The U.S. investor should be aware of the need to avoid activities that might be legal in the offshore jurisdiction but nonetheless illegal under U.S. law.

Flexibility to adjust to future developments is also important. If a trust is so drafted, the governing jurisdiction can later be changed and the trust moved elsewhere (e.g., from the Bahamas to the Isle of Man or vice versa). Although this cannot provide a complete guarantee against political, civil, or economic instability of the situs, it can provide one more layer of protection for the investor.

§ 4.8 Foreign Currency Investing and U.S. Bank Difficulties

The trustee of a foreign trust will often maintain accounts and make investments denominated in foreign currencies. This can create U.S. complexity.

Under IRC Section 985(a), a U.S. taxpayer's functional currency is the U.S. dollar. If a qualified business unit (QBU) of a U.S. taxpayer keeps its books and records in a foreign currency and that currency is the currency of the economic environment where it does a significant amount of its business, that foreign currency is the QBU's "functional currency." A trust is a QBU of its beneficiaries. Thus, a foreign grantor trust with a U.S. grantor and U.S. beneficiaries can have a functional currency other than the U.S. dollar. When a U.S. taxpayer receives or makes payments in a nonfunctional currency, there is a deemed sale and conversion of the nonfunctional currency into U.S. dollars. This conversion allows the IRS to determine gains or losses attributable to exchange rate fluctuations over a given period. The difficulty is in the conversion. Day-to-day banking activities and official conversion rates can have a negative impact on the offshore investor's interests.

If the foreign bank conducts its business in U.S. dollars, the U.S. offshore investor should be aware that some offshore entities require the participation of a local U.S. bank. In addition to investigating the integrity and fiscal soundness of a non-U.S. bank, the investor should determine whether such a bank has a subsidiary in the United States. If so, that relationship may allow the attachment of a client's otherwise protected assets.

§ 4.9 Asset Protection Trusts

The offshore product most commonly pursued by U.S. investors is the *offshore asset protection trust,* which is typically an irrevocable trust created under the laws of an offshore jurisdiction whose laws limit creditor remedies, whether by a statute of limitations or via high standards of proof, against assets within the trust (e.g., Caymans, Bahamas). These offshore trusts are generally irrevocable for a term of years (with or without provisions for extension of the term if a lawsuit exists), with a reversion to the maker, if he or she is living, or distribution to heirs at the end of the term. Depending on the jurisdiction, the maker and heirs both may be beneficiaries of the trust. Despite being irrevocable, these trusts are almost always structured to be grantor trusts for U.S. tax purposes (i.e., to be transparent) in order to avoid negative U.S. tax consequences. They do not confer any U.S. tax deferral or tax elimination advantages, since all trust income is annually taxable to the

U.S. grantor on his or her Form 1040. There is some additional U.S. tax reporting (on Form 3520) but very little complexity.

According to tests set forth in U.S. State Fraudulent Transfer Acts, asset protection trusts do not protect assets from U.S. creditors if they were set up "with actual intent to hinder, delay, or defraud" or if they were set up with less than reasonably equivalent value and the transferor was insolvent, was engaged in an undercapitalized business, or intended to incur debts that could not be paid. A fraudulent transfer, if it is to be challenged under U.S. federal bankruptcy statutes, must be filed within a year of the bankruptcy.

A major advantage of an offshore trust is that most offshore jurisdictions require a creditor to relitigate any lawsuit that it might have won in the United States. Another advantage of offshore planning is that many offshore jurisdictions have an anti-duress clause in their trust laws. An anti-duress clause prevents a trustee in an offshore jurisdiction from complying with a trust maker's instructions if those instructions are given under duress. Thus, if a U.S. court attempting to reach the assets of an offshore trust orders a U.S. trust maker to instruct the trustee to return the assets to a U.S. jurisdiction, the trustee will be unable to comply with the instructions because the instructions are given under duress. The assets are under the control of the foreign trustee; therefore, provided a U.S. court does not have jurisdiction over the foreign trustee, the putative U.S. creditor cannot levy upon the assets in the offshore trust.

A successful creditor in U.S. litigation therefore has many hurdles to overcome before it can get to the trust's money. First, it must file a new suit in the offshore jurisdiction. To be successful in this suit, the creditor must file before the local statute of limitations expires, usually one to two years from trust creation. The creditor must also have standing to sue. That is, the creditor must be an actual creditor whose claims against the trust maker existed at the time the offshore trust was set up and were known to the trust maker. The burden of proving this is on the creditor.

In addition, most offshore jurisdictions do not allow contingent-fee litigation. Therefore, the creditor has the burden of finding a non-contingent-fee attorney licensed in the offshore jurisdiction; this means the litigant must pay a retainer to that attorney. Some jurisdictions require that the plaintiff (creditor) post a cash bond with the court to cover the defendant's legal fees and court costs in case the defendant is successful in his or her defense. (Under the "English rule" prevalent in many offshore jurisdictions, the loser must also pay the winner's legal fees.) The litigant must also overcome jurisdictional hurdles, in that the debtor will not be likely to own assets outside the offshore trust that are within the offshore jurisdiction and the trust is a separate legal entity from the debtor (i.e., the defendant may not be "present" in the jurisdiction).

If a creditor decides to litigate in the offshore jurisdiction, the trustee might move the assets to another offshore jurisdiction before the litigation is completed. In many cases, this will force the creditor-litigant to start litigation all over again in the new offshore jurisdiction.

In determining situs for the creation of a trust, some investors turn to local U.S. "offshore" jurisdictions. Alaska and Delaware have attractive domestic U.S. trust asset protection laws; however, many U.S. advisers believe that the courts of other states (e.g., New York or California) might not fully respect these protective provisions. All in all, being truly offshore seems a more secure alternative.

Another consideration for the trust settlor is control. Although the trustee has a fiduciary duty to make investment decisions on behalf of the trust, the founder of an asset protection trust has a few ways to maintain some control over the trust investment. The founder may use a nonbinding letter of wishes to maintain a degree of de facto influence or control over investment decisions. Such a letter of wishes often requests the trustee to consult with the settlor of the trust before making important decisions. The settlor may also reserve powers in the trust instrument, such as the power to issue investment instructions, with which the trustee must comply. Another option is to retain the power to change trustees, which may be restricted by trustee qualification requirements. The founder must always be careful to respect the separate legal relationships created in the trust context. If too many "strings" are kept, a court might treat the trust as a sham.[2]

Finally, the U.S. courts will not have jurisdiction over property (*in rem* jurisdiction) if liquid property (e.g., money and investments) is moved offshore. In an asset protection trust, the courts of the offshore jurisdiction typically have exclusive control over the trust property and only the laws of the offshore jurisdiction will be applicable to determine the validity of the trust. U.S. courts usually cannot exercise jurisdiction over non-U.S. real estate owned by a foreign entity.

§ 4.10 Offshore Life Insurance Products

A transfer in trust of liquid assets, which are then used to buy an offshore-issued life insurance policy, is a useful option for minimizing or eliminating

U.S. or other income and estate tax while preserving intergenerational wealth. There are two main advantages to an offshore life insurance policy: (1) the U.S. reporting requirements are less stringent and (2) the U.S. excise tax (1 percent on premium contributions) applied to offshore policies is significantly less than the taxes applicable to domestic policies. In comparison, a U.S. domestic life insurance product is subject to a deferred acquisition cost (DAC) tax of 1 percent of the premiums as they are contributed and a state premium tax, which varies from state to state and averages approximately 2 percent. In addition, U.S. domestic products usually levy a one-time administrative fee and overhead charge.

Although domestic U.S. products have higher one-time charges, overall ongoing charges are comparable. Insurance in the United States is very closely regulated, and the cost of regulatory compliance is passed on in higher premiums. In offshore jurisdictions, the regulation of insurance companies is usually less burdensome; thus, the cost of insurance and administrative charges (and hence premiums) can be much lower.

Maintaining a minimum level of life insurance coverage in the investment contract means that there will never be any U.S. income taxation on the underlying investments during the life of the insured. Funds can be accessed during life on a tax-free basis as withdrawals, up to the tax basis in the policy if the policy is a so-called non-MEC (modified endowment contract) policy. After the policyholder's death, there is no income taxation on the proceeds of the insurance. If the policy is structured appropriately, there may be no U.S. estate tax for one, two, or more generations.

There are a number of variations of offshore life insurance to consider. The following discussion considers a U.S. domestic donor as the insured with a non-U.S. beneficiary, compared with a U.S. domestic donor as the insured with a U.S. beneficiary. If there is a U.S. domestic donor and a U.S. domestic beneficiary, the trust would be treated as a grantor trust for income tax purposes as long as there is a U.S. beneficiary. The trust could be set up to be outside the taxable U.S. estate of the grantor, but premium contributions would be treated as gifts.

If there is a U.S. domestic donor and a non-U.S. beneficiary, the trust could be treated as a nongrantor trust. A U.S. donor could enter into an agreement with the trustee whereby the premium obligation is split. The U.S. donor's contribution would then be treated as an interest-free loan, due and payable back to the donor. There would be no income tax issue because during the life of the insured there would be no tax on the cash value increases and therefore no taxable income at the trust level. If the trust had separate assets to pay its share of the premium, there would be no U.S. gift tax. The amount of the loan would remain in the estate of the U.S. benefactor, but the death benefit in excess of that (or the entire death benefit if the loan had been repaid) would pass into the offshore trust U.S. estate tax free.

§ 4.11 Entities Available Abroad

Offshore jurisdictions apply different laws and different procedural approaches, many of which offer unique advantages. There are dozens of offshore jurisdictions, each offering a broad range of offshore entities. Since the laws of each jurisdiction are different, they should be reviewed before any assets are moved offshore. The differences between entities based on civil law (European continental law) and common law (English law) are quite significant. Most continental European and Latin American jurisdictions are based on civil law and their forms of legal entities are quite different from U.S. forms of legal entities.

For example, a U.S. investor interested in offshore planning might consider a civil-law *stiftung,* which is a form of private interest foundation. Many U.S. investors have turned to stiftungs because of the U.S. reporting requirements incumbent on the grantor or beneficiary of offshore trusts. A stiftung shares some of the features of a corporation and some of the features of a trust and can be used for asset protection and to achieve testamentary goals. A stiftung achieves legal separation of assets while reserving in an individual the ability to retain a high degree of operations control. Thus, a person can create a stiftung and maintain control of its assets without occupying a publicly disclosed position within it.

The stiftung was originally established in Liechtenstein, and since then it has been adopted in Panama, where it is known as a *Panamanian foundation* (PF). Panamanian law grants PFs greater confidentiality than Liechtenstein law grants to siftungs. The process of establishing a PF gives insight into how the creator can maintain both control and heightened confidentiality. To create a PF, one must file a memorandum of foundation containing basic corporate information at the public registry. This memorandum appoints the initial member of the PF's governing council, which is composed of three natural persons or one juridical person (such as a corporation). The PF founder can maintain control of the PF by retaining the power to appoint the council, by serving as a member of the council, or by serving as a member of a supervisory board. The founder can also elect family members to serve on the council or can have the PF adopt regulations (like bylaws) and appoint a protector.

While the founder can maintain control of the entity, he or she does not need to publicly record in Panama the connection between the PF and the founder. Moreover, an outsider can obtain information about the beneficiaries of a PF only by obtaining an order from a Panamanian court and would need very good cause to obtain this information. Persons involved in PF activities have an obligation to maintain secrecy, and a breach of this obligation results in a six-month jail term and a fine of $50,000. From a U.S. tax reporting perspective, the PF may be treated either as a disregarded entity, a partnership, or a corporation, with differing tax reporting and tax payment obligations.

PFs are superior to stiftungs in certain circumstances. Stiftungs are subject to strict annual accounting and requirements; PFs are not. Creditors and heirs may attack stiftungs but not PFs. Contributions to stiftungs require disclosure to the local government; PF contributions may be made privately with no public record of transfer. Finally, a PF is available for a fraction of the $25,000 it normally takes to create a stiftung.

Stiftungs require a public record of the founder; to avoid this requirement some investors use an attorney or other agent to serve in this capacity. A PF, on the other hand, is a juridical person whose existence and identity are separate from those of its founder or any other person. Thus, PF property is separate and independent from property of the founder and other persons who transfer assets into it. Lawsuits against the founder or beneficiaries of a PF cannot attach or seize PF property, short of fraud. The statute of limitations for fraudulent transfers is five years.

An advantage of a PF over a trust is that a PF may own property in its name or through another entity. A trust, on the other hand, holds property indirectly in the name of the trustee. If the trustee dies, resigns, or is removed, all trust assets must be retitled in the name of the new trustee; this can be an expensive and time-consuming task.

Another promising form of entity is the Nevis limited liability company (LLC). The Nevis LLC provides members of the LLC with full protection from entity obligations, as a corporation does, while providing flexibility of management, as a partnership does. (Anguilla is another jurisdiction that provides for the creation of LLCs with limited liability for members and income and losses passing through to members.) The Nevis LLC has a one-year statute of limitations for civil suits; no minimum authorized capital; no business license requirement; no income, Social Security, capital, duty, gift, death, estate, dividend, distribution, or inheritance taxes; and a requirement that a plaintiff in a civil suit must post a $25,000 bond. A Nevis LLC must have a Nevis-registered agent at all times.

Although a Nevis LLC offers tax transparency to a U.S. person, and hence simplicity, it only permits creditors a "charging order" against any distributed profits of the LLC and does not allow creditors to seize the LLC's equity. This gives rise to an interesting conundrum for the U.S. creditor: As a result of getting a U.S. court order awarding him or her the equity of the LLC, the creditor gets taxed on all the income of the LLC; however, it is unlikely that the LLC will ever give the creditor any dividend distributions to pay the tax, because the LLC is still under its original control. Thus, the judgment creditor may wonder why he or she bothered to go offshore looking for assets to seize.

Yet another investment option with tax planning features is putting assets into a charitable trust. This option is not without risk, since the IRS may categorize a charitable offshore trust as an "abusive" trust. Even if the trust is considered a charitable trust in the offshore jurisdiction (e.g., Cyprus), the IRS would view a charitable trust as an improper scheme if it is used to pay for the personal, educational, living, or recreational expenses of the owner or the owner's family. For example, the trust may provide for payments to an accredited university. Such a payment may normally be a deductible educational gift; but when it is used for the college tuition of one of the maker's children, it would not be deductible. The trust maker cannot effectively retain authority to cause the financial benefits of the trust to be directly or indirectly returned or made available to the trust maker or his or her family.

Another option is a *hybrid trust,* which is a trust in which the trustee has discretion as to the application of the trust income or capital but there is at least one beneficiary with a fixed interest in that income or capital that cannot be affected by the exercise of the discretion. Even though a hybrid trust has both fixed and nonfixed elements, the fixed payments can be tax free to U.S. beneficiaries if they qualify as a "pecuniary legacy."

---

1. IRC § 4371.
2. FTL v. Affordable Media, LLC, 179 F.3d 1228 (June 15, 1999).

Part 2. Major Applications

CHAPTER 5

Creation of a New Insurance Company

Richard H. Mayer, Michael M. O'Mara, Albert H. Swanke, Jr., David D. Avasthi, and Michael J. Burns

Synopsis

The Bermuda experience is offered as an illustration only of a country that has had significant experience in this area.

The client and the adviser planning for the affluent may consider the creation of a new insurance company as an investment opportunity or a source of needed insurance. Because of the recent rumblings in Washington, DC, by the U.S. Treasury and certain members of Congress attacking hedge fund life insurance wraps, reinsurance schemes, and Internal Revenue Code Section 817, it is important to make the distinction between the formation of a properly functioning life insurance company and certain recently established offshore companies. Most of the concern is focused on three issues: investor control, assumption of risk, and the adequate generation of new life insurance premiums. These points will be addressed in the following material.

There is ample opportunity for the ultra-high net worth investor to establish a life insurance company within the regulations and within what is believed to be the spirit of these regulations. By the time of the publication of this book, the U.S. Internal Revenue Service will have undoubtedly issued a Notice or some other type of pronouncement on this subject.

§ 5.1 Opportunity and Rationale for Forming an Offshore Life Insurance Company

The offshore life insurance company is playing a growing role in wealth preservation. One of the central issues of wealth preservation is tax efficiency, and there is no vehicle that can achieve tax efficiency under U.S. tax law as the insurance product can. The product's increasing flexibility and popularity, along with the advantages of offshore investing, make the offshore private placement insurance product one of the best vehicles for wealth preservation.

A new offshore life insurance company could be formed specifically to exploit the wealth preservation market by designing products targeting three submarkets. The first product would be a private placement product for professional client handlers, primarily corporate trustees. These individuals could be offered the opportunity to manage client money on a tax-efficient basis. The second product would be a service offered to asset managers. Through the life insurance company's capital structure, investment funds could be offered the ability to convert an ordinary income taxable yield into capital gains. Third, the company could create products designed specifically for executive compensation.

The central strength of any organization is its association with talented professionals. The principals of the new insurance company should therefore include those who have created close working associations with the offshore jurisdiction's top investment, legal, and insurance practitioners. These individuals should also be dedicated to the product design and services the new life insurance company would be offering.

§ 5.1[a] Mission

The life insurance company to be formed would secure an international reinsurer as its anchor investor and reinsurer. While the life insurance company builds its capital reserve, the reinsurer would be co-writer as well as reinsurer.

The life insurance company's mission would be

1. To provide asset managers and their most important clients with the ability to invest in the capital reserve of the life insurance company on a tax-advantaged basis while remaining able to manage a portion of the assets;
2. To allow all individual clients to invest tax efficiently within institutionally priced life insurance policies;
3. To provide funding for nonqualified executive benefit plans; and
4. To allow institutional investors to invest in the capital reserve of the life insurance company.

The new life insurance company could concentrate on mutual educational opportunities by working closely with the "five aces"—agent, attorney, accountant, actuary, and asset manager—to share ideas and to keep each group informed about the latest ideas in combining life insurance and investment strategies. These individuals in effect would become clients of the new insurance company and thus better serve their own clients.

§ 5.1[b] Operations

The new company would be divided into two separate but interrelated companies, insurance and investments. The insurance would be exclusively private placement variable universal life (PPVUL) and the investments would be determined by highly qualified asset managers in a clearly defined relationship with the life insurance company.

The investment team could develop its investment relationships by creating two opportunities: (1) the ability to invest in the capital reserve structure of the life insurance company while building the capital base of the new life insurance company, and (2) cross-marketing the expertise of the insurance group to the investment community's client.

§ 5.1[c] Marketing

The life insurance agent is changing and the life insurance product of preference is changing. Insurance companies have been cutting costs significantly to remain competitive and this trend is affecting the careers of all life insurance agents. Many have not survived the upheaval, but the successful ones have become completely independent, fiercely competitive, and even more successful than they already were.

Agents realize that the fundamental changes are beyond their control, but are adapting to them. The growth in personal wealth since 1987 has created an opportunity at the very top to shelter vast sums of money. In response, life insurance agents have become entrepreneurs. They have learned that the lowering of commission rates does not have to mean insufficient compensation when the product attracts larger sums of investment.

Furthermore, the new, independent agent is serving the wealthiest population ever known with a new financial instrument available to every successful independent agent, through the miracle of the microchip. The computer makes each skilled individual a formidable competitor. New products and services will overwhelm competition. The new life insurance company may want to identify 10 to 15 leading agents to work with at the outset.

A package underwriting system utilizing international consultants will be helpful in arranging offshore policies. Applications may be completed in the United States, but must be executed offshore and physical examinations must be completed offshore.

§ 5.1[d] Investment Services

The offshore insurance industry has evolved, allowing for a highly flexible investment selection within its products. This caused investment advisers to familiarize themselves with the tax and economic advantages of the offshore insurance company and its products. Subsequently, there have been a number of attempts by hedge funds to create insurance companies primarily for the purpose of sheltering their returns. Most hedge funds, however, hesitate to involve themselves in the management of unfamiliar insurance operations or to inherit the apparent tax risks of an offshore corporation whose existence as a legitimate insurance company may be questioned by the Internal Revenue Service (IRS). The ownership of an offshore insurance company by a hedge fund could carry with it substantial tax risks relating to the passive foreign investment company (PFIC) section of the Internal Revenue Code (IRC) because of the possible absence of a viable insurance operation and its inherent risks.

In the creation of the new life insurance company, one must recognize the offshore activity between insurance companies and the investment community as a clear indication of the potential for an insurance company to provide services to this market.

§ 5.1[d][1] Capital Structure. The new life insurance company will issue a preferred class of stock for its capital investors. This preferred stock will be one of the primary methods for accumulating capital reserves for the company. As a method of attracting capital, the preferred stock could be designed in such a way as to achieve greater tax efficiency. The capital must be exposed to any operating risks. Funds for this preferred stock must be under the investment control of the insurance company.

§ 5.1[d][2] Life Insurance Market. The strength of the insurance company relies not only on adequate capital, but on the ongoing development of a strong life insurance marketing team. Since 1992, certain life insurance consultants have designed some of the most sophisticated products for the investment community in the form of PPVUL. The great appeal of these products to investment experts and their investors is their tremendous investment flexibility and, of course, all of the attendant tax efficiencies of a life insurance policy provided under the IRC.

Three Caveats:

1. A life insurance contract will not allow for recognition of tax losses.
2. Withdrawals above basis are taxed at ordinary rates.
3. Surrender of the policy will trigger tax recourse on outstanding loans.

The PPVUL structure is particularly appealing for the following reasons:

- Tax-efficient compounding
- Tax-efficient reallocation or rebalancing of the fund
- Tax-efficient access to the investment fund. (To realize this potential advantage, it is imperative that the policy not be allowed to lapse or be surrendered prior to death. Termination before death triggers ordinary income taxation.)
- Tax-efficient death benefit for survivors
- In-kind payment of premiums and death benefits
- One-year delay in payment of death benefits

The addition of the PPVUL wrap as a service investment managers may offer to their clients may cause a substantial increase in assets under their management. PPVUL products may provide investment managers with one of their most powerful asset-gathering tools.

§ 5.1[d][3] Tax Deferral for Hedge Fund Managers. The last of the services to be provided to investment managers is tax deferral. Like their clients, the majority of investment managers have a business structure that provides little to no tax efficiency. The typical manager works as a general partner receiving a management fee in the form of unshelterable income. Exacerbating the problem is the managers' high profit margin over their base expenses. Consequently, most managers are faced with an incurable tax result.

The PPVUL product will fit exceptionally well as part of a family of products including the insurance wrap and the capital structure to service both hedge fund investors and their general partners.

§ 5.1[d][4] Support Services Department. The new life insurance company should create an independent department for the investment managers' services discussed above (see §§ 5.1[d][1]–5.1[d][3]). The initial activity of this department will be three-fold. First, the department's activities will center around coordinating legal and tax information from specialists with whom strategic relationships have been formed. This effort should be geared to addressing any issues that investment managers need to resolve in relation to the products and services mentioned above. Second, there should be consultants on staff who are professional marketing specialists with a history of providing services to the investment community. These individuals will work in an advisory capacity with both the investment managers themselves and insurance consultants who offer products that interface with the investment community. Third, the investment services department must possess a servicing staff for ongoing administration of both clients and the consulting network.

The services offered to the investment funds must be designed to address the concerns of the entire investment community—both onshore and offshore. Although some offshore life insurance companies have attempted to address some of the investment portfolio tax issues, some of them may have maintained a questionable tax position and indeed have fallen short of addressing the complete breadth of issues facing the investment community.

§ 5.2 Forming and Funding an Offshore Insurance Company

The keys to the successful formation and funding of an offshore insurance company are a compelling business case, including the justification for going offshore, and experienced and committed sponsorship. Both components are necessary from the outset to give the project any reasonable chance of achieving success.

§ 5.2[a] Business Rationale

If the sponsors of an offshore insurance company are primarily domiciled in the United States and have developed and tested a specific business rationale, why go to the not inconsiderable time, expense, and challenge of setting up and funding an offshore regulated financial institution? The answer resides in a positive and compelling business case, as opposed to an untested hypothesis or market inclination. Without a compelling business case, the undertaking will not yield the expected returns and will fail to meet investors'expectations.

Experience since 1987 in conceiving, creating, and funding new financial institutions, primarily insurance entities, suggests that the most successful have been those that were formed to address a specific market need. What is the market need? Market need in the property and casualty insurance industry is best exemplified by the ability to respond to market timing in a counterintuitive way. For example, the commercial property and casualty sector has historically been cyclical, with "hard" and "soft" market cycles, characterized by capital moves in and out of the market in reaction to premium pricing and rate adequacy, two key determinants of overall return on investment. A hard market results when existing capacity to write premiums shrinks and rates rise for the capacity that remains. Rising rates usually attract new capital to the industry with the promise of substantial investment returns. At some point, however, sufficient new capital materializes, so rate competition increases and rate cutting softens the market.

Major catastrophic weather events, such as hurricanes Hugo and Andrew, and California earthquakes are good examples of precipitators of a hard market. Existing primary carriers and reinsurers are immediately saddled with torrential claim volume, oftentimes resulting in immediate sale of securities portfolios, at depressed market prices. Such adverse developments often bring to light inadequate reserving practices. In 1992, Hurricane Andrew caused more than a dozen primary insurance carrier insolvencies and wreaked havoc on the worldwide reinsurance property market. Hence, many primary companies and reinsurers withdrew from property markets and from business that was deemed to have higher risk exposures to windstorms. Several new reinsurance entities were created offshore to fill this market void and take advantage of the resulting significantly higher premium pricing (e.g., Renaissance Re and Tempest Re). Several of these companies have either gone public or been sold to larger entities, yielding attractive investment returns for their original sponsors.

The terrorist attacks of September 11, 2001, changed the game, in that not only was the property market affected, but the liability, workers' compensation, business interruption, and sadly even the life insurance markets were affected to some extent. It is still too early to know the total of the September 11 loss, but by anyone's estimation it is the largest single (or multiple) insured loss event (or events) in history. So far over $12 billion of new investment has flowed into new offshore reinsurance entities that were quickly established to take advantage of the events of September 11. In fact, several of the new offerings were substantially oversubscribed, including one initially capitalized at $500 million, which had more than $150 million of commitments that could not be taken. Capital beyond that modeled in the business plan was turned away because the underwriters wanted to be certain that they had adequately priced premiums of the appropriate type (line of business) to provide the investors with the projected returns. Although they are not consistent across all lines of insurance, renewal premiums at year-end 2001 were multiples of rates being charged for the immediately preceding year.

More recently, the Enron debacle and related situations may give rise to investment opportunities in the professional liability areas of the business, particularly accounting and legal. It is too early, however, to determine whether investors will step up to address the "long-tail" liability nature of the exposures inherent in these lines.

Although the life insurance business is different from the property and casualty side, where insurance coverage is a requirement of commerce, a well-constructed business rationale for forming an offshore life insurance vehicle is just as critical. In other chapters of this book, a strong case is made for offshore private placement life insurance, with preservation of wealth as a prime determinant of one's need for such insurance. In the development of a plan for such a vehicle, the critical success element will be distribution, which will ensure that sufficient cases will be written into the new company to provide the investors with an attractive rate of return. Evidence to date suggests that the few new offshore life insurers formed to address the offshore private placement life insurance market for the super-affluent have been successful in securing business. Failure to do so lowers the overall attractiveness of the entity, and serves as a warning for sponsors to "get it right" in gauging production potential and to assess top-line revenue projections realistically.

Companies that were set up to "create" a market need (also known as "build it and they will come") have been markedly less successful. Addressing a market need is the driver of new revenue, and failure to do so is one of the largest contributing factors to the demise of young companies. For example, most of the online insurance sales initiatives of the 1999–2000 Internet frenzy, several of which raised meaningful capital and went public, have failed to develop into viable businesses. Another example is a group of supposedly agent-sponsored companies, where the agents initially formed the new carriers and supported them with investment and preferred business. The model worked well in a hard market, but once the market softened and the larger, better recognized national carriers reappeared, much of that agents' support disappeared and the companies were not successful.

§ 5.2[b] Why Offshore

The advantages of going offshore from the tax and trust perspectives are addressed in chapters 4 and 5.

The tax and operational advantages of each offshore domicile need to be examined individually and compared. Presently (and historically), Bermuda is the favored domicile for U.S.-related offshore insurance activity. The advantages of conducting such activity in Bermuda include but are not limited to the following:

- No corporate or individual income taxes
- Ease of incorporation
- Favorable regulatory involvement
- Favorable investment parameters for insurance companies
- Attractive infrastructure (i.e., skilled labor pool, excellent communications, and availability of quality support services)
- Favorable geographic accessibility

Perhaps the greatest negative factor with respect to Bermuda is cost, in that compensation and office, housing, and living costs are high, even compared with current New York City equivalents.

§ 5.2[c] Sponsorship

After constructing a focused business rationale, sponsor identification is one of the most important tasks underpinning success of the project. Sponsorship implies significant responsibility, in terms of time and financial commitment. Since insurance is often viewed as an arcane, specialized industry, investors with or without specialized industry knowledge look to the sponsors' track record of accomplishment and commitment to gain comfort in making their investments.

Sponsorship identifies parties who have an ongoing interest in the formation of the offshore entity and who are willing to be identified with the project going forward. Some may have roles that relate solely to formation and funding responsibilities; others will continue as directors, be part of management, or function as strategic alliance partners. It terms of time commitment, the project needs to be the foremost priority of the sponsors and can very easily become an exclusive, full-time commitment. The post-September 11 offshore entities were quickly established and operational before year-end to take advantage of the renewal cycle; however, three months is an exceptionally short time frame, with the more usual rollout being six to nine months, and sometimes up to a year, depending on the pace of the capital-raising campaign.

In terms of funding, the sponsors are responsible for providing the seed money, that is, for the fronting of expenses. The investor memorandum provides for reimbursement of expenses on closing, but in the interim the sponsors should have the financial interest and capability of funding the project. The required amount could be in excess of $1 million.

§ 5.2[d] Structure

Once the game plan is agreed on and the sponsorship is secured, the project focus shifts to structure. The following is an outline of an investor memorandum that was used to raise $500 million for an offshore insurance company:

- Investment highlights
- Summary of selected financial projections
- Summary of the offering
- Business
- Management—board of directors
- Sponsors—existing business entities
- Offering
- Description of common shares
- Risk factors
- Certain tax considerations
- Regulation

The appendix to the investor memorandum included these financial projections and related assumptions:

- Projected statement of income
- Projected balance sheet
- Projected premium and expense—by anticipated sources of business

To a considerable extent, the scope and format of the investor memorandum are dictated by both U.S. and foreign counsel, according to applicable securities laws.

The memorandum should include definitive hurdle rates of return for the investor, which for start-up private equity investments should be no less than 30 percent on an annualized basis. The keys to how quickly this level of return is achieved are the pace of revenue development and the underwriting experience on the business produced.

Deal structures sometimes are developed to attract a particular class of investor. For example, an offshore life insurance vehicle would favor issuance of preferred stock, with a capital structure that is designed to convert short-term capital gains into long-term gains with an insurance wrap to be favorable to asset managers (see § 5.1[d]). Exit strategies are also important and vary according to investor preference. Traditionally, private equity funds have a five- to seven-year investment horizon and look to either an initial public offering (IPO) or a sale of the business for their exit. One offshore offering on the property and casualty side provided for liquidation of the company and return of capital after the first two operational years if the premium rates softened, an innovative approach that especially appealed to hedge funds.

§ 5.2[e] Investor Solicitation

There are two types of potential investors for an offshore insurance opportunity, strategic investors and financial investors, both of which have specific financial parameters that they seek to satisfy.

Strategic investors usually have a parallel business interest in the new entity being created that would add value over and above that anticipated from a stand-alone investment. For example, an existing reinsurer may project ancillary business from an investment in a new underwriting vehicle. In another case, a bank or other financial institution seeking to enter the insurance business may gain valuable industry insight by investing in a new insurance entity; or a major claims-handling organization or data-processing company might feel than such an investment would secure additional revenue by seeding a client for its core business. Because of these anticipated additional benefits, strategic investors may be willing to accept less pure financial return from the investment itself, although they would deny doing so to outside parties.

Financial investors, on the other hand, focus closely on the numbers, weighing the opportunity at hand against others under consideration. They usually have little or no interest in ancillary benefits to their core business to be derived from the investment. It would be difficult to present an investment opportunity to a financial investor that would return less than 30 percent on an annualized basis.

§ 5.2[f] Solicitation Process

The usual time frame for a successful capital campaign is three months to a year. The sponsors, at the outset, should be prepared to fund and support an effort of this duration.

The solicitation usually proceeds as follows:

1. Initial call, which may be accompanied by a confidentiality agreement;
2. Indications of interest, which may be verbal or written;
3. Distribution of the investor memorandum;
4. Firm commitments, which are presented in writing;
5. Distribution of subscription documents; and
6. Handling of subscriptions, including overage (includes "managing the book," usually performed by the sponsor or its agent, for a fee).

§ 5.2[g] Closing Process

There are a lot of details inherent in the closing process, relating to wiring instructions, escrow agreements, closing and post-closing arrangements, and so forth. It is the responsibility of the sponsors to ensure that these details are properly addressed and executed.

§ 5.3 Sample Strategy Paper

There will be a newly capitalized insurance company and management company, respectively, created to exploit a clear and specific market opportunity:

1. XYZ will provide the most up-to-date, and sophisticated wealth management tools for institutions and high net worth world citizens and groups seeking to capitalize on global investment opportunities available in private investment fund products, including the latest insurance strategies using group and individual variable life and annuity planning. These strategies incorporate legitimate and well-regulated offshore vehicles into more traditional international wealth management structures. XYZ will be the fast-moving, pro-active organization that will recognize, define, organize, and participate in these strategies.
2. While the insurance company, XYZ, will be the insurer, a proprietary management company, NEWCO, will be the conduit to provide the above. It will design the products, conduct the marketing and education of various relevant audiences, and place reinsurance, etc., on behalf of XYZ.

Outlined below are the driving forces and clear objectives that XYZ and NEWCO will pursue.

OBJECTIVE: To provide the firm's clients with consistently superior insurance, investment, and estate planning strategies and products.

NICHE: To fill the void that currently exists in the availability of a one-stop shop offering high-end insurance and investment guidance executed by seasoned professionals with proven market capabilities.

STRENGTHS:

- *Global view*—global range of expertise to exploit opportunities across different markets, asset classes, and strategies
- *People*—seasoned team of well-known and successful insurance and financial industry executives
- *Flexibility*—private ownership and boutique structure allowing for quick decision making
- *Full service*—ability to leverage off of the infrastructure of an existing global reinsurance provider with a commitment to superior management systems and practices via exclusive and contractual relationships
- *Risk management*—serious team of professionals with hands-on experience in the design and management of world-class wealth management entities

ECONOMICS: NEWCO projects delivery in excess of $X billion in Gross Written Premium (GWP) over the next four years, with cash values of issued policies exceeding that amount.

I. INDUSTRY OVERVIEW

Wealth management—or, more particularly, wealth preservation as a financial service—is in greater demand than ever before. Both the dollar volume and the number of individuals in this marketplace have grown significantly. The wealth preservation marketplace has articulated two distinct needs. One is a low-volatility asset class providing a consistent return to protect wealth against asset deterioration. This need is being met by the broad acceptance of hedge funds as a stabilizing asset class.

The second need is a tax-efficient delivery mechanism, including a mechanism to deal with transfer taxes and asset protection. For the most part, this need is being addressed through private placement life insurance for individuals and/or their credit shelter family limited partnerships and trusts. The rapid growth in hedge fund investing has increased the attraction of offshore tax planning and wealth preservation strategies and has widened their scope.

By the end of 2003, more capital will flood into the insurance and reinsurance industries than in any other comparable period in history. The demand for finite risk reinsurance, other structured insurance and reinsurance techniques, and captive insurance will increase greatly, as insurance premium rates increase, new risks are recognized, and capacity runs low. High net worth investors who have seen their technology-heavy equity portfolios decimated are also seeking absolute return strategies to fulfill their (currently) reduced return expectations. Fund of funds vehicles are proliferating at an unprecedented rate to serve the rapidly increasing demand among both institutional and private investors in North America, Europe, and Japan. Investors in asset-backed securities (ABS) are searching for opportunities where the ABS investment ratings have been credit enhanced by well-capitalized insurers, many of which have been formed and based in offshore domiciles.

II. THE CURRENT LANDSCAPE—CAPITAL FLOWS

The influx of capital into the insurance industry will primarily be driven by a significant increase in future profitability; however, the industry will also need new capital to replace the capital erosion caused by a possible $100 billion in losses due to the events of September 11, 2001, even if profitability in the future matches that in the past. In a flight to quality, buyers will demand stronger balance sheets and ratings will be critical.

Pricing increases will largely drive the future spike in profitability. Swiss Re issued a report in July 2001 predicting that prices were hardening and expected them to increase by 23 percent year on year. Moreover, history shows that a cataclysmic event, such as that of September 11, 2001, causes people to reassess their needs and decide that they are underinsured. Prices per unit go up and the number of units also increases.

In light of this backdrop, individuals in general have a renewed sense of urgency to complete and fund insurance and estate planning strategies. This increased demand, coupled with reduced capacity, has created a unique opportunity.

III. THE OPPORTUNITY

A. A Reorganized Insurance and Management Company

Opportunities exist to reorganize existing insurance firms to serve the growing need of investors for diversified alternative investment exposure within tax-efficient investment vehicles run as offshore insurance companies or as segregated cells within those companies. Further, such companies would be able to assist corporations to access existing and new insurance carriers for their risk management needs. Through skilled management by well-known insurance personnel and by establishing a presence in Bermuda, a new company will have a unique view on customer needs and available capacity.

To date there are multifold deficiencies in the marketplace that will account for the company's competitive strength. These weaknesses have been identified in research via face-to-face interviews with a variety of audiences all across the United States:

1. Companies offering offshore facilities are also involved in direct writing in the United States, subjecting the insured to queries from tax regulators as to the necessity for going overseas.
2. Many of the offshore companies are poorly capitalized and obvious fronts for onshore companies that also conduct direct writing operations in the United States.
3. Very often the offshore company is located in a domicile of dubious reputation or in a locale that the majority of its target clients are not familiar with.

4. Because of the onshore companies' expensive marketing infrastructure (the sales forces) their fees are often higher than the fees of offshore companies.
5. The investment alternatives offered by onshore companies are very often far too limited for the tastes of the high net worth individual or the larger family trusts.
6. Policy face values offerable by current companies are far less than many insureds would like—closer to $25 million rather than the $50 or even $70+ million.

B. Competitive Advantages

There are a number of competitive advantages that will differentiate this management company from other nontraditional asset management companies:

1. *Proven management.* Be sure the principals have extensive experience in investing and managing large amounts of capital. Also have exceptional access to insurance and investment opportunities in the earliest stages of development.
2. *Affiliation with world class provider.* Obtain the backing of world-class, investment-grade insurance companies offering proprietary capacities and the benefit of their visibility and recognition.
3. *Established infrastructure.* Leveraging off of the infrastructure of an existing insurance company, for starters, will provide a high level of comfort to new investors in the hedge fund vehicles and insurance products, a clear differentiation from most of today's start-ups, which lack capital and infrastructure.
4. *Solid business plan.* Key personnel should have deep experience on both the buy side and the sell side. This will result in the rapid deployment of a well-thought-out business plan that can capitalize on the large amount of experience the founders have developed.
5. *Improved market conditions.* The environment has strengthened for both alternative risk transfer mechanisms, traditional insurance responses, and alternative investments.

C. Proposed Product Offering

In the life arena, XYZ will start with one basic product: individual private placement variable universal life where the initial minimum premium will be

$1 million over four to five years, with the minimum quickly growing to $2 million over the four- to five-year period.

NEWCO will educate the insurance market and attract submissions directly as well as from other sources, which will then be underwritten by XYZ and its lead reinsurer(s). Because of XYZ management's experience and qualifications, besides the life products mentioned above, products may also include the following:

- Kidnap and ransom
- Reputational covers
- Professional liability

These additional lines would flow out of the primary insurance focus and would offer a natural extension of business relationships with ultra high net worth individuals and corporations.

IV. DECISION CRITERIA

A number of key criteria must be considered prior to establishing XYZ. The main decision points are outlined below.

A. Ability to Attract Revenue

The go/no-go decision must be based on the ability to attract sufficient revenue to make the endeavor economically viable. There must be initial premium commitments within the first two years of at least $200 million to ensure ample fees to cover initial fixed expenses. To create a truly successful business, however, a premium level closer to $400 million would be more realistic.

There are a number of ways to "test the waters" before making significant commitments to infrastructure and personnel. Meetings could be scheduled with a number of key insurance brokerage firms that are seeking new sources of offshore life insurance capacity. The principals should satisfy themselves that at least $400 million of premiums can be secured by XYZ through initiation of new business.

B. Clearly Defined Strategies and Policies

Research conducted over the past several months indicates that the offshore life insurance industry has been constrained by several significant shortcomings:

- Lack of well-rated life reinsurers that do not have direct life writing businesses in the United States
- Lack of offshore insurers that do not have a predominant portion of their reinsurance placed in the United States
- Being based in less attractive domiciles—less attractive due to distances or reputation
- Uncompetitive cost structure
- Insufficient face values

V. CONCLUSIONS

A significant opportunity exists to create new insurance and investment advisory companies that can capitalize on the knowledge, experience, and relationships that the principals have developed through their careers. There are opportunities to attract substantial sums of investment capital and subsequent insurance revenues if the product is properly structured and managed. If successful, such an entity can be extremely profitable, and the leverage inherent in the business is impressive.

§ 5.4 Marketing Plan

The new life insurance company's marketing program should incorporate several singular features that will enable it to wrap billions of dollars of investment assets. This will generate very profitable margins for the company.

§ 5.4[a] Tax-Efficient Investing

Investing through variable life insurance leverages the tax efficient compounding effect because earnings will accumulate tax free until they are withdrawn. If earnings are accessed via policy loans, there is no taxable event. Since there is no mandatory age at which one must begin taking distributions from a variable life insurance account, taxes can be deferred indefinitely. For portfolios with high turnover rates (the opposite of buy-and-hold strategies) and correspondingly high tax payments on short-term gains, the benefits of tax-deferred growth can be dramatic. However, there are several caveats. The U.S. Treasury and Congress are taking an increasingly critical look at PPVUL policies. By the time this book is published, Treasury may have issued a Notice regarding PPVUL and Congress may have proposed legislation. It is imperative that the underlying investments not be the same as an investment available to the public outside the contract. The investment must be cloned or otherwise identified as a distinct asset and separate from any other. The intent of the investment cannot be solely for the purposes of the tax advantages.

Withdrawals are tax free under current law up to basis (equal to the amount of total premium paid in). Funds extract above basis are taxed at ordinary rates. If the excess funds are obtained by loan they are considered tax free. Caution: if funds are borrowed and the contract subsequently terminated, except by death, full recourse of the loan portion will be taxed at ordinary rates.

If borrowing occurs, sufficient funds have to remain in the contract and sufficient investment yield has to be generated to keep the policy in force, otherwise potential adverse tax consequence can occur. The tax efficiency of a life policy will not accommodate investment losses, either short- or long-term, against outside income.

From an estate planning standpoint, the advantages of variable life insurance extend far beyond tax deferral. The death benefit from variable life insurance will not trigger appreciation taxes if the policy is held until the death of the insured.

§ 5.4[b] Hedge Funds

Hedge funds, as a group, have historically outperformed mutual funds and broad market indicators, and many of them are run by some of the world's top investment advisers. Classical hedge fund strategies rely on long and short selling to produce gains that do not depend on a rising market. By definition, they tend to be tax inefficient.

§ 5.4[c] Maximum Investment Flexibility

Generally, insurance companies that issue variable life insurance policies allow policyholders to select an investment adviser from a menu of possible choices made available through the insurance company or to allocate assets among multiple advisers. With a private placement policy, policyholders are allowed to suggest the names of individual advisers that they would like to be on the insurance company's list of advisers.

This broader choice of fund managers provides flexibility to help a policyholder generate healthy investment returns. In addition, a policyholder may reallocate assets periodically among existing fund managers or transfer funds to new managers. Typically, a policyholder may borrow against the cash value in his or her account. The cost ranges between 25 to 50 basis points depending on the carrier.

§ 5.4[d] Lower Expenses

Private placement variable life insurance is generally less expensive than retail insurance because it is not burdened by the overhead and expense of government regulation, large distribution systems, and high sales commissions.

This product is available at a cost not to exceed 100 basis points based on the net asset value of the policy. Participating life brokers, attorneys, and accountants may add additional fees.

§ 5.4[e] Commitments

The life insurance company should endeavor to secure several commitment letters from top-line producers to generate premium. In return, the carrier should accommodate these brokers with a product design enabling the brokers to differentiate themselves in the marketplace. A successful marketing effort will include plans to obtain several such commitment letters annually. To build the organization, the life insurance company must obtain commitments from trust and estate attorneys and accountants (devoted to their wealth management practices) as well as life insurance brokers.

§ 5.4[f] Direct and Indirect Marketing

The life insurance company should market directly to asset managers for their high net worth investors. Life insurance makes their investment tax efficient. The average policy results in $10 million of premium for the top-line agent, attorney, and accountant.

The company should also develop a program for property and casualty insurance marketing organizations. This represents a broad market opportunity. A custom-made program designed for one firm includes a pilot project to be kicked off with a few of its offices. The firm expects to enroll 50 lives in 60 days, for a total of $50 million in assets. If this program works, the offer is likely to be repeated, with all of the offices participating. Over $200 million of Gross Written Premium (GWP) is anticipated. These scheduled premiums will be paid in over a period of four years.

Verbal authorization was obtained from major European reinsurers to provide the reinsurance to enable this specialized product to be underwritten with an offshore carrier. A similar product is used by the leading life agent in the nation wrapping hedge funds; since 1995, he has wrapped in excess of $4 billion in assets. A new life insurance company should endeavor to obtain commitments of this type of production before attempting to raise capital. The keystone to building a life insurance company is the generation of new, quality life insurance premiums.

§ 5.4[g] Fees

The fee schedule developed by one of the successful domestic life insurance companies serving the investment community uses a formula of 100 basis points for its minimum premium sale of $2 million paid in over a period of four years. Many companies provide significant volume discounts.

§ 5.5 Reasons for Going Offshore

There are two startling statistics that clearly demonstrate the vitality of the offshore industry in relation to international finance:

1. The various offshore jurisdictions together play a role in more than $1 trillion worth of business annually, be it in the way of funds under management, offshore banking deposits, insurance premiums, or the amounts involved in finance deals.
2. There are some 680,000 companies incorporated in "offshore" jurisdictions, together with, probably, double that number of private trusts.

How is it that a sector composed of jurisdictions that are often looked at as tax havens or, worse, as somehow "dodgy" not only survives but thrives on such a scale? Surely, only tax-evading fly-by-nights use exempted companies incorporated in sun-drenched atolls? Nothing could be further from the truth. The truth is that every Fortune 500 company, most of the Fortune 1000 companies, and thousands of other enterprises and associations of individuals, or simply wealthy private persons, take advantage of the facilities offered by small islands and purpose-made international financial centers around the world. One has only to examine the annual reports of most listed companies to discover in the notes, or in the list of subsidiaries, that there are affiliates in Bermuda, Guernsey, Dublin, or Luxembourg. Even that does not tell the whole story. Off-balance sheet transactions now account for a growing portion of offshore business, so the true scale of the uses that sophisticated businesses make of the offshore centers is not apparent from their public documents, but it is real, and it is very important to the financing of international business in a world of uncertainties about taxes, creditworthiness, litigation, and privacy in commercial transactions.

Of particular interest are the booming offshore insurance markets. More and more captives are being formed in Bermuda, the Cayman Islands, Guernsey, Isle of Man, Dublin, and Luxembourg. This is because offshore jurisdictions have been able to offer a low-tax and -regulatory environment, but with sufficient controls to maintain confidence. Onshore companies seek to manage their own insurance risks and retain the premium by creating a captive, and then access the reinsurance market, which has a high concentration of providers of coverage offshore. Further, certain specialized forms of coverage—for example, finite risk insurance—are principally available only offshore.

What is meant by *offshore?* Surprisingly, *offshore* does not mean merely an island somewhere in the Caribbean or the English Channel. Indeed, there are a number of jurisdictions firmly anchored in a mainland somewhere that, for some purposes, are considered offshore. For example, nondomiciled individuals resident in England enjoy very favorable tax treatment; for them, the United Kingdom is a tax haven. Further, Scottish limited partnerships can supply particular benefits to American investors by taking advantage of the double taxation treaty between the United Kingdom and the United States. In North America, landlocked states such as Vermont and Colorado and the Canadian province of British Columbia have established themselves as captive domiciles giving special regulatory treatment to this offshore type of company. Luxembourg, Dublin, and Israel are clearly physically onshore, but they treat certain transactions differently than the major industrial jurisdictions do and provide, to the residents of those other jurisdictions, an opportunity to profit.

Obviously, the word *offshore* must have come from somewhere. Indeed, it was coined to describe the islands off the shore of the United States that, as early as the 1930s, offered locations from which American businesspeople could conduct their international affairs and thereby minimize their tax and regulatory exposure back home. As is evident from the discussion above, the term has been extended to any jurisdiction offering tax or regulatory advantages that are significantly different from those in the major economies; however, to understand what an offshore jurisdiction is, one needs to look at the reasons why offshore jurisdictions developed.

§ 5.5[a] Taxation

For the professional, going offshore is a structural tool in the efficient management of a company's affairs. The principal efficiency, and the one that has given rise to the loaded expression *tax haven,* is obviously taxation. To the legitimate businessperson, however, going offshore for tax reasons does not mean tax evasion, as many wrongly suppose it does. The governments of the mature economics have made escaping the tax net extremely difficult when the activities of a business or an individual's income are wholly connected with one jurisdiction. When businesses are multinational or when income comes from a variety of sources around the world, however, it is easier to position oneself in a tax-neutral or low-tax jurisdiction, and doing so has very powerful advantages. Why pay more tax than one is legally obliged to pay?

Thus, the tax question these days is a matter of setting off against each other the provisions of the tax laws of different jurisdictions, all or parts of which may govern aspects of a company's business. Sometimes this is known as treaty shopping; sometimes it is more a matter of arbitraging the differences in regulations between onshore jurisdictions. One simply exploits territorial limits of fiscal systems for legitimate businesses. That is, the lack of worldwide harmonization of fiscal systems, particularly with regard to unilateral and treaty relief measures, produces a situation in which factors—persons, places, and events—connected to a tax consequence not only are of jurisdictional relevance but also may give rise to problems of double taxation or, through a deliberate change of one or more parameters, permit the reduction of the global tax burden. It is the lack of uniformity that makes it clear that there is no intrinsic sanctity regarding taxation; revenue authorities create devices and it is perfectly proper to determine whether the devices apply in given circumstances. In this context, tax havens offer significant tax minimization opportunities, since the location of a taxable person or taxable event in a tax haven may

1. Sever or interrupt the formation of a connecting factor with regard to one or more high-tax jurisdictions; and/or

2. Reduce the tax burden falling on a taxable person with regard to a taxable event subject to taxation by one or more high-tax jurisdictions, simple examples of this being sales between two taxing jurisdictions for physical goods and products and services, or value-added tax (VAT) triangulation through the Isle of Man.

Further, despite the best efforts of the mature economies, there are still ways in which residents can achieve some tax economies offshore, particularly where the legal form of the offshore vehicle, for example, a partnership, allows the enterprise to roll up profits, but the owners are treated as individuals for tax purposes so that they do not suffer double taxation—first at the enterprise level and again at the personal level.

To escape the tax net where legally possible is self-evidently desirable, and it is clear that where the criteria that define the application of the taxing provisions are not met, an opportunity exists to mitigate the effect of taxation. What is curious about the expression of high-tax countries' attitudes is that they omit reference to state-owned companies that have offshore vehicles, a recent example being that of a French state-owned company that has set up a Bermuda captive insurer.

Seeking the most efficient approach to taxation is one of the principal reasons for going offshore, fraught though it may be with complexity.

§ 5.5[b] Regulation

Particular trades or businesses may want to operate offshore to disentangle themselves from red tape at home. This is especially true of insurance companies, particularly captive insurance companies. Some exchange-listed companies can also reduce their regulatory burden by incorporating offshore. NASDAQ, for example, has more relaxed rules for foreign-incorporated companies. Likewise, the absence or simplicity of takeover codes in offshore jurisdictions has appeal to some. Within the offshore jurisdiction it is likely that there will be sufficient regulation to ensure propriety but a much reduced reporting and compliance burden, making life simpler and easier for business executives. For example, an international business corporation incorporated in the Bahamas or British Virgin Islands requires "no maintenance," that is, no annual general meetings, filings, or other administrative burdens. This may not be appropriate for many, but it has its place in certain private client matters or in "static" finance transactions where it is unnecessary and expensive to be involved in corporate maintenance when the corporation is simply to hold a single asset for a number of years until a lease-financing transaction matures.

§ 5.5[c] Ease

Offshore jurisdictions generally make it easy to form companies, although certain of the offshore jurisdictions have confidential disclosure of ownership requirements that make the process slightly more complicated, but no slower. Ease also extends to the type of entity to be created. Whereas in the United Kingdom or Canada it might be more of a struggle to incorporate a company limited by guarantee, it is very simple to do so offshore. Guarantee companies are attractive to some in that they have no equity owners and so escape some tax systems or sidestep anti-avoidance legislation.

§ 5.5[d] Speed

Transactions that can take months or years onshore, such as the formation of an insurance company, can be accomplished with astonishing speed offshore. This is not necessarily through lack of effective oversight, but because the offshore jurisdictions are specifically in the business of facilitating enterprise and, instead of taking a hostile, bureaucratic approach, they engage industry professionals to review structures for them and dedicate civil servants to helping to achieve efficiencies. Generally, the lack of complex regulation speeds up affairs.

§ 5.5[e] Innovation

The relative simplicity of the legislation in the truly offshore jurisdictions, namely the small islands, allows for creative business executives to design new forms of commercial vehicles, whereas in their home jurisdictions the absence of enabling laws or the strictures of collateral regulation reduce the scope for innovation. In Bermuda, it is possible to obtain private legislation from the Bermuda Parliament to provide, for example, for bond-financed insurance companies, where the value of the bond tracks the underwriting performance of the company. Public legislation can also be introduced relatively quickly at the suggestion of overseas clients to provide, for example, for limited duration companies of cross-border amalgamations, all of which have value to overseas clients and are seen to be in the public interest in that the smaller countries have cutting-edge statutes. Particularly useful are offshore systems that can quickly adapt to developments in the United States, where the vogue is currently for U.S. tax transparency; hence, offshore jurisdictions respond with legislation providing for limited duration, unlimited liability companies, and modern limited partnerships. The flexibility of the legal structures available offshore enables the practitioner to structure transactions to meet the requirements of two or more legal systems and thereby achieve tax or regulatory efficiencies.

§ 5.5[f] Privacy

Takeover battles, bankruptcy rescues for major companies, and sensitive home government projects can all involve the use of an offshore entity. Clearly, in commerce, secrecy is both important and usually a right; however, it cannot always be ensured onshore. Thus, one distances the sensitive elements from home base. In certain cases, usually involving drug-related funds tracing, there may be exchange-of-information treaties. Ordinarily, however, offshore jurisdictions will have strong secrecy laws or enable nominee arrangements.

§ 5.5[g] International Arbitration and Litigation

It is a fact of life in commerce that there will be disputes. In international finance, the parties to a relationship may come from several different jurisdictions and it will be desirable to find a neutral ground where disputes can be resolved. The more sophisticated offshore jurisdictions have modern arbitration laws, as well as the high level of professional expertise required to litigate or arbitrate. The offshore jurisdictions that are British overseas territories also have final appeal to the Privy Council.

§ 5.5[h] Off-Balance Sheet Transactions

In structured finance and asset securitization transactions, it is almost inevitable that the facilities of an offshore jurisdiction will be employed to provide distance, secrecy, and data and creditor protection.

§ 5.5[i] Specialty Insurance

Offshore jurisdictions, particularly Bermuda, are renowned for their insurance industries. Bermuda is the third largest reinsurance market outside London and New York. A principal reason for the success of Bermuda in attracting insurance and reinsurance companies to its shores has been a regulatory environment that fosters innovation and creativity in responding to the emerging needs of the insurance and reinsurance markets. Bermuda's growth as an insurance and reinsurance center has been a direct result of crises or shortcomings in the established markets onshore. As a center of innovation, companies in Bermuda have been, and continue to be, able to provide risk financing solutions where others have failed. From the development of mechanisms such as captives in the 1960s, through the formation of excess liability carriers ACE and XL and the development of finite risk reinsurer center solutions in the 1980s, and through the formation of property catastrophe companies Mid-Ocean Re, Partner Re, and others in the 1990s, Bermuda has been, and continues to be, a center for innovation in the insurance market. New alternative risk transfer solutions such as risk swaps, special purpose vehicles for exchange-traded catastrophe bonds, and other insurance-related derivative products are also finding fertile soil in which to germinate and develop their creative solutions to capacity and other crises that insurance markets, in particular, are facing. Bermuda's track record of success in being a place in which innovation and creativity can flourish make it well-placed to continue to fulfill this vital function to the global financial markets into the future.

§ 5.6 Bermuda as the Premier Jurisdiction for Offshore Life Insurance and Annuity Products

Bermuda has long been known as a center of excellence and innovation in the world of insurance. Nowhere is this more evident than in the rapidly growing field of offshore life insurance and annuity products. There has been a dramatic upswing in interest in such offshore products issued by Bermuda insurers, which has translated into a high level of activity by large institutional players (mainly U.S. insurers and investment houses) seeking to establish new long-term insurance facilities in Bermuda.

Buying life insurance and annuity products to protect one's life and assets is by no means new. What is ground-breaking is the use of insurance as an alternative means of achieving the goals of investment appreciation, asset protection, and tax planning. Insurance techniques and structures can be a key tool in achieving planning goals for international clients, whether they are individuals seeking to provide for their families' future or companies looking to provide pensions or employee benefits.

Products offered in Bermuda are frequently tailor made to meet the needs of wealthy, sophisticated purchasers seeking an efficient means of minimizing taxes while safeguarding and growing assets for future generations. Bermuda insurers also often offer innovative product enhancements that are not available onshore.

There are many reasons to incorporate in Bermuda. These include the frequently cited ones, such as Bermuda's superlative infrastructure and professional expertise, cutting-edge telecommunications, and speed of response time. With respect to offshore life insurance and annuity products, there are also very special reasons for selecting Bermuda.

§ 5.6[a] Blue-Chip Financial Center

Bermuda is recognized the world over as a blue-chip offshore financial center. This has been cited as the number one reason why many of the world's largest institutional players have selected Bermuda as the domicile for their new life insurance and annuity companies. For example, Bermuda companies are well known to and readily accepted by the world's major stock exchanges. Professionals can therefore be confident of securities commission reviews that reflect high confidence in the selection of Bermuda. Likewise, investors have confidence in the probity of Bermuda's English common law-based legal system and its ability to protect their interests. This is reflected in the fact that large numbers of Bermuda's companies are registered on major stock exchanges around the world.

Since Bermuda is the third largest reinsurance market in the world after London and New York, enormous professional resources are readily available; many of the world's largest insurers and reinsurers have fully functional offices in Bermuda. Accordingly, it is possible to effect all aspects of a transaction in Bermuda on a one-stop-shopping basis. Adequate levels of reinsurance may be of particular importance to a newly formed life insurance and annuity vehicle, and the ready proximity of Bermuda's reinsurance players may, in turn, reduce structural costs as well as the professional time necessary to effect such arrangements.

§ 5.6[b] Flexible Yet Responsible Regulation

Bermuda's reputation rests on sound but flexible regulation. There is sufficient oversight to ensure probity and solvency; however, the government does not mandate the business methods of Bermuda companies. Thus, policy forms and rates for insurers are left entirely to the discretion of management. Additional flexibility may be achieved even in relation to statutory matters for insurers by way of a Section 56 direction under the Insurance Act of 1978 (the Act) from the Minister of Finance. These directions allow variations from the solvency and accounting rules in appropriate cases.

The issuing of life and annuity contracts falls within the meaning of long-term business under the Act. Hence, a life insurance and annuity company will need to be licensed under the Act. The minimum capital and surplus requirement for a long-term insurer is $250,000. In practice, however, this amount will almost invariably be much higher. The exact capitalization will depend on various considerations, including marketing and reinsurance arrangements.

Unlike general business insurers, long-term insurers in Bermuda are not subject to a liquidity ratio requirement. A long-term insurer must appoint an approved actuary, who must provide an actuarial report annually.

A long-term insurer is also required to maintain its accounts with respect to a long-term business separate from any accounts it has with respect to any other business. It may not reduce its total statutory capital by 15 percent or more below that included in the previous year's financial statements without the consent of the Minister of Finance. The only Act restriction on dividends is that the long-term insurer must be in compliance with the minimum solvency requirement at the time of payment of a proposed dividend.

§ 5.6[c] Investment Flexibility

Bermuda long-term insurers have wide latitude with respect to the investment of surplus funds. Moreover, there are no substantial restrictions on the nature or type of investments that can be made by a long-term insurer. They also have far greater freedom as to the nature and compensation arrangements of their investment managers.

§ 5.6[d] "Designer" Companies and Products

Bermuda is unique in being able to offer clients the ability to petition the Bermuda Parliament for the enactment of special legislation in favor of a client company. Private legislation is frequently instrumental in effecting innovative structures that a client may propose but that would otherwise not be permitted under either the Companies Act of 1981 or common law. Thus, recent life insurance and annuity products have been structured by "designer" companies created for the purpose, with a private act obtained to give unique characteristics to the policies as well as the corporate powers of the new company. For example, special provisions are now almost routinely enacted in appropriate cases to permit the payment of both premiums and death benefits in kind as well as in cash, to expand the meaning of insurable interest, and to extend the usual 30-day death benefit payment rule.

§ 5.6[e] Segregated Accounts

Since 1990, Bermuda has been enacting private acts of Parliament to enable life insurance and annuity companies to operate segregated accounts. Bermuda has more experience with such companies than any other jurisdiction. Although other offshore jurisdictions have rushed to enact public legislation providing for "protected cell companies," they have found it necessary to amend their statutes within a year of enactment to deal with the complexities they cause. Bermuda has chosen to watch and wait, with the result that the accumulated body of knowledge has now been put to use in drafting a definitive public statute that effectively segregates assets and liabilities per client account but protects general creditors and the public. Indeed, the intended Bermuda statute, which was tabled in the Bermuda Legislature for first reading on July 14, 2000, and is known as the Segregated Accounts Companies Act of 2000, is structured to ensure maximum recognition in foreign jurisdictions by employing trust and contractual concepts recognized under the Hague Convention and international private law. The new segregated accounts statute was enacted November 1, 2000, and will be effective for any type of company, not just those engaged in insurance.

The obvious benefit of segregated accounts as they relate to life insurance and annuity companies is that they provide each policyholder with statutory "fire-wall" protection against risks arising in other client accounts or in the general account of the insurer itself. In this regard, many clients express high confidence in the integrity and effectiveness of Bermuda segregated account structures. This is particularly important when the funds in a segregated account represent the life savings of an individual insured and are held in an account or financial instrument outside of Bermuda.

§ 5.6[f] The Life Insurance Act of 1978

Almost invariably, the policies issued by a Bermuda life insurance and annuity vehicle will be governed by the general provisions of Bermuda law and, in particular, the Life Insurance Act of 1978 (the Life Act). This is a crucial threshold issue for a new insurer and will take the form of an express provision providing for the Life Act as the choice of law to govern the policy. In making this selection, many clients have been persuaded by the comprehensive legislative framework established by the Life Act as well as by its overwhelmingly beneficial rather than restrictive nature.

The Life Act applies only to contracts of life insurance made after the commencement of the Life Act and to all such contracts made in Bermuda unless the parties agree that some other law will apply. The Life Act, among other matters, prescribes the contents of policies, defines insurable interest, and includes specific provisions dealing with the payment of premiums, default in paying premiums, the duty to disclose, incontestability, designation of beneficiaries, the right to sue, the assignment of policies, and the general powers of a court in relation to disputes between an insurer and one of its insureds.

§ 5.6[g] Modern Trust Law

The law of trusts in Bermuda, which is grounded in the common law of England, has been continually refined and amended over the years in response to the needs of Bermuda's international clients. For estate planning reasons, policies issued by offshore life insurance and annuity companies are often purchased by a trust or placed in a trust for the benefit of the heirs of the insured. It will be crucial to consider why the purchase of an insurance policy may be important to a client's personal or estate planning. If the client lives in a country where there is economic or political instability, then the ability to purchase, hold, and possibly borrow against a life insurance or annuity policy in a stable currency such as the U.S. dollar may be very attractive in terms of both asset protection and investment appreciation.

Such policies may be owned by any legal entity (e.g., the individual client, a company, a partnership, or a trust). When the client does not want to own the policy in his or her own name, the option of an alternative ownership should be explored. How the ownership is structured will depend on the planning advice given in the individual's home jurisdiction and on the reasoning behind the purchase of the policy.

The trust has the benefit of being flexible, of imposing a number of checks, balances, and other controls that can be drafted into the trust deed, and of passing the benefit of assets to one or more persons without the necessity of going through probate.

A master trust (which is nondiscretionary) will often be created in order for the trustee to hold a group policy. The most important reason for using a master trust to purchase policies is to ensure that the customer does not directly purchase the policy.

§ 5.6[h] Responsible Asset Protection Law

Bermuda has never sought to be a leading contender among offshore jurisdictions in the area of asset protection. *Asset protection* can mean many things (e.g., protection from exchange controls, taxation, or expropriation), but the term is most commonly used in legal circles to mean protection from one's creditors. It may be possible to achieve such protection by transferring assets to a trust (or to a company owned by a trust) established in Bermuda. In contrast with the legislation of certain other common-law jurisdictions, including the Cayman Islands and the Bahamas, which have restricted the rights of creditors, Bermuda has taken a more moderate approach, attempting to establish a reasonable balance between the interests of the well-intentioned individual and those of that individual's legitimate creditors. The Bermuda legislation in this regard is widely viewed as fair and sensible in international circles, and mandates the selection of Bermuda as a jurisdiction for legitimate arrangements.

§ 5.6[i] Robust Anti-Money Laundering Law

In keeping with its long-standing commitment to keep out the unscrupulous, Bermuda enacted sweeping anti-money laundering legislation in 1997. The Proceeds of Crime Act of 1997 (the Proceeds Act) was based on its modern counterpart U.K. legislation and complies with the recommendations of the Financial Action Task Force established by the G7 countries in 1989. Bermuda has embraced the passage of the Proceeds Act and its subsequent amendment. Compliance has not proved difficult for most client companies, since Bermuda (unlike several of its offshore competitors) has always had a deep-seated "know your client" culture. Nevertheless, since the Proceeds Act applies to companies with segregated accounts and long-term insurers (excluding reinsurance, life insurance, and disability insurance), it will be important for such "regulated institutions" to establish and observe appropriately high standards of client identification and verification, recordkeeping, internal reporting, and employee training.

In this regard, many large blue-chip institutional clients have welcomed the opportunity to be (and to be seen to be) subject to such standards of business conduct as clearly being in accord with their own high operating standards in the international life insurance and annuity marketplace.

§ 5.6[j] U.S.-Bermuda Tax Convention

Bermuda has a tax convention with the United States that offers insurance companies relief from certain U.S. taxes, if they qualify under U.S. rules. Some U.S. carriers have found they can benefit.[1]

§ 5.6[k] Tax Assurance

Bermuda does not levy income or capital taxes. By way of assurance to foreign-owned companies incorporated on the island, a certificate is routinely issued by the Minister of Finance confirming that no such taxes will apply to the company until at least 2016. Regular extensions of the time limit are made.

§ 5.7 How to Form a Bermuda Insurance Company

A Bermuda insurance company is established and enabled to commence business by a process that includes (1) making application for consent to incorporate the company (which includes a pre-vetting of the proposed insurance programs of the company), (2) incorporating the company, (3) organizing the company, and (4) registering the company as an insurer under the Insurance Act of 1978, as amended (the Insurance Act). What is required with respect to each of these steps is outlined below.

Further, if the insurance company wants to obtain legal segregation of assets and liabilities—which are useful, for example, for rent-a-captive programs—it will need to obtain a private act of the Bermuda Parliament. The procedure to obtain a private act is also detailed below.

§ 5.7[a] Application for Consent to Incorporate the Company

A company formation questionnaire must be completed at the beginning of the incorporation process. A retainer of $10,000 (U.S. dollars) is normally requested at this stage.

The availability of the proposed name of the insurance company should then be checked with the Registrar of Companies, and if the proposed name is available, it should be reserved on a request sheet. Once the name is reserved, the Registrar of Companies will stamp the request sheet. This registration is valid for three months but can be renewed, at any time before the expiration of the three months, for another three months.

Before beginning the formal application process, the principals of the proposed new insurance company will have spent days or weeks in consultation with both onshore and offshore advisers, developing a business plan and completing various forms.

Once this preliminary work has been completed, the formal application process is ready to begin. There are four distinct governmental or quasi-governmental bodies involved in the application process:

1. Application must be made to the Minister of Finance to request consent to incorporate the company, since the business of an insurance company falls within the definition of restricted business activities under the Companies Act of 1981, as amended (the Companies Act).
2. The permission of the Bermuda Monetary Authority (the BMA) to issue shares must be obtained.
3. The documentation must be reviewed by the Registrar of Companies.
4. The Insurers' Admissions Committee (the IAC) must review and approve the proposed insurance program of the applicant.

In practice, one application supplied in counterparts to the BMA will accomplish the four-way submission.

Therefore, the applicant (usually but not necessarily represented by a firm of attorneys), in the same letter, applies to the Minister of Finance, through the BMA, for consent to incorporate the company, and applies to the BMA for permission to issue the shares to the beneficial owners. The letter is copied to the Registrar of Companies for internal review and for circulation to the members of the IAC. The application letter must be accompanied by the following:

1. Form 1, Application for Registration/Continuation;
2. Form 2, Memorandum of Association of Company Limited by Shares;

3. The requisite application fee;
4. The pre-incorporation information form; and
5. A business plan that must contain the following information:
    a. Type of business being written, limits, attachment point, and retention,
    b. Class of registration,
    c. Ownership structure, including intermediate and ultimate beneficial owners of the proposed company (A net worth statement and personal declaration form are required for any shareholders or beneficial owners who are proposing to own 5 percent or more of the company. For shareholders that are corporate bodies, the most recent audited financial statements (private companies) or the most recent annual report (public companies) must be submitted.),
    d. Financial projections (including a pro forma balance sheet and income statement) for five years of operations with substantiation of loss assumptions,
    e. Proposed level of capitalization, and
    f. Reinsurance plan (if any).

The information provided in the pre-incorporation information form summarizes the information contained in the business plan.

Fourteen copies of the application materials are sent by the applicant to the Registrar of Companies, who keeps one copy for internal review and forwards the remaining 13 copies to the members of the IAC.

The IAC is a subcommittee of the Insurance Advisory Committee and is composed of insurance industry executives, and representatives from both the Insurance Division of the Registrar's office and the BMA. The IAC meets weekly on Friday mornings to conduct a pre-incorporation inquiry into the soundness of the proposed insurance programs outlined in pending applications. An application must be filed by no later than 5 p.m. on Monday in order to be considered at the meeting of the IAC on the following Friday. Ordinarily, it will not be necessary for the applicants or their attorneys to appear before the IAC. Requests for further information, or clarification, will usually be put to the attorneys by one of the technical officers of the Insurance Division of the Registrar's office, following the meeting.

The result of the IAC's review will normally be communicated by a technical officer of the Insurance Division to the BMA and the attorneys either on the day of the IAC's meeting or on the following Monday. In practice, the attorneys frequently contact the Insurance Division directly for news of the IAC meeting.

The BMA invariably waits to hear the IAC's views at the conclusion of its Friday morning meeting before making its recommendation to the Minister of Finance, but technically the BMA is not bound by the IAC's views. If the BMA is satisfied with the financial integrity of the proposed beneficial owners, a favorable recommendation will be made to the Minister of Finance for the granting of his or her consent, which will be endorsed on the memorandum of association. The confidentiality of all information received by members of the IAC is protected by Section 52 of the Insurance Act.

Once the application is approved, the Minister of Finance will issue his or her consent for the company to be registered as an exempted company under the Companies Act. Ordinarily, the Minister of Finance's consent is granted within ten days from the date of the application to him or her. The consent is delivered directly to the Registrar's office, which holds the incorporation papers with respect to the company that were submitted at the time of the application for consent to incorporate.

§ 5.7[b] Incorporation by Registration of the Company Under the Companies Act

An insurance company is usually incorporated in the same manner as other Bermuda companies, that is, pursuant to the registration procedure set out in the Companies Act.

The Registrar of Companies will have received the incorporation papers from the applicant's attorneys at the time of the submission of the application for consent to incorporate, but will not incorporate the company until all the necessary consents are obtained.

A government fee, based on the assessable capital of the company, must be paid within 30 days of incorporation. In practice, this fee is paid immediately after incorporation.

The Registrar of Companies will then issue a certificate of incorporation and the memorandum of association and consent granted by the Minister of Finance.

§ 5.7[c] Organization of the Company

The company can be organized (the term *organized* refers to the formal establishment of a company's internal corporate structure) at any time following its incorporation. Typically, organizational meetings are held on the day of incorporation. A company's organization involves convening and holding the following meetings:

1. Meeting of the provisional directors (i.e., the subscribers to the memorandum of association), at which, among other things, the bylaws are presented and the minimum share capital is allotted (if the company is a joint stock company);
2. Statutory meeting of the shareholders, at which, among other things, the bylaws are confirmed, the directors are elected, and the auditors are appointed; and
3. Meeting of the first board of directors, at which, among other things, the officers are appointed, the financial year-end is determined, the registered office is determined, the accountants are appointed, the bankers are appointed and signing authority is established, the insurance managers and principal representative are appointed, the secretary is instructed to apply for a tax assurance certificate (see below), and authority is granted for initiating the application for registration as an insurer in one of the classifications under the Insurance Act.

A notice must then be filed with the Registrar of Companies stating the address of the registered office (Form No. 13). A letter of application is then sent to the Accountant General (care of the Registrar of Companies) for a tax assurance certificate (i.e., a confirmation that the company will not be taxed in Bermuda on capital gains or profits, or be subject to other taxes of a similar nature). The Minister of Finance will then grant an assurance (effective until March 2016) under the Exempted Undertakings Tax Protection Act of 1966. Once the organization is complete, and the capital paid up (as referred to in the pre-incorporation information form), the company is in a position to make an application to the Registrar of Companies for registration under the Insurance Act so that it may commence underwriting.

§ 5.7[d] Registration of the Company Under the Insurance Act

On proof of receipt of the company's capital as confirmed by the attorneys, application is made to the Registrar of Companies for registration under the Insurance Act. The application must include the following:

1. Form 1B (i.e., the executed pre-incorporation information form);
2. The requisite application and registration fees;

3. A letter of acceptance of appointment from each of the principal representatives, the insurance manager, and the auditors; and
4. A letter of acceptance of appointment from the approved actuary and/or the loss reserve specialist, where required, together with their curricula vitae.

Although as a matter of law the Minister of Finance has the discretion to refuse to register the company under the Insurance Act, in practice such discretion is rarely exercised when registration is based on the insurance program presented and approved by the IAC before incorporation. If the Minister of Finance registers the insurer under the Insurance Act, he or she then issues a certificate of registration.

§ 5.7[e] Obtaining a Private Act

The procedure for petitioning for a private act is set out in detail in Exhibit A. In brief, the private act (in bill form) must first be formulated and drafted. It is at this point that the private bill would be tailored to suit a client's specific needs. The private bill must then be advertised locally and submitted to the Clerk to the Legislature, the proposer (a member of Parliament) in the House of Assembly (the lower chamber of Bermuda's bicameral legislature), and the proposer (a senator) in the Senate (the upper chamber). The Joint Select Committee on Private Bills, on the advice of various regulatory bodies such as the Registrar of Companies and the Attorney General's Chambers, will then review and approve the bill with or without amendments. Thereafter, the bill goes through three readings in the House of Assembly and three readings in the Senate. Once the bill has been signed by the Speaker of the House of Assembly and the President of the Senate, it is passed to the Governor for the purpose of receiving royal assent. On being signed by the Governor, the private bill is formally enacted into law.

Exhibit A. Timetable for Passing a Private Bill in Bermuda (total time: six to eight weeks)

1. Preparation of the private bill:
   a. Send a draft of the private bill to the printing company requesting that the company produce a first printer's proof of the private bill (24 hours).

b. On receiving the printer's proof of the bill, check for any errors (24 hours). If there are any errors, request a second proof. (Two days' lead time to advertise.)

c. Advertise the preamble and text of the bill in a local newspaper that is published at least once a week—either the *Royal Gazette* or *Bermuda Sun* should be used—not less than ten days before the first reading if the bill will first be read in the House of Assembly; or not less than 15 days before the first reading if the bill will first be read in the Senate. Although the Senate rules require the bill to be advertised three times, the practice is to advertise it once.

d. Prepare the following documents (one to two days):

- Explanatory memorandum
- Questionnaire (which will be signed by the law firm)
- Petition addressed to the Speaker of the House of Assembly, which must be signed by two directors and dated and the company seal affixed (The directors' names must appear in block letters below the signatures.)
- Petition addressed to the President of the Senate, which must be signed by two directors and dated and the company seal affixed (The directors' names must appear in block letters below the signatures.)
- Letters and required documentation to the Clerk to the Legislature, the proposer of the bill in the House of Assembly, and the proposer of the bill in the Senate

Note. The proposer in the House of Assembly or the Senate must not be a minister or an officer of either house.

2. Submit the following:

a. Letter to the Clerk to the Legislature for the Joint Select Committee on Private Bills together with 20 photocopies of the printer's proof of the private bill, 20 copies of the explanatory memorandum, 20 copies of the questionnaire, the original petition to the House of Assembly, the original petition to the Senate, and an original clipping of the advertisement; and

b. Letters and required documentation to the proposer of the bill in the House of Assembly and the proposer of the bill in the Senate.

3. The Clerk to the Legislature will vet and approve all submitted documentation.

4. Passage through Joint Select Committee on Private Bills (five days). On receipt of the private bill documentation by the Clerk to the Legislature, the bill will be tabled in the House of Assembly (on a Friday) and the Senate (on a Wednesday) at the next sitting of each (if the bill is received on a Monday or Tuesday). The Joint Select Committee on Private Bills will meet to review all private bills submitted when there is sufficient business to warrant a meeting. It is suggested that one not expect a meeting to be held for at least three weeks.

   Note. The attorney responsible will be required to attend and may need to speak about the bill before the committee.

   Note. As the sitting session of Parliament draws to an end, there are deadlines that must be met to ensure the bill is passed before the House of Assembly breaks for summer, winter, and Easter recesses.

5. Procedure in the Bermuda Legislature. The petitions are thereafter, as soon as is practicable, tabled in the houses by the proposers of the bill.

6. Procedure following approval of the bill (two days)

   a. The private bill (with or without amendments) must be sent to the printer with a request to produce 65 printed copies of the private bill and three overprints. (Overprints are copies of the private bill with notations on the front page as to the dates to be inserted—when the bill was approved by the House of Assembly, the Speaker of the House of Assembly, and the President of the Senate, and when it was assented to by the Governor.)

   b. The copies of the bill are then sent to the Clerk to the Legislature (65 printed copies plus four overprints) for distribution to the members of both houses before the first reading.

7. Procedure for the passage of the bill through the Bermuda Legislature:

   a. The copies of the bill are distributed to the members of both houses.

   b. The House of Assembly will proceed through the first, second, and third readings of the bill at its next sitting.

   c. The bill is signed by the Speaker of the House of Assembly and sent to the Senate.

   d. The Senate will normally approve the bill after two sittings.

e. If the Senate approves the bill, it will be signed by the President of the Senate and then forwarded to the Premier.

f. The bill is signed by the Premier and forwarded to the Attorney General's Chambers for final vetting.

g. The bill comes before the Governor and, having received his or her signature of assent, the bill is gazetted as having been passed and is now a private act of the Bermuda legislature.

h. The Clerk to the Legislature will send the private act to the printing company for printing.

---

1. See U.S.-Bermuda Tax Convention of 1986, art. 4.

CHAPTER 6

Home Security and Qualified Personal Residence Trusts

Kenneth A. Ziskin

Synopsis

A qualified personal residence trust (QPRT) can substantially reduce the transfer tax cost of leaving a home to heirs. A properly structured Home Security Trust™ (HST) strategy (essentially, an installment sale of the home to a defective grantor trust, coupled with a fair market value rental of the home) will usually produce better income, estate, gift, and generation-skipping transfer (GST) tax results for most families.

§ 6.1 Introduction

QPRTs, authorized by Section 2702(a)(3)(A)(ii) of the Internal Revenue Code (IRC) and Treasury Regulations Section 25.2702-5(c), may be one of the best ways to leave the family home, or its value, to heirs at minimal transfer tax costs. In fact, QPRTs offer so many advantages to taxpayers that the Clinton Administration proposed that Congress legislate QPRTs out of existence in its fiscal year 1999 and 2000 budget proposals.

Families considering the use of a QPRT should also consider an HST strategy. The HST strategy involves a partial gift and a partial sale of the family home to one or more intentional grantor trusts, with the grantor usually renting the home from the trust or trusts for a fair market rental. The property in a properly structured HST should not be treated as owned by the grantor for estate and gift tax purposes, but should be treated as owned by the grantor for income tax purposes.[1]

Both the QPRT and the HST strategy derive most of their transfer tax benefit from "freezing" the gift tax value of the residence used to fund the strategy at the value at inception of the trust. This freeze can be enhanced if undivided interests in the residence are used to fund the trust, so that their values can be frozen at a discounted level. Of course, each strategy really involves a "leaky" freeze. In the QPRT, the grantor gets back the "value" of occupying the residence rent free during the term of years. In the HST installment sale, the grantor gets back interest and principal on the installment note, offset by rent paid.

§ 6.2 Benefits Common to the QPRT and HST

Many grantors whose current or anticipated estate exceeds the amount that can be protected from transfer taxes by the applicable credit amount seek strategies that will reduce transfer taxes. When the grantor's home represents a significant part of his or her net worth, both the QPRT and the HST can save substantial transfer taxes with minimal intrusion on the grantor's lifestyle.

Benefits common to both QPRTs and HSTs include the following:

1. The grantor can pass the value of a principal residence (and a vacation home) to heirs at a substantial discount.
2. The grantor can continue to occupy the home.
3. The grantor can maintain the ability to use the exclusion from capital gains taxes on the sale of a principal residence.[2]
4. The grantor as trust can retain the home for life, can sell it and replace it with another home of equal, lesser, or greater value, or can sell it and move to a rental home.
5. The equity in the residence is protected from future creditors.

§ 6.3 Comparison of Benefits: QPRT vs. Installment Sale to HST

An installment sale to an HST should generally achieve better wealth transfer results than a QPRT. In fact, the benefits of a QPRT pale in comparison to the benefits that flow from the use of an HST strategy. The HST strategy has these advantages:

1. The HST generally uses less of a grantor's applicable credit amount (unified credit equivalent) than a QPRT uses.
2. The HST avoids the risk inherent in a QPRT that the home will come back into the grantor's estate at full value if the grantor does not survive the term of years selected at inception of the trust. The greatest drawback to the use of a QPRT results from the fact that if the grantor of a QPRT dies during the term of years during which he or she retains the right to use the property transferred to the QPRT, IRC Section 2036(a) causes inclusion of the property of the QPRT in the grantor's estate. The property will be valued as of the date of death and that will eliminate any benefit of the attempted freeze.
3. The HST allows for more efficient use of GST tax exemptions than the QPRT does. Since the value of the residence in a QPRT will be included in the estate of the grantor if he or she dies during the term of years, the estate tax inclusion period (ETIP) rule of IRC Section 2642(f)(3) prevents allocation of GST tax exemptions until the term of years lapses. Even if the grantor survives the term of years, however, the value of the home after the term of years elapses (presumably with appreciation at the rate of inflation) measures the value for GST tax exemption purposes. Thus, the QPRT allows for no GST tax freeze whatsoever during the term of years.
4. The HST provides a means to obtain a step-up in basis in the event of death, which the QPRT regulations purport to prohibit. Treasury Regulations Section 25.2702-5(c)(9) mandates that the governing instrument of a QPRT prohibit the transfer of the residence to the grantor, the grantor's spouse, or any entity controlled by the grantor or the grantor's spouse. For this purpose, the regulation treats a grantor trust whose property is deemed owned by the grantor or his or her spouse for income tax purposes as an entity controlled by the grantor. This regulation was intended to preclude a grantor from substituting other assets for the

residence just before death in order to obtain a step-up in basis at death. Although there may be some question whether the Treasury Department can limit the gift tax use of a QPRT based on income tax consequences, planners generally structure QPRTs on the assumption that the regulation is valid. No similar restriction applies to an HST.

5. The HST avoids most of the technical restrictions imposed on the QPRT by the Treasury regulations. Unless a trust's governing instrument meets all the technical requirements of Treasury Regulations Section 25.2702-5(c), the trust will not be considered a QPRT.
6. The HST allows greater flexibility in structuring cash flow issues for the grantor than a QPRT does. Generally, the note payments will be close to the amount of rent paid by the grantor to the HST. After the note is repaid, the grantor may be able to remain as the beneficiary of the HST with proper structuring, so he or she can either get distributions that offset some or all of the rent or use the rent as a way to transfer further wealth outside the transfer tax system.

§ 6.4 How a QPRT Works

QPRTs are a form of split-interest trust specifically authorized by Treasury Regulations Section 25.2702-5(c). Split-interest trusts allow a grantor to divide the value of an asset over time between (1) a current benefit (either income or use of the property) for a specified term of years and (2) the future benefit of ultimate ownership (a remainder interest).

The property in the QPRT is like an orchard. The QPRT split-interest trust lets the grantor keep the right to harvest a specified amount of fruit from the orchard, in the form of free use of the property, for a specified term of years. At the same time, it allows the grantor to give away the ultimate ownership of the orchard to his or her heirs.

When a grantor establishes a QPRT, he or she retains the right to live in the home placed in the QPRT for a fixed term of years that he or she selects (that is the fruit). The Internal Revenue Service (IRS) does not impose any minimum or maximum term of years. Usually, the grantor also keeps a reversion in the home so that the home, and any applicable credit amount used in connection with giving the home to the QPRT, will be returned to the grantor's estate in the event of the grantor's death before the end of the term of years.

The grantor can act as trustee of the QPRT. Grantors generally can benefit from continuing the QPRT after the end of the term of years. Continuing the QPRT after the end of the term of years ensures the grantor's ability to continue to occupy the home for payment of a fair market rent and protects the assets in the QPRT from claims of creditors of the beneficiaries and from the risk of loss in the event that a beneficiary's marriage fails.

If the grantor were not required to pay a fair market rent, the retained occupancy right would cause inclusion of the home's value in the grantor's estate at death. The IRS, however, in a statement accompanying the adoption of 1997 amendments to the Treasury regulations on QPRTs stated: "If the residence is leased for its fair market value rental, the grantor will not retain the economic benefit of the property for purposes of section 2036(a), since the grantor will be paying adequate consideration for the use of the property."

The IRC treats the creation of the QPRT as a gift to the other beneficiaries of the QPRT. Since the grantor keeps the right to live in the home for the term of years, however, the IRC does not use the full value of the home to determine the amount of the gift. Instead, it discounts the full value of the home by subtracting an assumed value for the right to live there for the term of years, and subtracts the actuarial value of the reversion. Although planners could calculate these discounts from IRS tables, inexpensive commercially available software allows a complex set of calculations to be completed in minutes.

The discounts increase as the term of years and the age of the grantor increase. Selection of the term of years requires careful planning and a little bit of luck. A grantor gets better discounts with a longer term of years; however, if he or she dies before the end of the term of years, the full value of the home (at the date of death, as opposed to the value at the date of the gift to the QPRT) will be included in his or her estate. That means the grantor's heirs risk loss of all of the estate tax benefit of the QPRT, although the applicable credit amount used for the QPRT gift will also be restored on a premature death.

The effective QPRT discount also increases when the rate of interest under IRC Section 7520 increases, since the assumed value of the grantor's retained occupancy right increases.

The following table shows selected QPRT discounts (the percentage of the value of the residence that will be subtracted to compute the taxable gift) for grantors who keep a reversion if they die before the end of the term of years at selected ages, based on the IRS tables and interest rates in effect in January 2000.[3]

Selected APRT Discounts

Age	*Term of years* 5 Years	10 Years	15 Years
55	33%	57%	73%
65	37%	63%	80%
75	45%	74%	90%

§ 6.5 How an HST Works

§ 6.5 [a] Basics

In the HST strategy, the grantor gives a portion of his or her home to an HST and sells the rest of his or her ownership to the HST in exchange for a promissory note equal to the value of the portion sold. The HST should be an irrevocable trust, and the grantor should not retain any rights in the trust that would cause inclusion under IRC Section 2036, 2037, or 2038.

Generally, two HSTs are created. For married grantors, the husband establishes one HST and the wife establishes the other. For single grantors, each HST has different remainder beneficiaries or other terms.

Grantors will normally structure each HST as an intentionally defective grantor trust. Under IRC Section 671, the property of such a trust is deemed to be owned by the grantor for federal income tax purposes; however, by not retaining for the grantor any of the rights listed under IRC Section 2036, 2037, or 2038, the grantor avoids inclusion of the trust property in his or her estate.

§ 6.5[b] Avoiding Estate Tax Inclusion

As long as the HST does not retain for the grantor any right to possession or enjoyment of the trust property, any right to income from the trust property, or the right to designate the persons who can possess or enjoy the property, IRC Section 2036 should not cause inclusion of the trust property in the grantor's estate on account of the terms of the trust.

Similarly, substantial precedent establishes that a promissory note given in connection with a sale of property does not cause inclusion in the seller's estate.[4] The obligation under the promissory note should not be charged to the transferred property and either the promissory note should be a personal obligation of the purchaser or, when a trustee does not want personal liability, the trust should have assets other than those sold to the trust, to provide equity "coverage" for the note. The IRS has informally indicated that other assets equal to, or exceeding, 10 percent of the amount of the note should be sufficient.[5]

In the alternative, the HST can provide the coverage to establish the bona fide debt nature of the note through a guaranty from one or more of the beneficiaries. This technique was used with favorable results in Letter Ruling 9515039, where the guarantor had sufficient wealth to satisfy her personal liability and neither the size nor the obligation to make payments related to the performance of the underlying property and its earnings. The guaranty by a beneficiary could, however, be deemed to be a gift to the HST, unless fair consideration is paid by the HST for the guaranty.

Similarly, IRC Section 2037 should not apply to a discretionary trust, because the trustee can distribute all of the principal to another beneficiary during the grantor's lifetime. Thus, the beneficiary can acquire ownership without surviving the grantor. Furthermore, since the grantor's interest as a beneficiary (if the HST is a self-settled discretionary trust) cannot be valued, no inclusion under IRC Section 2037(a)(2) is possible.[6]

IRC Section 2038 will not apply to cause inclusion as long as the grantor does not retain or share the power to alter, amend, revoke, or terminate the trust. Generally, if any powers to determine distributions from the trust are granted to the trustee, prudence suggests that the grantor not serve as a trustee in order to avoid Section 2038 inclusion.

§ 6.5[c] Achieving Grantor Trust Status

Grantor trust status under IRC Section 671 derives from one or more of the powers set forth in IRC Sections 673 to 677. Care must be taken, however, to use only the powers that do not cause estate tax inclusion. Among the powers that often work are the power to borrow without adequate security,[7] the power held by a nonadverse party to add beneficiaries,[8] the power held by the grantor to substitute assets in a nonfiduciary capacity without the approval or consent of any person in a fiduciary capacity,[9] and power held by any person, other than the grantor, to purchase assets of the trust for less than adequate consideration in money or money's worth.[10] When the grantor gives someone the power to add beneficiaries in order to achieve grantor trust status, the class of persons eligible to be added can be appropriately limited (e.g., to spouses of other beneficiaries). If the grantor allows beneficiaries to purchase assets for less than adequate consideration, the grantor can limit the discount (e.g., to 80 to 90 percent of fair market value) to prevent dissipation of the trust's assets and can require that approval of a nonadverse party be obtained as a condition to such a discount purchase.

§ 6.5[d] Undivided Interest Discounts

The use of two different trusts enhances the discount through the use of undivided fractional interests in real estate. The IRS has long taken the position that the sole basis for determining undivided interest discounts is the pro rata cost of partitioning the property;[11] however, if such right to partition has been waived before the gift or sale to the trust, the hypothetical willing buyer will be locked into the property unless, and until, the other co-owners agree to a sale, and such a hypothetical buyer should therefore further discount the value of the residence. In any event, the courts rarely follow the IRS theory (even when the right to partition clearly exists), and recent cases suggest that discounts as high as 44 percent should apply to undivided interests in real property.[12] As a result, the IRS has modified its position somewhat, and now appears to contend that a discount based solely on the cost to partition is merely one, as opposed to the only, acceptable method of determining the discount for undivided interests in real property.[13]

As a result of the unique characteristics of single-family residences, where the exclusive use of the property provides most of the economic utility and high rates of income are unusual, few purchasers would buy an undivided interest without a substantial discount. Grantors can enhance the discount argument by recording a covenant that waives the right to partition before making any sales or gifts. Experience reviewing numerous appraisals of undivided interests suggests that knowledgeable appraisers generally find undivided interest discounts of between 35 to 45 percent on single-family residences.

§ 6.5[e] HST Example

Assume Mr. and Mrs. Miller (both age 65) have a home worth $600,000. Each of them sets up an HST and gives a 10 percent undivided fractional interest in the home to his or her respective HST. In many cases, if the grantor is also conducting an installment sale of other assets to an income tax defective grantor trust, no separate HST will be required; instead, the other trust can be structured to hold the home and the other assets without losing the tax advantages of home ownership.

The ownership rights accompanying a fractional interest in real estate generally do not have a value equal to a proportionate amount of the value of the entire real estate. Appraisers suggest that the discount should be at least 40 percent, particularly when the grantor has waived the right to partition and the waiver is a covenant that runs with the land. Therefore, a 10 percent interest in the Millers' home could have a value of $36,000 ($600,000 × 10% × 60%). Thus, each of the Millers would use $36,000 of his or her lifetime exemption in connection with the gift to his or her HST. Valuing the gift this low using QPRTs would require the use of 15-year terms, taking each of the Millers to age 80. Actuarial tables suggest that Mr. Miller has only a 54 percent chance of surviving to that age and Mrs. Miller has a 69 percent chance of surviving that long.

Each of the Millers then sells a 40 percent interest in the home to his or her HST in exchange for a nine-year promissory note with a principal amount equal to the value of the 40 percent interest sold. Each sale has no federal income tax consequences, since the property is sold to an income tax defective grantor trust.[14] Each note has a principal amount of $144,000, calculated under the same valuation principles as those used in valuing the gift.

The outstanding principal balance of the promissory notes will be included in the Millers' respective estates, but can be reduced each year as the HSTs make principal payments. The notes bear interest at the applicable federal rate (AFR) under IRC Section 1274, which will approximate normally 80 percent of the Section 7520 rate used to discount values in the QPRT. For a note due in 20 years, the AFR in January 2000 was 6.3 percent with interest compounded quarterly. Thus, each trust must repay (or accrue) interest in the approximate amount of $9,070 per year, which represents less than 3 percent of the pro rata value of the home.

Normally, the notes would be structured to require interest-only payments until maturity, but would allow for principal to be amortized or repaid in advance of maturity, depending on the cash flow needs of the grantors. If market rates of interest fall substantially, the HSTs may elect to borrow from a conventional lender and repay the promissory notes to the grantors or renegotiate the term and interest rate. The aggregate of both notes represents only 48 percent of the value of the whole home. Such a low loan-to-value ratio may justify preferred mortgage lending rates.

The Millers then execute a lease to rent the home from the HSTs. As noted in the discussion of QPRTs (see § 6.4), the IRS does not contend that rental of the property for a fair market rent is a retained interest causing estate tax inclusion under IRC Section 2036. Therefore, the actual amount of the rent should equal the fair market rental.

If the trust charges less than fair market rent, the property of the trust could be included in the grantor's estate under IRC Section 2036(a). If the grantor pays more than fair market rent, he or she may be deemed to be making additional taxable gifts with each rental payment. Therefore, prudence suggests that the trust charge a rental based on an appraisal of fair rental value by a qualified appraiser. Some grantors may, however, elect to avoid the cost of an appraisal by getting a written estimate of the rental value from a knowledgeable real estate broker. Although an estimate by a real estate broker provides some evidence of the fair rental value, it will not be as probative as an appraisal by a qualified real estate appraiser in the event the IRS elects to argue for estate tax inclusion.

Fortunately, under the principles of Revenue Ruling 85-13 (which generally provides that transactions between a grantor and his or her grantor trust have no income tax effect), the payment of rent by the grantor to the HST has no income tax consequence. Further, at a fair market rental rate, there is no gift for gift tax purposes. The result is that rental payments to the HST transfer wealth free of both income tax and transfer tax consequences. This is an ideal estate planning result.

Assume the fair market rent for the Millers' home is $3,600 per month, or $43,200 per year, divided equally between the HSTs. Thus, each HST collects $21,600 per year in rent. (Generally, appraisers and brokers in Southern California estimate fair market rent at about 0.5 percent to 0.7 percent of the home's value per month; the mean of this range has been used in this example.) The lease for the property should provide for increases in rent from time to time, as any arm's-length transaction would (based on appraisal, inflation adjustments, or a fixed periodic increase).

Each HST pays its grantor not less than the interest on the note (about $9,072 per year before amortization of principal). If the Millers want the HSTs to amortize the note over a nine-year period, the note payments would need to be about $20,900 per year for each HST, or just a little less than each trust's share of the rent collected. At this amortization rate, the notes would be fully repaid in nine years.

If the home appreciates at 4 percent per year, it would be worth approximately $854,000 at the end of the nine-year period, and all of that value would be outside the Millers' estates. To get this asset outside their estates, the Millers would have used just $72,000 of their combined applicable credit amount, with an immaterial negative cash flow impact. That leverages the Millers' applicable credit amount approximately 12 to 1. Similar leverage applies for GST tax purposes if the Millers allocate their GST tax exemptions to the initial gift to the HSTs.

Even better, the Millers could accept interest only from their HSTs (rolling them over at each nine-year maturity). This would allow them to reinvest the difference between the rent and the interest payments. If the Millers earn 12 percent per year on the value of the funds in the HSTs and the HSTs remain grantor trusts throughout the relevant period, the trusts would accumulate the values indicated in the table below at the end of each period.

Number of Years Completed	*Projected Value of HST Assets, Net of Promissory Note Balance*
5	$ 615,180
10	$1,078,551
15	$1,808,867
20	$2,990,932

If the Millers properly allocate their GST tax exemptions to the original gift, all of these values should pass free of estate, gift, and GST taxes, with each of the Millers having used only $36,000 of his or her applicable credit amount and GST tax exemption. Part of this benefit derives from the accumulation of rents in excess of interest on the promissory note and reinvestment of these funds with the income taxes paid by the grantors.

§ 6.5[f] Cash Flow Impact After Notes Have Been Repaid

Of course, the rent will normally continue long after the note has been repaid, in which case wealth continues to transfer to the HST for the benefit of the grantor's heirs. Since the HST is income tax defective, the transactions between the grantor and the grantor's HST will have no income tax effect. The payment of fair market rent enhances the wealth transfer benefits of the HST, since such payment should not be treated as a further gift for transfer tax purposes.

To reduce the cash flow burden after the notes have been repaid, one grantor spouse can be a beneficiary of the HST established by the other grantor spouse. Thus, half of the rent can be repaid to the beneficiary spouse. If the trusts are sufficiently dissimilar in terms, or time, to avoid application of the reciprocal trust doctrine, each grantor spouse could be a beneficiary of the other's HST. Alternatively, each of the grantors could be among the permissible beneficiaries of his or her own trust if the HSTs are established under the law of one of the jurisdictions that does not allow a grantor's creditors to reach assets in a self-settled discretionary trust.[15]

In any event, for grantors needing this planning, distributions from the HSTs back to either grantor spouse will not normally be necessary, and should normally be avoided unless the grantors' cash flow situation changes and they need the funds to maintain their lifestyle.

§ 6.6 Comparison of QPRT and HST Strategies

The principal weaknesses of QPRTs include the following:

1. All the transfer tax savings of the QPRT disappear if the grantor dies even one day before the end of the term of years. In the HST, only the remaining principal balance of the note, reduced each year by the installment note principal payments if any, should remain in the grantor's estate. Normally, the note will be fully repaid during the grantor's lifetime and nothing will be included in the grantor's estate.
2. The QPRT does not allow efficient allocation of GST tax exemptions, but the HST does. If the property in the HST is not spent by the grantor's children and the grantor allocated his or her GST tax exemption to the initial gift to the HST, the property in the HST can pass to his or her grandchildren free of GST tax.
3. The Treasury regulations on QPRTs forbid the grantor from buying the home back from the QPRT before death to get the step-up in basis at death. In the HST, if the grantor becomes ill, he or she can buy the home back from the HST in exchange for a promissory note and get a step-up in basis at death on the entire home. The purchase has no income tax consequences, since it is made from the grantor trust. It would have no transfer tax consequences if the note (or other consideration) equaled the value of the home. The promissory note can then be repaid by transferring back to the HST the ownership of the home.
4. The HST gives the grantor and the planner flexibility to adjust cash flow between the grantor and the trust. The HST can enhance its cash flow by

slowing the amortization of the promissory note so that rent payments exceed note payments. Grantor spouses can limit the negative impact of rent on their cash flow to the extent that one or both grantor spouses are permissible beneficiaries of the HSTs and the trustee elects to make distributions to them. The trustee of the HSTs could also borrow against the home and repay the notes in advance, or let a conventional lender finance the purchase of the home from the grantors at the outset.

5. In most cases, the QPRT uses more of the grantor's applicable credit amount than the HST uses. For the Millers (see § 6.5[e]), nine-year QPRTs would use about $150,000 of their lifetime exemption, as opposed to $72,000 with the HST, even though the anticipated value of their home, at life expectancy in 22 years, would be more than $1.15 million with 3 percent annual inflation, excluding any accumulations from investment of the net rentals. With a properly structured HST, about 95 percent of the home's value passes to heirs at this life expectancy, free of estate tax and exempt from GST tax.

On the other hand, the QPRT offers a clear road map to its tax benefits in Treasury regulations and numerous letter rulings, and the grantor can remain the trustee of a QPRT (at least during the term of years) without adverse tax risks. Although substantial authority exists for the use of the HST strategy's sale to an income tax defective trust in exchange for a promissory note, there is no case law or revenue ruling directly on point.

Nonetheless, the numerical measures of tax benefit so favor the HST strategy that, in light of the strong precedents supporting the principles behind it, this strategy deserves serious consideration by anyone who wants to reduce the transfer tax burden on the value of a residence.

---

1. The principles that justify the favorable transfer tax treatment of an installment sale to a grantor trust have been well publicized in recent years, and most commentators believe they offer better transfer tax consequences than grantor retained annuity trusts (GRATs). For an explanation of the typical installment sale to a defective trust, see Belcher and Bridgeman, "Defective May Be More Effective: The Tax Advantages of Intentional Grantor Trusts," 7 *Prob. & Prop.* 24 (1993); van Hoffen, "Planning for Flexibility with Intentionally Defective Grantor Trusts," 9 *Prac. Tax Law.* 31 (1995); Mulligan, "Sale to a Defective Grantor Trust: An Alternative to a GRAT," 23 *Est. Plan.* 5 (Jan. 1996); Nicholson, "Sale to a Grantor Controlled Trust: Better than a GRAT?" *BNA Tax Mgmt. Memorandum,* Feb. 22, 1996; Mulligan, "Sale to an Intentionally Defective Irrevocable Trust for a Balloon Note—An End Run Around Chapter 14," 32 *U. Miami Est. Plan. Inst.* ¶ 1500 (1998); and Mezzullo, "Freezing Techniques: Installment Sales to Grantor Trusts," 14 *Prob. & Prop.* 17 (Jan/ Feb 2000).

2. IRC Section 121 allows an income tax exclusion for up to $250,000 of gain ($500,000 in the case of a married couple) on a personal residence owned by a taxpayer. Both the QPRT and the HST are grantor trusts covered by IRC Section 671. As a result, the assets of each are, for income tax purposes, deemed owned by the grantor of the trust, and should be eligible for the exclusion of IRC Section 121 if the exclusion would have applied had the residence been owned by the grantor directly.
3. These discounts were calculated using 120 percent of the mid-term applicable federal rate, which is set monthly by the IRS in a revenue ruling. The Section 7520 rate for January 2000 was 7.4 percent. Rev. Rul. 2000-1. The discounts in the table were computed using Brentmark Software Inc.'s Estate Planning Tools.
4. Rev. Rul 77-193, citing favorable Estate of Bergan, 1 T.C. 543, Acq. 1943 Cum. Bull. 2; Security Trust & Savings Bank, Trustee, 11 B.T.A. 833; Seymour Johnson, 10 B.T.A. 411; and Hirsh v. U.S., 35 F. 2d 982 (1929). *See also* Cain v. Comm'r, 37 T.C. 185 (1961), *acq.* 1961-2 Cum. Bull. 4; Estate of Becklenberg v. Comm'r, 273 F.2d 297 (7th Cir. 1959); and Estate of Fabric, 83 T.C. 932 (1984). On the other hand, in PLR 9251004, the IRS held, without distinguishing the contrary precedent, that a transfer of $5 million in stock in trust in exchange for a 15-year promissory note with a face value of $1.5 million left a 2036 retained interest since the transferor retained the "right" to interest payments of $165,000 per year.
5. *See* Abbin, "[S]He Loves Me, [S]He loves me not—Responding to Succession Planning Needs Through a Three Dimensional Analysis of Consideration to be applied in Selecting from the Cafeteria of Techniques," 31st Ann. U. Miami Phillip E. Heckerling Ins. on Est. Plan ¶ 1300.1 (1997); and Mulligan, "Sale to an Intentionally Defective Irrevocable Trust for a Balloon Note—an End Run Around Chapter 14?," 31st Ann. U. Miami Phillip E. Heckerling Ins. on Est. Plan. ¶ 1505.1 (1997). Mulligan notes the correspondence between this 10 percent standard and the 10 percent standard in IRC Section 2701(a)(4) for assignment to growth equity.
6. See Commissioner v. Irving Trust Co., 147 F.2d 946 (2d Cir. 1945).
7. IRC § 675(2).
8. IRC § 674(a), (b)(5)(A), (c), (d).
9. IRC § 675(4)(C).
10. IRC § 675(1).
11. *See,* e.g., T.A.M. 9336002.
12. *See* Hall, "Should the IRS Surrender Cost-to-Partition Discounts for Undivided Interests," January/February Valuation Strategies 25 (1998) for a good analysis of discounts for undivided interests in real property. The author represents that his firm has gathered information on 40 actual undivided interest transactions, showing average discounts of approximately 34 percent, with non-income or low-income producing properties, averaging 38 percent. Several tax cases support these discounts as well. In *Estate of Williams v. Comm'r,* TCM 1998-59, the Tax Court accepted the taxpayer's claim of a 44 percent undivided interest discount, rejecting the IRS's attempt to limit the discount to 5 percent. In *Williams,* the taxpayer's experts derived the 44 percent discount using factors for lack of control, lack of marketability, and the cost and difficulty of partition, as well as marketing time and costs. *See also LeFrak v. Comm'r,* TCM 1993-526 (30 percent discount allowed, explicitly rejecting the cost-to-partition approach, in a case where the IRS argued for a 15 percent discount, but where the IRS's own expert opined to a 30 percent discount); *Cervin v. Comm'r,* TCM 1994-550 (20 percent discount allowed, where IRS asserted discounts should be 6.54 percent on one property, and 8.20 percent on another); and *Barge v. Comm'r,* TCM 1997-188 (28 percent discount, calculating present values of anticipated cash flows from partition, using a 10 percent capitalization rate). *Estate*

of Lopes v. Comm'r, TCM 1999-225 confirms that real property interests held for the benefit of the decedent in two separate trust (a QTIP and a survivor's trust) need not be aggregated for valuation purposes, and therefore entitle the estate to a fractional interest discount, even though both interests were includable in the estate.

13. See T.A.M. 199943003.
14. The IRS has ruled that the existence of a wholly grantor trust should be disregarded for income tax purposes, and transactions between the grantor and such trust have no income tax consequences. Rev. Rul. 85-13. Some commentators suggest that the death of the grantor while the installment note is outstanding causes the recognition of any gain with respect to the outstanding balance of the note under the rationale of *Madorin v. Comm'r*, 84 T.C. 667 (1985), but without corresponding increase in basis.
15. As of this writing, Alaska, Delaware, and Nevada have enacted such legislation. For a discussion of why a self-settled trust in Alaska should not be included in the grantor's estate, see Hompesch, Rothschild and Blattmachr, "Does the New Alaska Trust Act Provide an Alternative to the Foreign Trust," *Asset Protection*, July/Aug. 1997, at 9. See PLR 9737007, which found a gift to a self-settled trust for the benefit of the grantor and her living descendants, established under Alaska law, to be a completed gift for federal gift tax purposes. While the PLR does not reach the possibility of inclusion in the grantor's estate, the article cited in this note makes it clear that no grounds for inclusion exist in a properly drafted Alaska self-settled trust. However, if the residence is located in a state that does not protect the assets of a self-settled discretionary trust from the settlor's creditors, the residence should first be converted to personal property in order to take advantage of the self-settled trust rules (e.g., by the contributing the residence to a single-member LLC or other pass-through entity). If not so converted, conflict of laws principles may prevent application of the law of the trust situs, and instead apply the law of the situs of the residence. The latter technique may not be desirable if the property is located in a state that imposes any significant income or franchise taxes on an LLC (such as California).

CHAPTER 7

Evaluating and Investing in Hedge Funds

Barclay T. Leib

Synopsis

Acknowledgment. Portions of this chapter were adapted from articles by the author first published in *Plan Sponsor* and *Global Custodian* magazines. The author is grateful for permission to quote from these sources. The author also gratefully acknowledges permission to use excerpts from *Grant's Interest Rate Observer* regarding hedge fund leverage.

There is little doubt that hedge fund investing is something that every wealthy individual will at least consider at some point. The impetus may come from a neighbor who brags about the 26 percent compound returns that he or she has stacked up investing with a particular hedge fund manager, from a friend who is a hedge fund manager and overtly solicits funds, from a professional money manager or estate planner talking about diversification, or from one's own desire to create smoother, less volatile returns on investment assets than traditional mutual fund or private equity investing will ever allow. Although the source of the impetus may vary, it will likely be worth at least considering a foray into hedge funds. This is because hedge funds—which are typically private limited partnerships set up by entrepreneurial traders executing a variety of relative value strategies—can often produce better risk-adjusted returns than traditional buy-and-hold investing styles. Hedge funds also tend to perform well in a wider variety of market environments since their managers are generally less dependent upon a given equity or fixed income market advancing in price.

Most family fortunes are created via a concentrated industry exposure but, once made, are best maintained by proper diversification. Hedge funds, through their wide variety of flexible trading styles and ability to match long exposures with equally robust portfolios of short positions, as well as their ability to become involved with other asset classes such as foreign exchange and commodities, can represent a singularly strong allocation choice. A properly constructed portfolio of hedge funds can deliver a steady stream of future returns and preserve capital in a variety of friendly and hostile market environments.

§ 7.1 Hedge Fund Managers: Who They Are

Hedge fund investing, or so-called alternative investing, has its roots in the desire to work for oneself and be entrepreneurial. Money managers, traders, and analysts who toil for years at large investment banks typically have but one goal: develop enough experience, make enough industry contacts, and create enough "edge" in their investment approach to set up their own shop. This is because while investment banks pay lucrative salaries and bonuses, few ever give a money manager a direct profit sharing equation, and those that do seldom offer bonus pools greater than 10 to 15 percent of net profits.

Hedge funds generally work on a 1 percent management fee and 20 percent profit sharing basis, so even a hedge fund manager successful in raising just $10 million in assets to trade can generally make a living. The 1 percent management fee pays the daily bills while the manager hopes that performance will land him or her a substantial portion of the investment profits at the end of the year. With just $10 million in assets under management, and at a 22 percent return on assets, a fund manager charging standard fees would make $320,000 a year in total compensation. With $100 million under management, the manager would earn $3.2 million.

Given such large potential rewards, new hedge funds are continually being set up, particularly since the barriers to establishing a hedge fund are quite low. Generally, it is a simple matter of paying some legal fees for an offering memorandum and disclosure document, and raising some seed capital. Sometimes hedge funds even get set up as the next step in an individual's career after that person has been fired from a previous position. Once displaced, entrepreneurial sorts often figure that the easiest way to get a new job is to create one. In other instances, an individual who is very successful at a large institution completely fails when striking out alone.

Reputational risk is the biggest risk these people face, for one failed hedge fund foray does not typically beget a second attempt. Savvy traders may thus agonize for years before setting up their own business. Their personal and professional lives have to be just right for them to make a full effort at a hedge fund endeavor. In more ways than one, it is very difficult to go back to a traditional Wall Street firm after one has left to hang out one's own money management shingle.

As a first rule of hedge fund investing, it is important to realize that just because a money manager has been a success in a big firm, there is absolutely no guarantee of similar success as a hedge fund manager. Whether people will admit it or not, every individual working at a Goldman Sachs or a Merrill Lynch has an advantage over an individual working alone in a small office. How important this institutional edge is will vary greatly by individual and investment strategy and will determine how portable a manager's skills are. There is also no general rule that a hedge fund manager with $1 billion under management is necessarily any better than one with $5 million under management. To the contrary, diminished returns tend to follow managers who grow their assets under management too quickly.

One scary statistic (according to research done by the University of Reading) is that only 59 percent of hedge funds that existed five years ago exist today. This means that out of roughly 6,000 hedge fund managers currently managing approximately $500 billion in assets, one might expect that over the coming five years 40 percent of these funds will close their doors for one reason or another—often related to poor performance. These managers are widely dispersed across North America, Europe, and Asia, with assets under management ranging from a few hundred thousand dollars to over $10 billion. By law in most countries, hedge funds—which typically are structured as private limited partnerships—cannot advertise, and by nature, many managers purposefully maintain a low profile. Therefore, finding these many firms is not an easy task, and finding the ones that will survive and flourish is even harder.

To make matters more difficult, there is a "ticking clock" element involved in the hedge fund search process. Many of the best managers will close their funds to new investment once a sufficient mass of capital under management is reached. Thus, good managers need to be found relatively early if finding them at all is to be of any use.

As this chapter progresses, it will discuss in more detail how exactly to locate and choose good hedge fund managers in an organized and systematic manner, but first it is important to understand what hedge funds are not.

When the term *hedge fund* comes up in conversation, any number of famous managers may come to mind: Julian Robertson, George Soros, Paul Tudor Jones, or perhaps Michael Steinhardt or Bruce Kovner. These are relatively high-profile managers who rose to prominence in the 1980s and 1990s making large "macro" bets on the global economy. Each ended up with enough money under management to become almost world famous.

The story of how Soros took on the Bank of England in the 1992 European ERM crisis by selling billions of pounds short and eventually forcing a pound devaluation is now legendary. Robertson likely played a similar hand in the 1997 devaluation of the Thai baht, before hitting rough times during the 1999–2000 technology bubble. Jones is known mostly for making a small fortune in the 1987 stock market crash by using "analog pattern match" techniques to predict the very week and day that Black Monday occurred. Steinhardt and Kovner are best known, perhaps in a bit more villainous light, for working together to corner the two-year note Treasury market in 1993.

All of these men have a delicate instinct for the markets and a long-term proven ability to make money in a variety of market environments. Are they representative of the hedge fund world? They are certainly not. They are instead the exception.

Most hedge fund managers are not managers betting on large macroeconomic events—currency dislocations, equity crashes, bond squeezes, and the like. Most hedge fund managers can better be viewed as niche specialists—often so-called arbitrageurs—picking up pennies and dimes left along kinked yield curves or from spurious short-term noise between highly correlated stocks that momentarily drift apart. Some are highly trained stock pickers that pair value equity positions against overpriced brethren. Others make money exclusively on the short side of equities looking for flawed or fraudulent accounting statements and business plans.

Yet others tend to be event driven; that is, their positioning is driven by some event such as a merger, a spin-off, a bankruptcy reorganization, or a lawsuit that is perhaps about to be settled—definable situations in which the hedge fund manager spies a potential valuation impact yet to be recognized by others.

If hedge funds sound like a game of inches, they are. The two best characteristics that one could look for in a good hedge fund manager are a repeatability of style and an ability to limit risk to within definable parameters. A good hedge fund manager will not stray far from the basic manner in which he or she has extracted money from the market in the past. Although hedge fund managers will certainly never be successful in every position taken, successful managers are able to size positions correctly with appropriate stop-loss and other risk control measures to avoid mark-to-market disasters. As a rule of thumb, no single position within a portfolio should be allowed to cost an entire fund more than 1 percent or 1.5 percent. The manager who can accomplish this type of risk control will likely be around for a long time.

Conversely, the worst characteristic that one could look for in a hedge fund manager is a combination of large ego and a large amount of money under management. That combination can be deadly, as investors in John Meriwether's failed Long Term Capital Management found out in 1998. All the warning signs of excess ego were there—a certain hubris—that this "dream team" of former Salomon Brothers stars, combined with quantitative aficionados such as Myron Scholes, were too smart too fail. It was bad enough that the outside world believed the hype; the problem was that the Long Term Capital Management team believed it as well.

§ 7.2 Hedge Fund Styles

A variety of different hedge fund styles are described below. It is important to be familiar with the wide diversity of approaches available when choosing a particular style and manager.

Long only. While long-only equity approaches dominate the mutual fund world, they are not particularly common in the hedge fund world. When they do exist, they tend to have a specific focus of large-, mid-, small-, or micro-capitalization, or a given sector specialization: technology, biotechnology, energy, and so on.

Dedicated short. These types of managers run a fully loaded portfolio of short equity positions at all times. Most tend to focus on stocks with deteriorating fundamentals and cash flow issues, although any dedicated short will also look for outright fraudulent companies. As a rule, they do not tend to try to time the overall market. Instead, they deem it their responsibility to be short 100 percent of the time. They are often hired as an insurance policy representing just 5 percent of a diversified portfolio to provide portfolio alpha in down market environments. As such, there is very little latitude allowed these managers to expand or contract their total short exposure at any moment in time. Dedicated shorts can effectively only rotate shorts between different opportunities and sectors. A reasonable goal of these funds is—through astute stock picking—to break even or lose just a small amount of money in up markets, and to hit 40 to 50 percent positive returns in sharp market downdrafts.

Short biased. These managers run portfolios of equity positions that on a net basis have gross short positions 0 to 70 percent greater than their gross long positions, but they do typically maintain some longs. There is also some latitude afforded these managers to expand and shrink their short exposures as the manager may deem prudent in different market circumstances. Before the 2000–2001 equity meltdown, it was not easy to find short-biased managers who would judiciously run a portfolio more short than long most of the time. Such funds have increasingly sprouted up since. A reasonable goal for these managers is to make 7 to 10 percent returns per year no matter what market environment exists and to make 20 to 30 percent returns in market downdrafts.

Long-short diversified. By far the most common type of hedge fund, long-short diversified funds scout for opportunities on both sides of the market across a wide range of industries and companies of varying market capitalizations. The drawback of this strategy is that it can be difficult to conduct an in-depth analysis into a variety of diverse industry groups. No one can be an expert on everything. The advantage is that small missteps likely will not hurt the overall portfolio in a significant way as long as a manager has reasonably good insights in general. A typical profile of a diversified manager is one who runs a portfolio between 30 and 70 percent net long, uses some leverage from time to time (but typically not more than 90 percent gross long, 60 percent gross short), and regardless of market environment hopes to achieve 10 to 20 percent returns per year without substantive drawdowns along the way. Some managers tend to focus on growth companies; others are more value oriented.

Long-short small-capitalization, long-short mid-capitalization, and long-short large capitalization. These managers are very similar to their long-short diversified brethren except that they add an extra filter of specialization. These managers concentrate their stock selection within certain types of stocks with specific levels of market capitalization. Managers specializing in small-capitalization stocks are most common. Each of these managers can subspecialize in either growth or value situations. Market exposures tend to range from 30 to 70 percent net long, with varying degrees of leverage used.

Long-short global. These fund managers run their portfolios much like other long-short managers, except that they also typically promise to maintain a portfolio with at least a 30 percent exposure to non-U.S. markets. Such exposure may also be as large as 80 percent, with country exposures periodically being shifted to greater or lesser exposures as the manager may deem most opportune considering relative equity valuation levels and macroeconomic circumstances.

Long-short country specific. This manager is similar to other long-short equity managers except that the focus of stock selection is a geographic locale. Japan-only, East Asia-only (excluding Japan), and European-only long-short funds are the most common.

Long-short sector specific. Instead of trying to conquer the world, or even a particular country, some managers feel most comfortable limiting their universe to a particular market sector (e.g., health care, banking, or retail). These managers tend to be more valuable as a straight function of an industry's complexity. It is thus not abnormal to find many hedge funds that specialize only in a field such as biotechnology. Market exposures can vary from 20 percent net long to 120 percent net long, with varying use of leverage.

Regulation D or private equity oriented. Getting aboard a hot young stock before it has even gone public is, of course, the dream of many equity investors, and buying privately placed Regulation D securities often allows hedge fund managers to get sweetheart deals. The risk of this style is the illiquidity of the positions, the amount of time necessary to allow positions to mature, and the hit-or-miss type of payoff pattern that occurs on these types of securities in the end. Longer lockup periods and higher net market exposures are the norm here, but a well-managed Regulation D manager in a generally equity-friendly environment may have an easier time getting to 25 percent annual returns than other managers.

Value driven, market and sector neutral. Many normal long-short managers are largely market neutral in their approach, but they make no guarantee to always be so, instead allowing their market and sector exposures to swing as opportunities present themselves. To advertise oneself as "market and sector neutral" is to guarantee to keep the fund beta near zero and exposure to any single industry group near zero at all times. The focus becomes ranking stocks (typically using a value approach) within each sector and then shorting the overvalued stocks by sector and buying the stocks deemed undervalued. This strategy may seem to some to be a bit like trading with one's hands tied behind one's back, but it appeals to many institutional investors searching for funds with a very low overall market exposure that can be added to a more traditional portfolio of stocks and bonds without large risk of increasing overall equity market exposure. This concept is called portable alpha and it is increasingly in demand. The strategy tends to do better in value-friendly environments as opposed to growth environments.

Statistical arbitrage driven, market and sector neutral. With the advent of electronic trading platforms, plus the speed with which modern-day computer algorithms may continuously test individual equity price movements for two- and three-standard deviation moves vis-à-vis highly correlated peer stock groups, a new hedge fund strategy style has emerged in recent years: statistical arbitrage. Statistical arbitrage managers worry primarily about relative price movement; very few use any multifactor fundamental data in their decision making. Individual trades tend to be small and incremental vis-à-vis the entire portfolio size, with statistical arbitrage managers acting almost as modern-day liquidity providers or market makers much as New York Stock Exchange (NYSE) specialists have done historically. This type of strategy tends to do well in volatile and noisy markets, but with a strong element of mean reversion. Thematic, trending, and quiet markets tend to be less kind to this strategy, particularly if themes within the market continuously pan out as opposed to dissipating. The absolute level of returns to be expected from this type of manager will thus vary greatly depending on the market environment that prevails. The strategy is generally market neutral in normal two-way markets but has shown some proclivity to perform poorly when stressful markets lead to extreme and statistically abnormal behavior. An environment with a great deal of merger activity can also be difficult for these managers.

Convertible bond arbitrage. To save on interest costs, corporations often issue convertible securities. The imbedded optionality to convert to common shares means the company can pay less in interest costs than it can by issuing straight debt. Because convertible bond tenors tend to be five to ten years, however, the market hardly ever pays corporations a fair price for the imbedded option. Instead, underwriters typically demand a discount in the imbedded option's "implied volatility" when compared to the equity's actual observed volatility. Convertible bond arbitrage managers try to spot situations in which this discount is large enough to merit buying the convertible bond versus selling a proportion of the simple common equity against it. The manager will then adjust this hedge in a beneficial manner as the underlying equity price moves higher and lower. Because convertible bonds often still carry a significant coupon and a rebate benefit also accrues to the manager from the stock short sale, trades may often be set up with positive carry attributes. By definition, the properly balanced trade of long bond versus short equity is largely market neutral. The Achilles heel of the strategy is that one is still buying a fixed-income instrument and thus incurring some exposure to interest rate movements and to credit risk. Although there are derivative contracts available that can hedge both exposures, using such tools can be costly. In general, therefore, environments with widening credit spreads and rising interest rates tend be difficult for convertible bond arbitrage managers. Conversely, in a volatile equity environment with benign interest rate movements, a good convertible bond arbitrage manager should be able to achieve 12 to 15 percent returns annually unleveraged, or 20 to 25 percent returns annually when added leverage is applied.

Options arbitrage. Options arbitrage managers typically trade listed individual equity options and index options. Some may also trade options on futures, particularly options on equity index futures or fixed-income futures. The game here is almost always to buy undervalued options such that premium expense is less than subsequent delta hedging opportunities that subsequently arise from underlying price movements. In other instances, managers may sell options in an attempt to earn time decay in excess of prudent hedging costs. Yet another variation is to combine portfolios of both activities into a premium-neutral portfolio. Finally, some managers systematically try to buy a batch of options on individual equities on a beta-adjusted basis versus selling equity index options. Because equity index puts typically trade at a premium price (portfolio insurance types almost always covet them), a market-neutral portfolio can often be created, but with an expected positive value or return. The manager then benefits if index volatility compresses vis-à-vis individual equity volatility, or if excess delta hedging value is extracted from individual equity positions as a result of equity-specific movement and so-called security-specific jump moves. In general, since managers may approach options in many ways, each with very different risk implications, this type of manager must be chosen with particular care and due diligence.

Event driven or opportunistic. This type of manager searches for situations in which, in the manager's opinion, a given corporate event—whether a spin-off, reorganization, merger, court case resolution, or simply a piece of news about a new product—will result in added or changed value for the corporation's shareholders, and the value is not yet recognized by the market. Positions are taken in anticipation of the event, and since a catalyst has already been defined to unlock value, a manager can typically look to unwind his or her position once the event has transpired. Many fine "special situation" event-driven managers have produced consistent 20 percent returns in recent years, often doing so regardless of market conditions.

Merger arbitrage. A specialized form of the event-driven category, the merger arbitrage fund manager focuses solely on announced merger deals, handicapping the probability that deals will actually be consummated (after legal, regulatory, financial, and other hurdles are surpassed) against the spread price available between the acquiring company and the target company. The level of these spreads and the actual number of mergers to choose from and participate in typically determine the attractiveness of this strategy. Merger arbitrage also has some sensitivity to periods of equity weakness when the probability of previously announced deals being scrapped increases. Because individual deal spreads are relatively narrow, but the certainty that most announced deals will close is relatively high, managers of this type typically use a fair amount of leverage. Merger arbitrage can thus produce steady returns most of the time, but hit significant occasional potholes.

Fixed income arbitrage. Managers focused on the fixed-income markets almost always are focused on some degree of relative value across either the shape of the yield curve or the spread between securities of similar duration but different credit quality or geographical location. Occasionally one will find a fixed-income manager who takes outright directional bets on the fixed-income market's overall direction, but most of these managers belong in the market timing or macro category. In addition, because people usually want to be paid to carry a position rather than to pay away carry costs, most fixed-income arbitrageurs engage in some amount of credit spread arbitrage where they will buy a lesser credit that has an attractive yield-to-maturity while shorting U.S. Treasury securities against it. Although managers can and do position themselves the other way around when credit spreads become overly compressed, in general fixed-income arbitrage managers typically show some vulnerability to periods of market stress and widening credit spreads. In addition, because the fixed-income markets typically involve a large degree of over-the-counter swap and option trading, some counterparty risk and access to reliable lines of credit can become an issue for the strategy. Since the spread relationships are typically measured in minute changes, a fair amount of leverage must also be used to produce attractive returns. Fixed-income arbitrage is best considered in environments where credit spreads are already quite wide and the interest rate environment is already volatile as opposed to quiet.

Mortgage-backed arbitrage. A specialized form of fixed-income arbitrage, mortgage-backed arbitrage attempts to position various tranches of mortgage-backed pools and securities relative to each other and to equivalent duration Treasury securities. This is a highly specialized area that is filled with both large positive carry opportunities and "negative convexity" issues, since the duration of mortgage-backed securities can shift as a result of interest rate and prepayment trends. Whether prepayments accelerate or abate can have serious impacts on any mortgage strategy, and higher default risk on certain asset pools always lingers behind the scenes as an important issue. Finally, managers typically use a fair amount of leverage in this area. Therefore, this is not a strategy for the timid or unsophisticated.

Multi-arbitrage. Arbitrage opportunities have a tendency to shift from time to time, and when they do, a hedge fund investor can either overtly shift manager allocations (typically on a lagged basis) or invest from the outset with a firm that engages in various styles of arbitrage. The usual multi-arbitrage firm has the ability to become involved with convertible bond arbitrage, merger arbitrage, statistical arbitrage, long-short paired trading of like securities, option arbitrage, and distressed investing. Capital within these funds tends to get allocated to areas in which the managers discern the best opportunities; but often at least a portion of the assets is deployed to each strategy all of the time. This has the attractive attribute of return smoothing. The downside of this strategy is that it may be difficult for a multi-arbitrage manager to be good at everything at once. Sometimes a significant staff is required to cover multiple areas, and then sophisticated risk management systems are needed to keep that staff from building too much autocorrelated market risk across the different strategies. Notwithstanding such hurdles, a good multi-arbitrage manager likely deserves a place in any hedge fund allocation.

Mutual fund market timing. If picking the immediate direction of the market at any given moment in time is a difficult enough task by itself, doing so with the liquidity to trade only once a day via a mutual fund subscription or redemption might initially seem an even sillier idea. Yet that is exactly what mutual fund market timers do. The primary twist that gives them their edge is the difference in global time zones together with the institutionalized willingness of most large mutual funds to accept subscriptions or redemptions on all of the funds they manage up to a fixed time in the afternoon, New York time.

> **Example.** Consider a day when the Asian markets quietly trade lower before closing for their day at 3 a.m. New York time; then the U.S. equity markets open and, for whatever reason, rally tremendously. There is a good statistical probability that the Asian markets will follow the U.S. market action in the subsequent trading day, and a mutual fund market timer can take advantage of that. Until 3 to 4 p.m. New York time, a mutual fund market timer has the ability to buy an international Asia-only mutual fund at a net asset value calculated from prices that prevailed in the Far East before the New York trading day even started. Such a position can be held for at least one day with a high probability of success.

This is the type of trading many mutual fund market timers engage in, typically adding on top of obvious statistical time-zone opportunities a variety of momentum models to gauge market health and help decide whether a position should subsequently be held or liquidated. Typical holding periods are two to three days, although some market timers can move more slowly and hold positions for two to three weeks. The overall endeavor is to be invested in mutual funds for as many up days as possible, while avoiding investment for as many down days as possible. The biggest drawback of the strategy is that is not very tax efficient: Short-term gains and losses reign here. The biggest constraint on the strategy is mutual fund capacity. Mutual fund companies dislike this type of trading behavior, and when they detect it, can limit or ban timer access to whole mutual fund groups. Dealing through third-party brokers and insurance companies has become a secondary avenue for some market timers, but how long these avenues will remain open is not clear. As a result, some mutual fund timers, stripped of their investment capacity, sometimes can be found adapting their models toward rotational basket and sector trading. One should be suspicious of the performance repeatability of any manager forced to do this. Overall, choosing a truly robust mutual fund market timer to add to a hedge fund portfolio requires some care, and once the investment is made, ongoing attention to possible capacity issues or style drift is warranted.

Basket trading. Applying sophisticated momentum and trending filters to baskets of similar stocks, some managers—particularly those coming out of a mutual fund timing background—try to pounce on different market sectors for short periods of time. They trust in their models to reveal enough daily price autocorrelation to extract a positive expected return over time. This has not historically been a common hedge fund strategy, but it has recently become more prevalent.

Pairs trading. A cousin to statistical arbitrage trading but usually simpler, pairs trading involves the buying and selling of two stocks within the same industry that are highly correlated with each other but trade at significantly different levels of valuation. While statistical arbitrage trading tends to be short term in nature and dominated by simple price action, pairs traders tend to have a more intermediate-term focus and be more fundamental and value oriented in their portfolio construction. Often they will try to have a fundamental catalyst in mind when establishing a paired position, trying to anticipate events that could cause a spread relationship between two companies to change suddenly. If a portfolio of 20 or so paired positions can be established, a certain smoothing of otherwise volatile daily spread movements can be achieved. This is a good solid strategy, albeit often with a value bias.

Short-term technical or swing trading. Markets can be repetitive in nature, and quite often a savvy trader—with the help of a good charting system—will see short-term price setups that historically yield a consistent type of ongoing price action. Often the basis of such trading is simply a coiling price pattern whereby market highs and lows are contracting as supply and demand eat away at each other, until finally a breakout occurs. A one- to three-day unidirectional run in such an asset is not uncommon. At other times, a short-term trader may spy a "key outside-day reversal" where the open and high of a given day are above the high of the prior day but prices close below the low of the prior day. Statistically this often suggests several further days of immediate weakness. Short-term traders are often looking for such technical setups that may coincide with other fundamental news about a company. Some short-term traders are more technically driven than others, but almost all consult a chart before pulling the trigger on any trade. Positions are typically held for one to ten days, and because opportunities may present themselves on both the long and short side of the market, short-term traders have generally proven themselves to be noncorrelated to overall market behavior. For trading success, however, some amount of trending behavior to the markets with a reasonable amount of volatility is helpful.

Emerging markets. These managers invest primarily in smaller countries outside of the United States, Western Europe, and Japan, searching out equities with modest market capitalizations plus high growth prospects, or buying corporate and sovereign debt that carries attractive yield characteristics and where the manager believes that the risk of credit default is exaggerated. At various points during the past decade, this style has been the best performing style among hedge funds, and at a few points (notably the 1994–1995 Latin American crisis and the 1997–1998 Asian and Russian crises), it has been the worst performing style. Since it is often difficult (and expensive) to borrow emerging-market securities in order to short them, most emerging-market managers are more long-only in their orientation. They are thus more sensitive to broader macroeconomic impacts and general market behavior. By definition, all emerging-market managers are also exposed to currency movements and potential devaluations, and how a manager hedges such risk is of some importance in choosing this style of manager. There have been instances in the past when foreign equity markets have advanced significantly in local domestic terms, but in currency-adjusted terms have shown negative returns to foreigners with no currency hedge. South Africa is one country notable for this type of return profile for the past two decades.

Distressed investing. This type of manager is a specific type of event-driven manager specializing in the securities and obligations—equities, bonds, and bank debt—of companies in or near bankruptcy. Sometimes the manager can spy sufficient corporate assets to almost guarantee that if bankruptcy proceeds, at least senior debt obligations will be paid off, even if common shareholders are wiped out. In other instances, a manager will buy senior debt, hoping to have it converted to new debt and equity in a reorganized company on favorable terms. There are two styles of distressed investing: One is passive and the other is more pro-active. The latter involves accumulating enough shares or bonds to influence the turnaround process, often with the help of legal counsel and other investors. There are also a variety of balance-sheet levels where managers become involved. Some play primarily in senior debt obligations, where seeing a bond converge back to a par payoff may not result in a huge trading gain but is a high-probability event. Others specialize in buying junior debt obligations and common shares of distressed companies, looking for bigger home runs that often may take a greater amount of time to achieve full success. Some managers trade different levels of a corporation's capital structure against each other as a hedged relative-value position. Others actively try to find companies in distressed situations that look serious enough to merit short sales of the companies' securities in hope that the bankruptcy truly proves terminal; however this path involves paying away carry, so typically it is limited to a small part of any manager's portfolio. Distressed investing thus carries some positive beta to the market in almost all instances, although the degree of this positive beta can vary greatly.

High-yield investing. Somewhere between investment-grade fixed-income trading and distressed securities investing is the high-yield universe of fixed-income investing. When companies are downgraded by rating agencies, quite often by charter, bank and insurance companies are forced to sell securities in the downgraded entity. This may create a temporary dislocation and often overshoot in these securities' declines. High-yield investing managers will then step in to buy these orphaned securities, often shorting against them other investment-grade securities that the manager believes may be ripe for a future rating agency downgrade. The success of this type of manager depends on his or her overall skill at picking solid credits and anticipating corporate or rating agency events that may change current debt valuations. Because some securities that become high yield go on (almost by definition) to become distressed, a high-yield manager does not have as much of a natural and definitive backstop to position taking as a distressed manager must have when looking at the underlying assets of a company already in liquidation.

Global macro. By far the most visible and well-known of the hedge fund managers, global macro managers tend to formulate a variety of fundamental economic views, and then step in to purchase securities and assets—equity, fixed-income, and foreign exchange—that are deemed particularly attractive based on the manager's underlying perception of macroeconomic trends and tendencies. Often, global macro managers may find themselves believing that a governmentally imposed policy—be it with regard to interest rates or currency behavior—will not be sustainable in the long run. At other times, they may be taking advantage of an economic policy that guarantees the attractiveness of a certain carry trade. Because positions may be taken in a number of different asset classes in a variety of markets, global macro managers do not tend to exhibit a high correlation to individual equity indices. To the extent, however, that global macro managers all become convinced of an asset's under- or overvaluation, or take too many carry trades at the same time, either reaping rewards or not, global macro managers have shown a fair degree of correlation to each other in past years. Both the 1994 and 1998 markets were particularly difficult for many global macro managers because both equity and fixed-income markets fell at the same time. Global macro managers tend to do better when one of these markets is going up and the other down, with a definable trend to interest rate and equity markets.

Foreign exchange-only. Foreign exchange is a borderline area between hedge funds and commodity trading advisers (CTAs), with the over-the-counter cash market effectively unregulated by either the Securities and Exchange Commission (SEC) or the Commodities Futures Trading Commission (CFTC). To the extent that a manger trades foreign exchange futures or options on foreign exchange futures, he or she will be considered a CTA and be regulated by the CFTC. These managers largely fall into one of three categories: fundamentally driven, short-term trading driven, and trend-following driven. Fundamentally driven foreign exchange-only managers could also be considered global macro managers, although they may choose to limit their fundamental bets to within the foreign exchange universe. Short-term traders are looking for temporary market moves that are driven by cross-border merger activity, capital flows, or hedging activity and that are creating noticeable dislocations or breakout moves in currency pairings. Trend followers typically try to trade a wide variety of currency and currency cross-rates (both currency legs being non-U.S. dollar) in an effort to capture significant market movements. Foreign exchange-only managers are far less common than other hedge fund managers, but they can provide a portfolio of hedge fund investments with an added degree of return alpha given the different underlying asset class. Significant leverage is also possible in foreign exchange-only funds as a result of the depth and liquidity of most currencies. It is not abnormal to see currency managers carry nominal face positions 10 to 20 times the size of the investable capital base. Defined stop-loss orders or margin calls from banks and exchanges are typically the limiting factor that managers must work within to limit market exposure.

CTA—technical or systematic. For over two decades now there have been a variety of CTA managers who extract value from commodity and foreign exchange markets by using sophisticated technical trading tools and models. They have done so by trading in a variety of markets. Some managers may limit themselves to a particular sector such as financial futures; others trade in an all-inclusive range of markets, including zinc and nickel, pork belly, sugar, natural gas, and other contracts. The concentration on markets other than traditional fixed-income and equity markets allows these managers to provide any hedge fund portfolio an added degree of diversification and alpha to its return stream. As long as all markets are not mean reverting and trendless at the same time, and exhibit at least a reasonable amount of price movement, systematic CTAs can do well. Systematic CTAs have, however, traditionally exhibited more volatility in their return stream (and thus a lower average Sharpe ratio) than most hedge fund managers. In addition, systematic CTAs can often have a high correlation to each other; many managers' models are somewhat similar in construction, with only a varying degrees of leverage use and slight differences in risk management. For this reason, adding one or two systematic CTAs to a portfolio of hedge funds is an alpha-producing move, but adding multiple systematic CTAs is unlikely to push a portfolio's alpha up commensurately. A good systematic CTA's annual return can range from –10 percent to +50 percent depending on prevailing market conditions. There is some academic evidence that these return streams can be somewhat cyclical in nature—two or three very good years being followed by two or three difficult years.

CTA—fundamental or sector specific. Once upon a time, the entire world of commodities was very much agriculturally oriented, and agricultural markets continue to be among the most susceptible to changes in fundamental conditions—principally the weather. For this reason, within these markets one tends to find at least some managers taking a purely fundamental approach. These managers tend to keep an eye on global weather patterns, U.S. Department of Agriculture crop reports, shifts in international trade and protectionist policies, and the like. Conversely, because of the volatility of the agricultural markets, some CTAs completely avoid them, using other methodologies to trade only financial, metal, energy, and index futures. On occasion, one will find a CTA who specializes only in the energy sector and its many product components—perhaps trading the spread between crude oil versus jet fuel, or crude oil versus unleaded gasoline, or similar fundamental price relationships.

CTA—short-term pattern recognition. A handful of CTAs trade in the commodity markets in a fashion similar to the short-term swing manager described above. The concentration here—which in some cases can be systematized—is to search for short-term bar-chart setups that in the past yielded high-probability outcomes over a one- to three-day time horizon. The advantage of these CTAs is that they tend not to be correlated with trend-following CTAs, thus offering yet another avenue of potential alpha for a hedge fund portfolio. The downside of these CTAs is that if market volatility becomes excessive for a short period of time, historical norms in market behavior may fail to materialize.

§ 7.3 Commodity Trading Advisers

The listing of strategies above ended with CTAs—a subclass of hedge funds that deserves some special attention. These entities are typically domiciled onshore and are regulated by the CFTC and a futures industry self-regulatory group, the National Futures Association (NFA).

CTAs do not typically trade stocks; instead, they trade from within a relatively wide universe of futures and futures options products; physical commodities such as oil, precious metals, and grains; and foreign exchange and foreign exchange futures and options. Fixed-income futures and stock index futures are often an important part of their repertoire.

Like hedge fund styles, CTA styles can vary greatly, but the majority of CTAs have developed computer-driven trend-following models and trade a basket of different commodities. The concept is that over long periods of time, commodity and futures markets may tend to be mean reverting, but over shorter intervals, significant autocorrelation of price action exists between today's price behavior and tomorrow's. If a computer model can filter through price behavior to recognize periods when the market is trending, and others when it is not, then jumping aboard trends early enough can reap statistically robust rewards.

Although this may sound like black-box hocus-pocus within a world where markets are supposedly an efficient zero-sum game, it is anecdotally notable that many firms such as John Henry & Co., Campbell & Co., and Chesapeake Capital have developed successful track records that now span two decades following such an approach. Each of these firms has grown to manage several billion dollars, and they are constantly joined by many smaller CTAs with newer and often more sophisticated multisignal models.

Trend-following CTAs tend to do well when definable bull and bear market moves transpire over 2- to12-month time horizons. Almost by definition, they do less well in choppy, nondescript markets with lower volatility.

In general, CTAs are more regulated than hedge funds and tend to be more transparent. Although limited partnership CTA structures certainly exist, CTA investments are often set up as simple managed accounts with complete transparency to the investor of the underlying positions and account value. Whereas a hedge fund may report results to investors only once per calendar quarter and allow funds to be withdrawn only at discrete redemption dates, many CTAs provide this information on a daily basis, and all provide it at least monthly. Redemption provisions also tend to be less restrictive. Accounts can typically be closed instantaneously without significant advance notice.

§ 7.4 The Role of CTAs and Hedge Funds in a Diversified Portfolio

Since 1990 the amount of assets under CTA management has increased from $7.8 billion to approximately $40 billion. During this time, the equity markets experienced both positive and negative periods of performance, with the downdrafts that began in August 1990, February 1994, October 1997, July 1998, and March 2000 being particularly trying to traditional fund managers even within a broader upswing in financial asset prices. The fixed-income markets saw their worst annual decline in over 20 years in 1994, and a similarly difficult environment in 1999. All financial futures prices experienced high volatility (particularly within these corrective periods); at other times within the decade there was a compression in volatility, which was most notable perhaps in the metal markets of 1992–1993 and the foreign exchange markets of 1995–1996. Thus, while the overall advance in equity markets during the 1990s was very much unprecedented, the futures markets presented a relatively diverse and normal set of different market environments within which both CTAs and hedge funds traded.

Throughout these diverse environments CTAs on average not only delivered significantly positive returns but also delivered returns statistically uncorrelated to traditional equity and fixed-income investing.

In 1999, it was easy perhaps to look at a histogram of equity valuations and argue that equity markets were overvalued. The two charts in Figure 1, saved from that period, clearly show this.

Figure 1. Price-to-Book Ratio and P/E vs. Dividend Yield

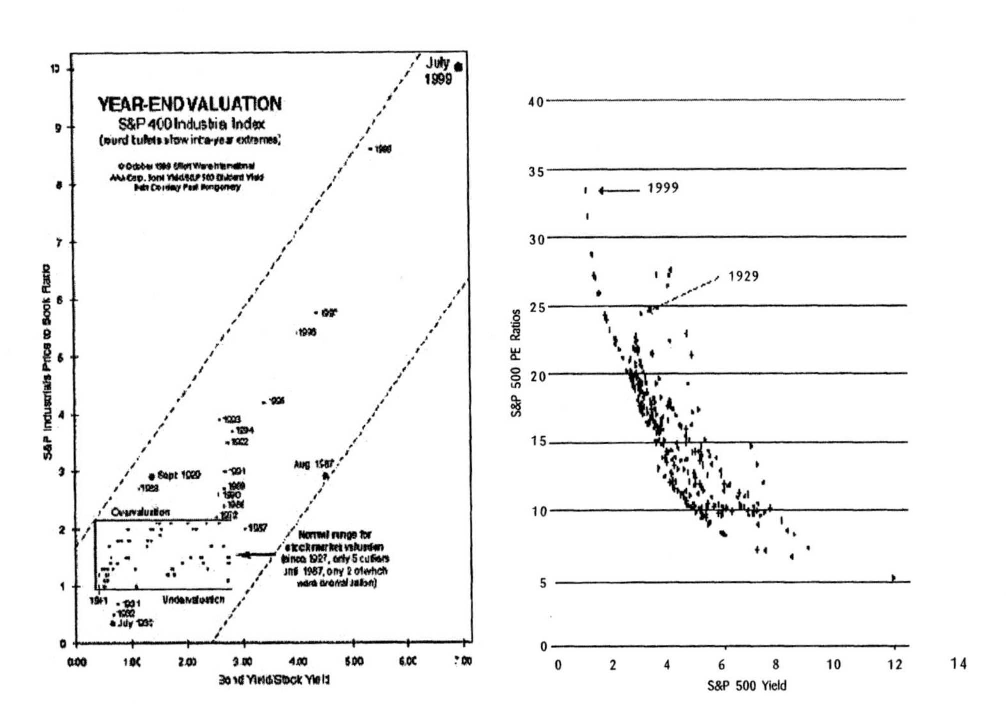

Source: Elliott Wave International.

Source: The Leuthold Group.

Even in early 2003, at a time when equity valuation levels have certainly normalized somewhat, the current level of corporate valuations stands near

130 percent of annual gross domestic product (GDP)—still far higher than historical norms. Over the past 100 years, most major equity lows have seen this percentage fall more toward 30 percent of GDP before significant equity lows have been found.

One can thus argue that in the current environment, diversifying into alternative investment vehicles such as CTAs may be particularly appropriate. Whether one concurs with this macroeconomic assessment or not, all of the existing research argues that the addition of managed futures trading into any portfolio increases the overall alpha or risk-adjusted return of any equity or fixed-income portfolio.

In 1983, Professor John K. Lintner of Harvard University presented a landmark paper, "The Potential Role of Managed Commodity-Financial Futures Accounts (and/or Funds) in Portfolios of Stocks and Bonds," to the Financial Analysts Federation. The paper stated:

> The improvements from holding an efficiently-selected portfolio of managed accounts or funds are so large—and the correlation between returns on the futures portfolios and those on the stock and bond portfolio are so surprisingly low (sometimes even negative)—that the return/risk tradeoffs provided by augmented portfolios . . . clearly dominate the tradeoffs available from portfolios of stocks alone or from portfolios of stocks and bonds.

Using the composite performance of 15 trading advisers, Lintner showed that the return-risk ratio of a portfolio of trading advisers (or futures funds) was higher than a well-diversified stock and bond portfolio. Furthermore, he found a low correlation between the returns of trading advisers and those of stocks, bonds, or a combined stock and bond portfolio. Lintner's study was limited, however, because he examined only the period July 1979 through December 1982.

Over a decade later Managed Account Reports (MAR), a hedge fund research organization, followed up on Lintner's work in a more in-depth manner. It studied the performance of the *entire universe* of CTAs over a substantially longer period (January 1980 through December 1992). MAR combined a portfolio of managed futures with (1) a portfolio of stocks, (2) a portfolio of bonds, (3) an efficiently selected portfolio of stocks and bonds, and (4) an efficiently selected portfolio of stocks, bonds, and Treasury bills. Managed futures investments were tested in two ways, through (1) futures trading advisers and (2) futures funds or pools.

As a portion of its results from this study, and as one can see from Table 1 below, MAR determined that to obtain the greatest risk reduction and highest return, the ideal mix within a portfolio of stocks versus CTAs was 61.8 percent stocks and 38.2 percent managed futures. Adding CTAs to portfolios of stocks and bonds also proved most advantageous.

Table 1. Minimum Variance Frontier for Standard & Poor's 500 Index and MAR Trading Adviser Qualified Universe Index

Return (%)	*Standard Deviation (%)*	*Return Std. Dev.*	*Allocations— S&P 500 Index (%)*	*Allocations— MAR Group Trading Adviser Qualified Universe Index (%)*	*Risk Reduction (%)*	*Risk Reduction (%)*
15.96	15.99	1.00	100.00	0.00	0.00	0.00
16.04	15.56	1.03	97.15	2.85	0.43	2.69
16.08	15.07	1.07	93.75	6.25	0.92	5.75
16.14	14.46	1.12	89.20	10.80	1.53	9.57
16.23	13.70	1.18	82.35	17.65	2.29	14.32
16.32	13.13	1.24	75.50	24.50	2.86	17.89
16.41	12.79	1.28	68.65	31.35	3.20	20.01
16.50	12.69	1.30	61.80	38.20	3.30	20.64
16.59	12.84	1.29	54.95	45.05	3.15	19.70
16.67	13.23	1.26	48.10	51.90	2.76	17.26
16.76	13.84	1.21	41.25	58.75	2.15	13.45
16.85	14.64	1.15	34.40	65.60	1.35	8.44
16.94	15.60	1.09	27.55	72.45	0.39	2.44
16.97	15.98	1.06	25.09	74.91	0.01	0.06

Source: MAR.

Overall, therefore, and despite the popular perception that futures trading is the domain of a handful of speculators, modern portfolio theory would strongly argue for its inclusion in an optimally balanced portfolio of assets.

§ 7.5 Choosing Hedge Fund Managers Oneself

It is easy to list the different styles of hedge funds, and it is even relatively easy to discuss the pros and cons of each strategy (see § 7.2), but deciding which strategy is best at any moment in time, or which particularly appeals to an investor's tastes and risk preferences, is a far trickier endeavor. Some people hire consultants to construct a well-diversified portfolio of hedge funds. Others choose to outsource this process fully to "fund of funds" alternative investment managers in order to obtain not only expert advice and due diligence on managers but also broader manager diversification and the ongoing monitoring of managers. Both paths have merit. This discussion, however, assumes that a wealthy individual (or his or her family office) not only has the time but also the resources and general inclination to choose hedge fund managers without outside help. The fund of funds path is discussed later in the chapter (see §7.6[c]).

§ 7.5[a] Legal Structure and Considerations

As opposed to CTAs where individually managed accounts are the accepted norm, hedge funds are almost always set up as either offshore asset pools or onshore limited partnerships. Offshore funds provide no tax accounting, whereas onshore funds are required to provide their investors with an annual Schedule K-1 (Form 1065) of investment partnership returns in time for tax season. This effectively makes most offshore funds inappropriate for domestic investors.

Under the Investment Company Act of 1940, and if a limited partnership accepts no more than 100 investors and at least 65 of those investors are so-called accredited investors, it is not necessary for a hedge fund manager to register as an investment adviser. Some general partners of hedge funds elect to register as investment advisers anyway; others do not. A nonregistered adviser can launch a hedge fund simply by issuing a private placement Regulation D security. Whether or not the general partner is registered, the Investment Company Act gives limited partners certain protections against outright fraud. The SEC, however, will investigate a registered investment adviser a bit faster than an unregistered manager who has issued a limited partnership as a Regulation D security. If a limited partner has a complaint against an unregistered hedge fund manager, a petition to the courts is often the better means of first recourse, although it is usually a costly and time-consuming process. Thus, there is something to be gained by choosing a manager who is a registered investment adviser.

The word *accredited* can at times cause confusion. The most basic qualification for being considered accredited is to have income in excess of $200,000 per year for each of the two most recent years or a liquid net worth (excluding property) in excess of $1 million. Other types of investors are automatically deemed accredited no matter what their net worth, including corporations, defined benefit plans, trusts, banks, entities such as a fund of funds, and the principals of the general partner managing the limited partnership being invested in.

Almost all limited partnerships are offered by a formal offering memorandum that typically includes a description of the investment program and its manager, various indemnity clauses and disclaimers, a limited partnership agreement, and a subscription document.

A hedge fund may present an investor with an offering memorandum that is 70 pages long. This is not abnormal. An investor who can find the time to wade through this document from cover to cover will be bored to tears but should do so for each fund manager. The legal templates of these offering memoranda are similar enough, however, that to the more experienced hedge fund investor, knowledge of the law firm that produced the document and a review of the "Summary" section can also be sufficient to understand the terms of most limited partnerships.

The important elements in these documents (beyond the nature of the investment program and the qualifications and integrity of the general partner) include initial lockup periods (6 to 12 months is not abnormal); redemption provisions (monthly is desirable, quarterly is typical, yearly or longer is some cause for hesitation); advance notice required of redemption intent (30 days is normal, 45 or 60 days occasional); special charges for early redemption (early redemption may cost 2 to 5 percent payable to the limited partnership for the disruption to the portfolio that a redemption may cause); management and incentive fees (the latter often being known as a performance allocation); high-water marks and special hurdle rates that may exist before incentive fees are payable; the minimum subscription amount; and the handling of partnership expenses.

In general, a 1 percent management and 20 percent incentive fee structure is normal; however, management fees sometimes range as high as 3 percent and incentive fees as high as 25 or 30 percent. A higher fee structure is not by itself a sufficient reason to eliminate a manager from consideration, but it does obviously offer more of a drag on potential returns. In general, a potential hedge fund investor must ponder whether a manager is special enough to deserve higher fees, or whether another manager with the same style and lower charges can be found.

Managers who do not offer high-water marks before incentive fees should be avoided, as should managers who reserve the right to allocate significant operating expenses to the partnership. Having the limited partnership charged for accounting and auditing is normal. Allowing for accruals of initial legal fees to set up a partnership is also commonplace. Even having a limited partnership absorb marketing fees is normal. Paying for a manager's office space, salaried employees, and/or travel expenses, however, is not normal and any provision toward such an end is a warning to stay away from that manager.

Another important part of the offering memorandum is the transparency and reporting frequency that a limited partner is to expect. In the past, hedge funds sometimes got away with only quarterly or yearly reporting of investment returns. These days monthly reporting is more normal, with informal e-mail updates given weekly or at least biweekly. Some managers like to write detailed monthly letters about the fund's positions, with a useful attribution of the recent profit and loss. Others hardly give investors any detail of portfolio exposures.

A potential investor should know what transparency to expect before getting involved with any hedge fund. The provision of more information rather than less is usually comforting to the investor. Even if the information is not fully studied and absorbed by the investor, at least it is there to explain away large monthly swings in performance or long periods of quiet or dormant returns.

Another feature to look for is the willingness of the hedge fund manager to offer limited partners quarterly conference calls to ask questions and generally stay abreast of the limited partnership's investment activities. If quarterly conference calls are not offered, an investor should ensure that unfettered access will be allowed to a manager either by phone or in person.

§ 7.5[b] Prenegotiation

By definition, hedge funds are less regulated and more secretive than many other traditional investments. Limited partnership agreements are drafted to give general partners much flexibility and a large degree of indemnification for their actions. Therefore, the only way to avoid many nasty back-end problems on a hedge fund investment turned sour is to provide for as many of these problems as possible *before* making the initial investment. In short, the potential investor should always consider asking for special terms outside of an offering memorandum's boilerplate.

In the words of Chicago-based hedge fund lawyer Wesley Nissen, "In my extensive work with investors and fund of funds managers, when I have seen them ask for something special in a side letter, they may not get all of that they ask for, but they will usually get something."[1] Along these lines, Nissen suggests asking for special transparency, liquidation, and redemption rights before investing. "It is often possible to get a stop-loss provision within an LP agreement or within a side letter whereby a fund must shut down if it loses 20 percent or more," says Nissen. This is a very useful provision to avoid having one's capital held hostage within a poorly performing limited partnership. Nissen admits that in the case an investment under $1 million, it may not be possible to negotiate any special terms unless the hedge fund is a nascent one, but he says that he has seen many bigger investors ask for and receive a most favored nation provision, guaranteeing an investor the best rights given to any other investor in the fund.

Establishing a separately managed account is also a way to increase transparency and liquidity rights for a large investor. In this instance, a simple phone call to the prime broker can shut an account down, but a separately managed account also increases an investor's potential liability beyond a finite amount of the initial investment. For this reason, many hedge funds eager for capital may agree to open a completely separate stand-alone limited partnership for a large investor.

Other lawyers suggest that the inclusion of an arbitration agreement in limited partnership agreements, or in initial side letters thereto, can be an attractive clause investors should strive to see included. In the words of one attorney, "Dispute resolution via arbitration is far more cost-effective than litigation. It also offers a defined timetable to resolve a given matter. More investors should look for the inclusion of such terms or demand them. Unfortunately, you likely won't get a hedge fund manager to agree to arbitration in advance unless you are a big investor."[2]

In general, thinking ahead about contingencies can prevent a lot of problems later on if a hedge fund subsequently falters. Simple steps are often very important in the end. For example, having prenegotiated monthly liquidity as opposed to quarterly or annual liquidity can avoid many further problems and allows an investor to pull the remaining value of an investment out of a fund without months of potential agony.

No matter what advance steps are taken to avoid future problems, nasty situations will of course still arise from time to time. When they do, it is important to realize that all limited partnerships, whether managed by a registered investment adviser or not, are subject to certain anti-fraud provisions of the Investment Advisers Act of 1940. "There are certain standards of care that need to be adhered to," explains Nissen. "If fraud or gross negligence can ever be established, a General Partner won't be able to source his own legal expenses from the partnership, and will need to make restitution to the fund of earlier legal advances."

According to Nissen, Delaware law—under which many limited partnership agreements are written—also "specifically provides that upon demand, any Limited Partner shall be provided with a list of other Limited Partners. Failure of a General Partner to do so could be adequate grounds for a judge to mandate compliance, or even issue a temporary restraining order against a General Partner." "But in most instances a judge is not going to do more than the minimum required," continues Nissen. "To get a temporary restraining order with any teeth to it, you must demonstrate that there are further problems that money alone won't solve. The General Partner must be deemed to have abrogated some specific responsibility. If the General Partner is simply losing money, but without willful neglect of his responsibilities to the investor, then a judge may rule that any damages related to this loss of funds can await the award process at the end of a case."

§ 7.5[c] Hedge Fund Databases

There is little that a group of hedge fund managers and experienced hedge fund allocators would likely agree on more than the fact that major hedge fund databases are seriously flawed. For one thing, there are too many databases with different clusters of managers within each, but no all-encompassing data source. When no single database has a fully inclusive list of hedge fund managers, creating appropriate benchmark indices is nearly impossible.

"The data simply stinks," says Jon Lukomnik, a pension fund consultant and former pension manager for the city of New York. "I'm honestly very skeptical of the value or professionalism of current hedge fund benchmarks."[3] Among the problems industry experts continuously bemoan is a "horrific" survivorship bias, no obligation or willingness of some of the bigger managers to report their returns, the miscategorization of managers within certain pigeon-holed styles, and the inclusion of managers in some of the databases that are already closed to new investment. While Lukomnik believes that many institutional and private hedge fund investors "now have an investment process that in terms of sophistication has developed far faster over the last few years than at any time since the introduction of Markowitz modern portfolio theory," he ironically suggests that the underlying data on which such analysis must be run remain a major problem. "Sure you can peruse different managers," says Lukomnik, "but take your first step toward peer group analysis or benchmark analysis and you will hit major problems."

These complaints and problems are real ones, but the situation used to be even worse. A few years ago, there were hardly any databases at all, and the industry was treading forward very slowly in an effort to determine from the SEC and CFTC whether third-party hedge fund databases offered over the Internet would be deemed an unacceptable form of hedge fund advertising. In a series of "no action" letters that started in 1998, the SEC finally specified that as long as access to such databases and Web sites was password delimited to only accredited investors, the SEC would indeed take no action on this topic.

Since that time, various databases have developed, some more extensive than others, and some more expensive than others. These include HFR.com, CSFB/Tremont (found on the Web under Hedgeworld.com), MAR/Zurich Capital (MARHedge.com), InvestorForce.com (originally known as Altvest.com), Stark, Barclays, and Hedgefund.net.

Obtaining access to at least a few of these databases is indeed a good first step for a potentially serious hedge fund investor, and Hedgefund.net is likely as good a starting point as any because subscription to the Web-based service comes at no cost.

All that is required at Hedgefund.net is to attest on the Web that the investor is indeed an accredited investor and declare whether the investor is onshore or offshore. A password accessible database—split between onshore funds and offshore funds—then becomes available covering over 1,800 hedge funds and over 160 funds of funds. Hedgefund.net also offers its own benchmark sector strategy indices and the ability to sift and sort through managers and indices in a variety of ways. These sorting criteria include sorting by strategy (Hedgefund.net offers 31 different strategies) and subsorting by best current-year return, best prior-year return, best current-month return, average annual return, and Sharpe ratio.

One can also filter to see only funds that have been profitable in more than 90 percent of the months, or peruse the "most visited" funds over various time horizons. There is a search capability by fund name, a section where one can establish a "watch list" of funds, a limited amount of hedge fund industry news, and occasional managers interviews. Managers choosing to post their returns on the site provide a brief qualitative description of their fund style (something very useful, which several other databases fail to offer), and enter their returns as either confirmed or estimated, with total fund and manager assets posted as well. Basic fee terms and contact information are also provided, as are various calculated statistics such as a fund's alpha, beta, R, R-squared, and annualized Sharpe ratio.

Overall, for a free service, Hedgefund.net is very easy to use and quite extensive. Unfortunately, only about a quarter of all the hedge funds that exist choose to be listed on it.

The next least costly database service that may appeal to potential investors is InvestorForce.com. This hedge fund site was the original brainchild of family office manager Jeff Tarrant, who wanted to combine in one easy-to-use format all of the statistical data on hedge fund managers that he possibly could. He found support for his platform from various other large family offices, and used the weight of the subscriber base to persuade a large number of hedge fund managers to list their funds. InvestorForce.com, like many dot-coms, is still searching for an appropriate and lasting revenue model, but at present its basic service costs only $1,000 per year. For that cost, InvestorForce provides a very basic alphabetical listing of over 2,400 hedge funds and funds of funds with contact information, monthly fund performance, and statistical information similar to that provided by Hedgefund.net. For reasons that are not immediately clear, InvestorForce.com also tends to be more rapidly updated each month than several other databases.

One helpful feature that InvestorForce.com provides in its basic service is the ability to compare a manager's returns and statistical performance side by side with a manager-designated benchmark index—whether that index is a broadly defined Standard & Poor's (S&P) 500 Index or perhaps a more narrowly defined Amex Biotechnology Index.

As one slight negative, InvestorForce.com provides a less useful free-form description of the manager's approach as Hedgefund.net. The small sector and industry fields that managers must fill in are far too short to convey much information. In addition, the 13 fund classifications (macro, growth, value, event-driven, emerging markets, etc.) and 15 sector-specific designations (technology, biotechnology, health, commodity, etc.) are not quite precise or extensive enough to be particularly useful. Missing from the list until recently have been whole categories such as statistical arbitrage, options arbitrage, merger arbitrage, convertible bond arbitrage, multi-arbitrage, and short-biased managers.

The ability to sort and screen the database by various criteria (style, performance, drawdowns, etc.) and to maintain strategy group pages come at an added cost under a second, far more robust tier of service named Altvest Trak. Above that, Altvest Edge and Altvest Edge Plus allow for a certain amount of hedge fund analytics—the combining of manager groups and the production of "optimal" allocations between groups of managers. Alvest Edge contains over 100 different charts and tables that can be produced to analyze portfolio risks and to help produce portfolio pro forma analysis. It is relatively easy for one to take a group of funds and produce an immediate risk-reward efficient frontier, moving the mouse to create optimal portfolio allocations at a desired level of return and risk. Downloads to Excel are available from all versions except for the basic Altvest Connect.

All of this premium service comes at a premium price. Altvest currently charges $5,000 per year for Altvest Trak, $6,500 for Altvest Edge, and $8,000 for Altvest Edge Plus (which includes some extra reporting features). Of these options, Altvest Edge is likely the best bargain for the reporting and portfolio analytical flexibility provided. One key problem remains: While InvestorForce's analytical platform is a very user-friendly one, the data is limited to approximately one third of the total hedge fund universe. Users do have the option of creating their own personal data files on managers who do not report to InvestorForce on their own, but some sort of ability within this system to access outside data from other sources—even if such data were to be stored on one's own computer—would help to make this system truly great.

This is why many serious hedge fund investors and fund of funds groups opt for another path—using the Hedgefund.net and InvestorForce databases, together with various other databases, but placing on top of all these databases a piece of analytical software produced by Strategic Financial Solutions called PerTrac (www.PerTrac.com).

PerTrac is a wonderful piece of desktop software that allows one to search for managers using a variety of style and performance criteria, produce peer group analysis between managers, optimize portfolios, run Monte Carlo risk simulations on portfolios, and produce customizable statistical and performance charts and templates. The price for this software starts at an annual licensing fee of $5,000. The only problem is that with the exception of the free Hedgefund.net database with which PerTrac is integrated, one must also pay for the other data sources to use with PerTrac. It is also necessary to download all of these other data sources into a format acceptable to PerTrac. The data maintenance and merging process here is occasionally somewhat complicated and certainly time-consuming. Thus, if one truly wants to create a robust single hedge fund database, one will have to work at it and spend a bit of money to get it right.

One of the longest and most extensive databases available is that maintained by Tremont/TASS. It is accessible at hedge fund news site Hedgeworld.com and tracks over 150 fields of information for each of the 2,500 hedge funds in the database. It has Web-based search capabilities that allow one to search for hedge funds by name, by manager name, by performance, by primary investment style, and by risk-return criteria. Style can be set first and then subsearches can be run by performance or risk-return criteria, but notably not by multiple criteria all at once (as can be done with Altvest Trak). The analytical reports available from Tremont/TASS are extensive and well organized, with basic portfolio tracking and performance monitoring also possible. Unlike InvestorForce, however, Tremont/TASS has no portfolio optimization or pro forma portfolio construction tools, making this Web site potentially more robust in terms of its database but less sophisticated in terms of overall analytical capabilities. Its annual cost of $5,000 puts it in a price range close to InvestorForce for slightly less functionality.

Hedge Fund Research (www.HFR.com) is yet another database vendor and hedge fund consultant that provides Microsoft Access and Excel formatted semimonthly downloads from its Web site. Covered are only 1,800 managers with no direct analytics from HFR.com—just the data—at an annual cost of $6,000. Therefore, HFR is a nicety that most hedge fund investors should consider as a secondary—but not absolutely necessary—step after purchasing an analytical package such as PerTrac. There is, after all, some overlap to be expected between each of these databases. If a given hedge fund is not in Hedgefund.net, it will likely get picked up by InvestorForce or Tremont/TASS, and only in rare instances will a fund be listed only with HFR.com.

Those who prefer to have a bit more pro-active analysis done for them instead of doing it on their own may wish to consider a subscription to MAR/Hedge and access to the MAR Hedge/CISDM database. MAR/ Hedge is a monthly publication that on a rotating basis produces in-depth reports on different managers. It tends to write up only managers that it thinks well of, thus providing a filtering service for the investor. Available at a subscription price of $745 per year, these reports can be quite a useful due diligence starting point, but they are not the ending point. Many hedge funds featured by MAR/Hedge have still gotten into trouble.

MAR's database and focus have historically been slightly more CTA oriented than many of the other hedge fund databases. This database was recently sold to Zurich Capital, which subsequently gifted it to the Center for International Securities and Derivatives Markets at U Mass Amherst—which is currently working to modify and improve the MAR/CIDSM database and indices.

Another service that is very CTA oriented, the Barclay Group (www.barclaygrp.com), provides both qualitative written manager analysis and database services, and is likely the best CTA performance index. Barclay produces both an interesting newsletter, Barclay Managed Funds Report, and an analytical performance database of some 1,400 hedge fund managers and 500 CTAs (the two databases are offered separately). The database is delivered by disk via regular mail and allows comparative studies and filtering. Like the MAR/Hedge newsletter, the monthly newsletter produced by Barclays, which comes at an annual cost of $150, is a reasonable value, particularly for an investor with a strong CTA interest. The database, however, is likely something most can do without. It certainly is not the first database an aspiring hedge fund investor should purchase.

S&P offers much information, particularly on offshore fund offerings, at www.funds-sp.com and a group called CTA Research offers slightly lagged but free CTA performance data at www.hedgefund-index.com. These represent supplemental sites that a nascent hedge fund and CTA investor may want to spend a bit of time on, particularly since they are free. One word of warning: www.hedgefund-index.com requires a detailed registration process, and this often leads directly to an unsolicited third-party marketing call.

Not all hedge fund or CTA research has to be done on a computer or via the Web. MAR produces an annual listing of hedge funds available in book form, as does Nelson's Directory of Investment Managers (www.Nelsoninformation.com). Listed in Nelson's $560 annual publication are brief reviews of over 2,200 hedge fund managers. Daniel B. Stark & Co. (www.Starkonline.com) is another powerful resource in CTA research. In addition to quarterly 600-page booklets and a monthly newsletter, Stark produces a comprehensive database on 600 CTAs that is updated bimonthly. The annual cost for the latter package is $2,500. A London-based research and fund of funds group, Global Fund Analysis (www.GlobalFundAnalysis.com) also produces well-regarded monthly manager research reports. The hedge fund series of these reports has a subscription price of 1,500 British pounds per year. The firm's Web site also offers a free but not particularly robust database, industry news, various message boards, a comprehensive list of upcoming hedge fund conferences, and search capabilities. It is at least worth an occasional visit.

§ 7.5[d] Investment Bank Referrals

Investment banks are another important source of information on hedge fund managers. Most investment banks have their own in-house series of hedge funds and funds of funds (with varying degrees of competent allocation) and are playing an ever more important role in the hedge fund world in other ways. Via the prime brokerage function, they not only sit atop many hedge funds as a middle-office risk-management collection point but also play an important role in client capital introductions.

In 2002, Bank of America, Goldman Sachs, Lehman Brothers, Morgan Stanley, and Deutsche Bank, among others, held conferences designed to introduce hedge fund clients to potential institutional investors. At a Deutsche Bank affair held on Amelia Island, Florida, 400 people recently came representing funds of funds, family offices, endowments, and pension funds.

"Word of mouth and prime broker introductions are without a doubt the primary way a hedge fund manager gets my attention," explains one Toronto-based hedge fund allocator for a large pension plan. "Consultants are still important, of course, but less so than in the past."[4]

To date, investment banks have stopped well short of becoming straight third-party marketers—wary of any perceived conflicts of interest that fee sharing with hedge fund clients might cause. They instead remain content, at least for the moment, with the increased commission revenues generated from active prime brokerage clients that gain more assets under management from simple introductions.

According to some, this may change in the future. "We're not that far away from the day when one investment bank will make the leap to become directly paid by underlying managers," says one pension fund consultant. "Properly disclosed, there's really no reason that this shouldn't happen. Banks will eventually just say to fund managers: 'As long as you're paying third party marketers for high-net worth introductions, why not just pay us for more significant institutional access.'"[5]

Therefore, a potential hedge fund investor should not be afraid to call an investment banking colleague or friend for a referral to the appropriate capital introduction people on Wall Street. Although investment banks may end up tainted by conflicts of interest, for now they represent a good central source of information about successful managers.

§ 7.5[e] Using the Statistics

With databases established, contacts made at various Wall Street investment banks, and the various general styles of managers studied and understood, the process of evaluating managers both statistically and qualitatively truly begins.

On most database reports, a plethora of statistics will be shown, and it may be daunting at first to understand which ones are truly important and how to use them. Listed below, in descending order of importance, are the tools for a successful manager search and evaluation process.[6] It is assumed that using PerTrac, InvestorForce.com, Tremont/TASS, or some other system, separately or in combination, that the reader can automate at least some degree of manager filtering.

§ 7.5[e][1] Sharpe Ratio. To calculate a Sharpe ratio, a risk-free interest rate is subtracted from a manager's average annual return and the difference is divided by the standard deviation of the return stream. The result is an annual level of excess return for a given unit of risk. A manager who has produced a steady stream of returns with very little variation will have a high Sharpe ratio. A manager who has produced a steady stream of returns but with a few outlying losses along the way will have a lower Sharpe ratio. The higher the Sharpe ratio, the better. The calculation is as follows:

$$\frac{((1+GM)^{12}-1)-TBill_{ann}}{STD}$$

where STD = Annualized standard deviation

GM = Monthly geometric average

$TBill_{ann}$ = Annualized average T-bill rate

For a hedge fund, a Sharpe ratio above two is deemed exceptional, between one and one-half is good, and above one is acceptable. Because CTAs tend to be more volatile in their performance than hedge funds, a good CTA will have a Sharpe ratio above one, but it is next to impossible to find a CTA with a Sharpe ratio above two.

Sorting or filtering managers by their Sharpe ratio can be a good starting point in finding solid hedge fund managers. Looking at a manager's Sharpe ratio for his or her entire trading history would be a first step, followed by an examination of the manager's Sharpe ratio for the last 12 months and on a rolling 12- or 24-month basis. Comparing these numbers will show whether the manager's strategy is effective not only over a long period of time but also within a more current market environment.

Some hedge fund analysts bemoan the use of a Sharpe ratio because it will penalize a manager with dramatic upside spikes in returns as much as it penalizes a manager with dramatic downside spikes. This is indeed a problem with this measure. Looking at a Sharpe ratio is also relatively useless when dealing with performance records less than three years. Even given these caveats, taking note of a manager's Sharpe ratio is a responsible first step in analysis of a hedge fund.

§ 7.5[e][2] Standard Deviation. Used in the Sharpe ratio calculation but by itself less critical in manager selection, the standard deviation measures how widely monthly or annual rates of return are dispersed from the arithmetic average return over the same period.

In its annualized form, standard deviation is calculated as follows:

$$STDM = \frac{\sqrt{\Sigma (r_i - AM)^2}}{s - 1}$$

where STDM = Monthly standard deviation

r_i = Rate of return (net of all fees) for the i_{th} month

s = Number of months since inception

AM = Monthly arithmetic average

$$STD = STDM * \sqrt{12}$$

where STD = Annualized standard deviation

STDM = Monthly standard deviation

Since the S&P 500 as a whole tends to run with an annualized standard deviation of approximately 15 percent or more, good hedge fund managers should typically have standard deviations below that level. Some may succeed in achieving standard deviations as low as 5 percent, but more typically 8 to 14 percent is acceptable. The returns of a manager who has a standard deviation above 20 percent would have to be exceptional over time for that manager to merit any consideration.

One should start by looking at a manager's standard deviation over an entire trading history and then look at the standard deviation for the last 12-

month period and on a rolling 12- or 24-month basis. The latter step will indicate whether a manager's overall volatility of returns has been increasing or decreasing in the current market environment.

§ 7.5[e][3] Percentage of Months Profitable. Another filter to use when searching for good hedge fund managers is to look at a manager's month-by-month return profile for winning and losing months, or to filter through a database only searching for managers profitable in more than 60 percent of calendar months. There are managers who are profitable in 80 or even 90 percent of months, but setting such a high hurdle would undoubtedly eliminate some managers deserving of attention.

One note on this filter is that if one is searching for a specialty manager such as a dedicated short seller, asking for 60 percent monthly profitability may be asking too much. For the more neutral manager, it is not.

This tool is typically best used from the inception of a trading record.

§ 7.5[e][4] Benchmark Correlation (or R^2) and Beta. The R^2 coefficient measures the extent to which the performance of the fund and the performance of another fund or benchmark index are related. More specifically, the R^2 coefficient measures how much of the fund's variability can be explained by the performance of the selected fund or benchmark index. R^2 values should always range between zero and one.

R^2 values close to zero indicate a minimal relationship between the performance of the fund and the performance of the other fund or benchmark. R^2 values close to one indicate a strong relationship between the fund's performance and the performance of the selected fund or benchmark.

In general, less correlation to a major equity index such as the S&P 500 is better when striving to create all-weather hedge fund returns. Thus, searching or filtering only for managers with an R^2 to the S&P 500 below 0.40 may be a useful approach. There may be instances, however, when an investor may want to add positive equity exposure to an investment mix.

The equation to calculate R^2 follows:

$$R^2 = \frac{(\Sigma x_i y_i)^2}{\Sigma x_i^2 \Sigma y_i^2}$$

where x_i = Rate of return (net of all fees) for the fund for the i_{th} month

y_i = Rate of return for a selected fund or benchmark index for the i_{th} month

In general, R^2 is a slightly more useful measure to use than Beta, although one will hear many more references to a manager's beta in casual conversation. Beta represents a fund manager's systematic market risk and is equal to the change in fund performance in relation to the change in selected fund or index performance. It is thus similar in many ways to R^2 but less rigorous. A manager might have a high beta to the market, but whether there is any causality between market behavior and manager performance is not guaranteed. The high beta could be accidental. Only R^2 estimates a true causal relationship.

Beta is calculated as follows:

$$\beta = \frac{s\Sigma x_i y_i - \Sigma x_i \Sigma y_i}{s\Sigma x_i^2 - (\Sigma x_i)^2}$$

where x_i = Rate of return (net of all fees) for the fund for the i_{th} month

y_i = Rate of return for a selected fund or benchmark index for the i_{th} month

s = Number of months since inception

It is best to look first at a manager's correlation or beta statistics from a fund's inception and then compare those statistics to the statistics for more recent periods. A dramatically different correlation over more recent 12- or 24-month periods may indicate some amount of style shift that the potential investor should query.

§ 7.5[e][5] Average Annualized Return. In looking at past performance, one should not look just at recent performance figures but at average annualized return over any rolling 12-month period. If the hedge fund manager has at least three years of history, this number will be a better representation of what one might expect from the manager going forward than the number derived simply from extrapolating recent returns. Filtering to look only at managers with average annualized returns greater than 10 percent would be an appropriate methodology to use for all but specialty managers such as short sellers.

On an overall basis, it is important to look at streams of monthly returns—not quarterly or annual returns. Managers who present their returns only quarterly are likely trying to smooth the appearance of the underlying volatility of their returns. It has long been the norm to present return streams on a monthly basis. One should be a bit suspicious if a manager does not.

Average annualized return is best used from a manager's inception of trading.

§ 7.5[e][6] Largest Monthly or Cumulative Drawdown. Databases regularly list the largest single monthly drawdown that a manager has incurred as well as the greatest cumulative drawdown incurred without first recovering a high-water mark in performance. Obviously every investor would want the smallest negative numbers possible in both these figures, but realistically, every manager will lose money at some point and certain styles of investing more or less necessitate occasional drawdowns. In general, the bigger drawdowns that an investor is willing to face, the easier it will be to find managers capable of delivering truly superior returns. What level of acceptable drawdown to set in a filter is a matter of personal choice. Most people would likely not be comfortable with a manager capable of losing more than 12 percent in a given month. Others would have a lower risk threshold closer to an 8 percent loss. In terms of cumulative drawdown, a reasonable filter here should likely range between 20 and 30 percent. If a manager can lose more than 30 percent of an investor's money when things go amiss, he or she should likely be passed over.

Always using a manager's entire trading record is appropriate here.

§ 7.5[e][7] Performance During Periods of Market Stress. If one has filtered a hedge fund database by the above six techniques, a list of 2,600 hedge fund managers should have been pared down to fewer than 100—maybe only 50 if one has set a tighter drawdown allowance. This is a far more manageable database to examine on a case-by-case basis. When one does so, it is important to examine the performance of a manager during periods of market stress. August and September 1998 are two months to look at carefully, as are June and July 2002. Large losses during those months may indicate that a manager is less market neutral than he or she claims to be, with risk management techniques to be further queried. Much of 1994 was also a stressful period in both the equity and fixed-income markets, as was the recessionary period of 1990. If a manager has a record stretching back that far, a potential investor should take note of performance during those periods.

At the same time, one does not want to choose a manager who can get stampeded on short positions during a period of market ebullience. Hence, a quick look at a manager's performance during November 1998 to January 1999, as well as November 1999 to January 2000, may reveal something about a manager's true exposures. Losses during these months may indicate that the manager has a long value, short growth bias in his or her equity investing approach. Large gains during these periods may indicate that the manager benefited from an extraordinary bull market in many technology stocks, but may be unlikely to repeat that performance in more normalized ongoing markets.

In other words, one needs to determine not only the level of returns that a manager has achieved in the past, but also when and how the manager achieved those returns. One must then ask oneself, how likely is it that those market conditions will reoccur in the future?

§ 7.5[e][8] Correlation to VIX Index. Some managers benefit from market volatility, and others do not. Some benefit up to a point, and then beyond an upper threshold in volatility, their strategies start to fall apart from illiquidity. Although not every database and analytical toolkit may offer it, one may want to look at a manager's performance in terms of its correlation to the Chicago VIX Implied Volatility Index. If a manager's performance has a high negative correlation to higher levels of volatility, a potential investor should use extreme caution in considering that manager. Conversely, a high positive correlation may indicate that a manager will only perform well in volatile markets but could languish in quieter ones. A slight but not excessive positive correlation between fund performance and the Chicago VIX Implied Volatility Index is generally a favorable indication.

§ 7.5[f] Other Tools

There are other ratios and indicators, of course. The filtering path explained above is simply the author's way of looking at things, but for sake of completeness, more tools are discussed below.

§ 7.5[f][1] Downside Deviation. Downside deviation (DD by mean), also known as the semideviation, measures the volatility of monthly returns below the arithmetic average of monthly returns. Because the calculation looks only at periods of drawdown, it does not penalize upside performance volatility (a principal complaint about the Sharpe ratio). Downside deviation is calculated as follows:

$$DD_{bymean} = \sqrt{\frac{\sum_{i=1}^{s} \Delta_i^2}{s-1}} \quad \text{where } D_i = t - r \text{ for } t > r_i$$

$\Delta_i = 0$ for $t < r_i$

t = Monthly average return (AM)

r_i = Rate of return (net of all fees) for the i_{th} month

s = Number of months since inception

Downside deviation is best looked at first from a manager's inception of trading, and then compared to more recent 12- or 24-month periods for indications of style shift or a changed current market environment.

§ 7.5[f][2] Skewness of Return Profile. Based on the third moment around the mean, *skewness* represents the level of symmetry or lack of symmetry within the distribution of a fund's rates of return around the average rate of return. In other words, a fund's mean monthly return may be 1 percent, but how many observations exist above that mean, and how many below it?

Fund performance with a skewness greater than zero is said to be positively skewed and indicates that returns larger than the average rate of return are more widely distributed. This is a desirable characteristic.

Fund performance with a skewness equal to zero is symmetrical. Normally distributed rates of return have a skewness of zero.

Fund performance with a skewness less than zero is said to be negatively skewed and indicates that returns less than the average rate of return are more widely distributed. Such managers are generally best avoided.

The calculation for skewness follows:

$$\text{Skewness} = \frac{u_3}{u_2^{\frac{3}{2}}}$$

$$u_2 = \frac{\sum r_i^2}{s}$$

$$u_3 = \frac{\sum r_i^3}{s}$$

where r_i = Rate of return (net of all fees) for the i_{th} month since inception

s = Number of months since inception

§ 7.5[f][3] Kurtosis of Returns. Based on the fourth moment about the mean, kurtosis measures how flat or peaked the distribution of rates of return is compared to a normal distribution.

If the kurtosis is less than zero, it is said that the distribution of the rates of returns is platykurtic. Platykurtic distributions are flatter or more gradually distributed.

If the kurtosis is more than zero, it is said that the distribution of the rates of return is leptokurtic. Leptokurtic distributions are more peaked, that is, more concentrated in a single region.

If the kurtosis equals zero, the distribution of rates of return is mesokurtic (a normal distribution).

Other things being equal, a leptokurtic distribution of returns shows more consistency. Thus, it is good to have a return distribution be greater than zero and be deemed leptokurtic.

§ 7.5[f][4] Alpha. Achieving added alpha (α) to one's portfolio is what hedge fund investing is all about. *Alpha* is definable as the added amount of return—or excess return—generated by a portfolio at a given rate of risk compared to the performance of another fund or benchmark index. The more alpha created by a fund manager, usually the less correlated this performance is to traditional benchmarks, and the better it is for the investor.

From a conceptual point of view, the added alpha created by adding a portfolio of hedge fund managers to a more traditional mix of long equity and long fixed-income investments can be seen in Figure 2.

Figure 2. Why Hedge Funds and Funds of Funds at All?—The Goal

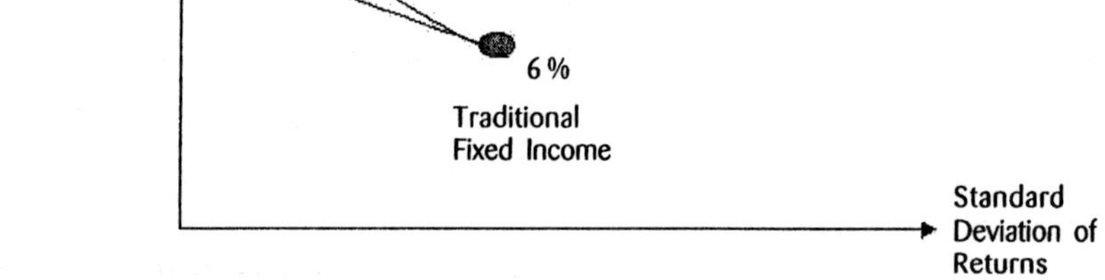

Same risk for greater overall return
Net Returns
Alternative Investments
17%
Equities
Same return with less risk
Alpha
6%
Traditional Fixed Income
Standard Deviation of Returns

Alternative Investments: Higher returns with lower volatility

Included in a stock-bond portfolio mix, alternative investments add alpha to the efficient investment frontier.

The calculation of alpha follows:

$$\alpha = \frac{\Sigma y_i \Sigma x_i^2 - \Sigma x_i \Sigma x_i y_i}{s\Sigma x_i^2 - (\Sigma x_i)^2}$$

where x_i = Rate of return (net of all fees) for the fund for the i_{th} month

y_i = Rate of return for a selected fund or benchmark index for the i_{th} month

s = Number of months since inception

Despite the importance of alpha, the alpha that a hedge fund manager produces is not usually an effective first sorting technique because differences in the cited benchmark can result in large differences in the reported alpha.

§ 7.5[f][5] Sortino Ratio. The Sortino ratio is similar to the Sharpe ratio, except that instead of using standard deviation as the denominator, it uses the downside deviation. This helps to differentiate between "good" and "bad" volatility. With the Sharpe ratio, if a fund is volatile to the upside (generally viewed as a good thing), its Sharpe ratio would still be low. The conservative assumption behind the Sharpe ratio is that if a fund can make large returns on the upside, it also stands at risk to lose them. Sortino concerns itself only with the amount of return above the arithmetic average of monthly returns per unit of downside risk. If a manager has an asymmetric return profile of occasional large gains but only small losses, the Sortino ratio may be a better way to evaluate that manager.

A Sortino ratio (by mean) greater than one and one-half indicates a strong rate of return per downside deviation (or high returns in terms of risk). The Sortino formula is as follows:

$$\frac{((1 + GM)^{12} - 1) - AAM}{DD_{bymean}}$$

where DD_{bymean} = Annualized downside deviation (by mean)

GM = Monthly geometric average

AAM = Annualized arithmetic average

§ 7.5[f][6] MAR Ratio. The *MAR ratio* is the ratio of the geometric annual return divided by the largest drawdown ever incurred. It thus gives a measurement of rate of return with respect to the historical worst-case risk involved to achieve that return. If a manager has a good Sharpe ratio, but a more questionable MAR ratio, it may be a sign of some inherent occasional vulnerability in that manager's risk management techniques.

The formula for the MAR ratio follows:

$$\frac{(GM + 1)^{12} - 1}{LD}$$

where GM = Monthly geometric average

LD = Largest drawdown

§ 7.5[f][7] Percentage Positive When Proxy Down. When examining a long-short manager or other absolute return arbitrage strategies, it may be useful to take note of the percentage of positive monthly rates of return when a selected proxy index (such as the S&P 500) is negative by some significant margin (perhaps –2 percent or worse). The higher this percentage, the more confident one can be that the hedge fund strategy truly is market neutral or completely uncorrelated. Since short sellers by definition are supposed to be up when the market is down, this is not a good tool of evaluation for a short-selling manager. It is, however, a very useful tool for looking at arbitrage managers, long-short managers, and funds of funds. Graphic representations of month-by-month relative performance during down benchmark periods can be a particularly effective way to see whether a manager truly is a solid alpha producer.

§ 7.5[g] Qualitative Factors

All of the quantitative tools discussed above can be of great use in narrowing the hedge fund universe from several thousand managers to a far more manageable number. Statistics alone, however, are never enough. Many times hedge fund managers can deliver steady returns for two to three years, before suddenly running into trouble—perhaps caused by a changed market environment or a hidden flaw in approach that eventually catches up to the manager. A visit to the manager to ask questions before investing is thus of absolute necessity.

§ 7.5[g][1] Overall Style and Demeanor. The main purpose of a hedge fund manager interview should be to determine the manager's general proclivities and beliefs.

Does the manager think that equities in the long term always go up, or that a reversion to the mean in equity valuations is inevitable? If the manager is a neutral long-short manager, one might ask why such a question is even relevant, but it is. The manager who believes the former will be quicker to buy a dip, quicker to allow a bit of positive beta to creep into the portfolio; the manager who believes the latter will be acting more defensively and working harder to be fully hedged at all points in time. The difference in attitude matters if an investor wants a truly market-neutral manager.

Overall, it is important to try to determine quickly how repeatable a manager's track record is likely to be. This is a function not only of the manager's trading strategy and skills but also of outside market conditions that may have favored that strategy for the past five years but will not necessarily do so in the near future. "Don't confuse a bull market with brains" is an old Wall Street adage that should always be lurking in the back of one's head. How dependent is this manager on momentum in his or her particular market? Did August to September 1998 show any vulnerability on this front?

As strange as it might sound, a potential investor should look for solid qualitative reasons *not* to invest. There are many small tests. For example, if a manager cannot remember the nuances in his or her own performance record, that is a bad sign. What exactly happened in April 1997 that caused a fund to drop 9 percent in a month, but a sister fund to lose only 2.3 percent? The manager should have an answer to that question on the tip of the tongue. Foggy memories of specific events can be indicative of future problems.

From the outset, the prospective investor should try to determine what makes the manager special. Is it a nifty execution technology that makes a statistical arbitrage strategy truly robust, or is it a group of analysts behind the manager that can deliver truly superior stock-picking advice? Is it a deep acquaintance with a particular sector or market that makes a manager special, or is it the diversity of positions and risk management rules that give this manager a special edge? On this front, the manager's willingness to share specific current views and strategies can be particularly useful in determining how the manager's mind works. A manager willing to talk openly about specific positions in an initial interview typically delivers fewer transparency problems later on.

Perhaps more than anything else, it is important to like the manager. Managers with an arrogant bravado may be moneymakers in the short term, but they breed trouble in the long term. A manager who is trying to rush an investor's investment decision process by talking about closing the fund, or a manager who talks too effusively about "other money pouring into the fund or earmarked to come in shortly" may not be a manager worth chasing after. A good manager should demonstrate a balance when handling potential clients: offering courtesy and a thorough explanation of the manager's process but not subsequently haranguing the potential client to invest. Over-aggressive marketing means the manager is focused on the wrong thing—pulling in more money as opposed to making money for current investors.

Sometimes deciding whether one trusts and likes a manager may come down to a small, accidental *faux pas* or admission, which may be as diverse as a statement about the manager's personal life or the dogged intellectual pursuit of a trading idea that repeatedly fails to deliver a profit. Managers starting new funds will very often suffer an exceptional early loss because they start the fund with their "one best idea," forgetting that that idea works best, from a risk control point of view, in a fully diversified portfolio. Therefore, funding start-ups requires even greater qualitative judgment because an investor is literally second-guessing the manager's money and risk management skills.

One small statement can often turn an interview around. For example, a manager specializing in distressed securities completes a fine 45-minute explanation of the ideas behind his current portfolio of investments. Several of these situations happen to involve near-bankrupt gaming companies. When casually asked at the end of the interview where he is headed for the upcoming long weekend, the manager says that he and his wife are flying to Las Vegas on an all-expenses-paid weekend gambling junket. Is a manager who is getting free weekend deals from the gaming industry and likes to roll the dice at the craps table a manager one wants running a portfolio of distressed gaming securities?

It is important to watch for the small admissions to see inside a manager's psyche.

§ 7.5[g][2] Operational Control and References. The prospective investor should also discuss more plebian matters during the interview process. Who handles the back office? If the manager relies on an investment bank as his or her prime broker and verifies their account figures each day using a spreadsheet, the investor must beware. Brokerage statements can be notoriously difficult to keep straight, and a single person working with a spreadsheet can fall horribly out of sync. Even fine investment banking firms make errors. How will these errors be caught? Conversely, if the investment bank that acts as the manager's prime broker feeds all of the manager's trades to a third-party administrator who then verifies the trades and produces a net asset value against information the manager separately provides to that administrator, the investor can feel more secure. A three-way sign-off process is far less prone to error and fraud than a two-way process.

One worrisome sign is a hedge fund that is itself a broker-dealer and self-clears. Although there may be legitimate reasons of cost savings for hedge funds to set themselves up this way, doing so has led to some disastrous consequences. For example, Manhattan Capital, a short seller, was able to manipulate its own net asset value figures because it owned one of the broker-dealers through which it traded, and thereby defraud investors. It is indeed reassuring to have a Morgan Stanley, a Goldman Sachs, a Bank of America, or a Deutsche Bank involved as a hedge fund's prime broker.

It is important to ask for references from the hedge fund's prime broker, as well as from its legal counsel, auditor, and several current clients. Prior employers of the hedge fund's principals should also be consulted. A glowing recommendation from a former boss speaks well of a manager's credibility. A more reserved recommendation or any hesitation to recommend may indicate potential problems.

> **Example.** "Joe is perhaps the most brilliant commodity trader that I have ever seen in a bullish crude oil market," a reference recently espoused about a commodity trader with a two-year track record of consistent performance. "But how does he typically do in a range bound market or a bearish market?" I asked. "He can become a bit stubborn," the reference responded. I liked Joe and thought his discretionary commodity orientation would make a nice addition of solid alpha to my portfolio, but a quick review of commodity charts showed Joe had been fortuitous in launching his hedge fund just in front of a huge oil market upswing. Why not wait and see how he performed during a retracement? I did so, only to see Joe take three consecutive monthly hits for a cumulative impact greater than –23 percent.

It is a fact that moving too slowly to make a hedge fund investment risks that a fund will get full and close. Many hedge fund managers with some previous pedigree of success are literally opening and closing their funds to new investment the first day. In general, however, showing some patience in the investment process—watching a manager for awhile before investing, reading at least a calendar quarter's worth of the manager's monthly letters, and taking time to place the manager within an appropriate peer group to compare real-time returns — can prevent the agony of making a poorly thought-out investment too quickly.

§ 7.5[g][3] Risk Management. A third part of the qualitative evaluation is to know something about how the portfolio is constructed. Does the manager keep concentrated positions in 10 to 12 stocks? Or is the portfolio a more diverse one with 30 to 40 stocks long and another 20 to 30 stocks short? What is the most that a manager will allow any one position to represent as a percentage of the total portfolio? What hard or soft rules exist to handle positions that start to move underwater? If a manager uses options in position taking, how do they add value to the portfolio and how are they managed from a risk control point of view? Does the manager have real-time access to profit and loss, beta-adjusted position exposure, market sector exposures, or volatility and time decay exposures? How liquid are the securities that the manager usually traffics in? How many days would it take to liquidate the portfolio in an orderly and noncostly fashion?

All of these questions point toward a single overall concern: Does a manager stand at substantive risk to "jump moves" in individual securities, and if so, how easy is it for the manager to recognize this exposure in advance and deal with it in real time? Even the simplest portfolio can benefit from having a real-time risk management system, and there is really very little excuse for not having such a system.

In general, the more stocks within a manager's portfolio, the better. Disasters tend to happen because of overly concentrated bets that represent more than 10 percent of a portfolio. A more solid approach is that no one position is allowed to grow to more than 7 percent of the total portfolio, and more typically should stand in the 3 to 5 percent range. A manager who tells an investor that no single position should ever cost the portfolio more than 1 percent is likely on the right track to dependable money management. This effectively means that the manager will not let a 3 percent position run by more than 30 percent against the fund, or a 5 percent position run by more than 20 percent against the fund. This still leaves much latitude within which to operate, but a known point where enough will be enough, and positions will be abandoned or at least significantly reduced.

The point is that even when the ideas behind a hedge fund are all thought out and fundamentally sound, how a manager trades a portfolio is of the utmost importance. Having good ideas is not enough. Having good ideas with good risk management is better. Having good ideas, plus solid risk management execution, plus some degree of actual trading acumen is best.

Some of the best hedge fund managers start with a fundamental premise in every investment, but will actively and opportunistically massage the size of their exposure to a given investment depending on short-term market conditions. The use of short-term technical analysis can be very useful in this regard.

> **Example.** XYZ Company has the greatest new ink cartridge technology, but just ran higher by 14 percent in three days and is now bumping up against prior highs. Its relative strength index may have hit 94 (on a 0–100 scale), indicating a short-term overbought condition in terms of the stock's momentum. Some managers would sit on their hands in this circumstance and trust that their long-term fundamental premise for investing in this company is simply playing out. Others might shave the position or temporarily exit the entire position, hoping to buy the position back on a significant retracement.

It is hard to make generalizations, but a more active trading approach shows a certain amount of nimbleness that is generally desirable in a manager. It shows a respect for market price action, and a desire to add value to the portfolio by trading around short-term excesses and market "noise." Having a full-time trader paying attention to actual market behavior, the pulse of the news, and the manner in which the stock is reacting to news and behaving relative to its peers is important. This is not to say that more static managers sitting in an ivory tower with their Reuters screens turned off will not make money. But the static manager will likely show more return variability over time, will risk falling out of touch with reality, and would be ignoring opportunities to extract value from the market around core ideas.

Must a manager use technical analysis to be successful? No. Must a manager have hard stop-loss rules in place at all points in time to avoid excessive drawdowns? No. There are no absolutes to successful hedge fund management. There are only general tendencies. A manager who respects market behavior enough to unemotionally abandon a position gone awry, or a manager who takes advantage of short-term market swings to increase or decrease an exposure opportunistically is simply more likely to make money in a steady fashion and survive over time.

§ 7.5[h] Style Drift

There is perhaps nothing more basic in hedge fund investing than understanding what one is investing in and then monitoring over time what is actually being delivered. There is nothing more dangerous than investing in a merger arbitrage manager who suddenly abandons that niche to take a few stabs at distressed investing, or to invest in a mutual fund market timer who—perhaps for lack of sufficient access to international mutual funds—starts dabbling in basket trading. Style drift usually spells trouble. If a manager says that a fund will typically run with a 0.30–0.50 net long overall beta, the investor should question whether the manager still deserves an allocation when the fund's beta exposure suddenly is taken up to 0.80 — even for good cause. Similarly, an investor should question a short-biased manager who completely misses a 7 percent equity downdraft. Underperforming a benchmark expectation is understandable from time to time; however, a manager who does not deliver any return at all when he or she is supposed to can be the first bad sign that the manager has drifted away from his or her core expertise.

Changing reporting habits can be another bad sign. Perhaps a well-written monthly letter suddenly turns into a more opaque quarterly letter. Perhaps a manager goes from divulging his or her top five positions to divulging no positions at all.

A large turnover of key staff members or the loss of a key analyst can also be cause for concern.

Not even the smallest of hedge funds can function effectively with just one person. There is always a need for at least two people, and most well-functioning funds have at least five or six people (perhaps two partners, two analysts, an operational officer, and a marketer-administrator). Losing just one, let alone two or three of these people, can prove very distracting to a manager. It can reduce the amount of time that a manager has to complete underlying company and market analysis and introduce new personnel hostilities and frictions into previously sound work environments.

Proper hedge fund investing is not as simple as finding a good manager and sitting back. Managers must be re-evaluated periodically. Has performance slipped vis-à-vis others in a hedge fund peer group? Are there any overt signs that the manager or his or her staff is changing? Is the overall market environment changing to the manager's potential detriment?

§ 7.6 Getting Help in Choosing Hedge Fund Managers

Proper hedge fund investing can be complicated. Compiling an appropriate database, filtering by the right statistics, and qualitatively evaluating managers using the right criteria can easily turn into a full-time job, and many affluent people simply do not have the time nor desire to pursue such a vocation. If this is the case, an affluent investor can turn to professionals for advice.

§ 7.6[a] Investment Banks

The first person an investor might consult is his or her stockbroker. All of the big investment banks have their own alternative-investment areas. As this is being written, Morgan Stanley has approximately $7 billion under management in alternative investments, JP Morgan Chase has $3.9 billion, Deutsche Bank has $5 billion, and Goldman Sachs has $4 billion. What they typically all offer are funds of funds—access to a variety of managers within a single pool of assets. That a large investment bank has approved the managers included in the pool and is watching managers from a risk management point of view are both reassuring aspects of investing in a fund of funds vehicle sponsored by an investment bank; however, large banks can also be bureaucratic and slow. They may move just slowly enough to miss some of the best upcoming managers and overallocate to large ones. In 1998 Citibank had $3 billion in alternative assets under management but allocated approximately 30 percent of its fund of funds to a few large macro managers, including Tiger Management. When Tiger Management ran into trouble in 1999 and early 2000 that eventually led to the fund's closure, Citibank's fund of funds performed abysmally.

Big investment banks also have a conflict of interest. Quite often they want to attract large hedge fund clients to execute more trading business with the firm. An allocation of other people's money on an investment basis can often cause hedge funds to reallocate such trade flows. Therefore, the motivation of investment bank fund of funds allocations can occasionally be called into serious question.

§ 7.6[b] Consultants

The second path an investor can take is to hire a consultant. If one has approximately $20 million or more to place into hedge funds, a variety of firms will be glad to provide due diligence assistance in choosing the best funds. Straight consultant names worthy of mention include Paradigm Partners of Clifton, New Jersey; Evaluation Associates of Greenwich, Connecticut; Lake Partners of Greenwich, Connecticut; and Tremont Advisers of Rye, New York. An investor can expect to pay approximately 25–50 basis points per year of the assets invested for the advice of any of these firms.

Of course, many institutions hire traditional consulting firms such as Watson Wyatt & Co. or William Mercer & Co. to advise them on hedge funds. Among endowments, Boston-based Cambridge Associates and

Tacoma, Washington-based Frank Russell & Co. are two favorite alternative investing consulting groups. Although these firms can certainly make generally good recommendations, they remain further removed from the hedge fund industry than the four specialty consultants mentioned above. They move more slowly and are more prone to recommend a manager who already has $2.3 billion under management as opposed to a potentially more skillful up-and-coming manager who has assets of only $40 million. In other words, they typically recommend the obvious.

Another problem with this route is that once a consultant makes its recommendation, the consultant tends to take the consultancy fee and walk away—responsible for recommending an initial allocation, but not typically responsible for ongoing monitoring and due diligence. The consultant is paid just as well whether a recommended manager turns into a star or a flop, and whether the client makes money or loses it. There is seldom any performance fee associated with consultancy contracts.

§ 7.6[c] Funds of Funds

The third path a wealthy investor may take to gain diversified access to a variety of hedge fund managers is an independent fund of funds. An independent fund of funds manager will choose a diversified group of managers and effectively compile them into one limited partnership. An investor not only receives the fund of funds manager's due diligence in picking the hedge fund managers but also ongoing monitoring and small sector adjustments to the allocation mix. The investor gets access to a wide range of styles through one vehicle and typically can invest as little as $100,000 in this vehicle instead of investing the $500,000 to $1 million minimum that most underlying hedge funds require.

It is thus fair to say that an individual with $10 million to place in hedge funds could obtain access to 10 to 15 managers, at most, when investing by him- or herself. The individual would also be taking on many monitoring headaches and would receive many annual K-1 statements during tax season—an accountant's logistical nightmare. Instead, this individual could invest in a fund of funds and potentially gain exposure to 40 managers with daily monitoring (thus achieving sector and style diversity) and receive a single K-1 during tax season. A summary of the various paths to hedge fund investing, outlining relative advantages and disadvantages, is given in Figure 3.

Figure 3. The Universe of Hedge Fund Investing

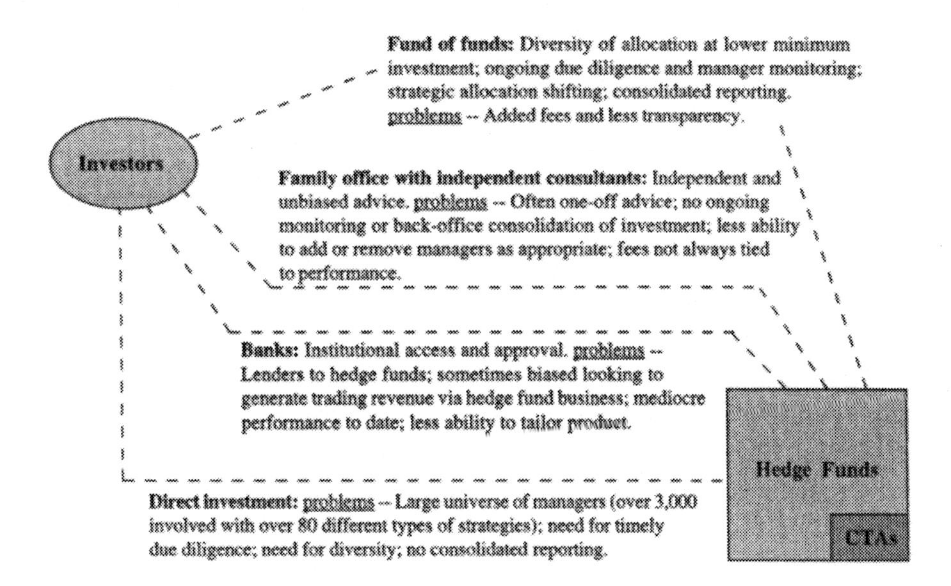

A sample fund of funds' pie allocation might offer the diversity shown in Figure 4.

Figure 4. Sample Fund of Funds Pie Chart Allocation

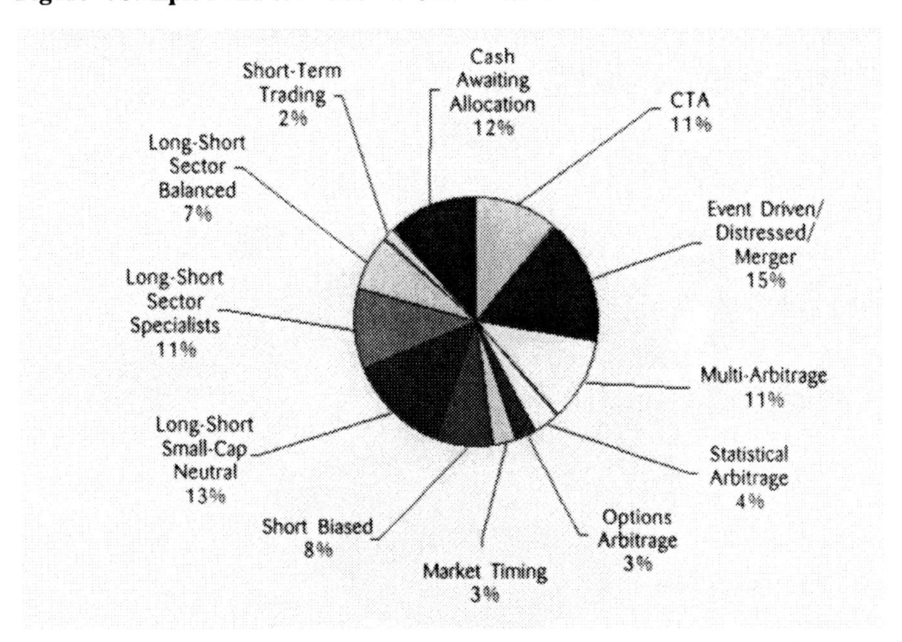

Of course, there is a catch. For amalgamating a portfolio and doing ongoing due diligence work and manager monitoring, funds of funds charge an extra level of fees. These fees typically range from a 50 basis point to 1.2 percent annual management fee and a 10 percent share of net profits reported to the fund of funds by individual managers. Added to the 1 percent/20 percent fees already being paid to underlying managers, some investors find this unappealing. There is even the tendency to do overly simplistic math and ask, how can one make any money at all paying away a total of 2 percent and 30 percent of profits?

Therein lies a slight wrinkle. If the fund of funds manager does a good job and has a limited partnership return of 22.2 percent gross after management fees for a year, the fund of funds is only charging its incentive fee on the return, not on the principal. The investor would thus net a 20 percent annual return, having paid the fund of funds manager a total of 3.2 percent for his or her services (a typical 1 percent management fee plus 2.2 percent of principal incentive fee). Thus, it might be fairer to say that the total fees associated with a fund of funds is closer to 2 percent/22.2 percent rather than the 2 percent/30 percent initial false presumption.

Another hesitation some investors have with funds of funds is that transparency into underlying manager names and performance can be limited. This is, after all, the fund of fund manager's competitive edge—being able to put together a robust portfolio mix—and few funds of funds will provide complete access to the managers being chosen. This may create a slight unease for some investors. Many fund of funds managers are asked where an investor's money has ended up, at which point they produce a chart such as the one in Figure 5.

Figure 5. Where Funds Actually End Up

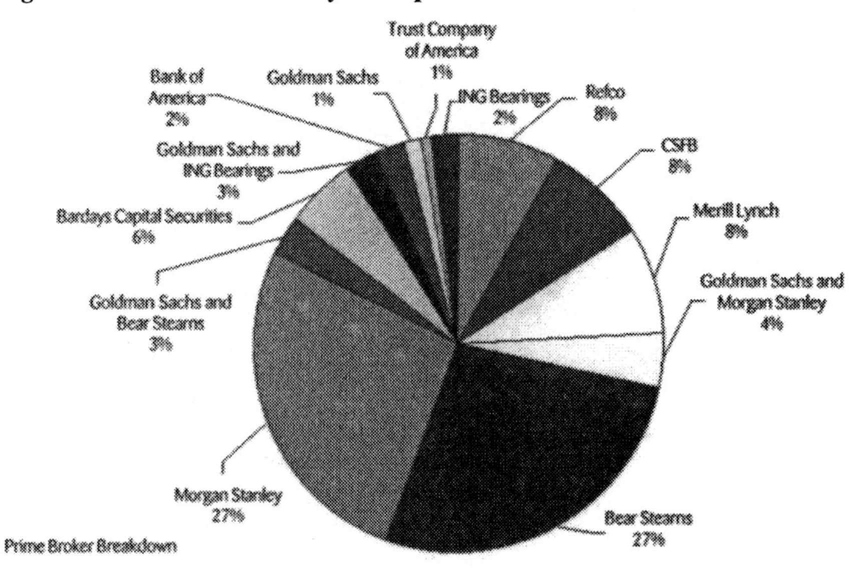

Although different managers control one's funds, the funds themselves all end up residing at major brokerage firms. This may reassure some hesitant fund of funds investors, but others may still feel unwilling to allocate "blindly." Funds of funds managers offer both their reputation and historical performance to potential investors, but sometimes that is simply not enough.

Using a consultant or a fund of funds is a matter of personal choice. With a consultant, a fee is paid and one knows the managers chosen, but without much support thereafter. With a fund of funds, a fee is still paid, but there is no direct access to the underlying managers. What a fund of funds investor does know is that the alternative manager to whom funds are entrusted is fully motivated to deliver robust performance.

Despite the added fee and transparency problems, a fund of funds can be a wonderful way to access the hedge fund world. The average fund of funds manager certainly can provide a huge amount of manager research and hedge fund portfolio construction for an investor. Fund of funds managers can calculate and quantify manager risks and correlations, and thereby construct and periodically rebalance portfolios far more correctly than most individual investors can. As shown in Figure 6, fund of funds managers can function as useful and logical middlemen to hedge fund investing.

Figure 6. A Better Way?

Fund of funds managers can also use a bit of common sense to make

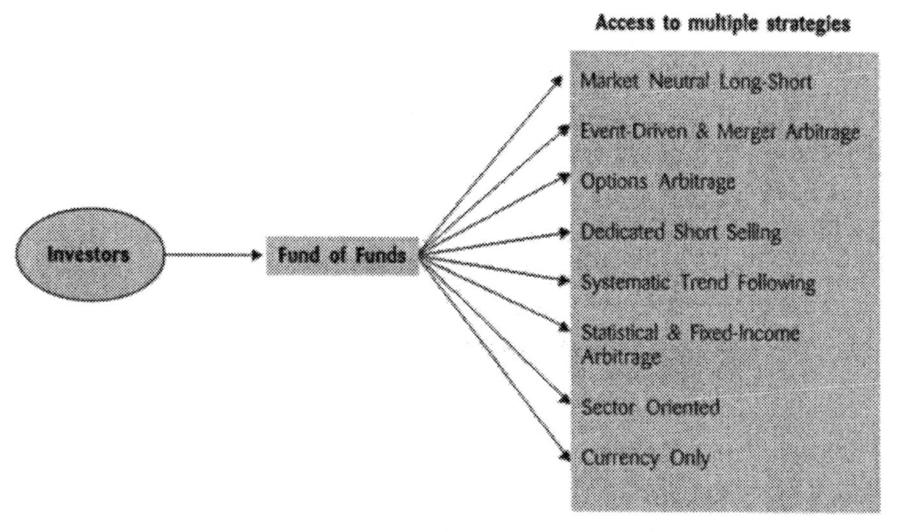

gentle shifts between hedge fund managers who use different styles. For example, merger arbitrage can at times be active, with many opportunities presenting themselves at attractive spreads. In other market environments, merger deals can quiet down and deal spreads compress to unattractive levels. An astute fund of funds manager will take either environment into account and divide the fund of funds' allocation accordingly.

On an ongoing basis, hedge fund investors can get huge advantages from fund of funds' continuous manager monitoring and search for new managers, as well as consolidated portfolio reporting. Hedge fund investing remains part art and part science, and the fund of funds manager is like a conductor of an orchestra—making something organized and efficient, and hopefully beautiful sounding, out of individual notes and melodies that could easily fall into chaos. A full depiction of the filtering and monitoring process that fund of funds managers typically employ is shown in Figure 7.

Figure 7. In-Depth Due Diligence: The Key to Finding Consistent Managers

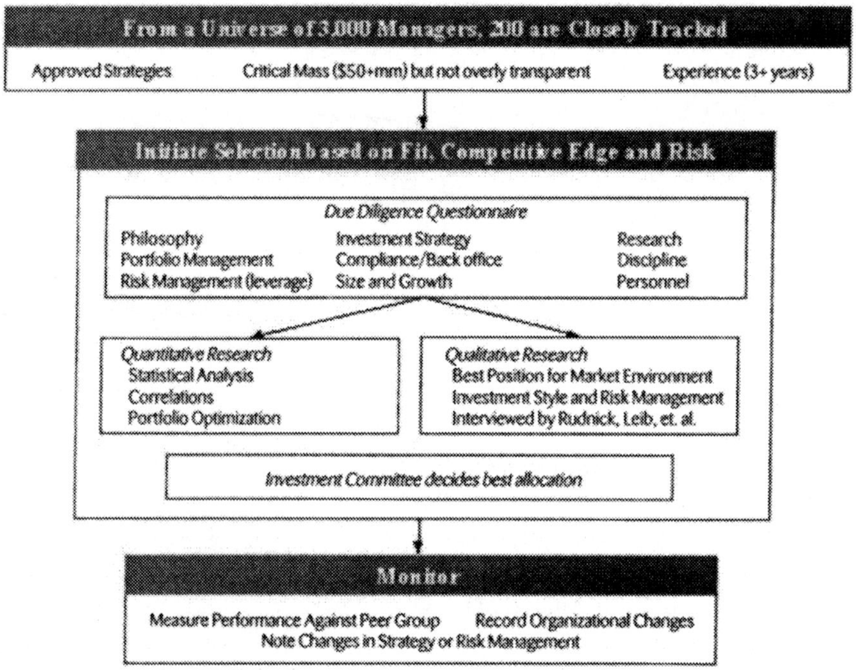

From a Universe of 3,000 Managers, 200 are Closely Tracked
Approved Strategies
Critical Mass ($50+mm) but not overly transparent
Experience (3+ years)

Initiate Selection based on Fit, Competitive Edge and Risk
Due Diligence Questionnaire
Philosophy
Portfolio Management
Risk Management (leverage)
Investment Strategy
Compliance/Back office
Size and Growth
Research
Discipline
Personnel

Quantitative Research
Statistical Analysis
Correlations
Portfolio Optimization

Qualitative Research
Best Position for Market Environment
Investment Style and Risk Management
Interviewed by Rudnick, Leib, et. al.

Investment Committee decides best allocation

Monitor
Measure Performance Against Peer Group
Record Organizational Changes
Note Changes in Strategy or Risk Management

§ 7.7 Choosing a Fund of Funds Manager and Product

Choosing a good fund of funds manager is a bit easier than choosing a basket of hedge fund managers by oneself, but still involves some work. In the average hedge fund database, interspersed with actual hedge fund managers, one will find more than 400 funds of funds. Some of these offerings are very good and some are very bad, and some of the better funds of funds will not even be listed.

The first step in finding a fund of funds manager is to determine the investment orientation of the fund of funds. Does it strive to maintain a market-neutral position, or does it allow its beta to creep up to 0.40 or even 0.60? Both styles of managers exist. Does the fund of funds contain mostly simple long-short managers or more arbitrage-oriented managers who may use complicated over-the-counter derivative contracts? The latter may be able to deliver more consistent returns than long-short managers most of the time but be subject to occasional shocks during periods of extreme market stress. International Swaps and Derivatives Association (ISDA) documentation for over-the-counter derivative contracts can still have enough loopholes to result in messy litigious fights between counterparts, and hedge funds typically have fewer resources for fighting such court battles than the big banks have.

A good tool to use to determine investment orientation is a pie allocation chart of a fund of funds. A prospective investor should ask the fund of funds manager to explain the current sector allocation thought process and describe managers within each sector. For a large enough investment, a fund of funds manager should be willing to reveal the names and individual track records of each underlying manager. Even if the fund of funds manager is not willing to reveal individual hedge fund names, the manager should provide a summary performance table that includes each hedge fund within the portfolio listed under a generic title such as FX Manager 1, Long-Short Small-Cap Manager 2, and so on.

A fund of funds manager should also be willing to reveal the amount of manager concentration within a fund. Some funds of funds have only eight or nine managers in them, each representing 10 to 20 percent of the fund. Others may have up to 45 managers, with no one manager representing more than a 5 percent allocation. The return stream from the former may be dynamic but subject to occasional drawdowns of significant magnitude; the return stream from the latter, by definition, should be far smoother, but may never achieve outstanding years. Twenty to thirty managers with no one manager representing more than 10 percent of the fund is usually the right balance to look for. Dynamic returns can still be achieved without risking too much drag from overdiversification and manager mediocrity.

The prospective investor should also try to obtain an understanding of how a fund of funds manager makes decisions. Is the allocation a fairly static one, or are managers replaced and sector allocations changed with some regularity? If the latter is true, what would be the various catalysts for the fund of funds manager to make a shift? What general methodology does the fund of funds manager rely on to select hedge funds and strategies? Is the approach purely quantitative (perhaps even optimized), or more qualitative, or a combination of both? What are the fund of funds manager's general macroeconomic proclivities and assumptions, and how do they relate to the strategy and individual hedge fund selection process?

How does a fund of funds manager keep tabs on hedge fund managers with whom he or she has placed money? Weekly phone calls with formal biweekly performance updates are the norm, but the fund of funds manager should also physically visit every manager two to six times per year. Very few fund of funds managers have achieved 100 percent transparency into underlying hedge fund manager positions, but some funds of funds do require fully transparent separate managed accounts when making underlying hedge fund investments. More typically, actual position transparency only flows to fund of funds managers for a portion of hedge funds in their portfolio, with some good-faith reliance on managers to report correct numbers in the balance of instances. Obviously, the more transparency, the better; but this desire must be balanced by the fact that some of the best hedge fund managers offer little or no transparency.

Another fruitful line of questioning revolves around the use of added borrowing. When the fund of funds manager chooses underlying managers, what amount of leverage does the average underlying manager use? Does the fund of funds manager impose any leverage above this? If the answer is yes, one might want to proceed with caution. An individual hedge fund manager should be able to gauge the use of leverage properly, but a fund of funds manager adding more leverage on top of manager-level leverage can be very dangerous. Historical returns might look fabulous, but a modest three-month drawdown in such circumstances might prove disastrous.

Modest 1.2:1 leverage at the fund of funds level is probably acceptable because a fund of funds achieves more diversity; however, products where

2:1 or 3:1 leverage is used at the fund of funds level should only be considered if such a product also has a principal guarantee provided by a major bank. This guaranteed product exists (Societe Generale, Royal Bank of Canada, and Zurich Capital are leaders in this field) and is becoming more popular. Such a principal guarantee costs more in fees (typically an added 1 to 2 percent), and it is important that the underlying fund of funds get off to a solid performance. Without the fund of funds first building up a substantial return cushion, there is a chance that the bank performing risk management on the guaranteed product may need to pull assets from the fund of funds manager to invest in zero-coupon fixed-income instruments, and thereby ensure principal protection. Therefore, other things being equal, it would be best to invest in a leveraged guaranteed product at or near a significant market low rather than investing blithely at any time. One needs to minimize the risk of a poor start.

Certainly one should be careful of excessive leveraging. There has yet to be a financial accident from leveraged investment bank structured notes sitting atop hedge fund assets, but some day there will be. As financial columnist Jim Grant recently wrote: "Here's a puzzler: If you buy into a fund of funds on leverage, and the fund-of-funds manager purchases the underlying hedge funds with leverage, and some of those hedge-fund managers use leverage to buy stocks in companies that are, themselves, deeply in debt, how many real assets do you own for every dollar you invested? Most investors don't (and can't) know the answer to this question."[7]

Could a margin call at one level of leverage unwittingly lead to a margin call at another level? "Where that would stop, nobody knows," offers Jonathon Spring, an alternative asset manager interviewed by Grant. "We do know that in 1998, the use of 80-1 leverage at a single large hedge fund required the intervention of the Federal Reserve to prevent a widespread economic meltdown. My guess is that today, many people are indirectly and unknowingly utilizing similar magnitudes of leverage. Yet no one is in the position to add up all the pieces or discern the connections and the consequences."[8]

It is important to avoid this trap. Although placing a private placement variable life insurance contract around a portfolio of hedge fund investments is a very sound and advisable estate planning technique that can achieve substantial tax savings (despite the structure's added costs), not all investment bank structured notes are a good idea. Hedge funds can be volatile by themselves. Superimposing too much leverage on top of them can turn a good product into a toxic one in the wrong environment.

A prospective investor should also be just a bit cautious about the underlying prime brokers used by hedge funds. Some are more aggressive and more exposed to the industry than others. Bank of America, Morgan Stanley, JP Morgan Chase, and many other firms run conservative hedge fund prime brokerage operations, but Bear Stearns, Deutsche Bank, Zurich Capital, and Societe Generale have been far more aggressive in "lending their balance sheet" to their hedge fund customers and have guaranteed billions of dollars worth of hedge fund structures. The author can almost guarantee that this type of business will eventually get some of these firms into great trouble. Therefore, at the margin and in a perfect world, it is best to have Goldman Sachs or Bank of America as one's hedge fund's prime broker rather than one of the more aggressive firms.

Other questions that one might ask of a prospective fund of funds manager include the following:

1. What mistakes has the fund of funds manager made in the past, and how has the manager learned from these experiences?
2. How much of the fund of funds manager's own capital is invested in the fund of funds? Often the general partner entity of a fund of funds may have none, but one should make sure that at least the principals of the general partnership personally are investors.
3. Are there any potential conflicts of interest that the fund of funds manager faces in the allocation process? One should be aware that fund of funds managers occasionally receive fee rebates from the managers to whom they allocate. This creates a potential conflict of interest for a fund of funds manager and should generally be avoided.

§ 7.8 Funds of Funds to Consider

In the interest of full disclosure, the author of this chapter is a fund of funds manager and president of the alternative asset management firm Sand Spring Advisors LLC (Sand Spring). Sand Spring allocates to a wide variety of hedge funds on behalf of the Wimbledon Sand Spring Class L Fund LP, doing so in conjunction with Weston Capital Management (Weston Capital). Weston Capital has a fine track record of more than seven years, and $1.2 billion currently under management. The firm provides Sand Spring added due diligence and back-office services. Working together, Weston Capital and Sand Spring are most proud of the performance of the Wimbledon Sand Spring Class L Fund to date and the diversification mix of managers included in this fund. Those interested in learning more about our product may contact the author at BTLEIB@Sandspring.com.

Apart from the author's own activities, many other alternative investment managers exist, and it is only appropriate to give fair press to a variety of the best.

§ 7.8[a] Investment Banks

The investment bank route is often a wealthy investor's first inquiry, and certainly many investment banks such as Goldman Sachs, Deutsche Bank, Credit Suisse First Boston, JP Morgan Chase, and Deutsche Bank have attracted significant alternative assets. Morgan Stanley Alternative Investment Partners, based in Conshohocken, Pennsylvania, has grown to manage $7 billion in total alternative assets, and Zurich Capital is now offering a new group of tradable hedge fund indices developed in conjunction with the academically intensive Schneeweis Partners based in Amherst, Massachusetts. Over $1.3 billion has been committed to Zurich Capital for this new product.

Come and now gone but quickly trying to rebuild itself is Citibank's alternative investment group. This group was previously based in San Francisco, but Citibank's alternatives effort was buffeted both by Salomon Smith Barney merger squabbles and by the misfortunes of various macro managers, including Tiger Management, to which the group had a large allocation.

By comparison, JP Morgan Alternative Asset Management has fared better through the recent Morgan-Chase merger. Most of the group comes from the Chase side, but an increasing number of relationships are currently being developed through new ties to JP Morgan Investment Management. The group is currently 49 strong and includes 15 specialized researchers, a quantitative staff, and a fully separate risk management area. The firm's flagship JP Morgan Multi-Strategy Fund Ltd. currently includes 36 managers and boasts a solid seven-year track record.

There is no doubt that consultants such as Cambridge Associates, Watson Wyatt, and William Mercer & Co. are increasingly receiving mandates not only to suggest individual hedge fund managers but also to present a selection of possible fund of funds managers. The end result of these consultancy searches may from time to time still deliver a large investment bank for a client's consideration; but according to William "Doug" Douglass III, a partner of $1 billion New York-based fund of funds manager K2 Advisors,

LLC, "Most of the time the finalists in fund of funds competitions are not the big investment banks, but instead are the more specialized firms." In funds of funds, as in hedge funds themselves, bigger is not necessarily better.

§ 7.8[b] Chicago Rules

Historically, when endowments and foundations, as well as wealthy individuals, have gone shopping for fund of funds managers, the clear winners (notwithstanding the Greenwich, Connecticut-based Commonfund) have largely emanated from Chicago—Grosvenor Capital Management, Glenwood Capital Management, Harris Associates, and Mesirow Financial.

Grosvenor Capital Management has an impressive track record extending back to 1971 and $4.5 billion in alternative assets currently under management, but generally maintains a very low profile within the fund of funds community and does not publicly report the performance of its products.

Glenwood Capital Management, owned by the Man Group, has traditionally seen the majority of its clients come from Europe. The firm, which currently has $4.5 billion under management, received a well-publicized $1 billion alternative advisory mandate from the General Motors pension plan in 2001.

Harris Associates, manager of the $22 billion Oakmark series of mutual funds, has $2.3 billion allocated within alternative assets, with its Aurora series of multimanager funds consistently landing high in the fund of fund league tables. "But with a $1 billion now in one fund, it's often hard to make a new meaningful allocation without also pushing up our manager count beyond desired levels," explains Ron Rollighed, Harris's Director of Alternative Product Management.[9] Hence, the Aurora offshore fund closed to new investment in May 2002 and was replaced by Aurora Offshore Fund Ltd. II, similar in sector construction to the first fund but with a slightly different mix of managers. The original Aurora Fund currently allocates to a rather wide spread of managers— 46 different managers at present.

Mesirow Financial is a firm with $2.5 billion under management in alternatives and a solid historical allocation record; however, Mesirow has recently engaged Goldman Sachs to find a potential merger partner for itself. In theory, many larger institutions without an alternatives presence should be interested. At the moment, it remains to be seen where this venerable firm will find its longer-term niche.

Even if Chicago rules, capable fund managers pop up at other geographic locales across the country.

Long Island, New York-based Ivy Asset Management, part of Bank of New York since October 2000, is one manager that has won a boatload of alternatives mandates. The Ivy Defenders Fund and Ivy Rosewood Fund have been the product leaders for Ivy Asset Management, sporting Sharpe ratios of 3.58 and 2.79, respectively, since inception. The firm's assets now top $5.8 billion.

Lesser known in the United States, but particularly well-respected in Europe is GAM. Founded in 1989, GAM has $7 billion in assets. GAM is a bit different from many fund of funds managers in so far as it typically charges a relatively high flat management fee in lieu of charging any incentive fees.

New York-based Blackstone Alternative Asset Management has a particularly attractive institutionally oriented fee structure in the funds that it offers as opposed to the higher norms that prevail at more retail-oriented funds of funds. With a solid institutional toehold already in private equity, real estate, and mezzanine investing, this firm has accumulated over $3 billion in alternative hedge fund assets to date (not including an advisory mandate from the California Public Employees Retirement System), with approximately 25 percent of these funds coming from plan sponsors. Most of these investments have been made directly into the firm's menu of fund of funds products, as opposed to any private label or customized funds. Since 2001, the firm has been delivering solid fund of funds performance within a difficult market environment.

Finally, within a top tier of alternative managers, many point to Quellos Group LLC, a private client wealth management firm founded in 1994 that has increasingly secured institutional mandates within the alternatives space. Also highly regarded is Meridian Capital Partners. This firm's home base is Albany, New York, but its roots are in two investment management pension consultants, William Lawrence and Donald Halldin, who started choosing hedge fund managers for plan sponsors in the late 1980s. These two men then changed from consultants into full-fledged fund of fund managers in 1994 and have built an impressive eight-year performance record since. Meridian Capital Partners offers five different funds, one of which is offshore, and invests with a relatively tight group of 14 to 18 managers in each product. "We don't want to over-diversify ourselves to mediocrity," says John Sica, Director of Research. "We want to be more diversified than a statistical optimization process might advise, but less diversified than many of our competitors."[10] Meridian Capital Partners currently has $1.5 billion under management; although it makes small tactical shifts in its allocation mix over time, it tends to be a long-term investor in a core group of long-short and multi-arbitrage managers. The firm tries to keep a small long beta to its products near .20, although it has consciously allowed its funds' market exposure to float a bit higher or lower at different points in time.

§ 7.8[c] Others Abound and Lessons Learned

The above fund of funds may be preeminent but they also typically have high minimum investment requirements. A slew of other creative alternative managers could also find their way onto an able consultant's list of recommendations. Many of these have lower investment minimums.

Rye, New York-based Tremont Advisers has been a steady if somewhat middle-of-the-road consultant and fund of funds group that recently was acquired by Oppenheimer & Co. It advises on over $89 billion in hedge fund assets.

Two New York-based alternative firms of some repute are Archstone Partners and Arden Asset Management. Archstone Partners, in existence since 1991, has $1.3 billion under management. Its Archstone Market Neutral Strategies Fund and Archstone Partners Fund sport two of the best long-term track records in terms of absolute and risk-adjusted performance. The former is a relatively concentrated fund oriented to nine nondirectional arbitrage managers; the latter has 22 managers with a slightly more aggressive 65 percent tilt toward directional managers. As a matter of policy, Archstone openly shares all of the names of its underlying managers with its investors.

Arden Asset Management began in 1993, and has since seen its assets swell to just over $2 billion. The firm finds its special niche by running its fund of funds products with a lower allocation to long-short managers than many other alternative managers. Perhaps as a result, 50 percent of its customer base comes from institutions, with an increasing portion of these institutional flows being ERISA (Employee Retirement Income Security Act of 1974) money.

K2 Advisors, LLC is another New York-based alternative manager. This fund of funds group, in business since 1994, is run by William "Doug" Douglass III and David Saunders. The firm has grown to have over $1 billion in total assets under management, of which Douglass estimates 80 percent comes from institutions. Both Highland Associates and New England Pension Consultants have brought clients K2's way, with Highland Associates' Bill

Mills terming the firm's working relationship with K2 as "truly first rate in terms of transparency, manager oversight, and client education."[11]

The firm maintains an allocation of approximately 60 to 70 percent to long-short equity managers and 30 percent to other low-volatility arbitrage strategies. It makes no allocations to any macro or statistical arbitrage managers. "We invest in strategies that we understand," says Douglass, "and our true value-added is that we come from a trading background. We understand these strategies."[12]

Whatever K2 is doing right, it has shown up in terms of performance. The fund's long-short and low-volatility hedge funds have collectively delivered returns of 19.6 percent, 17 percent, and 19.2 percent over the past seven, five, and three years, respectively.

Certain alternative managers have learned lessons from the past.

Greenwich, Connecticut-based Paloma Partners faced stressful times in September 1998 during the Long Term Capital Management debacle. Many of its arbitrage strategies proved to have more market correlation than initially anticipated in that environment, and customer redemptions threatened the firm's survival. Today, however, Paloma, with $1.7 billion under management in its fund of funds, errs on the opposite side of caution, demanding fully separate and transparent managed accounts of all of its hedge fund managers, and including in its allocation mix certain managers that consistently maintain long-volatility strategies. "These managers represent our insurance policy during turbulent times," says John C. Snyder, a Paloma Managing Director.[13]

Starting with its own money, Paloma Partners has historically acted as an incubator to new trading talent, and in recent years has spent much research and development time on statistical equity arbitrage managers. The firm is particularly close to multi-arbitrage manager Amaranth Partners, in which Paloma Partners maintains a substantive investment and for which it provides certain back-office and risk management services.

The Paloma International LP, a diversified mix of market-neutral absolute-return strategies, has averaged 14.7 percent per year net of fees since inception with less than 6 percent volatility.

§ 7.8[d] Pacific Perspective

Tacoma, Washington is home to well-known hedge fund consultant and alternative manager Frank Russell Company—a firm that had $69 billion under management at the end of 2001 and is owned by Northwestern Mutual. Early to the concept of hedge fund investing to create added alpha, the company remains a formidable, if somewhat secretive, force. Nowhere will one find a public track record of the hedge fund portfolios that it has created for its clients. Notwithstanding this fact, many institutions and family offices head its way if not to invest directly in a fund of funds product, then at least for the firm's research advice.

Also in Tacoma is Paradigm Partners Northwest, manager of the Benchmark Plus group of funds. This firm is headed by Robert Ferguson and Mike Dunmire, two men who have been involved exclusively with alternative investments since 1986, when Dunmire first created the Frank Russell Alternative Investment Services department. Seven years ago, the two moved on to form their own alternatives practice, seeking to create a truly market-neutral portfolio by overlaying index futures against each manager's expected equity market correlation.

"Most people pair off long-biased managers versus short-biased managers, but in a real market crisis, correlations can often change, and those managing their risk in this manner can never be 100 percent sure how such a portfolio will behave," explains Dunmire. "By comparison, futures hedges are quite predictable; so in a crisis, I can look directly at my index futures profit and know that I have a certain amount of money already in the bank. We are trying to extract a pure alpha, and this is the best way that I know to do it. It avoids any illusion of hedges that aren't there when you need them."[14]

Dunmire has developed four "super-enhanced" index funds around his basic market-neutral fund. By using futures to create synthetic exposures, each fund offers a return approximating that of its underlying index (minus the T-bill rate) plus the Benchmark Plus Market Neutral Fund return. This approach plays directly into the demand by many investors for so-called portable alpha.

Amy Hirsch, Chief Executive Officer of hedge fund consultant Paradigm Partners (a New Jersey-based firm of no relation), is a big fan of the Benchmark Plus program. "I view what Benchmark Plus is doing as a true alpha extraction process," she offers. Hirsch has placed funds with the firm in recent years.[15]

Seattle-based Silver Creek SV LLC (known by many people as Dillon/Flaherty Partners, the group's original fund) has historically been a low-volatility, low-fee manager that targets its net performance at 6 to 10 percent above Treasury bills with no down years. Its original Dillon/Flaherty Partners Fund has delivered just this—a 12.79 percent average annual return since its 1994 inception. More impressive yet, it has done so with only a 3.36 percent standard deviation of returns, yielding an impressive 2.31 Sharpe ratio. Its worst monthly drawdown over an eight-year life has been a single –2.8 percent month. Amazingly, the fund has been profitable in over 95 percent of months since inception—a truly impressive accomplishment. Silver Creek SV currently has two open products: the Silver Creek Long/Short Fund and Silver Creek Partners Fund, both with offshore feeders, and the latter representing a re-opening of the Dillon/Flaherty Partners Fund.

Bill Gates is rumored to have been one of the firm's early clients, and if so, it is no wonder. Silver Creek has racked up a strong performance record, and its fee structure also comes with a less egregious bite than that of many East Coast competitors.

Ironwood Capital Management is one more West Coast firm producing impressive fund of fund returns. Run by Fred Gans, together with his son Jon Gans, Ironwood has a six and one-half year track record that has placed the firm's funds at the top of the fund of funds league tables again and again. Since inception, the Ironwood Partners Fund, one of the firm's four very similarly structured offerings, has delivered an average 15.56 percent return and a worst cumulative drawdown of – 4.84 percent. The firm currently has $400 million under management.

Ironwood allocates only to managers with very low market betas—as market neutral as possible—with Gans deeming his allocation to be so narrow in focus and well-defined in risk that the firm maintains no short sellers within its allocation mix. Gans also specifically avoids strategies such as mortgaged-backed arbitrage that he deems contain too much unquantifiable risk in high-volatility environments. There is a large allocation to established multi-arbitrage managers, some of which are now closed to new outside investment, with Ironwood using no leverage at the fund of funds level.

§ 7.8[e] Florida Shores

In Palm Beach, Florida, but with research offices in New York, San Francisco, and London, Lighthouse Partners LLC has emerged as a fund of funds manager specifically focused on managing volatility. The firm started as a simple family office in the late 1980s, but in 1999 opened itself up to outside investors and has since attracted approximately half of its $876 million of assets under management from institutions. The firm uses no leverage at the fund of funds level and works only for a fixed management fee. "We're very focused on capital preservation," says Managing Director and founding partner Dana B. Hall, "and many institutional clients like us because they see our process as truly repeatable."[16] By comparison, investors point to many funds of funds that have experienced significant staff changes and asset growth, causing one to question how repeatable track records will be going forward. Lighthouse Partners has recently been landing college endowment business. Smith College signed on with the firm in July 2001, followed by allocations from Hobart and William Smith Colleges, Texas A&M University, and Indiana University. For the conservative hedge fund investor, Lighthouse Partners may represent a particularly appropriate firm to explore.

Elsewhere, Cadogan Management and Ontario Partners are well-regarded funds of funds worthy of mention, and other names will surely evolve over time. The key point is that each of these groups approaches the hedge fund world a bit differently, and an investor should search for an allocation mix, a risk ethic, and a specific return profile within these various groups with which he or she will be most comfortable. Liquidity terms can also vary with funds of funds (monthly being optimal, but quarterly more common), as can fee structures. Investigative comparison of multiple funds of funds is still strongly advised.

§ 7.9 The Ten Mistakes Most Often Made in Hedge Fund Investing

Hopefully this chapter will have proved a useful tool to any high net-worth individual considering increased hedge fund investing. Before finishing, however, let us list the ten most common mistakes that we have seen nascent hedge fund investors make time and again.

Mistake 1: *investing the majority of one's money with one manager, often a macromanager, who is considered a god.* Managers come and go, markets change, and personnel change. There is no reason to become overly concentrated with one manager. Concentration of assets in a single endeavor helps to create fortunes, but proper diversification helps assets be preserved and grow over time.

Mistake 2: *investing in hedge funds that have just grown from $100 million in assets to $1 billion in assets, without consideration as to whether the greater assets under management will impinge on the hedge fund* *manager's style of trading.* Smaller, more nimble, and hungry managers are usually better. Maneuverability and performance tend to diminish with total assets under management. Hedge funds that have more than several billion dollars under management stand at particular risk of having their positions known by investment banks that can benefit from such knowledge.

Mistake 3: looking at an unblemished track record without regard for potential changes in the future environment. A collateralized mortgage-backed manager might have been able to earn steady positive returns for years by employing leverage and investing in BB debt. Such a strategy will have its day of comeuppance, however, no matter how savvy the manager, if the housing market turns sour and householders start handing in their keys on suddenly depreciated properties.

Investors should further be aware that an unblemished track record can also be achieved in other, more nefarious manners such as behind-the-scenes option writing. It is often only possible to detect such activity after the fact when the least bit of volatility strikes and a manager quickly incurs losses seemingly out of the blue.

Mistake 4: becoming impatient with a manager too quickly once invested. Like anything, quality hedge fund managers can hit 6- to 18-month patches of difficult market conditions from time to time, often making a few mistakes while adjusting to a changed economic environment. If performance is clearly outside of the manager's historical norm, an investor should certainly question it. If a good reason exists to change a previous positive opinion about a manager (change of staff, failed risk management techniques, style shift, etc.), a quick redemption is justified. More often than not, however, investors will bolt from a hedge fund manager too quickly and often just before a substantial recovery materializes. Certain styles of trading can be cyclical. CTAs in particular can try one's patience with long periods of drawdown, but over the long term they add diversity and alpha to any portfolio of hedge funds.

Mistake 5: investing without truly understanding what a manager does. There are many complex arbitrage and statistical strategies. It is not expected that every investor will understand every strategy, but the investor should have a general feel for the strategy and an understanding of its weaknesses—when and why the strategy may fail. Without knowing this, one should not invest in the manager. Yet many do, looking at historical performance alone.

Mistake 6: not adequately checking references. Sometimes one may have such a positive and effusive opinion about a prospective manager that checking references seems a cumbersome and unnecessary process. It is not. The current trading success of any manager means little if that manager is not inherently honest or is not a good business manager. In the interview process, it is important to glean the names of former colleagues and bosses and then to call them.

Mistake 7: *investing in start-up managers, particularly ex-investment bank trader start-ups.* Investing in any start-up hedge fund is usually a dangerous proposition. It is better to risk being shut out of a hedge fund because of capacity constraints than to rush into nascent hedge funds too quickly. Watching a manager perform in real time is never a bad thing to do. On top of this, if a manager was successful at a large investment bank, one should not assume that this holds much bearing as to how that manager will perform as a small start-up hedge fund manager. Unless one is getting some sort of extra sweetheart fee and profit sharing terms to be a seed investor, one should stay away. The probability for a blow-up, or at least investment disappointment, is much higher with start-ups than with well-seasoned managers.

Mistake 8: *not putting a manager within the proper peer group before investing.* There is a tendency to find a manager one likes, become excited about that manager, and invest too quickly before doing a full peer-group analysis of other managers of similar style. Money can, of course, be made investing in this manner, but one risks choosing a manager with a worse risk-reward return profile than a more detailed search would yield. In other words, without doing proper hedge fund homework, an investor may end up with a manager who, in terms of risk-reward, falls short of the Markowitz efficient investment frontier.

Mistake 9: *not being willing to litigate quickly when something clearly goes wrong.* Hedge funds turn sour all the time, and despite all the due diligence in the world, bad situations sometimes cannot be avoided. When bad times arrive, most investors will spend considerable time trying to extricate themselves from a hedge fund through negotiations with the fund's general partner. If there is any initial problem on this front, investors should move more quickly than they typically do to call in legal counsel and launch court motions. Dallying to get tough usually makes the investor's position worse.

Mistake 10: *not asking for important documentation concessions in advance.* Many back-end hedge fund problems can be avoided by front-end attention to detail. More investors should ask for added transparency provisions, better redemption rights, fund liquidation provisions on certain loss thresholds being reached, or advance arbitration agreements. Doing so avoids many headaches later on.

---

1. Leib, B.T; "Getting Your Legal Ducks in a Row," *Global Custodian Magazine*, Spring 2002, pp 112–114.
2. Id.
3. Leib, B.T; "The Quintessential Blend," *Plan Sponsor Magazine*, March 2002, pp 28–29.
4. Id.
5. Id.
6. All analytical formulas in § 7.5[e] were obtained from InvestorForce.com.
7. Grant, J., *Grant's Interest Rate Observer*, Grants Financial Publishing, Inc. Vol 20 No. 18, May 2002.
8. Id.
9. Leib, B.T; "Sorting the Fund of Funds Sheep from the Goats," *Plan Sponsor Magazine*, June 2002, p 82.
10. Id.
11. Id.
12. Id.
13. Id.
14. Id.
15. Id.
16. Id.

CHAPTER 8

Enhancing After-Tax Investment Returns Through Swaps—The Paradigm of Investment Tools

Robert N. Gordon and Thomas J. Boczar

Synopsis

Individual investors have two primary tax concerns regarding their investments. First, how can they enter into an investment in the most tax-efficient manner? Second, how can they exit from an investment in the most tax-efficient manner?

Investors are often able to enter into and exit from investments synthetically (i.e., through a financial derivative such as a swap) in a more tax-efficient manner than they can by consummating an outright purchase or sale. This opportunity is available to investors because current U.S. tax law provides for divergent tax treatment for economically equivalent financial instruments. The end result should be enhanced tax efficiency and therefore higher after-tax returns.

This chapter examines swaps and their potential application to private client portfolios. It describes several strategies whereby investors might use swaps to significantly enhance after-tax investment returns.

§ 8.1 Background

A *financial derivative* is a contract whose cash flows and value depend on the value of an underlying financial instrument, index, or commodity. In other words, the value of a financial derivative depends on, or derives from, the value of the underlying instrument. The four types of financial derivatives are options, futures, forwards, and swaps.

A *swap* is a contract in which two parties (the counterparties) agree to exchange streams of payments over a given period of time, based on the value of an underlying instrument. Subsequent periodic cash flows are computed with reference to a specific principal amount (called the *notional amount* because the amount does not actually change hands).

§ 8.1[a] The Swap Market

A swap can be custom tailored to satisfy the needs of the counterparties. The counterparties can, in essence, start with a blank sheet of paper and negotiate a contract that is completely dedicated to addressing their specific needs. The swap market is unregulated and investors must be "qualified swap participants" to assess the inherent risks.

To enter into a swap, one potential counterparty must first locate a counterparty willing to take the opposite side of the transaction. To be willing to take the opposite side, the swap dealer must be able to hedge the exposure inherent in the swap. Each of the counterparties must get comfortable with the creditworthiness of the other, since there is no exchange or other guarantor of performance. Many times collateral is posted by one or both of the parties. Because a swap is a privately negotiated transaction, a swap cannot be terminated early without the agreement of both parties.

Swaps were first used in the early 1980s to hedge interest rate and currency risks. Swap dealers soon recognized that swaps could be structured to deliver many other value-added solutions to investors, including private clients. Since then there has been an explosive growth in the use of swaps, primarily by corporations and financial institutions. If a swap dealer can get comfortable with the creditworthiness of the counterparty it will be facing, as well as its ability to hedge the underlying exposure inherent in the swap, it will often entertain the possibility of entering into a particular transaction.

§ 8.1[b] Tax Treatment

The basic tax treatment of swaps is fairly straightforward, but the implications of this treatment for taxable investors are stunning:

1. Any scheduled periodic payments made by the investor to the dealer under a swap should be currently deductible against ordinary income, subject to the 2 percent and 3 percent of adjusted gross income (AGI) limitations on miscellaneous itemized deductions. Any periodic payments received by the investor from the dealer should be ordinary income in the year of receipt. *Periodic payments* are those payable at intervals of one year or less throughout the term of the swap.
2. Any nonperiodic payments made by the investor to the dealer under a swap should be currently deductible against ordinary income in the year the payment was made, subject to the 2 percent and 3 percent of AGI limitations on miscellaneous itemized deductions. Any nonperiodic payments received by the investor from the dealer should be ordinary income in the year of receipt. *Nonperiodic payments* would include a single depreciation or appreciation payment scheduled to be made at the end of a multiyear swap.
3. If the swap is terminated or sold before its stated expiration date, any amount received by the investor from the dealer should be capital gain recognized in the year of termination. Any amount paid by the investor

to the dealer should be capital loss recognized in the year of termination. If the swap was held open for at least one year, the gain or loss should be long-term gain or loss.

Because payments made or received during a swap are ordinary income or loss but termination payments are capital in nature, the investor is given the opportunity to choose the tax treatment of the investment after the result is known.

For example, in the case of a loss on a swap that has been held open at least one year, the investor would likely choose to take an ordinary loss, which should be currently deductible against ordinary income at a 38.6 percent benefit, rather than take a capital loss, which would be deductible only against other capital gains and most likely at a 20 percent benefit. On the other hand, if the swap is profitable, the investor would likely terminate the swap before its stated maturity and generate a long-term capital gain taxed at 20 percent (18 percent if the swap was held open in excess of five years). Thus, a swap gives the investor the ability to keep 80 cents on the dollar of its winners but lose only 61.4 cents on the dollar of its losers! A swap is the only investment tool with this inherent advantage. Because of this "heads I win, tails you lose" advantage, swaps are truly the paradigm of investment tools.

§ 8.2 The Constructive Ownership Rules

Because of the above rules, many investors used swaps to synthetically own interests in hedge funds, which are notoriously tax inefficient. By doing so, investors were able to convert the ordinary income or short-term gains that would have been derived from direct ownership of the hedge fund into long-term capital gains, and to defer the recognition of income that would have been passed through if the investor held a direct ownership interest in a hedge fund operating as a partnership for federal tax purposes.

Section 1260 of the Internal Revenue Code (IRC), which was adopted as part of the Tax Relief Extension Act of 1999, was aimed at eliminating this tax planning opportunity. The enactment of IRC Section 1260, which deals with constructive ownership transactions, led many investors to believe that synthetically owning an investment through the use of a financial derivative can no longer alter the character of income or the timing of income recognition for federal income tax purposes. This is not the case.

The constructive ownership rules of IRC Section 1260 have limited application. They apply only with respect to derivative investments in certain pass-through entities. The term *pass-through entity* is defined under IRC Section 1260 to include a regulated investment company, a real estate investment trust, an S corporation, a partnership, a trust, a common trust fund, a passive foreign investment company, a foreign personal holding company, a foreign investment company, a real estate mortgage investment conduit, and a limited liability company. Thus, despite IRC Section 1260, it remains possible to use financial derivatives, including swaps, to acquire exposure to various types of underlying investments (as long as the underlying investment is not in the form of a pass-through entity).

§ 8.3 Entering an Investment Tax Efficiently Through a Swap

A taxable investor can use a swap to gain tax-efficient exposure (either long or short) to a single stock or an equity or fixed-income index, to a hedge fund index, and to an actively managed separate account.

§ 8.3[a] Investing in a Single Stock or an Index Through a Swap

By using a swap to economically establish a long position in the underlying stock or index, an investor is entitled to the economic attributes of ownership of the notional property; this means that the investor is eligible to receive any increase in the value of the referenced stock or index and any distributions made with respect to the stock or index. The investor is obligated to pay out any decrease in the value of the referenced stock or index, plus an interest equivalent based on the value of the referenced stock or index. Swaps are usually structured so that the interest-equivalent payments are made periodically throughout the term of the swap, but payments made with respect to the appreciation or depreciation in the value of the stock or index, as well as dividend-equivalent payments, are typically not made until the end of the swap. The cash that would have been directly invested in the stock or index is typically invested in high-quality, short-term fixed-income instruments, with the interest that is generated used to offset the interest-equivalent payments due under the swap. Exhibit A illustrates this structure, which is commonly referred to as the *long side of a total return swap.*

Exhibit A. Structure of an Equity Swap (Long Position)

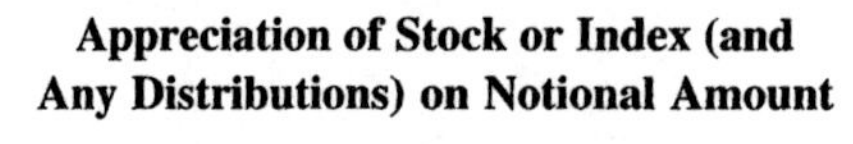

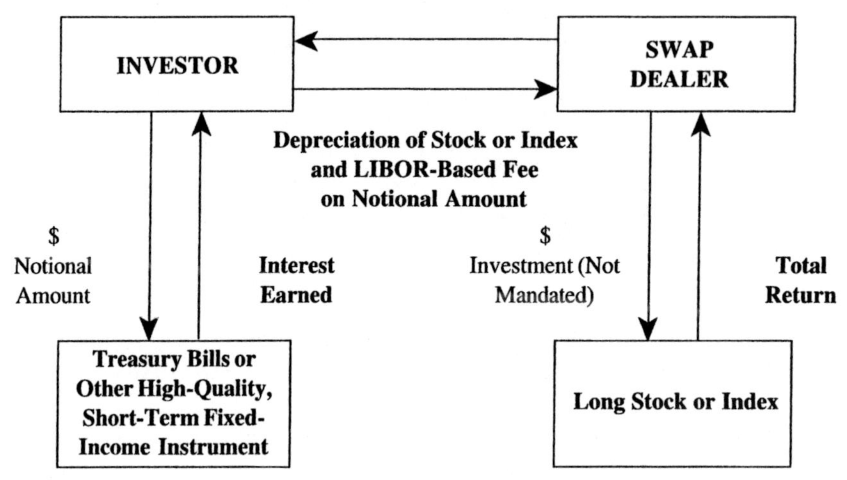

If the stock or index appreciates in value, the investor could terminate the swap before its stated maturity and generate long-term capital gain taxed at 20 percent (18 percent if the swap was held open in excess of five years). Alternatively, if the stock or index decreased in value, the investor could allow the swap to expire and generate an ordinary loss (with a potential 38.6 percent benefit).

An investor could also use a swap to economically establish a short position in a particular stock or index. Under this arrangement, the swap would be structured so that at the end of the swap the investor would pay the dealer any increase in the value of, as well as any distributions paid with respect to, the stock or index and would receive any decrease in the value of the stock or index. The investor would also periodically receive an interest-equivalent payment from the dealer (akin to the short interest rebate that is earned on short sale proceeds in a direct short sale of a security). Exhibit B illustrates this structure, which is commonly referred to as the *short side of a total return swap.*

Under IRC Section 1233, any gain recognized as the result of a direct short sale is generally treated as short-term capital gain regardless of the holding period. If the short seller were to establish the short position in the stock or index through a swap (instead of a direct short sale) and the swap were to remain open for at least a year, the investor could terminate the swap before its stated maturity and recognize a long-term capital gain on what would otherwise have been a short-term capital gain.

Exhibit B. Structure of an Equity Swap (Short Position)

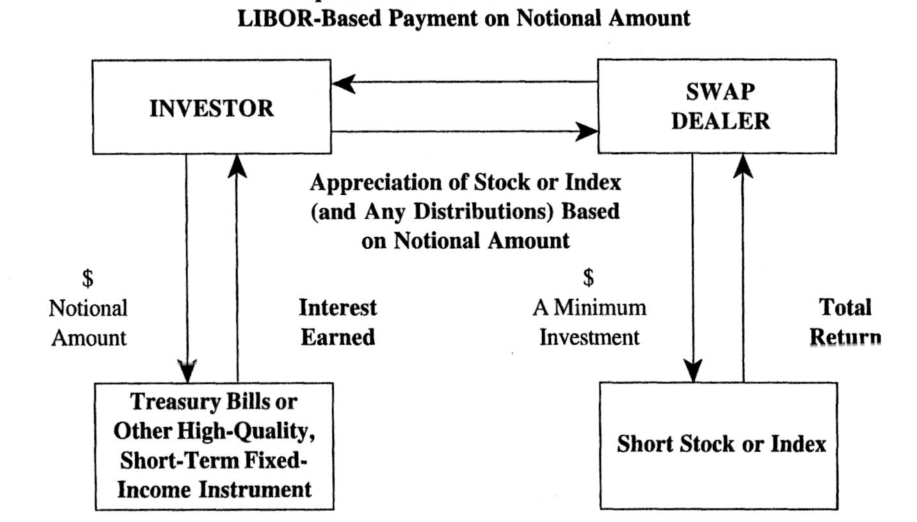

§ 8.3[b] Investing in a Hedge Fund Index Through a Swap

As discussed above (see §8.2), until 1999 investors often used swaps and other derivatives to synthetically own interests in particular hedge funds because of the tax advantages that were available (deferral of gain and conversion of ordinary income into long-term capital gain). Because of the constructive ownership rules, it is no longer possible for an investor to gain synthetic exposure to a particular hedge fund manager through a derivative in a tax-advantaged fashion.

Despite the constructive ownership rules, these tremendous tax advantages should still be available when investors employ a swap to participate in an index whose value is based on the composite performance of a number of hedge fund managers. More specifically, a properly structured swap should allow investors (1) to defer the recognition of all profits and capture these profits as long-term capital gains when the derivative is closed out and (2) to treat any losses as ordinary losses.

§ 8.3[b][1] Background on Hedge Fund Investing. In recent years investors have increasingly incorporated various alternative investments (especially hedge funds) into their asset allocation plans in an attempt to diversify their portfolios and reduce risk. Hedge fund managers typically specialize in a particular asset class or management style (e.g., merger arbitrage, convertible arbitrage, distressed securities, event driven, hedged equities). Most hedge funds are notoriously tax inefficient because there is usually a high degree of turnover in a hedge fund portfolio and investment income (e.g., short-term capital gains, dividend income, and interest income taxed at the ordinary rate) typically constitutes a significant portion of the total return of a hedge fund portfolio.

The way that most investors currently participate in the economics of hedge funds is through direct investment or through an actively managed fund of funds.

A second way of acquiring exposure to hedge funds, which is becoming increasingly popular with tax-exempt investors, is through an investment that has been specifically designed to deliver the total return of a particular hedge fund index. This passive approach offers investors diversification of managers within a particular style. The premise is that investors are more likely to improve portfolio performance by diversifying broadly across asset classes than by trying to identify active managers who can outperform benchmarks in their classes.

For instance, a 2001 study by Professors Amenc and Martellini found that within the most popular hedge fund index management styles, individual managers' performances tend to be similar. The study, entitled "The Brave New World of Hedge Fund Indexes," showed that for styles such as convertible arbitrage, emerging markets, event driven, merger arbitrage, short selling, and distressed securities, correlation among managers within the style ranged from 81 percent to 92 percent.

Based on this research, certain firms created hedge fund indexes based on the performance of a representative group of hedge fund managers that use a specific management style, including merger arbitrage, convertible arbitrage, distressed securities, event-driven multistrategy, and hedged equity. These firms then created a platform of separate accounts (with each account representing a different style of the hedge fund index), which they collectively oversee, with the objective of delivering the returns of the underlying index with minimal tracking error.

Although this approach lessens the risk of hedge fund investing by eliminating "specific manager risk," the investor does retain some degree of *basis risk* (which is the risk that the cash investment in the fund of funds does not perfectly correlate with the underlying index) and the approach is very tax inefficient, since the investor is taxed currently on any profits that are generated.

A third approach to acquiring exposure to hedge funds—a very intelligent one—is for the investor to gain exposure to one or more hedge fund style indexes directly (instead of to the account designed to track the index) through the use of a swap. This approach has three advantages:

1. It enables the investor to use a passive management approach to hedge fund investing.
2. It eliminates specific manager risk and basis risk.
3. It should greatly enhance the tax efficiency of the investment.

§ 8.3[b][2] Structure and Mechanics of a Hedge Fund Swap. The investor would enter into the long side of a total return swap with a derivatives manufacturer. For instance, if the investor wanted to make a $10 million investment in a hedge fund index, the dealer would agree to pay the investor any appreciation in the value of a $10 million investment, based on the performance of a specific hedge fund index. The investor would agree to pay the dealer any depreciation in the value of the index, and an interest-equivalent fee to compensate the dealer for the use of its capital. To offset the leverage inherent in the swap, during the term of the swap the investor could invest its $10 million of capital in short-term U.S. Treasury securities or some other highly rated, short-term fixed-income instrument. The interest earned would greatly offset (or possibly surpass) the interest-equivalent component of the swap. These securities would typically be pledged to the dealer as collateral. The dealer would most likely hedge itself by investing $10 million of its capital in the fund of funds that has been designed to track the index with minimal tracking error.

The swap could be structured so that the investor makes payments to the dealer periodically for the interest-equivalent fee and the dealer receives or makes only one payment to the investor on expiration of the swap. This payment would reflect the performance of the hedge fund index.

Exhibit C illustrates the basic structure of a hedge fund index swap.

Exhibit C. Structure of a Hedge Fund Index Swap

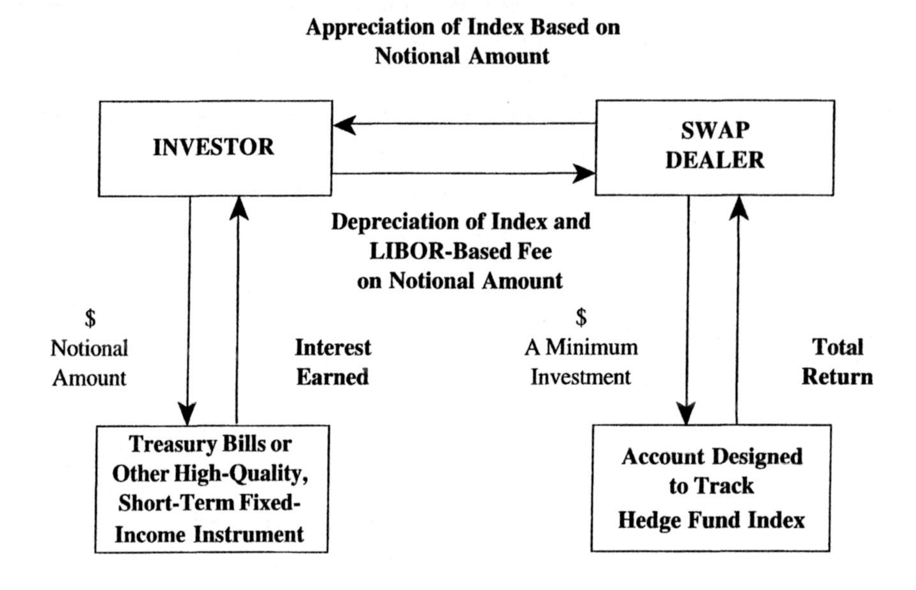

§ 8.3[b][3] Intriguing Tax Results. The constructive ownership rules should not prohibit an investor from using a swap (or other derivative) to gain exposure to a hedge fund index because their language limits their application to pass-through entities (see §8.2) and a hedge fund index clearly is not a pass-through entity. In general, profits (or losses) generated by derivative transactions, including swaps, are not taxed until they are closed out, so taxation of the hedge fund index returns should be deferred.

If a derivative is terminated before expiration, any gain (or loss) realized should be capital in nature. Thus, if a derivative contract is terminated after 12 months but before its stated expiration, any gain recognized at that time should be long-term capital gain. Therefore, investment income (such as dividends, interest, and short-term gains) that would otherwise be realized by the hedge funds and taxed currently at the ordinary rate (38.6 percent) should be deferred (until the derivative is terminated) and converted into long-term capital gain. Profits that would otherwise have been taxed currently as long-term capital gains should not be taxed until the derivative is closed out. Long-term capital gains are taxed at 20 percent if the derivative is held open less than five years and 18 percent if the investment is held open more than five years.

A benefit of a swap that is not available with other derivatives is that any periodic payments made under a swap by the investor to the dealer should be currently deductible against ordinary income (subject to the 2 percent and 3 percent of AGI limitations on miscellaneous itemized deductions). These would include the interest-equivalent fee and possibly a payment if the hedge fund index loses value during the term of the swap.

Similarly, any nonperiodic payments should be currently deductible against ordinary income. This would include a depreciation payment made by the investor on the expiration of the swap. Thus, if the swap is "underwater," the investor could let the swap expire and capture what would otherwise have been a capital loss as a deduction against ordinary income. This would not be the case if another type of derivative were utilized.

The overall effect of the hedge fund swap structure is to give the investment the look and feel of an investment within a tax-deferred annuity, with the added advantage that all profits are eventually taxed at the long-term capital gains rate but any losses could be currently deductible against ordinary income.

§ 8.3[c] Investing in an Actively Managed Separate Account Through a Swap

In recent years private clients and their professional advisers have increasingly used actively managed separate accounts in an effort to allocate and manage their investment assets more tax efficiently. The idea is that a separate account manager should be able to offset capital gains with capital losses, sell high-basis shares first, use lower turnover, and generally manage an individual's assets on a more customized and tax-friendly basis than a mutual fund or other pooled investment vehicle. Often more than one separate account is used (e.g., domestic large capitalization, domestic small capitalization, international equities, municipal bonds).

§ 8.3[c][1] Challenge Facing Taxable Investors Investing in Actively Managed Separate Accounts. Finding money managers that treat their taxable clients' portfolios significantly differently from their tax-exempt clients' portfolios is a most difficult undertaking. The universe of managers is small enough to warrant concern for lost alpha.

If a money manager could somehow manage its assets without concern for taxes, the money manager universe would not be constrained by tax considerations. A swap can be structured to accomplish this and managers can be selected on the basis of pretax returns.

§8.3[c][2] Structure and Mechanics of a Total Return Swap. The investor would enter into the long side of a total return swap with a derivatives manufacturer. For instance, if the investor wanted to make a $10 million investment with ABC Investment Advisers, the dealer would agree to pay the investor any appreciation in the value of a notional $10 million investment, based on the published performance of that investment adviser. (A problem arises if no official composite return is calculated.) The investor would agree to pay the dealer any depreciation in the value of the index, and an interest-equivalent fee to compensate the dealer for the use of its capital. To offset the inherent leverage of the swap, during the term of the swap the investor could invest its $10 million of capital in short-term U.S. Treasury securities or some other highly rated, short-term fixed-income instrument. The interest earned would greatly offset (and could possibly surpass) the interest-equivalent fee component of the swap. These securities would typically be pledged to the swap dealer as collateral.

The dealer would likely hedge itself by investing $10 million of its capital with ABC Investment Advisers. If the dealer invests, it will still run the risk that its account with ABC Investment Advisers will underperform the composite return that it is obligated to pay the investor pursuant to the swap.

Exhibit D illustrates the basic structure of a swap designed to gain exposure to the performance of a particular money manager.

Exhibit D. Structure of a Swap to Gain Exposure to a Particular Money Manager

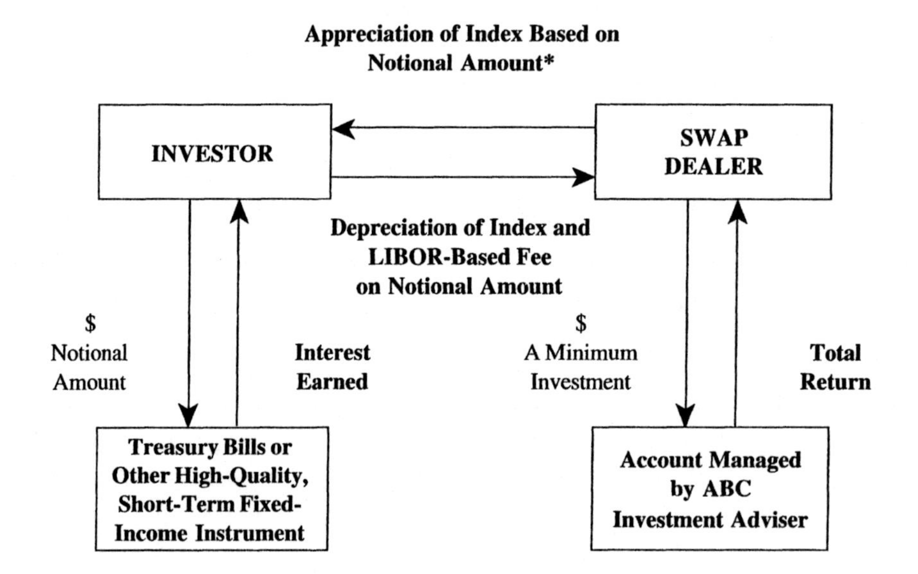

* The index is based on the composite performance of a group of accounts by ABC Investment Advisers with the same style.

§ 8.3[c][3] Intriguing Tax Results. Intriguing tax results are possible with swaps for taxable investors desirous of investing with one or more active managers.

First, the periodic payments (the interest-equivalent fee and possibly any portfolio losses) made by the investor to the dealer should be currently deductible against ordinary income, subject to the 2 percent and 3 percent of AGI limitations on miscellaneous itemized deductions. Therefore, capital losses, if any, should be effectively converted to ordinary deductions through the swap.

Second, if the swap is terminated before expiration, any gain or loss remaining in the swap should be capital in nature. Therefore, if the term of a swap exceeds 12 months and the swap is terminated at any time after 12 months, any gain remaining in the swap should be recognized at that time as long-term capital gain taxed at a rate of 20 percent. If the swap is terminated after five years, any gain should be recognized at that time as long-term capital gain taxed at a rate of 18 percent.

Therefore, investment income (such as dividends, interest, and short-term gains) that would otherwise be taxed currently at the ordinary (38.6 percent) rate should be deferred (until the swap is terminated) and converted into long-term capital gain. Likewise, gains that would otherwise be currently taxed as long-term capital gains should be deferred until the swap is terminated.

On the other hand, if the portfolio is underwater, the investor could let the swap expire and treat the remaining loss as a deduction against ordinary income.

IRC Section 1260 (the constructive ownership rules) should not prohibit an investor from using a swap (or other derivative) to gain exposure to a particular money manager (or managers) because its language limits its application to pass-through entities. Here the investor is not investing in a pass-through entity. Rather, the investment is in an index that is based on the composite performance of a group of accounts managed by a particular money manager with the same style.

§ 8.3[c][4] Summary of Tax and Nontax Advantages. A swap is a tool that allows taxable investors to synthetically invest with active managers and enjoy significant tax and nontax advantages. The potential tax advantages of gaining exposure to the performance of a particular money manager through a swap are as follows:

1. If the portfolio has appreciated, the investor can choose whether to receive ordinary income (by allowing the swap to expire) or long-term

capital gain (by holding the swap open at least 12 months and terminating the swap before expiration).

2. No taxable gain should be triggered until the swap either expires or is terminated before expiration.
3. Dividend income, interest income, and short-term capital gains that would have been earned in the account are effectively deferred and converted into long-term capital gains.
4. Gain that would otherwise be currently taxed as long-term capital gain should be deferred.
5. Portfolio losses should be deductible against ordinary income (subject to limitation), thereby converting what would otherwise be capital loss into ordinary deduction.
6. Wrapping the performance of a money manager with a swap should give the investment the look and feel of an investment within a tax-deferred annuity, with the added advantage that all profits should eventually be taxed at the long-term capital gains rate but all losses should be currently deductible against ordinary income.

The potential nontax advantages of this strategy are as follows:

1. Investors (and their advisers who assist in the asset allocation process) can evaluate portfolio managers solely on the basis of pretax returns, because tax efficiency should be achieved by virtue of the swap structure. The universe of managers that should be considered is therefore greatly increased.
2. Because a portfolio manager's buy, hold, and sell decisions are no longer constrained by tax considerations, one would expect the performance of the portfolio manager to be improved.

§ 8.4 When Swaps Are Not Respected

There are situations in which swaps are considered equivalent to the underlying investment for tax purposes:

1. *Wash sales.* Until recently tax practitioners thought that an investor with a sizable position in a depreciated security could sell shares and immediately reestablish the position by entering into the long side of a total return equity swap without running afoul of the wash sale rules. This belief was held on the basis that the rules applied only to stock and

securities and that swaps were not securities. On December 20, 2000, however, the wash sale rules were amended to include contracts that were settled in cash or property other than the stock sold. This amendment causes swaps to be captured by the wash sale rules, which disallow taking a loss if the investor enters into a contract to buy the same or substantially similar securities within 30 days.

2. *Constructive sale.* For instance, if an investor hedged with a total return equity swap, the transaction would be deemed a constructive sale. By embedding the economics of a collar within a swap (see §8.5), the swap can avoid being deemed a constructive sale if the possibility of gain or loss is retained by the investor.

§ 8.5 Exiting an Investment Tax Efficiently Through a Swap

As chapter 9 points out, there are two situations in which a swap (with the economics of a collar built into it) is clearly the financial derivative that minimizes the after-tax cost of hedging an appreciated stock position:

1. *Stock acquired before 1984.* If an investor acquired its stock before 1984, the straddle rules should not apply. In this situation a swap (with an embedded collar) is clearly the superior derivative tool for two reasons:

   a. If the underlying stock depreciates in value, the gain on the swap should be long-term capital gain. If the stock price increases, however, the loss on the swap can be ordinary (with a 38.6 percent benefit) or capital, whichever the investor chooses. Options-based collars and prepaid variable forwards do not share this latter advantage: Losses on either of these instruments would result in a long-term capital loss (with a probable 20 percent benefit).

   b. Because a swap is monetized through an explicit margin loan, the investor will incur investment interest expense that should be currently deductible against investment income (with a 38.6 percent benefit). By its very nature, a prepaid variable forward (which contains an implicit loan) defers and capitalizes (with a 20 percent benefit) the net carrying costs of the hedge.

2. *Hedging nonqualified employee stock options.* If an investor wants to hedge nonqualified employee stock options, the use of a swap (with an embedded collar) should deliver the optimal after-tax result. By using a

swap, if the underlying stock were to continue to increase in value (above the call strike embedded in the swap), there would not be a mismatch between the character of the income generated on the exercise of the nonqualified employee stock options (ordinary) and the loss generated on the expiration of the swap (also ordinary). Conversely, if an options-based collar or a prepaid variable forward was utilized to hedge nonqualified employee stock options, there would be a mismatch between the character of the income generated by the exercise of the nonqualified employee stock options (ordinary) and the loss generated on the closing out of the options or forward (capital). Since capital losses are deductible only against capital gains, unless the investor has capital gains the use of an options-based collar or a variable forward would result in an after-tax loss of 38.6 cents for every dollar rise in the price of the stock above the call strike of the hedge.

§ 8.6 Swap Spread

An individual investor who wants to (or is willing to) enter into a transaction betting on the relationship between two different investments should do so through two swaps (i.e., through a swap spread).

Two swaps can be managed to generate long-term capital gain and ordinary loss. Therefore, for an investor who has ordinary income, a swap spread should convert that ordinary income into long-term capital gain as long as the swap with the embedded gain is held open at least 12 months.

For the same reason, an investor who has capital loss carryforwards (and no offsetting gains) could use a swap spread to convert the nondeductible capital loss into a deductible ordinary loss. Here there would be no requirement that the transaction be held open for at least one year.

The basic concept is for the investor to enter into two offsetting swaps (e.g., a long and short position on two different underlying investments). The two positions must have material differences to provide economic substance for tax purposes. In addition, to achieve the desired tax result the position cannot constitute a straddle. A *straddle* exists when an investor holds one position that substantially diminishes the risk of loss of holding another position. To date, neither the statute nor the regulations have provided a clear definition of what constitutes a "substantial diminution" of risk; however, if the two positions leave the investor with substantial profit (or loss) potential, it is likely that the positions would not constitute a straddle.

If there were sufficient volatility, the swap with embedded gain would be terminated before its stated expiration, thereby generating a capital gain. The swap with the unrealized loss would continue until its stated expiration, thereby generating an ordinary deduction. The swap with the gain could be immediately replaced with an identical swap to maintain the economic integrity of the overall position. Here the wash sale rules should not be applicable because they do not apply to recognized gains. The flows on the replacement swap should also be treated as ordinary if the replacement swap is held to maturity.

Example 1. An investor who has a strong view regarding the relationship between interest rates on U.S. Treasury obligations and the London Interbank Offering Rate (LIBOR) might enter into the following transactions.

If the investor's tax advisers are confident that the transaction would not constitute a straddle, the investor would enter into two interest rate swaps with the same dealer. In one swap the investor would pay a floating amount and receive a fixed payment (long side of the swap). In the other swap the investor would receive a floating amount and pay a fixed amount (short side of the swap). The floating amount could be based on U.S. Treasury rates in one swap and could be based on LIBOR in the other swap. The fixed amount would be the same on each swap.

The use of the same counterparty can limit the amount of credit risk that the investor would have to assume to only the net profit on the two swaps.

As interest rates fluctuate over time, one swap should have a gain and the other swap should have a loss. If the relationship (spread) between the rates on Treasury obligations and LIBOR fluctuates, there will be either a net gain or a net loss on the overall transaction.

If the swap with the gain is terminated, the income recognized should produce a capital gain. The net payments made under the "loss" swap should continue to receive ordinary treatment (subject to the 2 percent and 3 percent of AGI limitations on miscellaneous itemized deductions). To preserve the economic integrity of the transaction, the investor could enter into a new swap (i.e., immediately replace the swap that was terminated).

According to Treasury Regulations Section 1.1221-2, interest rate swaps that are used to hedge a taxpayer's interest rate risk, if appropriately identified, should give rise to ordinary income or loss when closed; however, interest rate swaps that are entered into as an investment, or that are not appropriately identified, are not afforded ordinary treatment. In this transaction, the investor is taking a position with respect to two different interest rate indices, and the transaction is not identified as a hedging transaction. Therefore, the termination of the interest rate swaps should continue to give rise to capital gain or loss, as opposed to ordinary income, under the regulations.

Exhibit E is a spreadsheet analysis that examines the potential pretax and after-tax economics of swap spread. Exhibit E incorporates both the volatility of the underlying index, and the correlation (spread) between the long and short positions.

In general, the greater the volatility, the better, since more long-term capital gain and ordinary loss will be generated (and this generates the tax benefits). A change in the spread will result in either a net gain or a net loss. The risk is that the economic loss from a negative change in the spread will exceed the tax benefit resulting from the volatility of the underlying index.

Exhibit E. Hypothetical Swap Spread

Notional Value:	$160,000,000	Client Buys:	Swap on Treasuries
Ordinary Tax Rate $	39.1%	Client Sales:	Swap on LIBOR
Long-Term Tax Rate $	20.0%	Customer maintains a long exposure to the net spread.	

	Interest Rates		*Change in Net Spread* -6%	-4%	-2%	0%	2%	4%	6%
9.38%	**350**	Long Position	$15.0 mm	$15.0 mm	$15.0 mm	$15.0 mm	$15.0 mm	$15.0 mm	$15.0 mm
		Short Position	-$24.6 mm	-$21.4 mm	-$18.2 mm	-$15.0 mm	-$11.8 mm	-$8.6 mm	-$5.4 mm
		Net	-$9.6 mm	-$6.4 mm	-$3.2 mm	$0.0 mm	$3.2 mm	$6.4 mm	$9.6 mm
		After-Tax Net	-$3.0 mm	-$1.0 mm	$0.9 mm	$2.9 mm	$4.8 mm	$6.8 mm	$8.7 mm
6.25%	**340**	Long Position	$10.0 mm	$10.0 mm	$10.0 mm	$10.0 mm	$10.0 mm	$10.0 mm	$10.0 mm
		Short Position	-$19.6 mm	-$16.4 mm	-$13.2 mm	-$10.0 mm	-$6.8 mm	-$3.6 mm	-$0.4 mm
		Net	-$9.6 mm	-$6.4 mm	-$3.2 mm	$0.0 mm	$3.2 mm	$6.4 mm	$9.6 mm
		After-Tax Net	-$3.9 mm	-$2.0 mm	$0.0 mm	$1.9 mm	$3.9 mm	$5.8 mm	$7.8 mm
3.13%	**330**	Long Position	$5.0 mm	$5.0 mm	$5.0 mm	$5.0 mm	$5.0 mm	$5.0 mm	$5.0 mm
		Short Position	-$14.6 mm	-$11.4 mm	-$8.2 mm	-$5.0 mm	-$1.8 mm	$1.4 mm	$4.6mm
		Net	-$9.6 mm	-$6.4 mm	-$3.2 mm	$0.0 mm	$3.2 mm	$6.4 mm	$9.6 mm
		After-Tax Net	-$4.9 mm	-$2.9 mm	-$1.0 mm	$1.0 mm	$2.9 mm	$4.9 mm	$6.8 mm

	Interest Rates		*Change in Net Spread* -6%	-4%	-2%	0%	2%	4%	6%
0.00% $0.0 mm	**320**	Long Position	$0.0 mm	$0.0 mm	$0.0 mm	$0.0 mm	$0.0 mm	$0.0 mm	$0.0 mm
		Short Position	-$9.6 mm	-$6.4 mm	-$3.2 mm	$0.0 mm	$3.2 mm	$6.4 mm	$9.6 mm
		Net	-$9.6 mm	-$6.4 mm	-$3.2 mm	$0.0 mm	$3.2 mm	$6.4 mm	$9.6 mm
		After-Tax Net	-$5.8 mm	-$3.9 mm	-$1.9 mm	$0.0 mm	$2.6 mm	$5.1 mm	$7.7 mm
-3.13%	**310**	Long Position	-$5.0 mm	-$5.0 mm	-$5.0 mm	-$5.0 mm	-$5.0 mm	-$5.0 mm	-$5.0 mm
		Short Position	-$4.6 mm	-$1.4 mm	$1.8 mm	$5.0 mm	$8.2 mm	$11.4 mm	$14.6 mm
		Net	-$9.6 mm	-$6.4 mm	-$3.2 mm	$0.0 mm	$3.2 mm	$6.4 mm	$9.6 mm
		After-Tax Net	-$6.7 mm	-$4.2 mm	-$1.6 mm	$1.0 mm	$3.5 mm	$6.1 mm	$8.6 mm
-6.25%	**300**	Long Position	-$10.0 mm	-$10.0 mm	-$10.0 mm	-$10.0 mm	-$10.0 mm	-$10.0 mm	-$10.0 mm
		Short Position	$0.4 mm	$3.6 mm	$6.8 mm	$10.0 mm	$13.2 mm	$16.4 mm	$19.6 mm
		Net	-$9.6 mm	-$6.4 mm	-$3.2 mm	$0.0 mm	$3.2 mm	$6.4 mm	$9.6 mm
		After-Tax Net	-$5.8 mm	-$3.2 mm	-$0.7 mm	$1.9 mm	$4.5 mm	$7.0 mm	$9.6 mm
-9.38%	**290**	Long Position	-$15.0 mm	-$15.0 mm	-$15.0 mm	-$15.0 mm	-$15.0 mm	-$15.0 mm	-$15.0 mm
		Short Position	$5.4 mm	$8.6 mm	$11.8 mm	$15.0 mm	$18.2 mm	$21.4 mm	$24.6 mm
		Net	-$9.6 mm	-$6.4 mm	-$3.2 mm	$0.0 mm	$3.2 mm	$6.4 mm	$9.6 mm
		After-Tax Net	-$4.8 mm	-$2.3 mm	-$0.3 mm	$2.9 mm	$5.4 mm	$8.0 mm	$10.5 mm

After Tax NET assumes all gains are treated as long-term capital gains and all losses can be netted against ordinary income. There is no certainty of that, and investors should consult with their own tax advisers.

The net effect of a swap spread is that the investor will earn a profit if its views on the relationship (spread) between the two underlying investments proves to be correct. From a tax viewpoint, the transaction should produce capital gain and ordinary deductions. Thus, an investor with ordinary income could potentially convert that ordinary income into long-term capital gain and an investor with nondeductible capital loss carryforwards could convert these losses into currently deductible ordinary losses. As can be seen from Exhibit E, very little can be lost pretax in the swap spread before any after-tax profit is wiped out.

CHAPTER 9

Tax-Efficient Single Stock Concentration Risk Management—The State of the Art

Thomas J. Boczar

Synopsis

The extreme volatility the stock market has experienced has caused many investors who hold a single concentrated stock position with a low cost basis to explore strategies to enable them to hedge and monetize their positions without triggering a taxable event.

Most derivative dealers and investors seem oblivious to the fact that the economics of hedging and monetization can be achieved through several types of financial derivatives, including options, swaps, and forwards, and that each derivative tool can result in significantly different tax consequences depending on an investor's situation. For example, virtually the entire dealer community is currently touting an instrument called a prepaid variable forward as the preferred tool to use in almost every situation where monetization is the objective, even though that instrument will rarely deliver the optimal after-tax result.

This chapter assesses the alternative hedging and monetization strategies that currently exist in the marketplace and should help professional financial advisers select the diversification tool that achieves the desired economics while minimizing an investor's after-tax cost.

§ 9.1 Investor Objectives

Ideally, an investor holding a concentrated position in an appreciated stock would like to achieve the following:

1. Hedge—hedge against a decrease in the value of the stock;
2. Defer and eliminate capital gains tax—avoid triggering a current taxable event and still qualify for a step-up in basis at death;[1] and

3. Gain liquidity—monetize the position (i.e., currently receive in cash a substantial portion of the market value of the stock) to diversify into other investments.

§ 9.2 Short Against the Box Is the Paradigm

Before enactment of the Taxpayer Relief Act of 1997 (TRA '97) and the constructive sale rules, the short against the box strategy was the cheapest and most efficient tool for achieving the objectives listed in § 9.1.

Although the constructive sale rules have generally eliminated the use of the short against the box, it is important to have a basic understanding of its economics for two reasons. First, it remains possible for an investor, with respect to certain situations involving merger arbitrage, to establish a short against the box that should not be subject to the constructive sale rules. Second, the short against the box remains the paradigm that all financial derivative-based hedging and monetization strategies attempt to replicate as closely as possible without violating the constructive sale rules.

In a short against the box, the investor is simultaneously long and short the same number of shares of the same stock and therefore completely hedged.[2] The fully hedged position will earn close to the risk-free rate of return on 100 percent of its value. Because the position is fully hedged, the investor can borrow up to 95 percent (99 percent in certain situations) of its value. Although there is a cost associated with the borrowing, the income generated by the hedged position greatly offsets (and might even exceed) the cost of borrowing, making monetization very inexpensive. Before enactment of the constructive sale rules, the long and short positions were treated separately for tax purposes and therefore the capital gains tax was deferred; and because the long shares qualified for a step-up in basis at death, an investor who kept the short against the box open until death completely eliminated the capital gains tax.[3]

From a tax perspective, before enactment of the constructive sale rules, the form of the transaction (rather than its economic substance) controlled. Section 1259 of the Internal Revenue Code (IRC), commonly referred to as the constructive sale rules, focuses on the economic substance (rather than the form) of a hedging transaction.

Under the constructive sale rules, investors should engage in a three-pronged analysis to ensure that they use the most tax-efficient hedging strategy:

1. Can the investor establish a short against the box position that avoids the application of the constructive sale rules? If so, this is clearly the preferred choice.
2. If this is not possible, can the investor synthetically replicate the cash flows and payoff profile of the short against the box fairly closely without triggering a constructive sale?
3. Are there alternative strategies (to a short against the box or derivative-based solution) that might be appropriate in a particular case?

§ 9.3 Establishing a Short Against the Box Not Subject to the Constructive Sale Rules

It is common for one corporation to acquire another pursuant to a tax-free stock-for-stock reorganization (a merger). Establishing a short position in the acquirer's stock in an announced stock-for-stock merger presents an intriguing investment opportunity for investors who own an appreciated stock position in the target. If the merger occurs, the investor will have established a short against the box position that should not be subject to the constructive sale rules.

Under these rules, an investor is deemed to have made a constructive sale (which is a taxable event) of an "appreciated financial position" (e.g., low-basis stock) if the investor enters into a short sale of the "same or substantially identical property." The term *substantially identical* is not defined under the IRC.

If an investor owning stock of the target enters into a short sale of the acquirer's stock at a time when considerable deal risk exists (e.g., before regulatory approvals have been obtained and before the shareholder votes approving the transaction), for tax purposes the investor should not be deemed to have entered into a short sale of substantially identical property. Further, because there is no constructive sale, the provisions of TRA '97 that deny the step-up in basis to certain investors who have entered into a short against the box would not apply.

On consummation of a stock-for-stock merger, long positions in the target's stock are automatically converted into long positions in the acquirer's stock. Thus, if the investor starts out with a long position in the target's stock and shorts the acquirer, the end result (if the deal closes) is a short against the box in the acquirer's stock, which could be kept open for a long-term period (e.g., until death).

It is worth reiterating what is accomplished by establishing a short against the box. First, the investor is perfectly hedged; that is, it is no longer economically exposed to the stock. Second, a taxable event would not be triggered until the investor closes out the short position. In fact, the investor could hold the short against the box position open until death and qualify for the step-up in basis on the long position, thereby avoiding any capital gains tax on the appreciated long stock. Third, the investor could monetize (i.e., receive in cash) up to 99 percent of the value of the long position to diversify into other investments. Fourth, the cost of the monetiztion would be very cheap because the interest earned on short sale proceeds will greatly offset the cost of borrowing (and in certain circumstances can exceed it) and the straddle rules do not apply (i.e., it is clear that the interest expense that is incurred is currently deductible for tax purposes).

What is likely to happen if the deal collapses? On announcement of a stock-for-stock merger, investors and arbitrageurs typically purchase the stock of the target and sell (or sell short) the stock of the acquirer. Therefore, the stock price of the target typically increases while the stock price of the acquiring corporation often decreases. If the deal collapses, it is likely that the stock price of the target would decrease and the stock price of the acquirer would recover. In this case, an investor who is long the target and short the acquirer typically would suffer a loss. If, however, another potential acquirer entered the picture, offering a higher price for the target, the target's stock price would likely increase, benefiting the investor who is long the target.

Because the investor already owns shares of the target, there is no additional risk assumed on the long side; however, the investor will be naked short shares of the acquirer until the deal closes. (When the deal closes, a short against the box position is automatically established.) If the investor wants to hedge the risk of the short position, it could collar the short position with a reverse collar (i.e., sell a put with a strike price below the short sale price and buy a call with a strike price above the short sale price). Such a reverse collar could be structured to expose the investor to enough risk that the constructive sale rules should not apply.

In conclusion, if an investor holds an appreciated stock position in a target corporation that is involved in a tax-free stock-for-stock merger, the investor could establish a short position in the acquirer's stock before the completion of regulatory approvals and shareholder votes (i.e., at a time when the transaction is not yet a "done deal"). If the deal is consummated, the investor will have established a short against the box position with all its attendant benefits (allowing the investor to hedge, monetize, and defer taxes on the low-basis stock position) that should not be subject to the constructive sale rules. If the deal falls apart, the investor could realize a gain or suffer a loss, depending on the movement of the acquirer's and target's stock prices.

A similar opportunity could exist if the investor is long the acquirer and shorts the shares of the target. Additionally, owners of privately held companies whose companies are being acquired by public companies may be able to use the strategy to establish a short against the box in the acquirer's stock. In each of these situations, additional issues that are beyond the scope of this chapter need to be considered.

§ 9.4 Synthetically Replicating the Short Against the Box—Income-Producing Collars

If the merger arbitrage strategy is not available (and in most cases it will not be), the investor must examine what type of derivative-based strategy would deliver the desired hedging and monetization economics, as well as the optimal tax treatment.

Under the constructive sale rules, a particular type of equity collar—the income-producing collar[4]—has emerged as the preferred strategy because it remains possible to replicate the cash flows of the short against the box fairly closely while avoiding the constructive sale rules.

Specifically, by structuring an equity collar with a fairly tight band around the current price of the stock, an investor can minimize (within certain limits) exposure to price movement of the underlying stock, monetize the position, and generate positive cash flow that can be used to offset the cost of monetization, while deferring the capital gains tax and possibly eliminating it (by still qualifying for a step-up in basis at death).

To avoid a constructive sale, an income-producing collar should be no tighter than 15 percent around the current price of the stock. For instance, if a stock is currently trading at $100 per share, an investor might buy protection below $95 and sell off all upside potential above $110.

The House and Senate committee reports on the constructive sale rules both contain an example of what they deemed a standard collar. The example uses a 95 percent put/110 percent call equity collar. Although the committee reports express no view on whether this collar is abusive (and would therefore trigger a constructive sale), this example was most likely included to give investors some practical guidance as to what type of equity collar would not trigger a constructive sale. [H.R. Rep. No. 105–148 (1997); S. Rep. No. 105–133 (1997)]

The cash flows of this type of collar resemble a short against the box but should not trigger a constructive sale.

§ 9.5 Potential Impact of the Straddle Rules

Because the economics (hedging and monetization) of an equity collar can be achieved through the use of several tools (options, swaps, and forwards) and each of these tools can result in very different tax consequences depending on an investor's situation, investors and their professional advisers should engage in an analysis to ensure that the derivative tool that is used is the one most likely to minimize the investor's after-tax cost of implementing the collar. Whether or not the straddle rules of IRC Section 1092 apply is critical in the selection of the most appropriate tool.

A *straddle* exists when holding one position substantially reduces the risk of holding another. Because an equity collar substantially reduces the risk of owning the underlying stock, the stock and collar together should be treated as a straddle for federal tax purposes.

Investors face two negative ramifications from their stock and collar being deemed a straddle:

1. Any loss realized from closing one leg of a straddle must be deferred to the extent there is unrealized gain on the open leg. Thus, as a collar expires, is terminated, or is rolled forward, any losses must be deferred. Gains are currently taxed.
2. Interest expense incurred to "carry a straddle" must be capitalized (as opposed to being currently deductible). There has been (and continues to be) spirited debate about the methodology to be applied in determining the amount, if any, of the interest expense that must be capitalized under IRC Section 263(g).

§ 9.6 Analysis for Stock Acquired Before 1984

The straddle rules should not apply to stock that was acquired before January 1, 1984. Therefore, if stock was acquired before 1984, a collar can be implemented without triggering the straddle rules.[5] This creates significant tax planning opportunities.

§ 9.6[a] The Tools

The three hedging tools that can produce the economics of a collar are options, which can be either listed or over the counter; prepaid variable forwards; and swaps with an embedded collar.

In most situations the optimal tool to hedge and monetize an appreciated stock acquired before 1984 will be a swap containing an embedded collar monetized through a margin loan. The two other possible tools—options-based collars monetized through a margin loan and prepaid variable forwards—produce less favorable tax consequences.

§ 9.6[a][1] Options. Options-based collars involve the simultaneous purchase of puts and sale of calls on the underlying stock. The options eliminate the potential for loss below the put strike price and for profits above the call strike price.

> **Example.** An investor holding ABC Corp. shares that currently trade at $100 might buy a put with a strike price of $95 and sell a call with a strike price of $110 and then borrow against the hedged position (or other publicly traded securities) to monetize the position.

§ 9.6[a][2] Prepaid Variable Forward. A *prepaid variable forward* is an agreement to sell a security at a fixed time in the future, with the number of shares to be delivered at maturity varying with the underlying share price. The agreement effectively has the economics of a collar combined with a borrowing against the underlying stock embedded within it.

> **Example.** An investor holding ABC Corp. shares currently trading at $100 might enter into a prepaid variable forward that requires the dealer to pay the investor $88 at the start of the contract in exchange for the right to receive a variable number of shares from the investor in three years pursuant to a preset formula that embodies the economics of a collar (e.g., a long put with a $95 strike and a short call with a $110 strike).
>
> The formula would require the investor to deliver all its ABC Corp. shares if the price of ABC in three years was less than $95. If the price of ABC was greater than $95 but less than $110, the investor would deliver $95 worth of shares. If the price of ABC was above $110, the investor would keep $15 worth of shares and deliver the remainder to the dealer.[6]

§ 9.6[a][3] Swap. A *swap* is an agreement between an investor and a highly rated dealer with payments referenced to the price of a particular stock and covering a particular dollar amount (called the notional amount). Under a swap agreement, the investor could agree to pay the dealer any appreciation above a specified share price (e.g., the strike price of the embedded short call) plus any dividends paid on the stock. The dealer in turn could agree to pay the investor any depreciation below a specified share price (e.g., the strike price of the embedded long put) plus an interest-based fee on the notional amount.

> **Example.** An investor holding ABC Corp. shares currently trading at $100 could enter into a swap agreement to pay the dealer any appreciation above $110 plus any dividends paid on the stock while the dealer could agree to pay the investor any depreciation below $95 plus an interest-based fee on $100. The investor could then borrow against the hedged position (or against other publicly traded securities) to monetize the position.

§ 9.6[b] Tax Analysis

§ 9.6[b][1] Settling the Collar. Options-based collars and prepaid variable forwards are afforded essentially the same tax treatment.

A decrease in the price of the stock below the put strike will create long-term capital gain. Conversely, an increase in the price of the stock above the call strike will produce a long-term capital loss, which will be subject to the limitations discussed below.

Long-term capital losses are subject to very specific netting rules. Long-term capital losses must first be used to offset long-term capital gains that would otherwise be taxed at 20 percent. Only then can they be used to offset short-term capital gains that would otherwise be taxed at the ordinary rate.[7] Any remaining net capital losses can then be used to offset a maximum of $3,000 of ordinary income that would otherwise be taxed at the ordinary rate.

Unfortunately, because of the netting rules, when settling an options-based collar or prepaid variable forward where the stock price has appreciated well beyond the call strike, the investor will likely achieve only a 20 percent benefit (as opposed to a benefit at the ordinary rate) from the resulting loss.

> **Example.** In the example in § 9.6[a][1], the investor implemented a $95 put strike/$110 call strike collar. If the stock increases to $200 at expiration of the collar, the $90 difference between the then-current price

> ($200) and the call strike ($110) less the premium received will be treated as a long-term capital loss.
>
> Most likely the investor will sell $90 of the underlying stock to fund its settlement obligation. If the investor has achieved a long-term holding period on the shares that were sold and those shares have a zero basis, the investor will recognize a $90 long-term capital gain. Under the netting rules, the $90 long-term capital loss must first offset the $90 long-term capital gain. Here the $90 long-term capital loss cannot be used to offset other short-term gains or ordinary income that the investor might have generated. Thus, the value of the loss is only 20 percent.

Swaps receive more favorable tax treatment. All payments made or received under the terms of a swap agreement should generate either ordinary income or loss; however, a termination of a swap agreement should generate either capital gain or loss. Thus, with proper planning an investor using a swap should be able to recognize either capital gain or ordinary loss.

For instance, if the underlying stock declines in value below the embedded put strike, the investor could terminate the swap before its stated expiration date, creating long-term capital gain. If the stock increases in value above the embedded call strike, the swap could be allowed to run until its stated expiration, with the resulting loss treated as an ordinary loss, which should be deductible against ordinary income that would otherwise have been taxed at the ordinary rate.

It must be pointed out that the loss on the swap plus all of the investor's "other" itemized deductions must exceed 2 percent of the investor's adjusted gross income (AGI) to be deductible. After this hurdle is met, the deductible amount is reduced by 3 percent of the taxpayer's AGI. The deduction is also disallowed for alternative minimum tax purposes. Therefore, if the stock price exceeds the embedded call strike near expiration of the swap, the investor must determine whether it is better to generate an ordinary deduction, subject to these limitations, or a capital loss. The swap affords the investor the choice.

In this regard, it is worth pointing out that an investor who uses a swap will never be worse off than if he or she had used an options-based collar or a prepaid variable forward. That is, if the 2 percent and 3 percent of AGI limitations on miscellaneous itemized deductions prohibit the investor from receiving the full benefit of the ordinary deduction, the investor would simply terminate the swap before its stated expiration date and recognize a long-term capital loss, which is what the investor would have recognized anyway if he or she had used an options-based collar or a prepaid variable forward. Put another way, a swap can only deliver a potentially better result (never a worse result) than an options-based collar or a prepaid variable forward.

§ 9.6[b][2] Deductibility of Interest Expense. Because the straddle rules do not apply to stock acquired before 1984, there should be no question that investment interest expense incurred for the use of the monetization proceeds is currently deductible against investment income (e.g., dividends, interest, and short-term gains) otherwise taxed at the ordinary rate.

Because both a swap with an embedded collar and an options-based collar can be monetized through a margin loan (secured by the hedged position and/or other publicly traded securities), the investor will incur investment interest expense that is currently deductible against investment income. With a prepaid variable forward, however, the investor cannot achieve this favorable tax result. Instead, the investor is forced to defer and capitalize the net cost of borrowing.

> **Example.** In the example in § 9.6[a][2] the investor holding ABC Corp. shares currently trading at $100 entered into a prepaid variable forward embodying the economics of a collar (i.e., a long put with a $95 strike and a short call with a $110 strike) that required the dealer to pay the investor $88 at the start of the contract.
>
> The difference between the $95 put strike (i.e., the sales price) and the $88 advance is mostly the net cost of borrowing. Unfortunately, a deduction for this expense cannot occur until the underlying shares are actually delivered to close out the contract. Because the forward has a term of three years, the deduction will be deferred for at least this period.
>
> If the investor cash settles and rolls over the forward for another three-year term, the deferred expense merely increases the investor's basis in the stock. If the investor then dies, he or she will never receive the benefit of a deduction; there will simply be less tax forgiven at death.
>
> In addition, because the expense of borrowing is capitalized, the value of the deduction will be slashed from the ordinary rate to 20 percent. Assume that three years from now the price of ABC Corp. stock is less than $95 per share and that the investor decides to physically settle the forward by delivering shares to the dealer. The investor will then be taxed on the difference between the advance received up front ($88) and his or her basis in the stock that was delivered. That is, the investor is not taxed on the difference between the sales price ($95) and the amount received up front ($88). If the investor had achieved a long-term holding

period before entering into the forward, the benefit of the deduction will have been dramatically reduced.

§ 9.6[b][3] Tax Disadvantage of Swaps. Swaps have one slight potential tax disadvantage: Any payment received during the swap's term (whether an up-front payment or one received periodically) will be deemed ordinary income currently subject to tax. The only payment that the investor would be scheduled to receive (periodically) from the dealer during the term of the swap would be an interest-equivalent fee based on the notional amount.

§ 9.6[b][4] Recent Tax Developments. Proposed Treasury regulations published on January 17, 2001, with respect to the straddle rules would change the ground rules for hedging stock acquired after 1983. These proposed regulations should not, however, in any way impact stock that was acquired before 1984.[8]

In addition, the IRS released a field service advice (FSA) in 2000 relating to the taxation of a financial instrument that economically resembled a prepaid variable forward.[9] The IRS concluded that the investor was required to recognize gain on entering into the transaction. The IRS's rationale was that the benefits and burdens of ownership of the underlying shares had shifted to the purchasers of the instrument. This conclusion was reached notwithstanding that the investor retained the right to vote the underlying shares, was entitled to receive dividends paid with respect to the stock, and had the right to substitute collateral for the underlying shares.

Although the FSA is troubling with respect to prepaid variable forwards, it should not be fatal. An FSA is essentially an informal letter issued by the IRS National Office to an IRS examining agent. These letters are not considered binding on other taxpayers. In many cases, the analysis simply reflects the IRS's views on a particular transaction without the benefit of having competing positions thoroughly considered. Accordingly, the letters tend to side with the IRS examining agent. Nevertheless, the FSA points out that prepaid variable forwards are not immune from IRS attack.

Recent IRS Revenue Ruling 2003-7 concluded that prepaid variable forwards generally do not constitute constructive sales. The ruling essentially supersedes FSA 200111011, which suggested the opposite.

The ruling concerned a taxpayer who entered into a prepaid variable "forward contract"—defined by IRC Section 1259(d)(1) as a contract to deliver a substantially fixed amount of property for a substantially fixed price—on a holding of low-basis stock. Under the terms of the forward contract, a number of shares to be delivered on the exchange date was dependent on the market value of the stock on that date. Because of this variation, the ruling found that the forward contract did not cause a constructive sale under IRC Section 1259(c)(1)(C).

The ruling noted that the legislative history of the Code suggested that significant variation on the number of shares to be delivered would cause the contract to fail to meet the definition of a forward contract. In addition, the investor pledged the maximum number of shares for which the investment bank could require the delivery under the contract. The IRS ruled that the pledging of the shares (held by custodian, in this case) did not have an adverse tax effect on the transaction. This was due in part to the fact that the investor had the unrestricted right to substitute cash or other shares for the pledged shares and kept the voting right. This revenue ruling should ease concerns raised by FSA 200111011.

§ 9.6[c] Swaps—The Superior Tool for Stock Acquired Before 1984

Based on the above analysis, swaps are the superior tool for hedging and monetizing stock acquired before 1984. If the underlying stock depreciates in value, the gain on the swap should be long-term capital gain. If the stock increases in value, the loss on the swap can be ordinary or capital, whichever is more beneficial to the investor. In addition, because a swap is monetized through a margin loan, the investor will incur investment interest expense that is currently deductible against investment income. Options-based collars and prepaid variable forwards produce less favorable tax treatment.

Options-based collars receive essentially the same treatment as swaps if the underlying stock decreases in value; and because monetization occurs through a margin loan, the investor will incur investment interest expense that is currently deductible against investment income. Options receive less favorable treatment than swaps if the stock increases in value.

Prepaid variable forwards receive essentially the same tax treatment as swaps if the underlying stock decreases in value, but receive less favorable treatment if the stock increases in value. Prepaid variable forwards also require the investor to defer and capitalize the net cost of borrowing.

Although all three tools achieve virtually the same economics, for an investor who acquired his or her stock before 1984 swaps should usually produce a superior after-tax result.

Exhibit A compares and contrasts the tax treatment of the three available financial derivative-based hedging and monetization strategies—swaps, options, and forwards—for stock acquired before 1984.

Exhibit A. Tax Treatment of Alternative Hedging and Monetization Techniques for Stock Acquired Before 1984

	If an investor implements a monetizing collar through		
	Options and Margin Loans	*A Prepaid Forward (with an Embedded Collar)*	*An Equity Swap (with an Embedded Collar and Margin Loans)*
Should carrying costs be currently deductible against investment income (38.6% benefit)?	Yes	No	Yes
When the collar is a cash-settling collar and the stock price is above the call strike, what is the character of the loss?	Long-term capital loss	Long-term capital loss	Ordinary deduction or long-term capital loss at investor's discretion

	If an investor implements a monetizing collar through		
	Options and Margin Loans	*A Prepaid Forward (with an Embedded Collar)*	*An Equity Swap (with an Embedded Collar and Margin Loans)*
When the collar is a cash-settling collar and the stock price is below the put strike, what is the character of the gain?	Long-term capital gain	Long-term capital gain	Long-term capital gain or ordinary income at investor's discretion

§ 9.7 Analysis for Stock Acquired After 1983

The objective for the investor who owns stock that was acquired after 1983 is to mitigate the negative impact of the straddle rules (see § 9.5) as much as possible.

§ 9.7[a] Evolution of the Single-Contract Collar

Investors can address the first negative ramification of the straddle rules (i.e., getting "whipsawed"; see § 9.5) using an over-the-counter derivative contract that encompasses both a put and a call.

Example. Assume that XYZ Corp. stock is selling at $100 per share. The investor constructs a three-year zero-cost collar on the stock (with either listed or over-the-counter options), buying puts struck at $90 for $14 and selling calls struck at $160 for $14. If the collar expires with the stock price between $90 and $160, the investor faces a tax of $5.40 (38.6 percent of the $14 short-term capital gain) on each expired call; however, the investor cannot currently deduct the "wasted" $14 cost of the puts, which is a deferred long-term capital loss. The investor created economic protection and some potential for profit, but the after-tax cost is more than $5 per share (with no actual profits realized).

Suppose that instead of buying separate puts and calls, the investor hedges XYZ by employing a one-contract collar. With this approach, the investor could create the same economic structure—effectively buying puts at $90 and selling calls at $160; however, when a zero-cost collar is documented using a single contract, the price of the collar for tax purposes should be zero even if the straddle rules do apply. Thus, if the collar expires with the stock price anywhere between $90 and $160, the expiration should not create any taxable income or loss. The investor has created the same level of economic protection and potential for profit without being whipsawed for tax purposes.

Unfortunately, it is not currently possible to implement a single-contract collar with listed options because the documentation that is currently used by the options exchanges treats the put and call as separate contracts. Some practitioners are encouraging the exchanges to develop this type of collar. It is possible, however, to implement a single-contract collar with over-the-counter options.

With respect to a swap with an embedded collar or a variable forward, the amount received for the embedded call and the amount paid for the embedded put will also net against each other automatically because of the nature of those instruments.

In this regard, an equity swap with an embedded collar is slightly tax disadvantaged compared with an options-based collar or a prepaid variable forward because any payments received by the investor up front or during the swap's term will be taxed currently as ordinary income, whereas a single-contract options-based collar or a variable forward would allow such a payment to be part of an open transaction with the taxation deferred. During the term of the swap the investor would be scheduled to receive an interest-equivalent fee periodically from the dealer based on the notional amount.

No matter where the stock price is on the expiration date, an over-the-counter options-based collar documented as a single contract and variable forwards should receive essentially the same tax treatment when settling the collar.

Listed options are tax disadvantaged because of the current inability to net the option premiums.

§ 9.7[b] Tax Analysis—Deductibility of Interest Expense

In addition to hedging, most investors with appreciated stock want to generate liquidity to reinvest and diversify their investments. Often investors choose to monetize, or borrow against, their appreciated stock. Borrowing creates interest expense. If the borrowing cost occurs in conjunction with a straddle, the interest expense may need to be capitalized.

The proposed Treasury regulations published on January 17, 2001, with respect to the straddle rules make clear that if shares that are hedged by a collar are pledged as collateral for a borrowing, the interest must be capitalized;[10] however, the regulations do give an investor the right to specify which shares form a straddle and which are being leveraged. A careful identification of collateral will preclude the IRS from allocating (and therefore capitalizing) any of the borrowed proceeds against the shares that have been collared. Because of this "specific identification" rule, if an investor has publicly traded securities (other than the collared shares) to post as collateral, it would still be possible to deduct some or all of the interest expense.

> **Example.** Assume an investor with $100 of XYZ Corp. stock wants to hedge the stock with either an options-based collar or a variable forward that is not prepaid[11] and then monetize the maximum amount possible under the margin rules (Regulation T) in order to diversify. The investor could borrow $50 against the hedged XYZ position. If the investor diversifies into publicly traded securities, the investor could then finance the purchase of $100 of reinvestment securities through an additional $50 margin loan against the reinvestment portfolio. Under the proposed regulations, the interest expense incurred by borrowing against the hedged XYZ position must be capitalized, while the interest expense incurred by borrowing against the reinvestment portfolio is deductible.
>
> Suppose instead that an investor with $200 of XYZ Corp. stock wants to hedge $100 of XYZ with either an options-based collar or a variable forward that is not prepaid and then monetize $100 in order to diversify.

The investor could borrow $50 against the unhedged XYZ position. If the investor diversifies into publicly traded securities, the investor could then finance the purchase of $100 of reinvestment securities through an additional $50 margin loan against the reinvestment portfolio.

Under the proposed regulations, both the interest expense incurred by borrowing against the unhedged XYZ position and the interest expense incurred by borrowing against the reinvestment portfolio are deductible because there was no borrowing against the collared position.

Therefore, under the proposed regulations investors can readily monetize options-based collars (as well as variable forwards that are not prepaid and swaps with embedded collars) through margin loans and in most instances still achieve a current deduction for some or all of the interest expense incurred with respect to the monetization. In certain instances, however, it might be necessary to use a prepaid variable forward to achieve the monetization level that is desired because of margin rule (Regulation T) limitations.

Example. Assume that an investor with $100 of XYZ Corp. stock wants to hedge the stock with a collar and then monetize the maximum amount possible in order to diversify into a portfolio of investments that are not publicly traded (e.g., alternative investments, such as hedge funds).

If an investor hedges the XYZ position with an options-based collar, a variable forward that is not prepaid, or a swap with an embedded collar combined with a margin loan, a maximum of $50 could be borrowed against the hedged XYZ position under Regulation T. It will not be possible to borrow against the reinvestment portfolio because it consists of investments that are not publicly traded securities and hence cannot be given collateral value by a brokerage firm. Only $50 could be monetized, and under the proposed regulations all of the interest expense would need to be capitalized because the borrowing was incurred against a collared position.

If the investor instead used a prepaid variable forward, the investor would most likely be able to monetize between 85 percent and 90 percent of the value of the position because the Regulation T limitations do not apply to prepaid variable forwards. Although the nature of a prepaid variable forward effectively defers and converts interest expense into a deferred capital loss, in this instance there is no tax disadvantage because if margin loans were used to monetize the position, the interest expense would have to be capitalized because the borrowing is against the collared stock.

In sum, investors have the right under the proposed regulations to specify the collateral pledged to secure margin indebtedness. If the interest expense is incurred by borrowing against securities that are unhedged, the investor currently can deduct such expense; otherwise, it must be capitalized.

Therefore, the monetization structure that should deliver optimal after-tax results should be either an option-based collar or variable forward that is not prepaid combined with a margin loan. A prepaid variable forward is tax disadvantaged because its structure ensures that all net borrowing costs are deferred and capitalized.

§ 9.7[c] Optimal Tool for Post-1983 Stock Under the Proposed Regulations

If the proposed regulations with respect to the straddle rules become effective, it appears that for stock acquired after 1983, a single-contract collar combined with a margin loan should deliver the minimum after-tax cost in most instances.

Listed options are clearly disadvantaged because of the inability to net the option premiums, which can easily be netted with over-the-counter derivatives.

Prepaid variable forwards are clearly tax disadvantaged because of their structure, which gives an investor no choice but to defer and capitalize the net cost of carry. Prepaid variable forwards do, however, have several nontax advantages. First, the cost of the borrowing is fixed throughout its term, in contrast to a floating-rate borrowing typical of a margin loan. (Brokerages do, however, offer fixed-rate margin loans to their clients.) Second, because Regulation T is not applicable, a margin call would not be possible in the future. (A margin call is possible if margin loans are used.) Third, because Regulation T is not applicable, the investor is not limited to borrowing a maximum of 50 percent of the value of the hedged position if the purpose of the borrowing is to reinvest in other securities, as it would be if a margin loan were used. Fourth, because there are no "moving parts" (e.g., no interest payments because the interest has been prepaid, no interest rate resets because the debt is fixed-rate debt, and no mark to markets) until the expiration date, there are no monthly statements and other periodic communications from the brokerage firm (as there are with options and swaps) to confuse and frustrate a private client.

Exhibit B compares and contrasts the tax treatment of the three available financial derivative-based hedging and monetization strategies—swaps, options, and forwards—for stock acquired after 1983.

§ 9.7[d] Proposed Regulations' Negative Impact on Stock Acquired After 1983

The proposed regulations with respect to the straddle rules have mostly a negative impact on investors interested in hedging and monetizing appreciated securities. The regulations to some degree "level the playing field" among the various derivative tools that are available to hedge and monetize stock acquired after 1983. Under the proposed regulations, listed options no longer enjoy any advantage, and the fact that interest expense incurred by a borrowing that is collateralized by a hedged stock position must be capitalized narrows the possible advantage that a single-contract collar combined with a margin loan has over a prepaid variable forward.

Exhibit B. Tax Treatment of Alternative Hedging and Monetization Techniques for Stock Acquired After 1983

	If an investor implements a monetizing collar through		
	Options and Margin Loans	*A Prepaid Forward (with an Embedded Collar)*	*An Equity Swap (with an Embedded Collar and Margin Loans)*
Should carrying costs be currently deductible against investment income (38.6% benefit)?	Yes, at least partially	No	Yes, at least partially
When the collar is a cash-settling collar and the stock price is above the call strike, what is the character of the loss?	Deferred long-term capital loss	Deferred long-term capital loss	Deferred ordinary deduction or long-term capital loss at investor's discretion
When the collar is a cash-settling collar and the stock price is below the put strike, what is the character of the gain?	Long-term capital gain	Long-term capital gain	Long-term capital gain or ordinary income at investor's discretion

§ 9.8 Exchange Funds—An Alternative to a Financial Derivative Solution

Over the past few years a number of bills have been introduced in Congress that would eliminate the use of exchange funds as a variable strategy to diversify highly appreciated securities; none have been passed into law. Under current law, exchange funds can prove useful in two situations.

First, if a derivative-based solution is not available because of the characteristics of a particular stock[12] (e.g., the stock is difficult to borrow or is subject to liquidity constraints), an exchange fund might be considered the diversification tool of last resort.

Second, if an investor's objective is to diversify out of all or a portion of a highly appreciated stock position and into a passively managed portfolio that tracks a certain index (e.g., the Standard & Poor's 500), certain exchange funds should prove particularly useful. Certain exchange funds have historically exhibited a very high degree of correlation with the index they were designed to track and their "all in" cost compares favorably to what it would otherwise cost to monetize through a derivative-based solution and re-deploy the proceeds into an index fund.

Because of the constructive sale rules, derivative-based solutions generally have a maximum length of five years, at which time they must be rolled over to maintain the benefit of the tax deferral. Exchange funds are often structured with an unlimited life.

Since exchange funds have periodically come under attack, investors considering an investment in an exchange fund might want to act sooner rather than later to take advantage of current opportunities.

§ 9.9 Summary

Before the enactment of the constructive sale rules, hedging and monetizing a concentrated, highly appreciated stock position was fairly straightforward. The short against the box was the strategy that was most often utilized and it was very cheap and extremely effective.

The constructive sale rules currently in place require a much more sophisticated analysis to ensure that the investor selects the strategy and tool that deliver the optimal after-tax result.

If the investor is fortunate enough to own highly appreciated shares of a company that is currently involved in an announced tax-free stock-for-stock merger, it would behoove the investor to explore the potential of establishing a short against the box that should not be subject to the constructive sale rules through merger arbitrage. If successfully implemented, this strategy will clearly deliver the optimal after-tax result.

If the merger arbitrage strategy is not available to the investor, an income-producing collar would be the most appropriate strategy. This strategy can be implemented through various financial derivative tools, including options, a swap with an embedded collar, or a prepaid variable forward.

If the investor acquired its stock before 1984, the straddle rules would not apply and a swap with an embedded collar combined with a margin loan would clearly be the most tax-efficient solution.

If the investor acquired its stock after 1983, the straddle rules would apply and a single-contract, options-based collar combined with a margin loan should deliver the optimal after-tax result.

If the merger arbitrage strategy and the income-producing collar strategy are not available to the investor, it might want to consider an exchange fund.

---

1. Under the Economic Growth and Tax Relief Reconciliation Act of 2001 (EGTRRA), the step-up in basis at death would be eliminated beginning in 2010.

2. Following is an example of the mechanics of the short against the box:

   Assume that Investor owns 10,000 shares of XYZ Corp. and the current market price is $100 per share. Investor deposits 10,000 shares of XYZ into its account with Broker. Broker, on behalf of Investor, borrows 10,000 shares of XYZ from a third party and sells those shares into the market. Investor continues to own 10,000 shares of XYZ and receives all dividends paid on the shares. Investor pays to the lender of the borrowed shares an amount equal to all dividends paid on the shares (a substitute or "in lieu" dividend payment). Dividend flows are thus a wash. Proceeds of the short sale ($1 million) serve as collateral for the lender of the borrowed shares. Investor earns a money market rate of return (e.g., federal funds rate less 35 basis points) on these funds. Investor withdraws (i.e., monetizes) 95 percent (up to 99 percent in certain cases) of the value of the XYZ shares, or $950,000. Investor pays interest on this borrowing (e.g., federal funds rate plus 30 basis points). Investor is free to use or invest the $950,000 in any manner it wishes (i.e., there are no margin rule limitations on the use of the loan proceeds). The net financing cost will vary as the federal funds rate and the price of the stock change.

3. For a detailed discussion of the mechanics, economics, and tax treatment (before enactment of the constructive sale rules) of the short against the box strategy, see Boczar and Fichtenbaum, "Stock Concentration Risk Management Strategies," *Tr. & Est.*, June 1996, at 34.

4. There are three types of equity collars: income producing, zero cost, and debit. With an income-producing collar, the amount received for selling the call exceeds the cost of the put and this excess is used to subsidize the cost of monetization. With a zero-cost collar, the premiums for the put and call are equal. With a debit collar, the cost of the put exceeds the amount received on the sale of the call.

5. The straddle rules apply to any shares acquired after 1983. Therefore, most if not all of the investor's shares must have been acquired before 1984 to avoid application of the straddle rules. An unresolved issue arises when the original stock was acquired before 1984 but the shares being hedged were received for the original stock in a tax-free exchange that occurred after 1983.
6. A prepaid variable forward could also be cash settled. If this was the case in the example and the price of ABC Corp. stock was less than $95 per share three years from now, the investor would pay the dealer the then-current value of the ABC stock in cash. If the price of ABC stock was between $95 and $110, the investor would pay the dealer $95 in cash. If the price of ABC stock was above $110, the investor would pay the dealer $95 plus the difference between the then-current price of ABC stock and $110.
7. Under EGTRRA, the ordinary rate will be 39.1 percent in 2001, 38.6 percent in 2002 and 2003, 37.6 percent in 2004 and 2005, and 35 percent from 2006 through 2010.
8. See 66 Fed. Reg. 12 at 4746 (Nov. 18, 2001); Prop. Treas. Reg. §§ 1.263(g)-3(c)(2).
9. See FSA 200111011.
10. Prop. Treas. Reg. § 1.263(g)-3(c)(2).
11. A variable forward can be either prepaid or not. If it is prepaid, the investor has economically collared the position and receives an up-front payment from the dealer that is not currently taxed. If it is not prepaid, the investor has economically collared the position but does not receive an up-front payment from the dealer. In the latter situation, the investor could effectively monetize the stock hedged through the variable forward through margin loans.
12. If an investor hedges a long stock position through a collar, the dealer will be synthetically long in the underlying stock. To hedge this exposure, the dealer will typically establish a short position in that stock. To establish a short position, the dealer must be able to borrow shares from someone who currently owns them in order to be able to deliver shares to the buyer on the settlement date of the short sale. In addition, the stock must be sufficiently liquid to enable the dealer to increase or decrease its short position without significantly impacting the stock price.

Chapter 10

The Family Office

Martha Staniford

Synopsis

The opinions expressed in this chapter are those of the author and are not necessarily shared by Sontag Advisory LLC, its affiliates, or by its other employees.

The family office is a concept deeply rooted in history and is a topic frequently discussed in the high net worth marketplace. This chapter attempts to provide an all-you-need-to-know discussion of the topic.

§ 10.1 Origins

It is generally agreed that the concept of the family office originated in the late 17th century.

Baron Mayer Amschel von Rothschild, head of what was to become one of the most illustrious and wealthy banking families in the world, fathered ten children, including five sons. As his sons came of age, Baron von Rothschild dispatched them to Frankfurt, Paris, London, Naples, and Vienna to expand the family's banking operations. Although each son was responsible for his own banking enterprise, their father retained responsibility for the family's investments, which were centralized under his control in his native Germany.

The term *family office* was unknown at the time, and the Baron's centralized management entity was most likely referred to as a private investment company. In Britain, the royal family's office was known as the Office of the Exchequer, since it handled all the king's affairs.

As the Rothschild family's sphere of influence spread throughout Europe in the early 1800s, many other wealthy families, as well as European royalty, adopted the private investment company centralized approach to wealth management and preservation. These families also recognized that concentrating their wealth within their own country exposed their financial holdings to the risks associated with the country's economic, political, and social upheavals. In other words, these families recognized the benefits of diversification both by asset class and geographical boundaries.

Despite its acceptance in Europe, the concept of centralized administration of diversified family wealth was not adopted in the United States until the late 19th century and early 20th century with the emergence of such notable families as the Carnegies, the Rockefellers, the Pews, the Pitcarins, and the Mellons. As Andrew Carnegie (1835–1919) stated, these families understood the importance of and the difficulties associated with wealth preservation, "The problem with our age is the proper administration of wealth."

As a result of the expense of operating a single family office, only a relatively small number of wealthy families in the United States employed a centralized, diversified approach to managing their wealth during the first six or seven decades of the 20th century. Rather, most wealthy families in the United States depended on trust companies to handle their assets.

The fiduciary responsibility imposed on trust companies severely restricted investment opportunities available to families, so disillusionment with this type of structure began to grow. By the 1980s a new breed of first-generation millionaires had emerged and the family office concept became widely accepted in the United States. Some claim that the earliest reference to *family office* appeared in print in the 1990s at the same time *Forbes* magazine first published the Forbes 400, which identified the wealthiest families in the United States.

§ 10.2 Wealth Defined

The Spectrem Group, a leading market research firm based in Chicago, defines the three basic categories of wealthy U.S. individuals and families as follows:

1. Affluent—net worth of $500,000 or more exclusive of primary residence, and/or $100,000 in annual income;
2. High net worth—net worth of $1 million or more exclusive of primary residence; and
3. Ultra high net worth—net worth of $5 million or more inclusive of primary residence.

§ 10.3 Current Trends

Volatile economic and political market conditions in the early years of the 21st century have slowed the accumulation of personal wealth in the United States and throughout Europe and Asia. Nevertheless, the enormous economic growth of the late 20th century continues to be a major factor in the wealth management profession.

The bull market of the 1980s drove the United States and other world economies into a boom era, which spilled over into the 1990s. This economic resurgence, coupled with the leveraged buyout boom in the United States and the introduction of numerous technological innovations (the Internet, dot-coms, etc.) created an ever increasing number of high net worth individuals and families, especially in the United States. The economic boom of the 1980s and 1990s, however, accounts for only a portion of the recent growth of personal wealth in the United States.

There are other contributing factors, the most significant of which is the rapidly aging U.S. population. As Table 1 illustrates, nearly 50 percent of all current "wealth-creating events" are directly related to the hundreds of thousands of individuals in the United States who have reached or are nearing retirement age. This trend is accelerating and will likely continue to accelerate in the future.

Although, at 11 percent, inherited wealth occupies a relatively minor position among wealth-creating events, this source of wealth could also increase dramatically as the population ages. In fact, it is estimated that approximately $13 trillion will be transferred from one generation to the next from 2000 to 2010 in the United States alone.

Table 1. Wealth-Creating Events

Event	Percent
Inheritance	11%
Retirement distribution	12%
Insurance settlement	8%
Business sold	14%
Exercised stock options, restricted stock	16%
Liquidated individual retirement account (IRA)	14%
Liquidated life insurance policy	8%
Gift	9%
Divorce settlement, lottery winnings	8%

Source: The Spectrem Group, Chicago, IL, 1998.

Regardless of its source, the growth in personal wealth has resulted in a concurrent increase in the number of family offices, both in the United States and around the world. Although statistics are somewhat vague, estimates indicate that there are now more than 3,000 family offices in the United States, and an additional 2,000 throughout Europe, Latin America, and Asia.

§ 10.4 Family Office Benefits

The initiative for establishing a family office generally lies with the individual who has acquired or accumulated the wealth. This individual generally has an interest in preserving and enhancing that wealth as well as maintaining family unity, traditions, and values. As this individual generally intends to transfer some or all of the wealth to the next and/or succeeding generations, current tax and estate planning structures often suggest keeping the wealth centralized/amalgomated.

The benefits to the extended family of maintaining the integrity of that wealth by pooling it are several. First, economies of scale are available in such areas as legal and tax work, auditing, bookkeeping, recordkeeping, and other administrative functions. Generally, however, the greatest incentive for establishing a family office relates to asset management. A family with a large pool of investable assets typically benefits from reduced asset management fees, which are often comparable to appreciably lower institutional fees.

Second, pooled assets afford a family access to investment opportunities not generally available through standard retail channels. This is especially true in the areas of alternative (hedge fund) investments, private equity, venture capital, and real estate.

Third, tax efficiencies and certain estate planning techniques and structures become economically feasible when a family is working with a significant pool of assets.

Fourth, the family office greatly minimizes access to family members who might otherwise be besieged by unsolicited overtures from such vendors as investment "product pushers," "hot-tipsters," and a multitude of what might reasonably be characterized as questionable charitable organizations. Indeed, one of the key responsibilities of the head of a family office is to act as gatekeeper and to insulate the family from these and other types of solicitations.

Fifth, the family office offers family members the potential for a degree of anonymity. This is especially true when a family elects to establish a family limited partnership, private trust company, or limited liability company and uses a name unrelated to the family. The litigious nature of U.S. society and heightened security risks make the benefits of privacy and confidentiality afforded by the family office increasingly important.

Sixth, the family office offers the family an opportunity to concentrate and therefore maximize the benefits of its philanthropic interests. Focused giving can both preserve a family's legacy and serve as an educational and family participation tool for succeeding generations. Family foundations have multiplied greatly over the years as a result. These foundations serve as an excellent means of educating successive generations about the family, the source of its wealth, its goals and objectives, and the values and morals that constitute the family legacy.

Finally, because a family office is an outward sign that the family is truly wealthy, the family office represents a certain degree of prestige.

§ 10.5 Evolving Needs and Preferences

Historically, the primary focus of the family office was on managing financial assets, and many family offices remain primarily dedicated to providing asset management and investment management services. In addition, these investment management companies offer financial planning, asset allocation, and performance monitoring services.

Since the late '80s, market demands, the growing complexities in the U.S. tax and legal systems, and "information overload" have required family offices to offer a broader range of expertise, including expertise in such disciplines as wealth transfer planning, estate planning, business succession planning, tax planning, risk management services, and concierge services. Another area in increasing demand is the skill in the monetization of illiquid assets. This more recent demand is an outgrowth of the increasing number of investors who have concentrated positions in such illiquid assets as real estate, restricted and control stock, stock options, privately held businesses, and limited partnerships.

In addition, the business of managing wealth has become increasingly complex with the introduction of sophisticated new strategies and products, many of which involve the use of derivatives.

The family office in the 21st century also must be prepared to address a wide variety of what might be categorized as life management issues. Families now require a "holistic wealth plan," a wealth plan that coordinates all the disciplines associated with wealth management. These life management issues reflect the evolving needs and preferences of growing numbers of wealthy families that can well afford to pay for an increasing range of sophisticated professional services.

This vast array of services includes bill paying and cashflow management; hiring domestic help, nannies, tutors, and bodyguards; managing vacation and other properties; insurance reviews; negotiating jet plane leases; overseeing philanthropic activities; preparing business evaluations; and arranging for the purchase and sale of art, antiques, and other collectibles. The list of services the family office may be asked to provide is nearly endless.

That there are thousands of families who can well afford the services of a family office is reflected in the fact that gaining access to these services often requires a minimum of $10 million in investable assets. As recently as several years ago, that minimum was in the $3 million to $5 million range.

§ 10.6 Family Office Business Models: Surveying the Options

The total assets in the family pool generally will dictate which family office business model is most appropriate for the family. The four basic models are described below.

§ 10.6[a] Single Family Office

As may be apparent, the single family office is dedicated to representing the members of one family, extended or otherwise. Families electing the single family office business model generally must have a minimum of $250 million in investable assets to justify the considerable costs associated with operating the office. Many wealth management professionals might suggest that the asset pool be in the $500 million to $1 billion range to justify establishing a single family office.

The single family office generally is managed by a senior executive who may have either administrative or investment expertise, or preferably both. One family member assumes a key supervisory role or acts as an intermediary, although that individual does not assume the gatekeeper responsibilities.

In addition to the chief executive officer or chief investment officer, the staff will typically include a tax adviser, accountant, bookkeeper, and senior administrative assistant. Depending on the total assets under management and the requirements of the family, the permanent staff typically numbers between 5 and 25; it can, however, be larger.

The legal structure of the single family office may take any of a number of forms. These include a subchapter S or C corporation, a family limited liability company, a family limited partnership, a family foundation and/or a private trust company, or some combination of these, any of which can be registered as an investment adviser.

Regardless of the legal entity, one or more family members serve on the board. Often, one or more of the external advisers engaged by the family may also serve on the board. In any event, two major issues that must be addressed and resolved in the context of a single family office are family governance and succession.

§ 10.6[b] Multiple Family Office

The multiple family office is a fairly new phenomenon that has evolved in recent years largely as a result of the cost efficiencies and complexities associated with the wealth management business. These offices generally represent between 5 and 30 families, allowing the costs to be spread over a greater number of members. The size of the multiple family office also allows its members to benefit from "the best of breed" advice—financial planning, tax consulting, and other wealth management services.

Access to a multiple family office generally requires a minimum of $5 million in investable assets, or the near-term prospect of controlling assets in that range.

Rockefeller and Company is perhaps one of the better known examples of the multiple family office business platform. Originally dedicated to serving the interests of the Rockefeller family on an exclusive basis, the Rockefellers' single family office has become a multiple family office and now provides investment management, risk management, and wealth planning services to a number of families. Many multiple family offices, however, have been established as the result of a joint venture among wealthy families that have aligned themselves for this purpose.

The typical multiple family office staff might consist of a chief executive officer, a chief administrative officer, and a chief investment officer. Other staff members may include a tax adviser, an accountant, one or more bookkeepers, and one or more senior administrative assistants. The staff will also include as many relationship managers as are required to represent the various families.

Multiple family offices are most commonly incorporated as private trust companies or limited liability companies, and clients pay fees for asset management and other services they utilize. Representatives of each family often serve as trustees or board members of these companies.

The multiple family office is one of the fastest growing family office models because of the complexity of wealth management and because there are limited numbers of highly qualified professionals available to run family offices. The scarcity of these professionals has resulted in a significant increase in compensation costs.

§ 10.6[c] Commercial Family Office

Commercial family offices are also an outgrowth of the single family office structure and fall into one of three categories: small-, mid-, or large-scale offices. Entrée to a small-scale commercial family office requires a minimum of $1 million in liquid assets; mid-scale offices require approximately $2.5 to $5 million; and large-scale offices require $10 million or more. These numbers reflect the very high fixed costs of wealth management services.

Under the commercial family office business model, all of the disciplines associated with wealth preservation and life management services are provided by a full-time staff of professionals who work for and are compensated by a public trust company, the trust department of a bank, or some similar organization. Bessemer Trust, Fiduciary Trust, Glenmeade Trust, Pitcarin Trust, and U.S. Trust are high-profile examples of public trust companies that offer commercial family office services. Commercial family offices tend to have in-house money managers; provide credit, banking, and trust services; and prefer to act in the capacity of key adviser to their clients. In other words, commercial family offices offer all the benefits of a single source for all wealth management and related services.

Under the commercial family office business model, services are bundled with products, and fees are paid for assets under management. This business model is not new. It is an outgrowth of the commercial bank trust company business model, updated and restructured to reflect today's needs.

§ 10.6[d] Virtual Family Office

Like the multiple family office, the virtual family office is a relatively new concept. Families electing this option generally must have a minimum of $5 million to $25 million in investable assets. Many believe this segment of the market will experience the most rapid growth over the next five years.

Establishing a virtual family office involves forming alliances with a team of independent, outside professionals who represent a broad range of disciplines, including but not limited to investment management, tax planning, accounting, trusts and estates, legal work, and risk management. The permanent staff is minimal and might consist of a secretary, a bookkeeper, and a gatekeeper. Although a family member may assume the gatekeeper responsibilities, the gatekeeper is often not a family member but a chief executive officer who works exclusively for the family office. This individual is frequently referred to as the quarterback or consigliere.

Other members of the virtual family office team might include bankers, business agents, and individuals with expertise in such disciplines as investment management, risk management, education consulting, philanthropy, fine arts, antiques and collectibles, concierge services, and family psychology.

All of these advisers, regardless of their level of involvement, are compensated directly by the family office in accordance with a predetermined fee schedule.

Most services are outsourced. As a consequence of this arrangement, advisory costs are often easier to identify and quantify than they are when the other business models are used. Oftentimes, the overall cost to the family for accessing these services may be lower under this model than it is under the other models because the family pays only for the services it uses.

The virtual family office can afford the family access to top independent advisers from around the world; this means that a family can surround itself with those it believes to be the best professionals available in each field of wealth management. These independent professionals are engaged only when their expertise is required and are dismissed when they are not needed or are not performing. This ability to fire or otherwise dismiss advisers is a major benefit of the virtual family office.

In addition to being potentially more cost effective than the other models, the virtual family office business model is based on an open architecture platform, which lends itself well to engendering cutting-edge advice. Because there are generally few if any proprietary products or services associated with the virtual family office, the family and its chief executive officer are well positioned to make objective decisions regarding the advisers and the products and services used.

Depending primarily on the level of assets involved, coordination of the advisory team generally is provided either by a chief executive officer or by a member of the core team, such as the wealth management or investment adviser, the attorney, or the accountant. A family member may also be directly involved in certain aspects of managing the virtual family office, generally in conjunction with the chief executive officer. At the very least, one family member is required to invest the time required to represent and articulate the interests of the family. This individual must be prepared to participate in interviewing and selecting the advisers who will constitute the virtual family office team.

§ 10.7 Family Dynamics

Family dynamics can represent serious obstacles to establishing a family office.

Despite the commonality of interests that might inform and therefore direct their decisions, some family members may not be fully cooperative in resolving the details associated with establishing a family office.

It is neither necessary nor possible to cite all of the issues that may develop within families, especially those with considerable wealth. Nevertheless, certain basic issues can be expected to arise more often than not.

First, some family members may choose not to pool their resources. In that instance, it may be advisable to make some provision for allowing those individuals to join the family office at some future date. Conversely, provisions must be in place to accommodate family members who may elect to withdraw their assets from the pool at some future date and to disassociate themselves from the family office.

Second, the family must determine which family member or members will assume responsibility for representing the family interests in various capacities, as well as whether and how those individuals will be compensated for services rendered. The services provided by family members may range from acting as a gatekeeper to coordinating the team of professional advisers in a virtual family office (see § 10.6[d]) or serving on the board of a single or multiple family office (see §§ 10.6[a], 10.6[b]).

Regardless, the precise mission and goals of the family office must be articulated. The responsibilities the family member or members will undertake and the degree of authority they will assume must be clearly understood and agreed to by all parties. At the same time, there must be a provision for removing family members from positions of authority in the event they fail to meet the family's expectations.

The third area that must be addressed is educating succeeding generations. In this regard, external board members often act as mentors to younger family members. Family meetings or counsels often serve as a forum for addressing issues. These forums are a common approach to resolving continuity issues and to developing a shared control system when generations are linked together as a result of estate planning structures that have been put in place. The family must decide when succeeding generations will be invited to participate in the decision-making process and in what capacity.

The more successful a family is in resolving these delicate issues, the more likely it will survive as a unit into the fourth, fifth, and six generations and the more likely it becomes that the family will avoid falling victim to the tenet "Ashes to ashes in three generations." Like any organization that wants to retain its viability, the family office must continually review its reason for being, evolve in accordance with changing family needs, and avoid staying in business simply to be in business.

Experts in the fields of family psychology and family dynamics are well experienced in dealing with these types of issues. Often these experts are among the first advisers a family will need to engage when deciding whether to join or establish a family office.

§ 10.8 Professional Management: Compensation and Other Issues

The most senior employees in the single, multiple, and virtual family office business models hold many different titles. These titles may include chief investment officer, chief executive officer, chief financial officer, president, vice president, managing director, executive director, investment director, principal, and partner.

Regardless of their title, these senior managers discharge a variety of responsibilities. According to a 2001 survey of its members, the Institute for Private Investors (IPI) found that in various family office structures, these responsibilities include structuring asset allocation plans, dealing with wealth transfer issues, tax planning, and trust administration (see Figure 1). In other words, these senior managers are responsible for ensuring that the comprehensive wealth plan is executed and updated as and when appropriate.

Figure 1. 2001 Family Office Compensation Survey: Responsibilities (81 respondents)

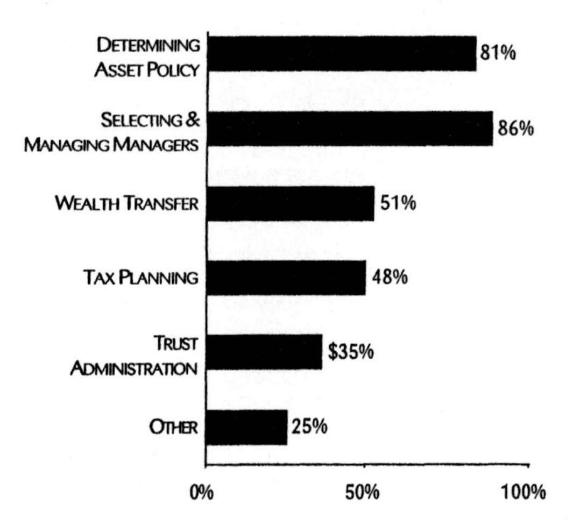

Source: Institute for Private Investors, New York. Family Office Survey conducted in the summer of 2001.

According to the same study, approximately 40 percent of senior executives surveyed oversee direct investments and 60 percent manage independent money managers.

In considering the single, multiple, or virtual family office alternatives, families must first determine whether their pooled asset base is sufficiently large to attract and retain qualified employees, especially at the upper management levels. Because individuals in senior positions may be subject to the whims of a single family member, these positions tend to be categorized as high risk. This, of course, makes the recruitment process more difficult.

There are also many challenges facing the family office in the area of compensation. The Institute for Private Investors survey indicates that these challenges include the effect of down markets on assets under management, the lack of comparative information on compensation benchmarks, the degree of difficulty in measuring employee performance, and retaining employees in a highly competitive marketplace.

As illustrated in Figure 2, base salaries among those participating in the aforementioned survey generally range from $100,000 to more than $350,000.

Figure 2. 2001 Family Office Compensation Survey: Base Salary (81 respondents)

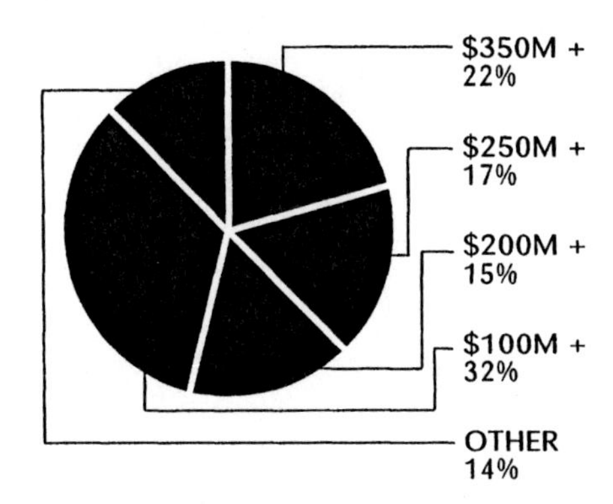

Source: Institute for Private Investors, New York. Family Office Survey conducted in the summer of 2001.

As a result of the competitive marketplace, there is a general trend among family office operations to give senior executives a variety of incentives beyond their base salary. According to the Institute for Private Investors survey, the incentives most commonly offered as a means of rewarding and retaining senior executives are above-average compensation, funded retirement plans and similar benefits, bonuses, profit sharing, and performance incentives. Fifty-nine percent of the family offices participating in the survey also indicated that they allow certain senior employees to co-invest with the family or families.

Despite the Institute for Private Investors survey, the dearth of information regarding compensation benchmarks and the difficulty of accurately measuring executive performance continue to cloud this important issue.

§ 10.9 Technology and the Family Office

Among the many issues surrounding family offices, perhaps the most complex involve technology and questions of account aggregation, performance monitoring, information dissemination, and information security.

§ 10.9[a] Account Aggregation and Performance Monitoring

Developing, maintaining, and monitoring a comprehensive picture of a family's assets can be a very challenging undertaking.

To assess overall portfolio performance accurately, information relating to accounts managed by various outside advisers must be submitted to the family office in a consistent manner and format; however, numerous methods are used in structuring performance reports. Some performance reports are based on trade dates, some are based on settlement dates, and still others are based on specific cut-off dates, such as month-end. In addition, there may be discrepancies among managers' performance benchmarks. Some benchmarks reflect management fees; others may not. Some benchmarks are based on pretax numbers; others are based on after-tax numbers. In the case of offshore investments, there may be discrepancies in approaches to reporting multicurrency transactions and holdings.

To compensate for these reporting vagaries, reports from the various money managers must be aggregated. That is, the data must be cleansed when they are transmitted electronically. Although data cleansing provides a common basis for assessing performance, the software technology utilized in this process is relatively new, very sophisticated, expensive, and not yet perfected.

All these issues must be identified and addressed, and the costs associated with data cleansing can be significant.

The costs associated with the multiple, virtual, and commercial family office business models (see §§ 10.6[b], 10.6[c], 10.6[d]) are, of course, shared by a number of families. That is not the case with the single family office model (see § 10.6[a]).

The virtual family office also requires a technology platform sufficient to support coordination of the advisers. Families utilizing a virtual office approach must be careful about the manner in which proprietary information is shared among the various advisers, especially when the information is available online.

Advent/Kinexus, TechFi, and By All Accounts are reputed to have the most advanced systems, and a number of family offices have created their own systems; however, no one seems to have developed the perfect technology platform.

§ 10.9[b] Information Security and Privacy

In addition to addressing account aggregation and data cleansing, those considering establishing a family office must decide where data pertaining to their investments, as well as other pertinent and proprietary family data, will be warehoused. One option is to contract with an independent party to provide data warehousing services. Another option is to assign responsibility for data warehousing to one portfolio manager, although doing so gives that manager access to proprietary information. Access to the holdings in other portfolios may prompt the manager to make unsolicited overtures to the family about products in which the manager has a vested interest. A third but expensive option is for a family to establish its own data warehouse.

Regardless of where the data are stored, families must be concerned about who has access to what ultimately will prove to be a significant volume of highly personal information. This information is not necessarily limited to financial information about the family. The family office data bank will include such information as tax records, academic records, insurance records, medical and perhaps mental health records, private telephone numbers, personal and business travel schedules, police records, legal correspondence and documents, birth dates, and so forth.

In other words, there will be a wealth of very powerful information in this database; in the wrong hands, this information could be very damaging. It also is important to recognize that the security and privacy of family data must be maintained not only vis-à-vis individuals outside of the family but also vis-à-vis individual family members.

The final area to consider is how to maintain communications with family members who may be dispersed throughout the United States and around the world. In addition to family meetings and reunions, e-mail and dedicated family Web sites may be used to communicate. Regardless of the method used, communication channels should be available to all family members so that all can be located and kept current on relevant family matters and family whereabouts.

§ 10.10 Family Office Cost Components

For many reasons, there are no reliable figures on the actual and highly variable costs associated with any of the family office business models, and it is extremely difficult to provide quantitative cost data.

The following are general estimates based solely on informal conversations with family office staff and on presentations made at various family office conferences in the United States and abroad.

Labor is the highest cost component of many businesses, and the family office is no exception. The number of employees in the family office and their positions of responsibility bear significantly on the costs associated with each of the family office business models.

Although they provide some basis for comparison, the absence of reliable information is apparent in the wide ranges in Table 2.

§ 10.11 The International Family Office Market

Despite the fact that the family office originated in Europe, the growth in the number of family offices outside of the United States has not been as dramatic as it has been in the United States. Many foreign families that own a business prefer to run a family office in conjunction with that business. Additionally, because of the lesser tax impact, family offices outside the United States generally tend to be structured more like U.S. endowments and foundations and/or private investment companies. Foreign families, however, have been dealing with social and political upheavals and other risk management concerns for many generations. These families undoubtedly can be of assistance to U.S. families in addressing these types of issues.

Over the next decade or so, as more American, European, and Asian families sell their family businesses, more family offices will likely be established, and the largest incremental growth of family offices will no doubt occur in Latin America, Europe, and Asia.

Table 2. Family Office Costs

	Type of Family Office					
	Virtual	*Single*	*Multiple*	*Small-Scale Commercial*	*Mid-Scale Commercial*	*Large-Scale Commercial*
Incorporation expenses	\$5,000–\$50,000	\$50,000–\$100,000	\$150,000 +	\$250,000 +	\$1 million +/–	\$5 million +/–
Fixed operating expenses	\$10,000 +	\$100,000 +	\$250,000 +	\$1 million	\$10–\$20 million +	\$30–\$50 million +
Management information system (per system)	\$10,000–\$50,000	\$100,000–\$250,000	\$250,000 +	\$1 million	\$5 million +	\$10–\$15 million +
Personnel (annualized)	\$150,000–\$300,000	\$300,000–\$1 million	\$1 million	\$5 million	\$15–\$20 million +	\$40–\$50 million +
Full-time staff	2–3	2–10	5–20	15–30	20–40	40 +
Minimum assets required	\$5–\$25 million	\$250 million +	\$500 million + (Generally \$5–50 million per family)	\$1 million (per family)	\$2.5–\$5 million + (per family)	\$10 million + (per family)
Target fee range (exclusive of asset management fees)	10–60 basis points	35–150 basis points	35–100 basis points	60–150 basis points	60–150 basis points	50–150 basis points

According to research published by Cap Gemini, Ernst & Young, and Merrill Lynch, the number of wealthy U.S. investors grew by 1.8 percent from 2000 to 2001. In comparison, Latin America registered the largest growth at 12 percent. This growth in Latin America occurred despite the economic and social problems in Argentina and weak U.S. financial markets.

§ 10.12 High Net Worth Family Networking Groups and Organizations

Formal networking groups are growing in popularity in the United States, Europe, and Asia. High net worth families are also establishing small, less formal networking groups in cities such as London, Geneva, Atlanta, and Chicago.

There are also a number of organizations throughout the United States dedicated to supporting those engaged in the family wealth management business as well as the individuals and families that either operate a family office or are contemplating establishing one. These organizations maintain Web sites and sponsor conferences at which leading experts in the wealth management field make presentations on topics of interest to the high net worth community. These organizations include the following:

- The Institute for Private Investors
  74 Trinity Place
  New York, NY 10006
  212-693-1300
  www.memberlink.net

- The Family Office Exchange
  137 North Oak Avenue, Suite 310
  Oak Park, IL 60301
  708-848-2030
  www.familyoffice.com

- Family Firm Institute
  221 North Beacon Street
  Boston, MA 02135
  617-789-4200
  www.cof.org

- The Aspen Business Group
  100 Elk Run Drive, #200
  Basalt, CO 81621
  970-927-8555
  www.aspenfamilybusiness.com

- The Family Business Consultants
  318 Canyon Avenue, Suite 100
  Ft. Collins, CO 80521
  970-221-1910
  www.familybc.com

§ 10.13 The Future

The events of September 11, 2001, changed the world. Wealthy families as well as professionals in the wealth management business are engaged in responding to this new market environment. Issues that were important at the end of the 20th century remain important, but they are now viewed in a different context.

New issues have evolved as well, some of which are listed below:

1. Time may now be more important than money.
2. How much and for how long can one afford to lose on one's investments?
3. Is it possible to be overdiversified?
4. Finding appropriate managers rather than "the best" performers may be important.
5. Return expectations may need to be reassessed because economic growth may slow, thus driving returns back down to historic levels.
6. Finding objective, interdisciplinary advice may take on more importance.
7. Risk management on all levels must be reviewed—for example, business risk, personal security risk, market risk, and concentration risk.
8. How much is sufficient for heirs and their heirs to inherit is a question asked more frequently.
9. How does one assess the value of a family office? What are the mission and goals of the family office?
10. What criteria should be used to measure family office performance? Should they all be quantitative or are there qualitative aspects that must

be weighed? When should the family office be disbanded?

11. It is important to recognize and understand the human, social, and intellectual aspects of family wealth, not just the financial aspects.
12. Managing information, applying technology, and keeping current will become increasingly relevant and perhaps create vexing issues.
13. Competing against institutional clients for services, investments, and professionals will become more intense.
14. Providing education and leadership training and fostering entrepreneurial spirit will take on greater importance for a family and its succeeding generations.

These are just some of the key issues that need to be considered. Other issues include the ongoing consolidation among asset management providers and the need for product providers to team up with independent advisers to provide more comprehensive, integrated wealth plans.

These issues, combined with the increasing uncertainty in the world and the negative effect down markets have had on wealth preservation and enhancement, will undoubtedly impact the future development of the family office business and the future of the family wealth management business.

These issues point to a continued, albeit slower growth of the family office market, with the virtual family office (see § 10.6[d]) and the multiple family office (see § 10.6[b]) most likely gaining a larger market share. One thing, however, is certain. Regardless of how it may evolve, the family office is here to stay.

Part 3. Special Techniques

CHAPTER 11

Funding Nonqualified Deferred Compensation, Supplemental Executive Retirement, and 401(k) Mirror Plans

Charles C. Morgan

Synopsis

Nonqualified deferred compensation plans (NQDCPs) and supplemental executive retirement plans (SERPs), including 401(k) mirror plans, provide for the future payment of income to a select group of employees while allowing these employees to avoid current taxation at the time the income is earned. These plans do not receive the favorable tax treatment accorded qualified pension plans under the Internal Revenue Code (IRC) because they are discriminatory, covering only a segment of the entire employee base. For that reason, these plans are known as *nonqualified plans*. Nonqualified plans can be either funded or unfunded.

Funded and unfunded plans offer a mixture of advantages and disadvantages under the IRC and the Employee Retirement Income Security Act of 1974 (ERISA). In most cases, employers have a third option—informally funded plans—which bridge the gap between funded and unfunded plans and limit many of their potential disadvantages and capitalize on many of their advantages. Employers can enhance the appeal of these plans by purchasing life insurance (corporate-owned life insurance) or by using rabbi trusts investing in life insurance (trust-owned life insurance).

This chapter discusses the types of funding vehicles available to employers today; explains issues relating to both the IRC and ERISA; and examines funded, unfunded, and informally funded plans, with emphasis on informally funded plans. This chapter also explores the advantages and disadvantages of using corporate-owned or trust-owned life insurance as the investment vehicle in a SERP or NQDCP.

> **Note.** Congress is considering repealing the moratorium that currently prohibits the IRS from issuing regulations with respect to nonqualified deferred compensation plans (including rabbi trusts). That moratorium may have been repealed by the time of publication of this book. A tax advisor should be consulted to make sure the following treatment remains accurate.

§ 11.1 Nonqualified Deferred Compensation Plans

NQDCPs allow employees to postpone the receipt of earned income to a future period. These plans are attractive to employees because income received in a future period will often be subject to lower tax rates, especially if the employee is deferring income into retirement years. There should be no taxation of the deferred income until the end of the deferral period as long as the plan is properly structured.

NQDCPs help attract and retain highly qualified executives. Employers may mandate a deferral under some plan designs rather than providing employees with an elective deferral of current compensation. Under mandated deferral plans, an employer typically requires that income from bonuses or incentive compensation awards be deferred for some period. The employee can usually choose to defer this income for a period of time longer than the mandated period and there is generally a provision for payment in the event of death, disability, or involuntary separation from employment. This type of plan design is attractive to employers because it establishes financial incentives for employees to remain with the company. If employees leave, they forfeit a substantial amount of deferred compensation.

NQDCPs come in a wide variety of forms but can generally be categorized into the two types mentioned above: those initiated by employees and those initiated by employers. Variations in plan design are usually attributable to both the primary objective of the plan and the relative bargaining positions of the employee and employer. The number of participants, amounts deferred, and length of deferral vary among employers.

§ 11.2 Supplemental Executive Retirement Plans

SERPs provide additional retirement benefits to a firm's most highly compensated employees. Whereas NQDCPs may permit employees to receive benefits well before retirement, SERPs rarely, if ever, permit employees to receive benefits before retirement.

§ 11.2[a] Retirement Income Shortfall

SERPs provide retirement benefits in excess of the retirement benefits that executives receive from other sources. These other sources include Social Security, qualified pension plans (both defined benefit and defined contribution plans), profit sharing plans, and employee stock ownership plans. For a variety of reasons, the combination of these other sources often amounts to a smaller total benefit package than that required for an executive to maintain a consistent standard of living throughout retirement.

The formulas used by both Social Security and the IRC for qualified plans contain salary caps that are well below the total compensation levels of many executives. For example, the Omnibus Budget Reconciliation Act of 1993 reduced the maximum annual earnings that could be taken into account for purposes of qualified benefit plans to $150,000. The limit is $200,000 in 2003 and will be indexed for inflation thereafter. Additionally, executive compensation may include types of payments, such as incentive compensation (indexed for inflation) and bonuses, not usually recognized in qualified plan benefit formulas. A large percentage of an executive's salary and other cash compensation may not generate the qualified retirement benefits on which most employees rely. Although the qualified retirement compensation of executives will still be greater in absolute dollars than that of lower-paid employees, the postretirement difference will not be proportional to the preretirement difference. The effect of these rules is to discriminate against the highly compensated employees. SERPs mitigate that discrimination.

In the case of a qualified defined contribution plan, the executive is limited in the amount of contributions permitted to be made to the plan. The SERP used for the nonqualified excess benefit is referred to as a *mirror plan.* The nonqualified plan mirrors the investment options underlying the qualified plan. A 401(k) mirror plan cannot, however, exactly replicate the investment options underlying the 401(k) plan, since the investment options of a qualified plan governed by the IRC and ERISA cannot be used by either a nonqualified plan or a life insurance contract. Nevertheless, the same investment strategies and investment managers can be used for the mirror plan.

§ 11.2[b] Other Uses for SERPs

In addition to having higher salaries, executives face employment situations different from those faced by most employees, resulting in different needs for both the executives and their employers. Some of these special requirements can be addressed by SERPs.

For instance, SERPs may be established to help attract mid- to late-career executives who, because they will have short lengths of service with their new employers or have forfeited benefits on leaving their previous employers, would otherwise retire with less than full pension benefits. In addition, SERPs can be used as motivational tools by gearing future compensation to the achievement of short-term operational or performance goals. Finally, SERPs can be used to influence the career length of executives. They can either encourage retention by making the benefits forfeitable on separation from the employer or encourage early retirement by making full benefits available to those who retire early (as might be the case in a downsizing).

§ 11.3 Factors Affecting the Design of NQDCPs and SERPs

Several different factors affect the design and operation of NQDCPs and SERPs, chief among them being their status under the IRC and ERISA. To examine how the IRC and ERISA apply to these types of employee benefit plans, it is first necessary to understand the differences between qualified and nonqualified plans and the differences between funded and unfunded plans.

§ 11.3[a] Qualified versus Nonqualified Plans

Depending on an employee benefit plan's design, it will be classified as either qualified or nonqualified under the IRC. This classification determines the plan's tax treatment. A plan qualifies for special tax-favored treatment if the plan complies with the IRC qualification requirements. The special tax-favored treatment sought through qualification includes an employer deduction for plan contributions at the time of the contribution, tax-free growth of investment earnings, and deferral of taxation to employees until they receive their benefits.

Qualified plan regulations generally require that an employer establish a trust for the exclusive benefit of employees, in addition to mandating adherence to many other rules. One of the other important requirements is that employees may not be excluded from the plan based on an age requirement of more than 21 or a service requirement of more than one year. Qualified plans must be nondiscriminatory.

Nonqualified plans are plans that do not fulfill the requirements necessary to be a qualified plan. Nonqualified plans usually violate one of the two requirements discussed immediately above: either the assets are not secured (because they are not placed in a trust or because the trust is intentionally written so that the assets are not secure) or the plan discriminates in favor of highly paid employees.[1]

Since NQDCPs and SERPs are discriminatory, covering only a segment of highly compensated employees, they are nonqualified plans under the IRC.

§ 11.3[b] Funded versus Unfunded Plans

The IRC and ERISA classify employee benefit plans as either funded or unfunded. *Funded plans,* also known as formally funded plans, are plans that give the participants significant assurance of payment. *Unfunded plans* are plans that provide only an unsecured promise of future payment.

Under funded plans, the employer sets aside assets that are not subject to the claims of the employer's general creditors and gives the covered employees as a class a beneficial interest in the underlying assets. The assets of funded plans, and therefore the executives' future benefits, are fully secured to the extent of the funding.

In contrast, an unfunded plan provides only an unsecured agreement between the employee and employer. The employer promises to pay future benefits without providing any assurance that the funds to do so will eventually exist. The employee is given no beneficial interest in specific assets because none are set apart from the general assets of the employer, and the employer has no plan asset to match the liability. Ultimate payment of the benefits depends on there not being a change in management, or a change of heart about the need for the plan.

In a sense, no plan is ever unfunded. All plans, even so-called unfunded plans, are funded from the perspective of the plan and plan participants. The plan invests in an IOU from the employer. That IOU is a form of fixed-income security. It is also a nondiversified portfolio composed of a single investment instrument. This funding approach is risky from the perspective of the plan and plan participants and is expensive from the perspective of the employer.

§ 11.3[c] Implications of Qualification and Funding Status

A plan's status as nonqualified and either funded or unfunded directly affects the plan's treatment under the IRC and ERISA.

§ 11.3[c][1] Internal Revenue Code. In a qualified plan arrangement, both the employer and the employee receive tax-favored treatment if the employer's contribution to a trust will be used exclusively for the payment of employee benefits. The employer is eligible for an income tax deduction in the years that it contributes to the trust. Moreover, the employees do not pay taxes on the amounts contributed or on the earnings on such amounts until they receive the benefits.

In contrast, under unfunded or informally funded nonqualified plans, the employer gets no deduction until the employee receives the deferred amount as income. In addition, the IRC generally mandates that the employer pay current taxes on any plan earnings.

In the case of a funded nonqualified plan, the employer does get a deduction at the time of a contribution to the trust, but the employee will be taxed on that contribution. Depending on the nature of the trust, either the employer or the trust will generally be taxed on investment earnings.

The timing of the taxation of an unfunded, informally funded, or formally funded nonqualified plan is subject to the doctrines of constructive receipt and economic benefit. The doctrine of constructive receipt states that an employee is taxed currently on compensation to which he or she has access, whether or not the compensation is reduced to the employee's actual possession.[2] In other words, if compensation is segregated for an employee, and the actual receipt of the compensation is within the employee's control, then the employee is taxed in the year in which he or she is given unrestricted rights to its receipt. The employee is taxed when he or she obtains control of the receipt of the income, not when he or she chooses to receive the compensation. To avoid current taxation to the employee, therefore, the employee's control of the receipt of the compensation must be subject to substantial limitations or restrictions.

The doctrine of economic benefit extends the ideas inherent in the doctrine of constructive receipt one step further. It states that even where then is no actual or constructive receipt, an employee is taxed in the current period if monetary value can be attached to any conferred benefits. In other words, the employee need not even control the receipt of an asset to be taxed currently. He or she need only have an interest in, or rights to, specific assets.

Partly as a result of these two doctrines, funded and unfunded or informally funded nonqualified plans receive different tax treatment. Because formally funded plans not only segregate assets for the payment of future benefits but also give the participants a current, beneficial interest in these assets, they meet the test of economic benefit and may, depending on plan design, also be subject to the doctrine of constructive receipt. This results in a situation in which the participants in funded nonqualified plans are liable for current taxation on contributions to the plan when the employer can currently obtain an income tax deduction, whether or not the participants actually receive the contributions.

Funded plans are also subject to taxation under IRC Section 83, which taxes employees on the receipt of property that is not subject to a substantial risk of forfeiture. With an unfunded or informally funded plan offering only an unsecured promise of future payment, there is no current tax liability for the plan participants, the future benefits are not completely secure, and the employer does not obtain a tax deduction until the employee actually receives the benefit.

§ 11.3[c][2] ERISA. In addition to receiving different treatment under the IRC, funded and unfunded plans receive different treatment under ERISA.[3]

Under ERISA there are notable differences between NQDCPs and SERPs. A distinction must be made not only between funded and unfunded or informally funded NQDCPs but also between funded and unfunded or informally funded SERPs.

SERPs, which provide benefits in excess of the limits of IRC Section 415, constitute the more straightforward case. If SERPs are unfunded or informally funded, they are not subject to any ERISA requirements. If SERPs are formally funded, they are subject to extensive fiduciary rules and possibly to other rules as plan assets.[4]

The treatment of deferred compensation plans, whether NQDCPs or SERPs, depends on the plan design. All such deferred compensation plans, regardless of their funding status, are subject to limited reporting rules.

§ 11.3[c][3] Summary of Implications. In light of both the IRC and ERISA, it is clear that in most instances formally funding either NQDCPs or SERPs is disadvantageous to both employees and employers. Funded plans subject the participants to current taxes on benefits they will not receive until the future and require greater employer attention to ERISA requirements. It is no surprise, therefore, that the vast majority of NQDCPs and SERPs are either unfunded or informally funded. Moreover, it is not surprising that an unfunded or informally funded plan is not the ideal solution, since participants would prefer to have more than an unsecured promise of future payment. Although not the ideal solution, an informally funded plan generally is considered the best solution available for both the employer and the participant.

§ 11.4 Formal Funding Through a Secular Trust

A *secular trust* is an irrevocable trust that segregates assets solely for the purpose stated in the trust, which, in this context, is the payment of nonqualified deferred compensation benefits. A secular trust is essentially the same as a rabbi trust except that the secular trust does not have an insolvency or bankruptcy contingency. A secular trust not only protects the plan assets from takeovers, changes in management, or business strategy shifts, but also shields them from the employer's general creditors in the event of insolvency.

A secular trust often contains rules to which the employees must adhere in order to retain their right to benefits. Some common conditions include noncompetition agreements, geographical constraints, and limitations on the provision of consulting services. These restrictions must be genuine.

When the design of a secular trust gives nonspecific rights to the employees and places the assets or rights at a substantial risk of forfeiture, there will be neither constructive receipt nor economic benefit to the employees. Consequently, while the plan benefits are only somewhat more secure than the benefits under an informally funded plan, the plan participants may not be liable for current taxes. When the design of a secular trust does not impose any conditions on the employee's right to receive his or her deferred benefits in the future, constructive receipt, economic benefit, or IRC Section 83 may apply. In that case, while the plan benefits are absolutely secure, the plan participants will be liable for current taxes.

§ 11.5 Informal Funding Strategies

One solution that offers a compromise between the absolutes inherent in both formally funded and unfunded plans, and can address the disadvantages of adverse tax consequences and unsecured benefits, is the use of an informal funding vehicle. To fund a plan informally, an employer must either informally dedicate general assets to the plan through an accounting device (i.e., a bookkeeping entry or memorandum account) or segregate assets using a trust. There are several established techniques for informal funding that may or may not provide a measure of security or avoid current taxation to covered employees.

§ 11.5[a] Investment Accounts

To fund a plan informally without giving plan participants a beneficial interest in specific assets, an employer need only establish an account on the company books. The employer can then grow or draw down this account as needed to pay the required benefits.

The major disadvantage of informal funding through an accounting device is that the employee does not have any security that the amount "segregated" for payment of the deferred benefits will actually be used for that purpose. Informal funding using an accounting device does not provide the same level of security as a rabbi trust does but avoids current taxation to the employee. Despite this disadvantage, participants feel that memorandum accounts have significant value.

§ 11.5[b] Rabbi Trust

Rabbi trusts are currently undergoing examination by Congress and the IRS. As the rules may have changed significantly, a tax adviser should be consulted to make sure that the following treatment remains current.

To obtain greater security for employees, employers often establish *rabbi trusts*. Once assets have been committed to a rabbi trust, the employer can no longer access those assets. This provides a measure of security to the employees. The rabbi trust segregates the assets from the general assets of the employer but leaves them subject to its general creditors in the event of employer insolvency or bankruptcy. While the trust protects the assets from events such as hostile corporate takeovers, changes in management, or changing corporate strategies (where a large pot of assets might be tempting), the assets remain subject to substantial risk in the event of the employer's insolvency.

Informal funding of NQDCPs and SERPs using a rabbi trust can be a better option than a formally funded or completely unfunded plan, since it strikes a balance between the benefits and limitations of both plan types. It offers a significant amount of security to plan participants but retains enough risk that covered employees are not liable for current taxation.

There are several major advantages to the employer of informal funding through a rabbi trust. One significant advantage is a reduction in the volatility of earnings in the profit and loss statement. The volatility of earnings is introduced by the NQDCP and SERP liabilities changing from one quarter to the next as a result of the performance benchmarks used to credit the employee's account with investment gains or losses. The assets in the rabbi trust can be invested in portfolios using the same indexes as their performance benchmarks. The movement of the assets will parallel the movement of the liabilities and dampen or eliminate earnings volatility.

Other advantages to the employer include reduced pension expenses, stabilized pension cash flow, reduced corporate credit risk, enhanced budgeting for the pension expense, and improved employee morale.

The major disadvantage of informal funding through a rabbi trust is that the employer forgoes the use of the assets it dedicates to the trust and may not receive an income tax deduction until the plan participants are in constructive or actual receipt of the assets (i.e., until the employee is taxed). Moreover, the employer is taxed on any taxable earnings of the assets when they are in the trust. Despite these disadvantages, many employers that are concerned about providing an element of security for employees' future benefits choose to fund informally using a rabbi trust, rather than formally fund their plans; the advantages to the employer stated above and the advantages to employees in terms of security and taxation are normally considered to outweigh the disadvantages to the employer.

§ 11.5[c] Split-Dollar Insurance

Split-dollar insurance is currently undergoing significant examination by the IRS and is in a state of flux. The rules could have changed significantly by the time of publication of this book. Check with a tax adviser to make sure that the following treatment remains current.

Split-dollar insurance uses an agreement between the employer and the employee to split, or share, the cost of the insurance premium, the benefits available under the contract, or both.

The four basic agreements used to allocate the premium of a split-dollar plan are (1) the classic plan, (2) the level-basis plan, (3) the employer-pay-all plan, and (4) the PS-58/Table 2001 offset plan.[5] Under the classic split-dollar plan, the employer contributes the portion of the premium equal to the yearly increase in the policy's cash surrender value and the employee contributes the balance. Cash surrender values in this type of guaranteed cash value policy's early years frequently represent a small portion of the premium. In the early years, therefore, the employee pays a large portion of the premium and the employer pays a small portion of the premium. Under a level-basis split-dollar plan, the employer's cost is a level amount for a specified number of years and the executive pays the balance of the annual premium.

Employer-pay-all split-dollar plans are provided by employers that elect to pay the entire premium. PS-58/Table 2001 offset split-dollar plans are designed to impose on the employee a premium contribution just large enough to eliminate the employee's current tax liability for the value of the insurance coverage. This is accomplished by having the executive pay a premium equal to the PS-58/Table 2001 economic benefit (i.e., the imputed income value of the life insurance) and having the employer pay the remaining premium.

Under any split-dollar plan, the employee is deemed to be in receipt of taxable income on the value of the annual insurance protection for which he or she does not pay. This taxable income is derived from the PS-58/Table 2001 rates published by the Internal Revenue Service (IRS). Under some arrangements, lower term life insurance rates are used to compute the employee's imputed taxable income in lieu of the PS-58/Table 2001 rates.

There are two basic ways to implement split-dollar arrangements. Under the first, called the *endorsement method,* the policy is owned by the employer and the death proceeds are split in accordance with an endorsement to the policy. Under the second method, called the *collateral assignment method,* the employee is generally the owner of the policy, but the policy is assigned to the employer as collateral for its designated interest. Typically, the employer receives an amount equal to premiums paid plus, in many policies, an imputed interest factor for the employer's lost use of its money. Under these policies, the executive's personal beneficiary receives the balance.

A split-dollar insurance policy is often used to fund a NQDCP or SERP in the following manner: Throughout the deferral period, the employee will designate a beneficiary to receive the policy's insurance proceeds; the employer will receive the investment proceeds or the cash value of the policy as a reimbursement for its share of the premium payments. When the employee retires, the employer may surrender the policy and use its share of the cash value to meet its deferred income obligation or borrow against the cash value of a collaterally assigned policy to meet its obligation. Alternatively, the employee could transfer the policy back to the employer, in which case the employee would receive retirement income payments and the employer would receive the policy proceeds on the employee's death. More typically, however, the employer will roll out the policy to the employee by transferring its interest in the policy to the insured employee. Under IRS Notice 2001-10, the employee is taxed at the earlier of rollout or when there is no substantial risk of forfeiture.

The major disadvantage of split-dollar insurance is that the employer's interest in the cash value is subject to the claims of its general creditors and the employer's interest does not offer any security to employees.

§ 11.5[d] Life Insurance

Once an employer has chosen to fund its plan informally, it can avoid taxation on the earnings of the plan assets. The employer achieves tax-deferred earnings on the plan assets, or tax-free earnings on those assets if the earnings are paid out in the form of death benefits, by purchasing life insurance coverage on the plan participants. Earnings on the premiums grow tax deferred within the policy, creating what is often referred to as the *tax-deferred inside buildup* of insurance policies.[6] As a general rule, the contract holder pays no taxes on the earnings until the policy is surrendered or the earnings are otherwise withdrawn. More important, if the contract holder allows the contract to return both the principal and earnings through the insurance policy's death benefit, no income taxes will be payable on the earnings. Life insurance death benefits are generally paid to the beneficiary income tax free when a covered individual dies.

In practice, an employer implements this life insurance strategy in one of two ways: either by buying the insurance directly or by establishing a trust, which then buys the insurance. If the second method is chosen, the employer establishes a type of grantor trust,[7] most commonly a rabbi trust. The trust cannot be formed for the specific purpose of purchasing the insurance. It must be formed for the purpose of funding benefits. If the corporation chooses to purchase the insurance directly, the employer establishes an account on the company books to reflect the asset. The corporation then purchases life insurance on the plan participants, with the corporation, rather than the employees, named as the beneficiary of the coverage. When the corporation is the beneficiary-owner, the policy is known as *corporate-owned life insurance;* when the corporation establishes a trust which then purchases the insurance and the trust is the beneficiary-owner, the contract is referred to as *trust-owned life insurance.*

Premiums on the insurance coverage are paid over time, either directly by the employer or through the trust. Since the plans are nonqualified, the employer does not receive a deduction for these contributions. Concurrently, the plan incurs liabilities in the form of deferred compensation or retirement benefits for the plan participants. The employer can access funds to pay for the benefits in one of three ways: death benefits, withdrawals, or policy loans.

If a covered individual dies, the death benefit is paid to the beneficiary—either the corporation or the trust. The death benefit, which is tax free, can be used to pay the current plan liability. If the liability in the current year is less than the amount of the death benefits, the excess can be put back into a group contract as an additional premium. If, on the other hand, the death benefits in any year are not sufficient to pay the required benefits, the corporation or trust can make a withdrawal from the contract. Since the corporation's or trust's basis in the contract is generally withdrawn before the investment earnings are withdrawn (unless the contract is a modified endowment contract (MEC))[8], withdrawals are also tax free up to the basis in the contract. Finally, tax-free policy loans can be taken from the contract unless the contract is a MEC.

When the employer uses the funds from either a company account or the trust to pay the plan participants, it receives an income tax deduction, since the employees are in receipt of the payments and are currently liable for the taxes.

When used under a 401(k) mirror plan, an insurance contract will offer the same investment strategies as those offered under the 401(k) plan itself. Often the same investment managers will be employed as well.

A 401(k) mirror plan works as follows: The executive allocates his or her deferred compensation to the 401(k) mirror plan investment options. The employer maintains memorandum accounts reflecting those allocations on behalf of the executive and credits investment returns to the selected investment options based on the applicable benchmarks. The employer allocates cash to the life insurance contract investment options (either directly in the case of corporate-owned life insurance, or indirectly through the trust in the case of trust-owned life insurance) in the same proportion as the executive's allocations. The executive does not select the investment options under the life insurance contract in order to comply with the IRC and securities law constraints.

In summary, corporate-owned or trust-owned life insurance is an advantageous choice for informally funding employee benefit plans, since it allows either the deferral of taxes on the plan asset earnings, or tax-free earnings if plan asset earnings are paid out in the form of death benefits. As a general rule, withdrawals are not taxable to the extent the amount withdrawn does not exceed the corporation's or trust's investment in the contract unless the contract is a MEC. Loans are not taxable unless the loan is outstanding at the time of lapse or surrender (or unless the contract is a MEC). When the loan is taxable, it is taxable to the extent there is gain in the contract. Corporate- or trust-owned life insurance is the optimal funding vehicle for NQDCPs and SERPs because of the tax advantages of life insurance contracts. If the employer chooses other investment vehicles instead, it may incur a tax liability on plan investment earnings.[9]

---

1. This chapter highlights only two of the more important requirements for plan qualification; there are many more.
2. Treas. Reg. § 1.451-2.
3. Even though funded nonqualified plans must adhere to many ERISA requirements similar to the IRC requirements for qualified plans, they retain their nonqualified status and are not eligible for qualified plan tax treatment because they are discriminatory.
4. ERISA §§ 4(b)(5), 201, 301, 401, 501. Accrual and vesting rules may also apply.
5. PS-58 rates are generally used to calculate the value of the life insurance coverage to an employee under qualified retirement plans, tax-sheltered annuities, and split-dollar insurance policies. PS-58 rates are from a table of values assigned to life insurance by Pension Service Bulletin Number 58 released by the Internal Revenue Service (IRS). IRS Notice 2001-10 replaces the PS-58 rates with rates from Table 2001, which applies to all taxpayers in 2002 but could be used in 2001.
6. This may not apply to corporate-owned life insurance when the alternative minimum tax applies.

7. A grantor trust is a special kind of trust that is not taxed; instead, the employer is taxed on any trust earnings.
8. IRC § 7702A.
9. The employer would not incur a tax liability if it invested solely in municipal bonds. For a variety of reasons, however, including relatively lower returns and limited investment options, this strategy is not usually employed.

CHAPTER 12

Private Placement Variable Universal Life

Jay A. Harvey

Synopsis

The objective of this chapter is to explain an investment program that eliminates both income and capital gains taxes by wrapping an underlying investment portfolio with a private placement variable universal life insurance policy.

This chapter is an updated version of a half-hour speech presented in October 2001 at the Lido Wealth Management Conference at the Four Seasons, Aviara, in Carlsbad, California.

§ 12.1 Private Placement Variable Universal Life Defined

Universal life is a reserve, or cash value, plus a decreasing amount of term insurance. The two elements are combined to create the death benefit. A second form of universal life pays the initial death benefit (the *face*) plus the cash value at the time of death. *Variable* means the cash value is based on security market values. In an off-the-shelf variable insurance product, mutual fund-type clones are offered, managed by major investment firms or by the insurance company's own money managers. Universal life is a stop-and-go product; that is, as little as the term cost may be paid (minimal funding), or as much as is legally allowable without creating a modified endowment contract (MEC) (maximum funding).

Private placement variable universal life (PPVUL) is a thin, noncommissionable layer of life insurance wrapped around an underlying investment portfolio. One's personal investment portfolio, managed by the policyholder's favored investment manager, approved by the insurance company, becomes the cash value account of a product defined as life insurance under Section 7702 of the Internal Revenue Code (IRC). Therefore, no income tax or capital gains tax is paid on the gains in the portfolio (i.e., on the "inside buildup" in the policy's cash value.[1] A cost of 1.5 percent to 2 percent, above the 1 percent manager's fee, gets rid of all future taxation on ordinary income and capital gains, making PPVUL probably the simplest tax-efficient investment available by law in large amounts.

In addition, withdrawals from a private placement contract may be made on a nonreportable basis either by extremely low interest policy loans (interest is typically 50 basis points or less) or by withdrawals from the original principal (one's basis in the contract), and the death benefit passes to named beneficiaries income tax free and with a stepped-up basis.[2] The private placement client may purchase large amounts—$50 million to $100 million of premium investment deposit, per capita, depending on age, sex, health status, and type of private insurance structure chosen—and may refer a favored money manager, including a hedge fund manager, to the insurance company to serve as the portfolio manager of his or her separate account, subject to the company's approval.

In many ways, the benefit of an investment portfolio wrapped in a private placement contract could be compared to an unlimited Roth IRA (individual retirement arrangement) for the wealthy.

To obtain the desired tax treatment, the PPVUL must be considered life insurance as defined in the IRC. IRC Section 7702 requires that either of two methods be used to determine that the policy is not being bought as a pure investment vehicle: (1) the cash value accumulation test (CVAT) or (2) a double-edged test, consisting of the guideline premium test (GPT) and the cash value corridor test (CVCT).

The CVAT says a contract will qualify as life insurance if its cash surrender value, at any time, does not exceed the net single premium that the policyholder would have to pay at such time to fund the future benefits under the contract. The CVAT assumes the contract has a maturity no earlier than the insured's age 95 and no later than the insured's age 100.[3] The GPT is satisfied as long as the sum of the premiums meets the policy's "guideline premium limitation" at any given time.[4] The CVCT is satisfied as long as the death benefit at any time is not less than the applicable percentage of the cash surrender value. At age 40 the percentage is 250 percent; at age 100 the percentage is 100 percent.[5]

A policy that passes either the CVAT, or both the GPT and the CVCT, is not an MEC (modified endowment contract) and can be used to create extremely favorable downstream tax treatment of distributions from the policy.

The MEC rules were enacted in 1988 to counteract the use of single premium life insurance, which was being sold almost as a pure investment. Policies written after June 21, 1988, became subject to the seven-pay test, which basically sets forth the limitations on a life insurance policy's ratio of cash value to death benefit and how quickly premiums can be deposited into a life insurance contract. Policies that do not meet the seven-pay test are not life insurance. In §12.14, there are illustrations of two-premium-payment non-MECs. By increasing the death benefit, a two-payment plan can qualify as a non-MEC and still satisfy the 1988 seven-pay test.

A standard or non-MEC life insurance policy is taxed under the first-in, first-out (FIFO) accounting method. Thus, a policyholder needing a withdrawal for his or her own retirement or other investment purposes could withdraw all basis first (i.e., the amount of money the policyholder contributed to the policy), and if he or she needed further withdrawals (cash values *above* basis), these could be accessed as nonreportable policy loans (nonreportable events).[6] The policy loans used to make withdrawals of amounts above basis have exceptionally low loan spreads. Spreads are usually 0.5 to 1 percent, but could be as low as 0.1 to 0.25 percent. If the policy is not in force at death, any loans beyond basis become ordinary income. Great care must be exercised to avoid this.

Conversely, MECs and annuities are treated under the last-in, first-out (LIFO) method of accounting. Thus, any withdrawal from either produces ordinary income. Under a MEC, the death benefit is not subject to income tax. By contrast, on the death of the annuitant, an annuity leaves its beneficiaries subject to income tax on the gain in the contract.

§ 12.2 Investing the Cash Value Account

The ability to recommend a proven performer known to one's family office or other advisers is a key advantage of PPVUL. Of course, he or she will have to meet the requirements of the life insurance company and will be chosen on the bases of size of assets under management, years of verifiable experience, willingness to keep records in compliance with insurance company standards, and possibly willingness to accept money from new investors who become policyholders in the private placement offering. Once accepted by the company, the money manager recommended by the investor effectively becomes an employee of the insurance company, contracted to manage that investor's separate account. The money manager could limit the ability of other private placement investors who might want to have him or her as their investment manager merely by posting a very high minimum acceptable investment (e.g., $10 million), or by declaring the portfolio dead to new investors.

The minimum investment in a PPVUL contract is generally a commitment of $2 million, with a commitment of $5 million usually needed to recommend one's favorite money manager to manage the assets held in one's account. Under special circumstances, some carriers will accept annual premiums as low as $250,000 and a commitment of as little as $1 million to name a favorite investment manager.

An investor's selected money manager must manage the investor's account in compliance with IRC Section 817(h). IRC Section 817(h) provides that there must be no fewer than five separate investments, no one of which may exceed 55 percent of the separate account's assets, no two of which may account for more than 70 percent of the account's assets, no three of which may constitute more than 80 percent of the account's assets; and no four of which may represent more than 90 percent of the account's assets. Many people wonder what happens if one of the investments becomes 80 percent of the total. If no new money (premium) is added to the account and no rebalancing takes place, the policy continues to meet the diversification rules. It is the addition of new money or a change due to rebalancing that may violate the diversification rules.

The diversification requirements are tested at the end of each calendar quarter for the life of the policy. The Internal Revenue Code provides that a segregated asset account that satisfies the diversification provisions at the end of any calendar quarter is not considered to be nondiversified merely because of subsequent fluctuations in value. Therefore, once a portfolio is adequately diversified, it continues to meet the diversification rules regardless of market fluctuations.

There is a two-pronged safe-harbor test in IRC Section 817(h)(2). Both tests must be met for the account to fall within the safe harbor. The first test provides that an account will be diversified without any further showings if it meets the requirements mandated for regulated investment companies under IRC Section 851(b). A regulated investment company is diversified when at least 50 percent of the account is represented by cash and cash items, government securities, securities of other regulated investment companies, and "other securities," with the further limitation that not more than 51 percent of such other securities may be invested in any one issuer, and that no such investment may be greater than 10 percent of the voting securities of any one issuer, and not more than 25 percent of the account may be invested in any one issuer (other than government securities and other regulated investment companies), or in two or more issuers that the taxpayer controls and that are in the same trade or business or in similar or related trades or businesses. For the purpose of this two-pronged safe harbor provision, the term *control* means ownership of 20 percent or more of the total combined voting power of all voting shares.

The second test of the safe harbor imposes the additional requirement that no more than 55 percent of the value of the segregated account can be attributable to cash, cash items, government securities, and securities of other regulated investment companies.

These diversification rules mandate a broad-based approach to investing that will accommodate only a limited investment in venture capital and convertible preferred stock.

A policy owner is permitted to recommend and even change a money manager but must have no investor control of the selection of investments in the account. Although IRC Section 817(h)(5) is the guideline, in Letter Ruling 9433030, the IRS required certain taxpayer advance representations before it would issue the ruling. These included the following:

1. The policyholder does not have a legally binding right to require the insurance company or the segregated account to purchase a particular

investment and a prearranged plan regarding spebcific investments does not exist.

2. The policyholder does not have a legal or equitable interest in any investment in the segregated account and does not communicate directly or indirectly with the investment officer of the insurance company or its affiliates.

By extension, the policyowner must also avoid telling the chosen manager what to buy or sell, lest a policyowner trigger a violation of the investor control rules, thus turning the portfolio earnings into ordinary income. When there is a policyowner interest in an underlying security, the safe harbor of IRC Section 817(h)(2) allows an investment manager to include 25 percent of such securities as investments in the private placement contract.

§ 12.3 Protecting the Cash Value Account

An investor's segregated account is separate from the insurer's general assets. Since PPVUL is a private placement product, it is governed by Securities and Exchange Commission (SEC) rules. Offshore carriers are subject to similar separate account rules, based on the jurisdictions in which they are located. For added comfort, an investor should consider offshore companies that are subsidiaries of major U.S. carriers, comply with U.S. onshore regulations, and/or choose to be taxed as U.S. companies under IRC Section 953(d).

Whether the policy's cash value accumulation account (underlying investment portfolio) is protected from the investor's creditors, from the departing spouses of the investor's children, or from the children's creditors depends on policy ownership. A completed gift, irrevocable dynasty trust appears to offer protection against all three types of liabilities. If the policy is owned outright and is payable to a spouse or children, some states offer almost complete protection (e.g., New York, Illinois, and Florida); however, many states offer very limited creditor protection or no protection at all. If the policy is owned by a self-settled grantor trust (i.e., an Alaska or Delaware trust) and the trust is irrevocable, the policy appears to be insulated from most creditors. In this case, the creator of the grantor trust is responsible for any income taxes the trust incurs. Since the trust is usually incomplete for gift tax purposes, it will be included in the investor's estate and subject to any transfer taxes due. (A "side-by-side" irrevocable trust, usually containing only a life insurance contract, but outside of the estate and the transfer tax system, can be used to pay the estate tax liability of the private placement contract.)

Factors to consider in structuring the situs and ownership of the PPVUL contract include the following:

1. If deposits are within gifting range and removal of the death benefit from the estate is the primary objective, investors should consider irrevocable life insurance trusts (ILITs), split-dollar arrangements; family limited partnerships (FLPs), limited liability companies (LLCs), and related devices, as policyowners, to remove the death proceeds.

2. If large deposits are to be made and gift taxes are not going to be paid, residents of states that protect cash values from the claims of creditors should consider paying state premium taxes. For the one-time payment of the state premium tax, an investor who lives in a state that protects the cash value of a policy from the claims of creditors if the policy is payable to the insured's spouse or children has a very effective, simple plan:

    a. The policy and its underlying cash value stay in the name of the insured policy owner, with complete control vested in him or her.

    b. The owner has unfettered access to the policy's cash value through loans and withdrawals of original basis.

    c. The owner has the ability to change beneficiaries at any time.

    One state, Illinois, has a state premium tax of only 0.5 percent (50 basis points) and very strong resident asset protection rules. An Illinois resident purchasing PPVUL from an Illinois-domiciled company can take advantage of this. A nonresident, unfortunately, will be subject to the Illinois "retaliatory" tax rules. In other words, if a California resident buys from an Illinois company, he or she is charged 2.35 percent, not 0.5 percent, because California has a 2.35 percent premium tax and Illinois "retaliates."

3. If large deposits are to be made, residents of states that give cash values little or no protection from creditor claims should consider an Alaska trust or an offshore structure as the owner. Both domestic Alaska trusts and offshore trusts will probably be grantor trusts. An attorney can be very creative in such ownership designs.

§ 12.4 Taxes and Other Expenses

PPVUL investors generally pay the following taxes and other expenses:

- State premium tax
- Deferred acquisition cost (DAC) tax
- Company mortality and expense (M&E) charge
- Brokerage costs
- Investment manager's fee
- Cost of insurance (COI)

Those investing offshore must generally also pay a 1 percent federal excise tax, but avoid state premium taxes and may avoid the federal DAC tax. If the offshore PPVUL is Section 953(d) compliant, the DAC tax is paid *in lieu* of the one percent federal excise tax; however, the state premium tax is avoided.

Federal DAC tax. This tax is levied against domestic carriers in the *first* year of each *new* premium deposited into the contract (about 7 percent gross and 5 percent net) and forces the carriers to stretch out the deductions they take for acquiring new business. The companies pass the cost down to the policyholder; depending on how the company keeps its books, the company will usually charge the accumulation account 1 to 1.5 percent in the first year of each new premium payment, in effect making up for the company's lost opportunity cost of the early tax write-off of commission expenses to agents. Note that actual DAC taxes range from 0.7 percent to 1.75 percent.

State premium tax. State premium taxes vary greatly. In typical high-tax states the premium tax can run between 2 and 3 percent. It is paid as each new premium is deposited. Having a trust-owned policy in the right jurisdiction can greatly reduce state premium taxes. If a California resident invests $10 million in a life insurance policy premium, the insurance company must pay the state 2.35 percent ($235,000) in state premium taxes. If that California resident established a trust in Alaska or South Dakota and the trustee of that trust bought the same policy, the state premium tax would be approximately $12,600. Except for Alaska and South Dakota, all states have retaliatory premium taxes; that is, if a state has a 2 percent tax but the investor buys a policy from a company domiciled in a state with a 3 percent tax, the investor must pay the higher state tax.

Company M&E charge. The insurance company will levy an M&E charge generally ranging from 50 to 110 basis points, which usually include a broker's trail of 25 basis points. The M&E charge is frequently the only area of company profit in PPVUL. Domestic companies generally charge in the vicinity of 60 basis points; 0.35 percent to the insurance company and 0.25 percent to the broker is a typical distribution. Larger purchases and duration can create reductions. Smaller offshore carriers levy higher M&E charges. The larger U.S. subsidiary companies are similar in cost to their domestic counterparts.

Brokerage costs. The broker will typically charge 1 to 2 percent of the premium as a placement fee.

If the contract is issued offshore in Bermuda, Nassau, Grand Cayman, or another foreign jurisdiction, broker's expenses of $5,000 to $7,000 are not an unusual additional expense; however, an offshore contract allows the investor to avoid the federal DAC tax and state premium taxes (see below). One investing in an offshore contract should expect to spend a minimum of two workdays to meet company officers, be examined, and sign trust documents and applications (see § 12.5). In the offshore jurisdiction, the broker will probably spend a day before the investor arrives and a day after the investor departs, making sure the investor's instructions are carried out.

Investment manager's fee. The investment manager's fee will vary greatly, depending on the type of manager chosen. The fee, which depends on the size of the assets and the type of management required, usually ranges from 50 basis points for an index fund allocator to 1 percent plus 20 percent of the profits for a hedge fund manager. The manager's fee will usually be the second highest expense, after the COI over the life of the contract.

Cost of Insurance. COI also has a significant spread; 25 percent is not unusual. Are the rates passed through from the reinsurer or marked up? Are preferred rates or super-preferred rates available? Is there a separate rate on retained risks versus reinsurance? On jumbo risks, reinsurance is more costly in the higher bands, driving up overall costs. Health classification has a major effect on the COI. COI is generally in the vicinity of 1 percent for preferred nonsmokers. Smokers and those with ratable medical conditions will pay more. Offshore rates of smaller companies are usually higher and preferred rates may not be available. A company's reinsurance treaties, retention capacity, and profit spread are also major factors in COI pricing. COI can always be a profit center in any policy design.

U.S. citizens or residents purchasing an offshore policy are generally subject to a 1 percent federal excise tax but avoid state premium taxes and may avoid federal DAC tax. In Bermuda and Grand Cayman there are offshore subsidiaries of some major U.S. insurance companies. Frequently, these insurers are Section 953(d) companies, choosing to be taxed as U.S. taxpayers. These companies do not pay the 1 percent federal excise tax. They pay the U.S. DAC tax, but since the DAC tax they pay is frequently 1 percent, the same percentage as the excise tax, there is little effect on investment performance. There are a number of smaller but reputable offshore companies whose structure complies with U.S. law. If a U.S. investor purchases a policy in an offshore jurisdiction, he or she definitely will not be subject to state premium taxes, as long as he or she was not solicited illegally and did not undertake any prohibited activities onshore.

In general, the policies of small offshore carriers cost more to create and maintain. Independent offshore companies (those that are not U.S. offshore subsidiaries) generally have less capacity (see § 12.9) than their onshore counterparts and are frequently thinly capitalized. Some offshore companies mark up their COI, especially in the early years of a contract, as a profit center. One major offshore American subsidiary charges an extra 20 to 40 basis points if the investor chooses his or her own investment manager. If the M&E charge, COI, and administrative costs are all higher, that could have a marked effect on investment performance. An investor who can get his or her own money manager approved domestically, or by an offshore subsidiary of a large American carrier, should increase yield because of tax efficiencies.

Conversely, with recent mergers, profit margin targets can vary widely among carriers. One Section 953(d) compliant offshore carrier even has a DAC tax of only 0.3 percent (30 basis points). To complicate matters further, some offshore carriers have both Section 953(d) compliant and noncompliant companies and policies. A specialized private placement broker can provide insight into how each product is currently structured from an overall cost standpoint.

Whether offshore is Bermuda, Nassau, Grand Cayman, Isle of Man, or anywhere else, an offshore investment means travel costs, generally higher trustee fees, time lost from work, and extra charges for the broker's expenses.

§ 12.5 Purchasing an Offshore PPVUL Contract

There are many advantages to purchasing a PPVUL contract offshore, including the following:

- Asset protection
- Wider choice of investment options and managers
- Hedge fund managers not available in the United States
- Less stringent liquidity requirements (i.e., the ability to pay a death benefit in kind)
- A lower DAC tax if the offshore carrier complies with IRC Section 953(d)
- Possibly lower COIs
- Contributions in kind (although such transfer will be taxed as a sale and will probably trigger capital gains tax)
- Ability to operate a captive property and casualty insurer, perhaps having shares in that captive available as an investment for PPVUL portfolio
- Possibility of having a venture capital manager
- Possibility of employing an offshore annuity freeze (also known as the Swiss annuity ploy or the deferred private annuity structure; see § 12.12)
- Increased respectability if a major U.S. carrier buys a substantial interest in the offshore company

Conservative investors should review the contracts of the Section 953(d) companies first. These tend to be the larger offshore entities. Smaller offshore companies will be more likely candidates to accept "annuity freezes," venture capital fund managers, contributions in kind, and other creative structures. These aggressive techniques have been under severe IRS scrutiny since January 2002 and should be considered in the gray area. They should not be used without advice of counsel. If large investments are being made, an investor should also consider a private "opinion letter" opining a "more likely than not" success rate. The opinion letter allows the investor to avoid tax penalties if there is a disallowance.

Special securities and insurance rules apply to the discussion and presentation of an offshore private placement product. An attorney, certified public accountant (CPA), family office manager, or any other non-insurance-licensed or non-securities-licensed professional may present the pertinent facts to a client. Great care must be taken so that there is no solicitation of the offshore product on U.S. soil by any securities- or insurance-licensed person. The client-specific presentation must not be made on U.S. soil by the insurance broker. These licensing restrictions do not apply to domestic contracts.) Consequently, the offshore product presentation must be made by the client's attorney, CPA, or other unlicensed adviser from generic (i.e., non-client-specific) information.

The private placement broker will be invaluable in getting the unlicensed advisor through the maze of possible permutations, since many products will be compared and spreadsheets prepared. The adviser should describe his or her client and the client's objectives and profile to the broker and should discuss any related estate, tax, asset protection, and gift reduction techniques that may be contemplated. The client's identity should not be revealed to the broker.

The adviser should have hypothetical illustrations prepared by each carrier being considered. The illustrations should use uniform assumptions and the client's name should not appear on them. The broker will assist the adviser in obtaining the illustrations and will prepare the analysis for the unlicensed adviser's ultimate presentation to the client. Medical information should be gathered by the adviser. The broker will explain how to get attending physicians' statements so that the adviser has a good estimate of the insurance health underwriting classification of the proposed insured. The various proposals are then compared. The broker will explain line item differences, minimums, ability to accept the client's desired money manager, and so on. The ledger sheet proposal formats presented to potential buyers of offshore policies are amazingly short on details and the breakdown of each expense item, compared to those presented to potential buyers of onshore policies. The private placement broker's responsibility is to sift through the nuances of these policies and custom-design a product appropriate to the needs of each client.

If the plan interests the client, the adviser can suggest that the client meet the broker in Bermuda, Nassau, Grand Cayman, or other offshore site chosen for the purchase. The presentation to the insured, with the identity of the client and the company fully revealed, will be made by the broker in the chosen jurisdiction.

All U.S. subsidiaries of major companies require the prospective insured to have a physical examination offshore and that all paperwork be done offshore by the prospective insured. Some smaller offshore carriers will accept a power-of-attorney purchase. An attorney should be consulted to see how the investor's state views such purchases, and the required physical examination site should also be checked on.

An investor's offshore schedule might look something like this:

- Day 1
  —Arrive at airport
  —Be met by broker
  —Drive to hotel
  —Get settled
  —A dinner appointment explaining the next day's procedures
- Day 2
  —Physical examination, consisting of blood and urine tests (which require a 12 hour fast), treadmill test (usually means light eating and nonstressful prior activities), and medical history
  —Application process, consisting of application, trust document, and investor suitability questionnaire
  —Inspection report (a financial credit report), which is a phone call that takes place in the insurance company's office after the application is signed and involves basic financial questions, since a large amount of insurance will be issued

Before any documents are signed, a detailed review of any sales illustrations (which are merely hypothetical projections) and a review of policy details will be presented. Since documents will usually be signed at the home office of the offshore carrier (or a nearby trust company), a senior officer of the company will be there to assist the investor and the broker in understanding policy details.

§ 12.6 Role of the Law Firm and the Accounting Firm

Private placement offerings, onshore or offshore, are complicated matters. The investor will generally want his or her attorney involved in the whole process. If the firm has had little experience in these transactions, most brokers will supply a list of attorneys who are extremely competent in this area and who are willing to do "back-room" drafting of any needed documents. Frequently, the initial concept is presented to a client's law firm in a generic format. Knowing some of the estate and tax objectives will help the broker in ordering the proper formats and ledgers. If the plan involves an offshore purchase, the law firm rather than the licensed broker will generally make the initial presentation to the client (see § 12.5). The purchase will usually involve one or more trusts or other entities as policy owners. Since the private placement contract will house significant and possibly growing funds, great care should be taken in the trust or other ownership design.

The law firm will also generally know the details of business succession planning, charitable intent, generation-skipping plans, and the like. Since many domestic policies are written as Alaska trusts, the law firm should be familiar with Alaska regulations. South Dakota has recently joined Alaska as a very low state premium jurisdiction, so familiarity with South Dakota regulations is also a good idea. Because many trusts holding PPVUL are grantor trusts and no gift tax was paid, the proceeds of the private placement will be included in the estate of the insured. The law firm will frequently suggest a second, irrevocable trust, funded with completed gifts and out of the estate, containing an insurance amount large enough to pay the tax on the private placement trust.

If asset protection is a motivation, structures to hold title to the contract will have to be created by the law firm in the appropriate jurisdiction. "Self-settled" trusts allowing the donor to get his or her money back under certain circumstances are frequently used. Since only a few states (e.g., Alaska, Delaware) allow such trusts, an offshore jurisdiction is frequently chosen.

Much of the appeal of PPVUL hinges on the nonreportable nature of the cash value inside buildup, combined with the ability to make nonreportable, extremely low interest loan withdrawals on gains above basis. Therefore, the client's CPA firm will probably review all tax aspects. That the ultimate death benefit passes to the beneficiaries income tax free and that there is a step-up in basis on death are of major importance for both estate and income tax planning reasons. The client and CPA can view hedge fund management more favorably as an alternative investment. Short-term trading and sales that normally create a large amount of ordinary income create no income tax consequences in the insurance-sheltered structure of PPVUL. Both the CPA adviser and the client's law firm will use these facts in the overall design of the client's plan.

§ 12.7 Potential Buyers of PPVUL

Wealthy individuals who can commit $5 million or more have the most flexible choices in PPVUL. Wealthy buyers fall into categories, each of which may require a somewhat different PPVUL design:

1. A client who wants all funds working immediately and does not intend to make lifetime withdrawals. Here, passing the greatest transfer amount to heirs or charity is the prime motivation. In this situation, a single-payment MEC might be appropriate. A single-payment MEC will produce the largest policy face amounts if a death benefit rather than investment return is the sole objective.
2. A client who may need some lifetime withdrawals. In this situation, a two-payment non-MEC contract is a better choice. The initial face amount will be lower, but the added withdrawal flexibility may warrant the reduction.
3. An older client who is insuring children and/or grandchildren (individuals with a long life expectancy) in the overall plan. For this client, MECs and annuities, withdrawals from which are taxed at ordinary income rates, should not be used. Annuities are taxed under the LIFO method and create ordinary income on gains to heirs. MECs do not create ordinary income for heirs.
4. A client who is a young entrepreneur, hedge fund subscriber, or other aggressive investor willing to forgo normal capital gains and ordinary income now to create a very long future deferral of all taxes. For this client, MECs, annuities, or hybrid frozen cash value contracts may be appropriate. The downside is that on annuitization 20 or 30 years hence, all distributions will come out of the contract as ordinary income.
5. A buyer who is age 20 to 55. In this situation, illustrations should show withdrawals done in a number of ways—at retirement age; at an assumed rate; at a lower rate; for 15 years, 20 years, and longer durations; and with inflation increases. This seems like lots of work, but in the private placement arena all bases should be covered. Monte Carlo simulation (MCS) illustrations should also be considered. If withdrawals are to be made, the client is probably contemplating a retirement stream of income and probably wants to know the odds on achieving this goal.

   MCS software is designed to make an investor aware of the fact that there are many ways to achieve a given rate of return, and that varying assumed stock market actions will affect the end result. One of the problems with these programs is the period of time chosen as the norm (the period of time one would like to emulate in future performance).

   The following exercise demonstrates how random market volatility affects rates of return:

a. Look at any 20-year Standard & Poor's (S&P) 500 historical performance.

b. Reverse the performance figures (i.e., the year 20 becomes year 1, year 19 becomes year 2, etc.).

c. Calculate the ending balance, which can change dramatically.

PPVUL projections that assume a uniform rate of return are only rough guesses, and probably will not occur as shown.

Running illustrations at 8 percent versus the exuberant 10 to 20 percent used for the past several years will be a better reflection of the next decade's predicted performance. The SEC *still* allows a 12 percent illustration, but does *not* allow MCS.

6. A client with nondiversified holdings seeking diversification and tax efficiency in a parallel portfolio to offset the market vicissitudes inherent in a single large block of any holding (e.g., founders' stockholders, executives holding stock with large gains plus many stock options, or those owning locked-up stock in any market condition, volatile or not). For these investors, nonrestricted shares, usually with large capital gains, are monetized through the use of loans, collars, and prepaid forwards. Generally, Treasury regulations (Regulation T) will restrict loans against securities to 50 percent when such loans are used to purchase other securities. PPVUL is treated like a security in this respect. For wealthy clients, there are many bank-type loans available, based on the client's personal statement. The borrowed money is used to buy life insurance of the private placement variety, and a diversified portfolio inside the contract is used to offset the volatility of the single large stock position. As long as the performance of the investments exceeds the cost of interest on any loans and the portfolio is properly diversified, overall volatility should be reduced.

§ 12.8 Removing PPVUL from the Estate

Before and investor has any thoughts of purchasing a large PPVUL policy, many methods of discounting, fractionalizing, and gifting will probably have been employed by the investor's attorney, CPA, and other financial advisers in order to reduce estate and transfer tax liabilities. The private placement broker frequently discovers some or all of the following in place, before a request for information on PPVUL is received: FLPs, LLCs, limited liability partnerships (LLPs), grantor retained annuity trusts (GRATs), ILITs, intentionally defective irrevocable trusts (IDITs) and, frequently, installment sales to those IDITs containing interest-only notes with a balloon payment at the end, and the myriad of other sophisticated devices used to save estate taxes. In addition, these wealthy clients have income tax saving devices in place. These might include employee stock ownership plans (ESOPs), 412(i) plans (fully insured pensions), multiple defined benefit pensions in unrelated entities, and opportunity-shifting devices.

If most of these devices are already in use, the amount that can be removed from the estate without being subjected to gift taxes may be limited; however, the recent increases in the lifetime exemption amounts may make this the perfect time to consider additional gifting. An adviser might want to double-check to see if a client should be exploring additional discounting concepts. Unfortunately, the gift tax remains very much intact in spite of the recent changes in the estate tax arena. Investors frequently use grantor trusts that are incomplete for gift tax purposes as the private placement contract owner, whether the contract is purchased onshore or offshore. Domestically, many cases are written with an Alaska trust as the policy owner. In the form of grantor trusts, Alaska trusts are irrevocable and offer creditor protection during life, but eventually the proceeds of PPVUL will end up in the estate, because no gift tax was paid.

Many techniques are available for removing PPVUL from the estate, some of which are described below.

Split dollar. Family or private split dollar is often used with PPVUL. Family split dollar has been utilized for very large transfers when gift value reduction, rather than cash flow, is a primary objective. Even with the 2001 rules and the higher imputed gift values that will be imposed in 2003 and beyond, there is lots of tax leverage available through the use of family split dollar. A problem with all split-dollar plans is the later rollout, which in a corporate setting is the payback to the corporation for what was effectively an interest-free loan to an employee. Combining split dollar with a qualified personal residence trust (QPRT) creates the ideal repayment "crawl-out" method: The remainder interest in the QPRT is owned by the ILIT and rent payments from the client go to that grantor trust, which in turn receives the rent and pays off the split-dollar obligation. Of course, having more than one residence in a family makes the QPRT split-dollar transaction easier. Also worthy of exploration is the leverage in a second-to-die split-dollar plan utilizing Table 38 (Department of the Treasury "U.S. Life Table 38," recently revised in 2001) values as the measurement of the gift. Table 38 can be extremely helpful in gift reduction for survivorship planning.

Dual trust concept. An innovative plan has been designed to indemnify the trust owning the PPVUL for any transfer taxes it must pay. Arrangements have been made with a major financial institution to act as investment manager for all or a portion of the private placement assets. This institution will make a series of loans, at a half point below prime, to the trustee of a side-by-side irrevocable trust. These interest-only loans will be used by the trustee to purchase enough insurance to fund any transfer tax liability incurred by the private placement trust. The side-by-side ILIT will serve several purposes: paying transfer taxes at death, restoring lost investment values with cash in down markets, or allowing the investment manager time for portfolio restoration following a market decline.

GRAT versus installment sale to an IDGT. The IDGT comes out better most of the time, but the GRAT has more substantial tax authority. Software for this technique is available.[7] The GRAT allows a wealthy property owner to shift the appreciation in that asset to his or her children or to other individuals. As long as the value of the asset appreciates at a rate greater than the rates used by the IRS for valuation purposes, the asset appreciation will be transferred to the property owner's children without the imposition of a gift tax. The GRAT is highly effective with publicly traded and "pre-IPO" stock, which may be used to make the annuity payments "in kind." A recent court decision has resulted in short-term GRATS—two to five years in length—having zero gift tax consequences (a "zeroed-out" GRAT). In such an instance, the annual annuity rate must be set high enough to eliminate the gift value.

In contrast, the installment sale to an IDGT begins with a trust structured with the grantor as owner under rules set forth in IRC Sections 671 to 678. These trusts are defective for income tax purposes, but not for gift tax or estate tax purposes. These trusts are generally used to "freeze" the value of a closely held business or real estate owned by the grantor. The grantor then sells assets, which are usually subject to discounts (the closely held family business, limited partnerships, etc.) to the IDGT in exchange for an installment note for a term of years. As long as the assets appreciate at a faster rate than the interest payable on the rate, this is a very effective transfer technique. If life insurance is purchased by the trust on the grantor's life, the note should be interest only with a balloon payment, extended out until death of the grantor.

Crummey gifts to an ILIT. This method is reliable if the gifting power has not been used elsewhere.

Funded ILITs using lifetime exemptions and/or loans. Leveraged uses of the increased lifetime exemptions should be explored. London Interbank Offered Rate (LIBOR) rates are historically very low at this writing. Borrowing to reduce some of the gift tax problems appears to be a very attractive alternative to a cash purchase. For very sophisticated clients willing to subject themselves to interest rate risk combined with currency risk, a loan in a foreign currency such as the Japanese yen might bear an exceptionally low interest rate.

Loan to pay premiums. Clients with lots of assets and limited cash should consider obtaining a loan to pay premiums, either against a corporate balance sheet or a personal statement. Lenders like the liquidity in private placement policies. Since cash value is immediately 95 percent to 100 percent of the premium, there is no large "hit" to the corporate or personal balance sheet. Whether conventional split dollar, family split dollar, or a conventional loan with a very favorable loan rate is used, the immediate, high cash value of private placement makes a number of creative loan plans feasible. Regulation T limitations apply when borrowing to buy variable universal life policies. Only 50 percent of the cash value will serve as collateral. In contrast, if the loan is being used to provide estate liquidity, a regular universal life (UL) policy with high early cash values can use 100 percent of its cash value as collateral for a loan. If there is freed-up stock that cannot be sold because of built-in gains, the client should consider collars, prepaid forwards, and other creative loan structures. In these techniques, the liquidity is used to buy true death benefits and to pay transfer costs. The idea is centered on using the borrowed funds to create funds for investment rather than a death benefit earmarked for heirs or charity.

Life insurance liquidity. A well-known asset management institution will do the following for a client with limited cash: The client deposits $1 million of securities with the institution for management. The client's ILIT can get seven consecutive annual loans of $100,000 at a rate floating 0.5 per cent below prime for the purpose of life insurance liquidity. The loan is usually liquidated in year 8 with investment profits.

FLP owning the life insurance. Getting more gifted money into a FLP using the FLP's various discounts results in more money being available to pay premiums, increasing the ultimate amount transferred.

Using a dynasty trust as the "family bank." This technique gets assets permanently out of the estate and protected from family creditors. PPVUL is the ideal product to fund a dynasty trust. With many states eliminating the law against perpetuities, dynasty trusts, used as divorce and creditor protection devices, look better than ever.

There are many other ways to get insurance out of the estate. The problem to avoid in these cases is the payment of gift taxes on gifts or transfers into the various structures designed. Split-dollar arrangements, loans, term insurance, FLPs, and similar devices can help reduce the gift value. Frequently several of these devices are used in combination.

§ 12.9 Avoiding Force-Out

A *force-out* is a return of premium that occurs when the client's investments have done so well that the "corridor" above the cash value creates a total amount higher than worldwide reinsurance capacity. *Capacity* could be defined as the sum of all pure risk available through the carrier's addition of worldwide reinsurance arrangements to the amount it retains (its retention amount). Capacity goes down when reinsurers merge. Before September 11, 2001, reinsurance capacity was as high as $235 million per capita; now it is approximately $150 million per capita.

A force-out is subject to ordinary income treatment. Removing some of the cash value from the policy to an annuity by means of a tax-free Section 1035 exchange can alleviate the problem. For wealthy clients, the largest insurers are recommended since they are most likely to have first chance at worldwide reinsurance capacity and to have the largest retention amount. If several carriers come in close, choosing the carrier with the highest retention amount, even though its fees might be five basis points higher, is probably the best way to avoid a future force-out for investors considering commitments of $20 million or more.

Investors considering large premium deposits should be wary of purchasing a survivorship policy for two reasons:

1. Its lower premiums will purchase a very large face amount.
2. That face amount will count against any other insurance to be issued on both lives.

Since laws can change and an investor may want to make large deposits quickly, capacity is the top priority. Wealthy clients should also consider MECs, annuities, and various hybrid policies (e.g., frozen cash value types) as ways to reduce face amounts, thereby allowing larger premium deposits and greater wealth to be passed to heirs and charity.

§ 12.10 Investment Grade Publicly Available Variable Universal Life

A client who *insists* on investor control should not even consider PPVUL. For a client who wants to be in money markets or bonds on Monday, health stocks on Tuesday, and biotechnology stocks on Wednesday, there is a solution: investment grade publicly available variable universal life, which is basically standard variable universal life with 25 to 40 investment choices that allow the commission to be driven out to the point where the investment performance, with all expenses included, can nearly equal that of PPVUL.

This product allows the investor to switch funds frequently, without triggering taxes, since he or she is in a protected cash value environment, and probably can check values on the Internet everyday. The second-to-die version of this product produces the highest investment returns, since the COI for survivorship policies is lower than the COI on a single life policy.

Another use of this product is for a client who does not qualify for the minimums required in a PPVUL purchase. An easy way to know if a contract is true investment grade variable universal life is to compare the end-of- year cash surrender value to the beginning-of-year annual premium. If the cash value is 90 to 100 percent of the premium, the contract is either PPVUL, or standard VUL with commissions reduced to very thin levels and spread out to make it perform like PPVUL. A private placement product with a mere $100,000 minimum has recently been developed. The expenses for products with a lower minimum are, unfortunately, higher than the expenses for larger products.

Some carriers will issue a "honeymoon surrender" rider. The rider, which can be attached to a regular universal life or variable life contract, allows the policy owner to surrender the policy (usually during the first five policy years) for the "accumulation" value rather than for the "net surrender value." The accumulation value is the policy value minus the cost of insurance, without the commission backcharge (agent's compensation). The surrender values during the honeymoon surrender period are similar to the high surrender values of a private placement. As agents' compensation is reduced and spread, a client will have to request this feature.

§ 12.11 Private Placement Annuities

A private placement annuity is taxed under the LIFO method. Therefore, it will probably be used in only three situations:

1. In a large net income charitable trust with a makeup provision (NIMCRUT), where the annuity is used as the spigot to turn the income stream on and off.
2. In a pension plan considering a purchase of real estate with a mortgage on the property. There is an unrelated business taxable income (UBTI) problem in this situation. If a private placement variable annuity purchased the property, the pension could purchase the annuity as another investment of the pension plan and the UBTI problem should disappear.
3. In the case of a young, very wealthy investor who is willing to give up capital gains mixed with ordinary income today for future withdrawals totally taxed as ordinary income when withdrawn, usually 20 or 30 years in the future. For one investing in hedge funds or other ordinary income taxable investments, a private placement annuity might make great sense. At death, a large charitable contribution could solve the income in respect of a decendent (IRD) problem.

§ 12.12 The Offshore PPVUL Deferred Private Annuity Structure

Although widely used by smaller offshore carriers, the offshore PPVUL deferred private annuity structure (also known as a Swiss annuity) seems to be pushing PPVUL products beyond their intended use. In January 2002 the IRS announced that the techniques used with this structure were being carefully examined. Therefore, the following techniques should be considered very aggressive and likely to produce problems on audit. Getting the advice of a tax attorney is strongly recommended.

A client sells low-basis stock to a company owned in the variable subaccount of a life insurance policy that she has established on the life of someone else (e.g., on the life of an adult child, parent, or sibling). Rather than receiving cash for the sale, and thereby creating capital gains tax immediately, the client receives a deferred private annuity from the wholly owned company. The deferred private annuity will defer the recognition of gain on the sale of the stock for a period of years. When the client starts receiving the annuity payments, she will be spreading the gain on the sale of the stock over her lifetime. The company owned in the life insurance subaccount can sell the low-basis stock without recognition of gain and the proceeds can be invested in a diversified portfolio that will be earning returns tax free. If the stock was an initial public offering (IPO) and had a big jump in value after sale to the insurance structure, there could be a further boost to the account.

The following is a description of an offshore private annuity freeze.

The client is founder and majority stockholder in a company with a fair market value of $10 million. He anticipates going public in 24 months and assumes that his new antiterrorism X-ray machine will make the stock worth $200 million. The stockholder determines he will have plenty to live on and would like to transfer much of the new wealth to future generations. The client establishes a Delaware trust. (Delaware has abolished the rule against perpetuities, as have several other states.) The use of an offshore trust is being avoided in this situation, since it creates additional reporting requirements, and IRC Section 684 would impose a 35 percent excise tax on the net amount at risk at the insured's death. After the death of the insured, the situs of the trust could be moved offshore.

The first step involves the purchase of an offshore private placement life insurance policy by the trustee of the ILIT. To mitigate the gift tax consequences of the initial gift, a private split-dollar arrangement is used. The second step involves the transfer of the soon-to-be appreciated stock to a foreign entity in exchange for a private annuity with deferred payments. The third step involves the sale of a call option to the investment adviser of the private placement policy, which will allow the adviser to buy some or all of the assets of the foreign entity.

If the client has guessed correctly and his stock really is worth $200 million after the IPO, some of the stock may be sold after the SEC-imposed six-month lockup period is over. The gain on the stock is not subject to U.S. capital gains tax, since the entity is a foreign entity. If the investment adviser decides to exercise his call and purchase some of the stock from the foreign entity, his purchase will be based on the value at the time of transfer, the $10 million valuation. The annuity obligation will be based on the lower transfer value.

The exercise of the call option will transfer the assets of the foreign entity in the separate account of the policy. This transfer will cause a dramatic increase in the value of the policy's cash value, bringing it up to the fair market value of the IPO stock. At the subsequent death of the insured client, the proceeds will pass tax free to the client's dynasty trust, which is not subject to the rule against perpetuities.

There are at least a half dozen other interesting uses of private placement life, many involving split-dollar arrangements, deferred compensation, golden parachutes, and charitable uses.

§ 12.13 Factors Affecting Investment Return in a PPVUL Contract

The following factors affect the investment return in a PPVUL contract:

COI. The health underwriting classification is important because it affects the COI and reinsurance for the duration of the contract. Standard risks may be 25 percent higher than preferred risks. Smokers may have term costs twice as high as nonsmokers. Major health problems will change rates greatly. If a risk is uninsurable, a substitute life may be used. Age and sex are also major considerations. COI is marked up by many companies to create another profit center. This practice will reduce overall return.

Amount of insurance required under IRC Section 7702. At any age, the number of payments needed for a policy to qualify as a non-MEC standard policy may be reduced to two payments; but as the number of payments decreases, the amount of the death benefit must be increased. Thus, to get money into the contract quickly, an unwanted extra amount of death benefit may have to be purchased in the early years of the contract. Two factors can reduce the problem and increase the yield: the return on the early deposits and the fact that the death benefit may be reduced in year 8, reducing the COI.

Where the policy is written. State premium taxes are a factor that can be somewhat controlled by use of a trust-owned policy. Having a trust and trustee in Alaska or South Dakota will reduce the state tax and thereby increase yield. An offshore policy avoids all state premium taxes and the federal DAC tax but is subject to a 1 percent federal excise tax, and if trust owned, will generally have higher annual maintenance costs. Offshore contracts in smaller companies tend to have higher costs than policies of larger companies.

Overall cost of the insurance contract being offered. How and when costs are deducted from the accumulation account will affect overall yield. Costs may be fairly constant throughout the life of the policy or could be higher in the early years but lower in the later years. COI can be a pass-through item or may be marked up. Discounted costs for large purchases will improve yield. The overall combination of factors must be carefully weighed. If no withdrawals or only small withdrawals will be made from the policy, the yield on the ultimate death benefit will become much more important than the yield on the cash value (the accumulation account).

"Cross-over" year. If death occurs early, the yield on the death benefit becomes the key. Over many years, however, a policy written with the smallest possible face amount of death benefit will eventually grow in face amount as the underlying portfolio grows in value and the face amount is forced up by the corridor rules.

> **Example.** Assume that the same premium is deposited over the same time period in each of two policies. Policy A is written with the least amount of death benefit allowable under IRC Section 7702. (This is the pattern generally seen in private placement policies where withdrawal yields are emphasized.) Policy B is written with the maximum death benefit possible. Policy B's initial death benefit will far exceed the death benefit of Policy A if the yields on the underlying portfolios are the same. The year in which the death benefit of Policy A exceeds that of Policy B is referred to as the cross-over year. Since the cross-over may not occur for 30 years, clients seeking maximum estate transfer values can hedge by buying some of each type of policy.

Performance of the investment manager. A company allowing an investor's hedge fund manager or conventional fund manager of choice may be worth some extra basis points, since the single most important factor in an underlying portfolio's future value is the manager's performance. The manager's fees are a factor, but good performance will far outweigh reasonable costs.

---

1. IRC § 72.
2. IRC §§ 101(a), 1014.

3. IRC § 7702(b).
4. IRC § 7702(c).
5. IRC § 7702(d).
6. IRC V 72(e)(5).
7. See Oshins, "Dynasty Trusts: Beneficiary Control, Non-tax Benefits, Leverage and Opportunity Shifting Strategies," Nebraska Continuing Legal Education presentation, July 2, 2001 <www.oshins.com>; Oshins, "Opportunity Shifting," *J. Fin. Serv. Profs.*, May 1999, at 30; Handler and Oshins, "GRAT Remainder Sale to a Dynasty Trust," *Tr. & Est.*, Dec. 1999, at 20.
8. See R. Oshins and Blattmachr, "The Megatrust: An Ideal Family Wealth Preservation Tool," *Tr. & Est.*, Nov. 1991.

CHAPTER 13

Section 529 Education Plans

Edward Higgins

Synopsis

The Economic Growth and Tax Relief Reconciliation Act of 2001 (EGTRRA) has reinvigorated a somewhat sleepy college savings plan known as the Section 529 education plan, which was named after the section of the Internal Revenue Code (IRC) that created qualified state tuition programs. As amended, IRC Section 529 may change the way education costs are funded by affluent families. This chapter reviews the basic features of the revised Section 529 plan and describes the process used to structure a personal education plan for high net worth clients, incorporating the favorable features of Section 529 plans where applicable.

§ 13.1 Spiraling Education Costs

Costs at four-year U.S. colleges and universities have been skyrocketing at a rate that is two to three times the rate of inflation since 1982, and recent financial data show this trend is getting worse. Costs to attend college are estimated to grow at 5 percent per year; by this estimate, the total cost for a four-year undergraduate degree at a private university in 2019 will exceed $200,000. A bachelor's degree from a public institution will cost over $100,000.[1] Furthermore, according to the General Accounting Office (GAO), from 1980 to 1995 the average tuition costs at a public university increased 234 percent, but average family incomes rose only 80 percent.[2] Affluent family members who are currently paying for college costs are well aware that it is not uncommon to spend $40,000 or more per year for a top private college, before considering other college "essentials" such as cars, clothes, and vacations.

Unless they have had recent experience, few families know that even the cost of applying to college is on the rise. A *Wall Street Journal*[3] article points out that a total cost of $10,000 is not uncommon when the following expenses are factored in: application fees, testing fees, Scholastic Aptitude Test (SAT) prepatory courses and study books, college visits both during the application process and before the final decision, and supplementary application materials such as videotapes of athletic performances or color slides of an art portfolio. Finally, many parents do not hesitate to pay thousands of dollars to hire a college counselor.

For many families, education costs extend beyond the cost of a four-year bachelor's degree program. Graduate school is becoming the norm, and education costs for private schooling before college often begin with the cost of private nursery school for two-year-olds and last for 12 or more years before college. During this time, additional "education" costs are incurred in the form of ballet lessons, summer camps, piano lessons, singing lessons, sports camps, and athletic equipment. There is no limit to the process of obtaining a well-rounded educational experience.

It is not surprising that even the wealthiest families borrow funds or liquidate holdings not targeted for education to cope with this enormous expense. Education costs are often shifted to the child, as seen in the record levels of student loans. According to a report released in March 2002 by the Higher Education Project of the State Public Interest Research Groups, 39 percent of student borrowers graduate with unmanageable levels of debt. *Unmanageable* in this report is defined as monthly loan payments in excess of 8 percent of monthly income. This study also found that borrowing levels quadrupled among wealthy students from the 1992 academic year to 1999, with *wealthy students* being defined as dependents of families with at least $100,000 in annual income.[4] Investing in a Section 529 savings program can help reduce the occurrence of such incidents, if not eliminate them altogether.

§ 13.2 Summary of Section 529 Plans

Simply stated, a Section 529 plan in its present form is an investment plan operated by a state to help families save for future college costs. As long as the plan satisfies a few basic requirements, federal tax law provides special benefits. All 50 states and the District of Columbia either offer plans or were scheduled to do so by the end of 2002. One of the most appealing features of the present plans is that one does not have to live in a particular state or send a student to school in that state to participate in its plan. This has resulted in a lively race between the states to offer competitive plans, since they are a source of goodwill and often times revenue for depleted state treasuries.

The estate planning implications of Section 529 plans are enormous. Wealthy families have a new incentive to give away more money. In addition to using the special five-year gift tax exclusion that applies to Section 529 plans (see §13.2[d]), wealthy families can fund Section 529 plans without gift tax by choosing to use as much of their lifetime exemptions as they wish. (EGTRRA increased the exemption from $675,000 to $1 million.) A secondary estate planning benefit of a Section 529 plan is that the money in the plan can grow without increasing the donor's estate.

The simplicity of a Section 529 plan appeals to many clients, especially older family members. A Section 529 plan is much more straightforward than a complex estate plan. Older people cannot always get a good grip on an irrevocable trust with complex Crummey provisions or the various trusts that are the lifeblood of experienced and sincere estate planners.

Creditor protection is a topic of increasing interest in this litigious society and makes these Section 529 plans more advantageous than education funding plans that do not qualify for this creditor protection. About a dozen states offer Section 529 plan assets some form of protection from creditors of the owners, beneficiaries, or both.

Some of the main benefits of all Section 529 plans and some of their drawbacks are reviewed below.

§ 13.2[a] Tax-Free Growth

Once a Section 529 plan is funded by the donor, all earnings grow free of federal income tax. Thus, the investment strategy can be similar to the management of tax-advantaged 401(k) and individual retirement arrangement (IRA) rollover programs. This is an improvement over most traditional education funding plans such as UTMA accounts and trusts, which often involve the payment of federal taxes, which can be substantial if the funds grow through investment. (*UTMA* stands for Uniform Transfer to Minors Act, which is also known in some states as the Uniform Gift to Minors Act, or UGMA).

§ 13.2[b] Tax-Free Withdrawals

Beginning in January 2002, withdrawals from a Section 529 plan for qualified higher education expenses are free from federal income tax. The definition of these expenses is quite liberal. In general, qualified higher education expenses include tuition, fees, room and board, books, applications, and any equipment necessary to attend an eligible institution. Also included are costs incurred for the enrollment and attendance of a special needs beneficiary and to provide special services to such a beneficiary. There is no ceiling on the amount that can be withdrawn to pay for these qualified expenses, although there is a ceiling on contributions (see §13.2[e]).

To benefit from the tax deduction, the expenses must be expenses incurred at an eligible educational institution. To determine whether a school is an eligible institution, one should search for its federal school code, the identification number for schools eligible for Title IV financial aid programs, at the following Web site: www.ed.gov/offices/OSFAP/Students/apply/search.html. Section 529 funds can be used for graduate programs, including medical school and law school, as well as for programs at some foreign institutions. Since trade schools may qualify, Section 529 monies could be used to pay for training to become a chef, a fashion designer, or even an auto racer if there is an accredited auto racing school. Since a Section 529 plan is designed for higher education expenses, it should not be used as a source of funds to pay for private elementary school. Any nonqualified withdrawal loses the tax advantage and incurs penalties.

§ 13.2[c] Donor Control

Wealthy families have all heard the horror stories about children who divert funds designated for higher education expenses by generous donors—or have experienced the horror themselves. Section 529 plans allow the donor to give up most of the ownership of these assets designated for higher education expenses while retaining enormous control over investment of the plans, reallocation among other members of the family, and transferring Section 529 plan assets to other Section 529 plans. The owner authorizes all expenditures and can veto paying for a college that he or she does not like. With few exceptions, the named beneficiary has no rights to the funds. In this respect, Section 529 plans are dramatically different from traditional UTMA accounts, under which unspent monies automatically become the property of the named beneficiary when he or she reaches legal age, 18 to 21 depending on the state. Furthermore, a donor may open an account for the benefit of any U.S. citizen or legal U.S. resident, regardless of family relationship; however, if the donor changes the original beneficiary, the new recipient must be a member of the family of the previous beneficiary. The definition of *family member* includes the donor and goes beyond the immediate family, including relationships by marriage. The following are examples of individuals who may qualify as family members:

- A son or daughter or a descendent of either
- A stepson or stepdaughter
- A brother, sister, stepbrother, or stepsister
- A father or mother or an ancestor of either
- A stepfather or stepmother
- A brother or sister of the father or mother
- A son or daughter of a brother or sister
- A son-in-law, daughter-in-law, father-in-law, mother-in-law, brother-in-law, or sister-in-law
- The spouse of the beneficiary or the spouse of any individuals described above
- A first cousin of the beneficiary

Once a Section 529 plan has been selected, the investment allocations have been made, and a beneficiary has been selected, the plan is not static.

The donor is permitted to change the investment program once per year and the beneficiary at any time. If the Section 529 account is an UTMA rollover, however, the account owner loses the ability to change beneficiaries (see §13.4). A rollover to another Section 529 program for the same beneficiary is no longer considered a taxable transfer but is limited to one transfer per 12-month period.

§ 13.2[d] Generous Gift Tax Exclusion

In 2002 the federal gift tax exclusion increased to $11,000 per person ($22,000 per married couple). In addition, there is a special annual gift tax exclusion that applies to Section 529 plans. The special exclusion permits an individual to accelerate up to five years' worth of annual exclusion gifts. Thus, a donor can contribute up to $55,000 ($110,000 for a married couple) per beneficiary in any one calendar year.

Another consideration for Section 529 programs is the effect of changing the named beneficiary. If a donor changes the beneficiary, there are no gift tax consequences to the account owner or beneficiary provided that the new beneficiary is a member of the family. If the new beneficiary is in a younger generation, however, the previous beneficiary will have made a gift of the account value to the new beneficiary.

§ 13.2[e] Contribution Limits

Each state has a different Section 529 plan, and they all have imposed different dollar limits on the plan's original investment account. Some states have generous ceilings on the plans. For example, Virginia has a $250,000 ceiling. Therefore, although a married couple may have a $110,000 limit per beneficiary, other family members (e.g., grandparents) may contribute another $140,000 and stay within that state's ceiling. Since the monies from a Section 529 plan need not be spent for 30 years, establishing such a plan provides a tremendous opportunity to shift significant amounts from the donor's estate. Since the ceiling applies to the original investment amount, donors who are optimistic about the long-term growth potential of the account may want to make large contributions as early as possible to stay within the ceiling. All growth beyond the ceiling retains the aforementioned benefits (see §§13.2[a]–13.2[d]). This creates the opportunity for a wealthy couple to shift large amounts to other family members even after they have implemented other estate planning strategies. If a taxpayer has not used up his or her lifetime gift tax exemption, setting up Section 529 plans leaves him or her more room for the lifetime exemption than using alternative methods.

§ 13.2[f] Drawbacks

There are some disadvantages to Section 529 plans that require attention. Following is a brief discussion of some of the problems that are explicit in the legislation. The reader should be cautioned that these plans are absurdly complex and that each state's plan may have drawbacks that are particular to that plan.

First, the legislation that makes Section 529 plans tax free may expire in 2011. Under this last law, which President George W. Bush has asked Congress to extend beyond 2010, any distribution taken from a Section 529 plan to pay for college will be taxed directly to the student. This could be expensive, since withdrawals to pay taxes are not considered qualified distributions. Although many forecasters feel that it would be political suicide not to extend all or a portion of the changes made by EGTRRA to years after 2010, there are no guarantees. The worst case would be that the federal government does nothing, so that Section 529 plan earnings do become taxable after 2010. Unless a change is made, the money will grow tax free only through 2010.

Second, although an owner can withdraw all or a portion of the money in a Section 529 plan at any time for any purpose, if it is not used to pay for qualified higher education expenses, it will generally be subject to ordinary income tax and to a 10 percent penalty on the gains. The tax will be assessed at the account holder's or beneficiary's tax rate, depending on who receives the distribution. Even after paying taxes and the 10 percent penalty for a nonqualified withdrawal, however, an investor could still be benefit from years of tax-deferred growth.

Third, unlike guaranteed prepaid tuition plans that are available in some state-sponsored Section 529 plans, Section 529 plans do not guarantee funds sufficient to meet projected education costs. Therefore, the responsibility for the success of the program is on the owner and will depend on the performance of the investment, as is the case with a 401(k) plan. On the other hand, superior performance could create funds that exceed expenses. The donor could then direct the surplus to other beneficiaries. Once again, the worst-case scenario still provides for many years of tax-free compounding before profits not used for qualified higher education expenses are taxed.

Fourth, substantial administrative fees may be charged by both the states and the financial institutions that manage the funds (see §13.5[c]).

Fifth, a Section 529 plan may affect a beneficiary's eligibility for financial aid. On the surface this would not seem to be a deterrent for wealthy families, but the reality is that financial aid is not just for the needy. In addition, nobody can predict what the future holds, and private colleges are free to consider family Section 529 assets in any way they wish when awarding their own financial aid packages.[5]

Finally, the worst drawback of Section 529 plans for wealthy families is that they are generally subject to a mass-marketing approach and therefore there has been an abundance of nonprofessional advice given by uninformed advisers. Examples include misinterpretation of the drawbacks mentioned above, failure to analyze the effects of state income taxes (which can be especially problematic for wealthy families and families with residents in several different states), and failure to consider alternative measures. Wealthy families can afford to have specialized advice in this area.

§ 13.3 Defining Educational Goals

The first step in setting up an education plan for high net worth individuals is to define all the educational needs of the individual's family, including college. The family profile is viewed both vertically and horizontally, since anyone can set up a Section 529 plan and can name practically anyone as a beneficiary.

Parents and other financial supporters have different views on how their beneficiaries should be educated. In some cases, private education begins in nursery school at age two and continues for 20 or more years. Regardless of their wealth, some families believe in paying only for four years of college. As each family member's needs are defined, an adviser may discover some very interesting applications for a Section 529 plan:

1. The young college graduate who, after entering the workforce, decides to go to graduate school to enhance his or her career opportunities. The costs can be staggering and are often far in excess of the costs of undergraduate school. For example, a first-year medical student at Harvard Medical School (HMS) can expect to pay $47,750 for the 2002–2003 academic year alone. The total estimated cost of attendance for all four years at HMS exceeds $200,000.[6] The first year of the MBA program at

Columbia Business School is estimated to cost $58,510 for a single student.[7] Finally, law school at Stanford University costs an estimated $47,403 per year.[8]

2. The parents who originally funded a prepaid tuition plan for their children that required that the children attend the public state university in their state of residence. The family's goals for education have now changed. In large part because of the children's accomplishments, the family now expects that all will qualify for an Ivy League diploma. In addition to their academic accomplishments, children may have nonacademic skills—for example, in athletics and music—that give them an edge in applying to the college of their choice.
3. The parents who funded a state plan in the past with the wish that the child attend college in the state of residence. Although they did not realize it at the time, the qualified expenses are limited to tuition. They therefore set up a separate Section 529 plan to cover the expenses not covered by the plan they chose—for example, room and board, books, and other supplies.
4. The successful Wall Street investment banker who contemplates a life change, accepts early retirement, and enrolls in divinity school.
5. The corporate executive and his or her spouse who decide to retire early and enroll in culinary school and live out their dream to open a country inn.
6. The 60-year-old attorney who loved studying the classics in college and decides to go back to college after retirement and take many of the same courses.
7. The family that wants to reward their loyal housekeeper with a special gift at retirement. The housekeeper prided herself in her ability to save for her own retirement, but was most concerned that her two children would not be able to attend college if they qualified. A Section 529 plan is set up to give the housekeeper the right to allocate the funds in a manner that she can control.

§ 13.4 Reviewing the Present Education Funding Program

The most common vehicle for funding college expenses is the UTMA account or trust. Under present law, there are some federal income tax advantages when these accounts are small. Until the children are 14 years old, the parents' (presumably higher) tax rate applies only to investment income above $1,500 and the children's (presumably lower) rate applies after the child reaches age 14. When these investments are cashed out to pay for college, however, they are subject to taxes on the gains, which may be significant. Although a UTMA account's tax treatment has advantages compared to the tax treatment of the parents' accounts, the tax advantages cannot compete with a Section 529 plan's tax-free status.

The child becomes the owner of a UTMA account when he or she receives the UTMA funds, which may be as early as age 18 in some states and is no later than age 21 in all states. When the child receives the UTMA funds, he or she is free to spend the funds on college or on other, nonintended purposes, such as a sports car. Parents may consider closing one UTMA account and opening another, but such a course is not advisable. Below are a few ideas on what can be done when goals have changed after a UTMA account has been set up:

1. The parents can simply stop funding the UTMA account and set up a separate Section 529 account for college expenses.
2. The UTMA account can be used to reimburse the parents for legitimate expenses for a child that do not fall within the category of parental responsibilities (typically interpreted to mean necessities such as food, clothing, shelter, and medical expenses). As any parent knows, expenses for children before college run the gamut from private elementary and secondary school tuition to summer camps and karate lessons. Depending on state law, all these expenses could qualify for this strategy.
3. The UTMA account can be transferred to a UTMA Section 529 account. Since Section 529 plan contributions must initially be made in cash, however, the UTMA account must be liquidated, the taxes paid, and the proceeds transferred to the UTMA Section 529 account. The long-range tax benefits of Section 529 plans may make this a good strategy if the taxes on the liquidation are low. If the funds are paid out before the child reaches majority, the new, non-UTMA portion can be subject to the control of the donor.

In addition to UTMA accounts and trusts, other programs may help wealthy families accomplish some of the same objectives as Section 529 plans. Where grandparents have taken over the education needs of their grandchildren by funding the premiums for a variable life insurance policy on the lives of their children (at a much lower cost than policies on the grandparents' lives), they plan to use the cash values that grow tax free in the investment portion of the policy to pay for the college costs. If the parents die before the children go to college, the life insurance policy's death benefit pays for the grandchildren's education.

§ 13.5 Choosing a Section 529 Plan

After the education needs of each family member have been defined, present plans reviewed, alternatives explored, and a decision on the extent of the use of Section 529 plans made, the real work begins.

Almost every state has at least one plan and the states without plans were scheduled to set up Section 529 programs during 2002. Some states offer several management choices and even more fund options. New Mexico, for example, uses four fund managers and offers a total of 32 investment options. The plans that are already established are subject to change. This makes shopping for a plan somewhat daunting. Each plan has its own set of rules, investment options, and tax treatment. No single plan is right for everyone.

At the outset, a wealthy family planning to make a significant contribution to one or more Section 529 plans is well advised to engage a specialist in this area or at least to insist that its present adviser be reasonably conversant with this complex subject. The advisers should be encouraged to delegate to or share responsibilities with the specialist.

For families preferring to set up Section 529 plans themselves, there are a number of excellent books, articles, and Web sites that discuss planning concepts and the particulars of various plans. Some of these are better than others at updating their information for recent developments. The following is a list of Web sites that are good sources:

- www.savingforcollege.com
- www.review.com
- www.cfionline.com
- www.ed.gov
- www.collegesavings.org
- www.salliemae.com

- www.nast.net
- www.collegeboard.com

General guidelines for selecting a plan are discussed below.

§ 13.5[a] Start with One's Home State

A person affected by high state taxes should determine whether his or her state plan provides state income tax benefits. Some states offer hefty tax deductions for investing in their Section 529 plans, and some allow withdrawals that are free of state income tax. If the donor resides in one state and works in another, he or she may still qualify for a Section 529 deduction for the tax paid to the state where he or she works

§ 13.5[b] Choose the Investment Manager Carefully

Investors should beware that some of the financial institutions that have been chosen by the states to offer Section 529 plans have done a better job of marketing their plans to the states than they have done or are likely to do in managing the monies. In addition, a person may want to choose a financial institution where he or she already has a relationship and is comfortable.

Many of the institutions offer preschool age-based plans, possibly making the selection process simpler. Some advisers tend to favor managers who have set up Section 529 plans that offer the client and his or her adviser the flexibility to select from a broad array of funds. This customized approach, which allows the client the opportunity to integrate the choices with the rest of his or her portfolio, is most appropriate for wealthy clients who prefer a tailored approach to managing the family's assets.

> **Example.** An executive who made her fortune in the technology sector would be able to decide how educational funds are invested in a Section 529 program, since transparency is required in managing the plans. Therefore, if this executive did not want to risk her child's educational funds in the technology sector, even though it had been profitable in the past, a plan with more conservative holdings could easily be found through assistance from her financial adviser or through independent research.

§ 13.5[c] Keep the Expenses Low

Most states are selling plans through advisers; this can drive up fees and sales charges. Some of the mutual fund organizations are charging as much as a 3.5 percent upfront load with no reduction for large purchases and no links to non-Section 529 accounts that could help investors benefit from volume discounts. In addition, some of the ongoing yearly management fees are quite large. Finally, state treasuries see Section 529 plans as a source of revenue and are also charging yearly management fees and transaction fees (e.g., to change plans). Competition and disclosure, coupled with good advice, are likely to cause the expenses of Section 529 plans to follow the expenses of 401(k) plans, which have decreased dramatically over the years.

§ 13.6 Reviewing the New Plan

Once the education funding program has been agreed on and implemented, it is important that the adviser review it with the family each year. Some of the topics to cover may include the performance of the underlying funds and any reallocations within existing plans, changes in the family members' education needs (e.g., newly born family members), and changes among the suppliers. This gives the adviser the opportunity to establish a long-term meaningful relationship with a client in an area that is most important to the client and also permits an expansion of a partial relationship.

---

1. College Board, Trends in College Pricing, 2000–2001.
2. Rosen, "The 529 Plan," *Ticker,* Dec. 2001, at 29.
3. Asinof, "Hard Lesson: Cost of Applying to College is Rising, Too," *W.St.J.,* Feb. 28, 2002.
4. See http://www.pirg.org/highered/BurdenofBorrowing.pdf.
5. Wang, "Tuition Relief," *Money Magazine,* May 2002.
6. Estimated cost of attendance provided by the HMS Financial Aid Office.
7. See http://www1.gsb.columbia.edu/admissions/mba.
8. Estimated cost of attendance provided by the Financial Aid Office of Stanford Law School.

CHAPTER 14

Private Annuities

Karl N. Huish and Craig R. Campbell

Synopsis

The Internal Revenue Service (IRS) defines an *annuity* as a "contract which provides primarily for periodic installment payments to the annuitant named therein, and under which the death benefits at any time cannot exceed the larger of the reserve or the total premiums paid for the annuity benefits."[1] Basically, an annuity is a right to receive a stream of payments.

Annuities are divided into two types: commercial annuities and private annuities. A *commercial annuity* is a contractual arrangement between an obligor (an insurance company) and a contract holder that entitles a payee (annuitant) to periodic payments. For federal income tax purposes, the payments consist of a return of capital portion and an ordinary income portion.

Life insurance companies and brokerage firms derive substantial revenue from the sale of commercial annuities to their clients, whether the annuities are fixed or variable. In fixed annuities, each annuity payment is guaranteed; in variable annuities, the annuity payments vary with the performance of the assets—typically stocks and bonds or mutual funds—inside the annuity contracts. Commercial annuities are used chiefly to (1) provide tax deferral on the growth of the annuity contract and (2) shift investment or mortality risk from the annuitant to the insurance company or brokerage firm.

The other type of annuity—the so-called private annuity—is the focus of this chapter. Private annuities are generally used as an estate planning device pursuant to which property is sold, often by one family member to another, in exchange for a promise to make a fixed periodic payment for the life of the seller.

Private annuities are also used as an asset protection tool. There are many estate tax planning techniques that can be used to create annuities that may qualify as state bankruptcy exemptions. Even if the annuity payments are not exempt from creditors under state law, only the income payments are exposed to creditor attachment; the principal is ordinarily secure.

The taxation of private annuities is a bit more complicated than the taxation of commercial annuities, because a private annuity is treated as part sale and part annuity. The income from annuities is subject to varying tax rules but is often controlled by Section 72 of the Internal Revenue Code (IRC). For tax purposes, each payment to the private annuitant is broken down into (1) a tax-free return of capital; (2) gain, the character of which depends on the character of the property transferred and its holding period; and (3) ordinary income, provided the property is not secured.[2] This chapter provides an introduction to private annuities and related transfer techniques, which offer effective mechanisms for the transfer of significant wealth if they are structured properly.

§ 14.1 How Private Annuities Work

A *private annuity* is an arrangement whereby property is transferred in exchange for a promise to make periodic payments (annuity payments).[3] The obligor (the person who promises to make the annuity payments) is usually related to the annuitant (the person who transfers the property and is promised the annuity payments).

> **Example.** John has substantial stock in a corporation that he believes will rapidly appreciate in the future. He transfers the stock to Megan, his daughter, under the terms of a private annuity. The private annuity provides that Megan will make an annual payment to John until he dies. Within one year, the stock appreciates to ten times its value prior to the transfer. Megan makes annual payments to John under the terms of the annuity. She may need to fund the payments by borrowing against the value of the stock. After John's death, any remaining value in the stock has effectively been transferred to Megan, without any gift or estate tax. At John's death, the stock will not be included in his estate.

As demonstrated in this simple example, private annuities have several advantages, including the following:

1. They may reduce estate taxes if the annuitant dies before he or she is actuarially supposed to die.
2. The transfer immediately removes the property from the annuitant's estate, so it is not reachable by the annuitant's creditors (although the annual annuity payment might be reachable by creditors, depending on the dollar amount of such payment, and any available exemption under applicable state law).
3. The control of assets transferred can be retained by family members if they are the obligors.
4. Appreciation of the property transferred will not be included in the annuitant's estate, and the property remaining (i.e., the life estate) will also not be included in the annuitant's estate.
5. The annuitant is relieved of management duties.
6. Gain from the property is recognized over several years.
7. The obligor receives a step-up in tax basis equal to the amount of the annuity payments.

There are also several disadvantages to the use of private annuities, including the following:

1. There is no step-up in the tax basis of the property on the death of the annuitant (but, correspondingly, there are no estate taxes either, since the asset is not owned by the annuitant).
2. Payment of the annuity is unsecured and uncertain.
3. Property transferred is unprotected from the creditors of the obligor.

Generally, a transfer of property in exchange for other property, including an annuity, is a taxable transaction. If the annuity is unsecured, however, the tax is suspended until payments are made.[4] This is because an unsecured promise to pay an annuity creates an uncertainty as to whether payments will be made when required. On the other hand, when the annuity is secured by an escrow account, assets, or other device, the transfer of property in exchange for the annuity is treated as a taxable transaction in which the gain recognized is equal to the excess of the fair market value of the annuity over the tax basis of the property transferred in the exchange. Similarly, the transfer of property in exchange for a commercial annuity is a taxable transaction to the extent the present value of the payments to be made under the annuity contract exceeds the tax basis in the assets transferred.[5] For this reason, as discussed below, it is critical that private annuities are structured so that the payment is unsecured.

In the past, trusts were frequently used to secure annuities. Today, this tool has limited use because of the potential adverse tax consequences; however, when trusts were used to secure annuities, certain steps were taken—steps that can be effective if they are used today. The four steps are as follows:

1. A trust is established by someone other than the annuitant.
2. Property is transferred to the trust in exchange for an agreement to receive an annuity.
3. The property transferred to the trust is usually sold.
4. On the death of the annuitant, the remainder interest is held or distributed to the natural objects of the annuitant's bounty.

This configuration would appear to be subject to the anti-freeze estate tax rules of Chapter 14 of the IRC.[6] In addition, since the use of a trust in a private annuity secures payment of the annuity, such an arrangement would normally result in taxable income being recognized on the exchange. Current authority, although sparse, holds that whether a trust is being used to secure payments depends on whether the trustee has the power to dispose of trust property. If the trustee is free to dispose of the trust's assets by sale, the trust is not being used to secure payments and the transfer of property to the trust in exchange for a private annuity is not a taxable sale.[7]

For many clients, deciding between a commercial annuity and a private annuity need not be an "either/or" proposition; clients can use both. In light of the different tax treatment afforded to secured or commercial annuities and unsecured private annuities, it may be appropriate to establish two annuities: an unsecured private annuity for assets with a low tax basis so that the gain attributable to the assets can be deferred, and a commercial or secured annuity for property whose sale will not produce a significant tax (i.e., property with a relatively high tax basis).

§ 14.2 Income Tax Consequences of Unsecured Private Annuities

Revenue Ruling 69-74 describes the IRS's position regarding the income tax consequences of a private annuity. In general, if the annuity is unsecured, each annuity payment will have the following three components: (1) a tax-free return of capital; (2) gain, the character of which depends on the character of the property transferred and its holding period; and (3) ordinary income.

If the fair market value of the property transferred exceeds the present value of the annuity payments, the excess will be a gift as long as the transaction is not in the ordinary course of business. The tax cost basis of the property subject to the gift tax will be increased by the amount of the gift tax, but will not be increased to more than the property's fair market value.

> **Example.** Mary (the mother) transfers stock to Jason (the son) under a private annuity. The stock is worth $1.5 million at the time of transfer, but the annuity is structured such that Jason's payments are based on a $500,000 transfer of stock. The additional $1 million would be a gift to Jason, and result in gift tax to Mary. (Gift tax is generally paid by the grantor of the gift, not by the recipient of the gift.)

When appreciated property is transferred in exchange for a secured annuity, the exchange is taxable and the annuitant's investment in the contract is the fair market value of the property transferred. When the fair market value of the property transferred substantially exceeds the value of the annuity received, the excess is treated as a gift and the investment in the contract is limited to the value of the annuity. A loss derived from the worthlessness of an annuity is treated as a capital loss.

Payments made by the obligor are nondeductible. The obligor's basis is the present value of the expected payments; however, if additional payments are made, the tax cost basis will increase accordingly. The tax basis for loss purposes is the amount of the payments actually made, but payments made after the sale are treated as a loss in the year of payment. After the annuitant's death, the tax basis is adjusted to reflect what actually occurred.

§ 14.3 Effectiveness of Private Annuities for Estate Tax Purposes

Clients often try to retain the use and enjoyment of property that is ostensibly transferred through a private annuity. A private annuity is designed to remove the property transferred in the exchange from the annuitant's estate for federal transfer tax purposes. Since property is being transferred in exchange for an annuity, which is often paid, at least in part, from the property transferred, taxpayers who engage in such a transaction by necessity straddle the line between a valid annuity arrangement and a retained life estate that will render the property includable in the annuitant's estate. If the annuitant is treated as having a retained interest in the property, he or she will also likely be taxed on all of the income of the property; to the extent the transaction results in a partial gift of property, the retained interest will be includable in the annuitant's estate for federal estate tax purposes.

> **Example.** Howard attempts to transfer his house to his son William using a private annuity, but Howard continues to live in the house without paying rent to William. It is likely that the IRS will include the house in Howard's estate.

Whether the annuitant will be treated as having retained a prohibited interest in the property transferred in exchange for the annuity is determined on the basis of the substance and effect of the transaction and not on the basis of the subtleties of draftsmanship. Several factors are taken into account by the IRS, and no single factor is controlling. Generally, to avoid adverse tax consequences, the obligor should be personally liable for the annuity payments, which should not be chargeable against the property transferred and the amount of which should not be determined by the income of the property at the time of the payments. Other factors affecting this determination include the following:

1. The transaction should be in the form of an annuity.
2. The property transferred by the annuitant should not be the sole source of payment; there should be other assets from which the annuity could be paid.
3. The property transferred by the annuitant should be assignable. An asset that is nonassignable by the obligor implies control by the annuitant.
4. The obligation to pay the annuity should be unconditional and not limited to the property transferred or the income derived from the property.
5. The amount of the annuity should be determined in accordance with Treasury valuation rules. Any disparity between the value of the annuity and the fair market value of the property transferred is a factor, since the property would ordinarily be consumed in whole or in substantial part by the payments required. A disparity between these two amounts will not, however, be fatal, since a disparity merely establishes that there was a gift.

6. The annuitant should not retain control over the arrangement, including investment of the property.[8]

The tax calculations for private annuities are established according to IRS rules. The following two examples give some idea of the tax consequences to the annuitant.

Example 1.

Annuitant	Married couple, ages 65 and 62
Joint life expectancy	26 ½ years
Imputed interest rate[9]	7.00%
Fair market value of property	$1 million
Annuitant's tax basis in property	$100,000
Payment period	One annuity payment at end of each year
Annual payout to annuitant	$90,989
Tax-free portion	$ 3,846
Capital gain portion	$34,615
Ordinary income portion	$52,528

Example 2.

Annuitant	Single individual, age 85
Life expectancy	6.9 Years
Imputed interest rate	7.00%
Fair market value of property	$1 million
Annuitant's tax basis in property	$100,000
Payment period	One annuity payment at end of each year
Annual payout to annuitant	$221,990
Tax-free portion	$ 15,625
Capital gain portion	$140,625
Ordinary income portion	$ 65,740

§ 14.4 Private Annuities for Seriously Ill Taxpayers

A private annuity may be appropriate for a severely ill individual. The implications are obvious. If a terminally ill person establishes a private annuity, substantial assets can be transferred to family members without estate tax. If actuarial tables are used, a substantial portion of property can be excluded from the estate. The IRS, however, has taken the position that if death is imminent, the actuarial table will be disregarded.[10] Nevertheless, taxpayers have considerable flexibility. For example, in *Estate of Fabric v. Commissioner,*[11] the Tax Court upheld a private annuity established before the annuitant had open heart surgery. She died one year and five months after the surgery. The Tax Court stated:

> At the time of decedent's execution of the annuity agreement, it was not established that her maximum life expectancy was one year or less. In addition, while the decedent underwent open heart surgery five days later, she survived the operation by one year and five months. Furthermore, the uncontroverted testimony of decedent's physician was that as of late 1975 decedent should live several more years, possibly even five more years. . . . The evidence demonstrates that the decedent's death was not clearly imminent or predictable at the time she entered into the annuity agreement. Only where death is imminent or predictable will departure from the tables be justified.[12]

Similarly, in *Estate of McDowell v. Commissioner,* the decedent's death was imminent, but his life could have been prolonged by treatment. The court held that, since the condition was treatable, the fact that it "was not treated does not justify a deviation from the annuity tables."[13]

---

1. Rev. Rul. 55-639.
2. Commissioner v. Kahn, 174 F.2d 357 (3d Cir. 1949).
3. Private annuities are closely related to self-canceling installment notes (SCINs), which are installment obligations that expire (or cancel) on the death of the seller, and so are excluded from the seller's gross estate for estate tax purposes. The technical differences between SCINs and private annuities are beyond the scope of this chapter.
4. This treatment is similar to installment sale treatment.
5. Estate of Bell v. Commissioner, 60 T.C. 475 (1973); Lloyd v. Commissioner, 33 B.T.A. 903 (1936); Burnet v. Logan, 283 U.S. 404 (1931); 212 Corp. v. Commissioner, 70 T.C. 788, 802–03 (1978) (creation of annuity constituted "taxable transaction" because it was secured by real

estate transferred, obligation of lessee to pay rental with respect to the real estate, and confession of judgment); Rev. Rul. 62-136.

6. Treas. Reg. § 25.2702-2(a)(2) (1992) (Chapter 14 rules apply to transfer to trust).
7. Stern v. Commissioner, T.C. Memo. 1992-374. The *Stern* holding is questionable because the proceeds of any such sale would still be held in trust; consequently, the annuity payments would be secured to the extent of the proceeds.
8. Some of the key private annuity cases are Lazarus v. Commissioner, 58 T.C. 854 (1972), *aff'd,* 513 F.2d 824 (9th Cir. 1975); Fidelity-Phila. Trust Co. v. Smith, 356 U.S. 274 (1958); Ray v. United States, 762 F.2d 1361 (9th Cir. 1985); Stern v. Commissioner, 747 F.2d 555 (9th Cir. 1984); Lafargue v. Commissioner, 689 F.2d 845, 849 (9th Cir. 1982); Syufy v. United States, 818 F.2d 1457, 1465 (9th Cir. 1987); Bixby v. Commissioner, 58 T.C. 757, 790 (1972).
9. This interest rate is the Section 7520 rate, which is 120 percent of the applicable federal rate (AFR). The Section 7520 rate is a "hurdle" rate imputed by the IRS. The Section 7520 rate in existence when the private annuity is established remains throughout the annuity. The higher the rate, the higher will be the ordinary income portion of the annuity payment. For this reason, private annuities have additional benefits when interest rates are low.
10. Rev. Rul. 80-80.
11. 83 T.C. 932 (1984).
12. Id. at 942–43.
13. T.C. Memo. 1986-27, 51 T.C.M. (CCH) 319, 324 (1986).

CHAPTER 15

Long-Term Care

David L. Smith

Synopsis

It is only when a family member or friend requires long-term care that people feel the enormity of the impact of long-term care. The impact is emotional and social, as well as financial, and the need for long-term care is more common than one would think.

A Metropolitan Life[1] study reports that the number of households in the United States caring for family members tripled from 7 million to over 22 million between 1987 and 1997. Further, family caregivers provide an estimated $196 billion of free care annually and caregiving preoccupies one in every four households. As the U.S. population continues to age these numbers will increase.

Almost 50 percent of couples age 65 and older will spend some time in a nursing home. Close to 75 percent of people over age 65 will utilize long-term care services either at home or in a facility. About 40 percent of long-term care benefits are being paid to individuals between the ages of 18 and 64.

The costs are enormous! The average annual nursing home cost across the United States is around $48,000 and climbing. In the Northeast it is more than $80,000 per year. Home health care is usually less expensive, but it can approximate or exceed nursing home costs if round-the-clock care is required.

It does not take long for $1 million of assets to disappear when long-term care services are required. If long-term care costs increase at a compounded rate of 5 percent per year and an individual in the Northeast is spending $80,000 now, the costs will be about $123,000 per year in 10 years and over $200,000 per year in 20 years.

The point is that one has a 50-50 chance of needing long-term care at some point in one's life. The costs are high and getting higher. Should one take a chance and self-insure, or purchase private long-term care insurance?

§ 15.1 What Long-Term Care Is

The term *long-term care* is generally thought to be synonymous with the term *nursing home care* but it really means much more than that. It encompasses home care, community care, and assisted-living care as well as nursing home care and it affects all age groups, not just the elderly. Long-term care is care provided to help people remain independent.

Someone suffering from an accident, an illness, or a cognitive impairment (such as Alzheimer's disease) could need long-term care. Long-term care helps one live as one lives now; it may not improve or correct medical problems. It is quite different from traditional medical care.

There are also different levels of long-term care. *Skilled care* usually refers to care provided by medical professionals such as registered nurses. It is usually needed 24 hours a day, a physician must order it, and the care must follow an agreed-upon plan. Skilled care is usually provided in a nursing home, but it can be provided at home with help from visiting nurses or therapists.

Personal care or *custodial care* refers to care that helps people with activities of daily living. These activities include bathing, dressing, toileting, eating, and transferring (getting in and out of a chair or bed). It is this type of care that most people will need at some point, and it is not covered under most medical plans or Medicare.

§ 15.2 Ways to Pay for Long-Term Care

There are only three payment options:

1. *Self-insurance.* Self-insuring simply means paying out of pocket. Until recently many wealthy people opted for self-insurance; however, changes in the Internal Revenue Code (IRC) over the past few years, along with legislation being considered by Congress, have heightened interest in insuring the risk.
2. *Medicaid.* Medicaid is a welfare program. One must "spend down" all one's assets to qualify. This is not an option most want to consider.
3. *Long-term care insurance.* Long-term care insurance is becoming more popular as people begin to understand its role in financial planning. It has been around for the past 25 years, but it was not until 1997 that the government created tax-qualified policies and gave tax deductions to businesses offering long-term care programs to their employees. Tax deductions for individuals are minimal at the moment but it is expected that premiums will become 100 percent tax deductible in the very near future.

§ 15.3 The History of Long-Term Care

Long-term care is a recent phenomenon. At the beginning of the last century people were not concerned about retirement. The average life expectancy was only about 47 years. Back then families tended to stay close to home. If a family member lived longer than usual, one or more of the children provided whatever care was necessary. Today life expectancy in the United

States is approaching 80 years and family members, rather than being close to home, are often spread across the country.

Social Security was created in 1932. That was the first time many people even thought about the possibility of retiring. Medicare was created 33 years later—in 1965. Even then, Congress did not anticipate the longevity Americans enjoy today. Congress determined that Medicare benefits would begin at age 65, not having any idea that medical advances, better nutrition, exercise, and so forth would extend life expectancy as they have.

Only in the last 25 years have Americans begun to address issues relating to increased life expectancy: people who need care, people whose care is not covered under their health insurance plan, people who are shocked at how much the care costs. The Health Insurance Portability and Accountability Act of 1996 (HIPAA) was the first piece of legislation that provided incentives for businesses and individuals to own long-term care insurance.

U.S. legislative leaders have been aware for some time that Social Security and Medicare need some attention if they are going to be available for future generations. They have been the focus of many studies and debates. Long-term care issues, however, were not seriously addressed until the mid-1990s when the government began to realize the potential problems increased longevity is creating.

Medicare and traditional health insurance do not cover long-term care. They might cover some skilled nursing home and skilled home care, but only if the patient has been in the hospital for three days and only if the treatment is helping him or her improve and only for a limited period of time. The only government program that covers long-term care is Medicaid.

Medicaid is a welfare program. To qualify, an individual must "spend down" his or her assets to poverty level. Once at that level, the qualifier must typically relocate to a nursing home—a nursing home chosen by Medicaid and not necessarily by the individual or his or her family.

It is estimated that almost 80 percent of nursing home residents do not require skilled nursing care. They are there because they have used up their assets paying for care and now are on Medicaid.

As the government became aware of these facts, it also found that Medicaid spending was climbing dramatically. In Connecticut, for example, Medicaid spending for long-term care grew from $318 million in 1986 to $1.86 billion in 2001.[2] That is a six-fold increase in just 15 years.

U.S. leaders came to the conclusion that government could not afford to pay for long-term care along with Social Security and Medicare. They decided the best solution would be to encourage individuals and businesses to own private long-term care insurance policies and the best way to do that would be through tax incentives. HIPAA was the first step.

§ 15.4 The Government's Position on Long-Term Care

In the mid-1990s Congress began to realize that the U.S. population was living longer than had been anticipated. As people aged it became apparent that they needed more services and the services needed were not so much skilled nursing services as they were custodial services. *Custodial services* are typically services that used to be provided by family members when family members were available to provide them: bathing, dressing, getting around, toileting, and so on.

Many Americans are under the impression that their traditional health insurance or Medicare will cover these services. Unfortunately they are wrong. Medicare will cover skilled nursing care under limited circumstances and never for more than 100 days. Group health insurance plans differ, but they too are generally designed to target skilled care and only for relatively short periods.

As mentioned in §15.3, Medicaid expenses exploded from the mid-1980s to the mid-1990s. Those expenses have to be controlled and government leaders decided to tighten the rules for Medicaid qualification and to make it more attractive for individuals to own, and for businesses to offer, long-term care insurance.

The most effective means of accomplishing that objective is through tax incentives. HIPAA took the first step. It created a new class of long-term care insurance policies called *tax-qualified policies.* These policies came into being as of January 1, 1997. Essentially HIPAA provides that benefits paid under tax-qualified policies are income tax free to the insured.

HIPAA also provides that any costs an employer incurs in establishing a long-term care insurance program for its employees can be deducted—as any other medical expense can be. These expenses include any premiums paid by the employer. HIPAA went one step further: it allows an employer to discriminate and still deduct the premium. This means that the owner of a business can purchase long-term care insurance through the business just for him- or herself and his or her spouse. No other employees need to be covered and the business still gets the deduction. The amount of the deduction varies depending on the type of business (see Illustration 1).

Under most benefit plans an employer must treat all employees equally to qualify for a tax deduction, or the employer must divide employees into classes

Illustration 1. Income Tax Deductions for HIPAA Tax-Qualifying Long-Term Care Insurance

<table>
<tr><th>Type of Taxpayer</th><th>Premium Deductions</th><th>Taxation of Benefits</th></tr>
<tr><td>Individual Taxpayer Who does <u>NOT</u> itemize</td><td>No deduction[1]</td><td rowspan="9">Reimbursement benefits for qualified long-term care services are not taxed.

Per Diem or Indemnity benefits are not taxed except those benefits that exceed the greater of:[5,6,7]

• Total qualified long-term care services charged or,

• $220 per day (in 2003 and adjusted each following year for inflation)

Nonforfeiture Benefit (return of premium benefit):

• Available only upon total surrender or death.[10]

• May not be borrowed or pledged.

• Not taxable at death.[10]

• Taxable upon policy surrender to the extent premiums were deducted.[10]

———

NOTE: This document refers only to the tax treatment of Tax Qualified Long-Term Care Insurance Policies under the Health Insurance Portability and Accountability Act of 1996.

The tax treatment of Non-Qualified Long-Term Care Insurance policies, benefits and premiums is unknown.</td></tr>
<tr><td>Individual Taxpayer Who Itemizes Deductions</td><td>Treated as medical insurance premiums.[9]

Limited to the lesser of the actual premium paid or the amount per person from an age-related table of maximum deductible premiums. Table is adjusted annually for inflation. For the year 2001 and 2002, the maximum deduction per person is:
<table><tr><th>Age</th><th>2002 Max Deduction</th><th>2003 Max Deduction</th></tr><tr><td>Age 40 or younger</td><td>$240</td><td>250</td></tr><tr><td>Age 41 - 50</td><td>450</td><td>470</td></tr><tr><td>Age 51 - 60</td><td>900</td><td>940</td></tr><tr><td>Age 61 - 70</td><td>2,390</td><td>2,510</td></tr><tr><td>Age 71 and older</td><td>2,990</td><td>3,130</td></tr></table>
Premium deduction is effective to the extent that the deductible premium above added to taxpayer paid medical premiums and deductible out-of-pocket medical expenses exceeds 7.5% of the taxpayer's Adjusted Gross Income (AGI).</td></tr>
<tr><td>401K Plans</td><td>May <u>not</u> be paid through 401K retirement accounts.[11]</td></tr>
<tr><td>IRA Owners</td><td>Individual Retirement Account may <u>not</u> be used to pay LTCI premiums.</td></tr>
<tr><td>MSA Owners</td><td>Taxpayer <u>may</u> pay for LTCI premiums from Medical Savings Accounts.[1]</td></tr>
<tr><td>Section 125 Plans</td><td>LTCI premiums become <u>taxable</u> to employee if paid through Section 125 plan.[11]</td></tr>
<tr><td>Employees (Non-Owners)</td><td>Premiums paid by employees
• Deductible by the employee who itemizes as an individual taxpayer, above premiums paid by employer
• Deductible by employer[2,9]
• Not taxable to employee[8,9]
• Not limited to the age-related-cap maximum deduction
Applies to both individual policies and group insurance.</td></tr>
<tr><td>C Corporation Owners</td><td>If a corporate employee, treated as employee.[4]</td></tr>
<tr><td>Other Business Owners
• Sole Proprietors
• SUB Chapter S 2% or more owner
• Partners
• Limited Liability Corporation owners</td><td>May be treated as a business expense for medical insurance premiums.[12]

Limited to the lesser of the actual premium or the amount on an age-related table of maximum deductible premiums which are adjusted annually for inflation:[13]
<table><tr><th>Age</th><th>2002 Max Deduction</th><th>2003 Max Deduction</th></tr><tr><td>Age 40 or younger</td><td>$240</td><td>250</td></tr><tr><td>Age 41 - 50</td><td>450</td><td>470</td></tr><tr><td>Age 51 - 60</td><td>900</td><td>940</td></tr><tr><td>Age 61 - 70</td><td>2,390</td><td>2,510</td></tr><tr><td>Age 71 and older</td><td>2,990</td><td>3,130</td></tr></table>
Reduced to the Self-Employed medical insurance allowable percentage, by year:
<table><tr><td>2000 and 2001</td><td>60%</td></tr><tr><td>2002</td><td>70%</td></tr><tr><td>2003 and there after</td><td>100%</td></tr></table></td></tr>
</table>

The information provided herein is not intended as legal or tax advice. Consult with an attorney, accountant, or tax adviser regarding tax implications of purchasing long-term care insurance.

[1] HIPAA 1996, P.L. 104-49L	[4] IRC Sec. 106(a)	[7] IRC Sec. 104(a)(3)	[10] IRC Sec. 7702B(b)(2)(C)	[13] IRC Sec. 213(d)(10)(B)
[2] IRC Sec. 7702B(a)(3)	[5] IRC Sec. 7702B(a)(2)	[8] IRC Sec. 213(d)(1)	[11] IRC Sec. 125F	
[3] IRC Sec. 105(b)	[6] IRC Sec. 7702B(d)	[9] IRC Sec. 7702B(a)(1)	[12] IRC Sec. 162(l)	

and treat all employees in each class in the same manner to get the deduction. The fact that the government allows discrimination in the provision of long-term care insurance is taken to be an indication of the importance it places on offering private long-term care insurance through employers.

HIPAA also provides some tax deductibility for individuals; however, an individual can only deduct unreimbursed medical expenses in excess of 7.5 percent of adjusted gross income and the "eligible" expenses are limited by age. Although not useless, the deduction made available to individuals under HIPAA is very limited.

The good news is that HIPAA was only the first step. More needs to be done to attract people to long-term care insurance and take the pressure off Medicaid. In 2001 two bills that would give a 100 percent tax deduction for individuals' long-term care insurance premiums were introduced in Congress.[3] These bills would also allow businesses to offer long-term care insurance through cafeteria plans and flexible spending arrangements, effectively giving employees tax-free premiums. These bills, or others like them, will pass in the near future.

Bills are also being introduced in state legislatures with the same goal in mind: to reduce Medicaid spending. A bill was introduced in Connecticut in 2001 that would require municipalities, as a condition of receiving state aid, to form groups for the purpose of purchasing long-term care insurance for town and city employees.[4] That bill did not pass, but its introduction shows the concern Connecticut has about its Medicaid spending and indicates that it sees long-term care insurance as a means of solving the problem.

The federal government announced that it would begin offering long-term care insurance to its 20 million employees in the fall of 2002. John Hancock and Metropolitan Life agreed to create a group product for federal employees. The surrounding publicity generated lots of interest in the general population about long-term care and should be a boon to agents specializing in this market.

§ 15.5 The Market for Long-Term Care Insurance

Long-term care insurance is designed to protect assets. When a person requires assistance with activities of daily living at home or in a facility, there are substantial costs involved. When these costs exceed the individual's income, he or she will usually have to dip into savings, investments, or other assets to pay the bills. Once the individual accesses principal, a lifetime of savings can disappear very quickly.

By paying for the care received, long-term care insurance preserves the assets of the insured either for future use of the person receiving care or for his or her heirs. It also allows the individual to have choices about how to live and where to live. With little or no assets, the choices would be made for him or her and in most cases would not be the choice the individual would have made for him- or herself.

Since asset protection is the primary goal of long-term care insurance, lower-income people are not primary targets for this coverage. Deciding what constitutes lower income is very subjective; however, an individual whose assets (excluding the person's home) are less than $200,000 would probably not be a viable prospect. He or she would not have a lot of assets to protect and might find it difficult to pay the insurance premiums.

At the other end of the spectrum are the very wealthy. They have lots of assets and, presumably, a healthy income. The argument can be made that they do not need long-term care insurance because they can afford to pay for any care out of their own pockets. In other words, they can self-insure. On the other hand, an argument can be made that, although they may not need long-term care insurance, they would be foolish not to purchase it. Why would someone who can afford to pay an insurance premium take on the risk of having to spend $50,000, $100,000, or even $200,000 per year on home health or nursing home care? Statistics say about 50 percent of Americans will spend some time in a nursing home and almost 75 percent will receive some long-term care services. Injury, illness, and old age do not discriminate by income level.

The low-income population may not be able to afford coverage and the very wealthy may choose to self-insure, but those in between definitely have the need for long-term care insurance and the ability to afford the premiums. They might be defined as those with investable assets between $300,000 and $3 million. These are the people who enjoy a comfortable lifestyle right now, but who could face financial ruin rather quickly if long-term care costs are not insured.

Figures 1 through 4 are based on an individual who is age 55 and has $500,000 of assets earning 7 percent compounded annually. He also has a long-term care insurance policy with an annual premium of $2,000.

Figure 1 shows how his investment will grow if he never needs long-term care. In 40 years the investment would amount to almost $7.5 million if he does not take the insurance and to just over $7 million with the insurance premiums (and lack of earnings on them) taken into consideration.

Figure 1. Table and Graph Showing No Long-Term Care

Year	Without LTCI	With LTCI
0	$500,000	$500,000
1	$535,000	$532,688
2	$572,450	$567,665
3	$612,522	$605,089
4	$655,398	$645,134
5	$701,276	$687,981
6	$750,365	$733,828
7	$802,891	$782,884
8	$859,093	$835,374
9	$919,230	$891,539
10	$983,576	$951,635
11	$1,052,426	$1,015,937
12	$1,126,096	$1,084,741
13	$1,204,923	$1,158,361
14	$1,289,267	$1,237,135
15	$1,379,516	$1,321,422
16	$1,476,082	$1,411,610
17	$1,579,408	$1,508,111
18	$1,689,966	$1,611,367
19	$1,808,264	$1,721,851
20	$1,934,842	$1,840,069
21	$2,070,281	$1,966,562
22	$2,215,201	$2,101,909
23	$2,370,265	$2,246,731
24	$2,536,183	$2,401,691
25	$2,713,716	$2,567,497
26	$2,903,676	$2,744,910
27	$3,106,934	$2,934,742
28	$3,324,419	$3,137,862
29	$3,557,129	$3,355,201
30	$3,806,128	$3,587,753
31	$4,072,556	$3,836,584
32	$4,357,635	$4,102,833
33	$4,662,670	$4,387,720
34	$4,989,057	$4,692,548
35	$5,338,291	$5,018,715
36	$5,711,971	$5,367,713
37	$6,111,809	$5,741,141
38	$6,539,636	$6,140,709
39	$6,997,410	$6,568,247
40	$7,487,229	$7,025,712

If you never need LTC

$8,000,000
$7,000,000
$6,000,000
$5,000,000
$4,000,000
$3,000,000
$2,000,000
$1,000,000
$0
1 11 21 31 41
Year
Without LTCI
With LTCI

Printed with permission of Henrik Larsen, Advance Resources Marketing, Allston, Massachusetts.

Figure 2. Table and Graph Showing Long-Term Care Starting in Year 10

Year	Without LTCI	With LTCI
0	$500,000	$500,000
1	$535,000	$532,688
2	$572,450	$567,665
3	$612,522	$605,089
4	$655,398	$645,134
5	$701,276	$687,981
6	$750,365	$733,828
7	$802,891	$782,884
8	$859,093	$835,374
9	$919,230	$891,539
10	$840,865	$953,947
11	$749,921	$1,020,723
12	$645,098	$1,092,173
13	$525,072	$1,168,626
14	$388,385	$1,250,429
15	$233,458	$1,337,959
16	$58,580	$1,431,617
17	$0	$1,531,830
18	$0	$1,639,058
19	$0	$1,753,792
20	$0	$1,876,557
21	$0	$2,007,916
22	$0	$2,148,471
23	$0	$2,298,863
24	$0	$2,459,784
25	$0	$2,631,969
26	$0	$2,816,207
27	$0	$3,013,341
28	$0	$3,224,275
29	$0	$3,449,974
30	$0	$3,691,472
31	$0	$3,949,875
32	$0	$4,226,367
33	$0	$4,522,212
34	$0	$4,838,767
35	$0	$5,177,481
36	$0	$5,539,905
37	$0	$5,927,698
38	$0	$6,342,637
39	$0	$6,786,621
40	$0	$7,261,685

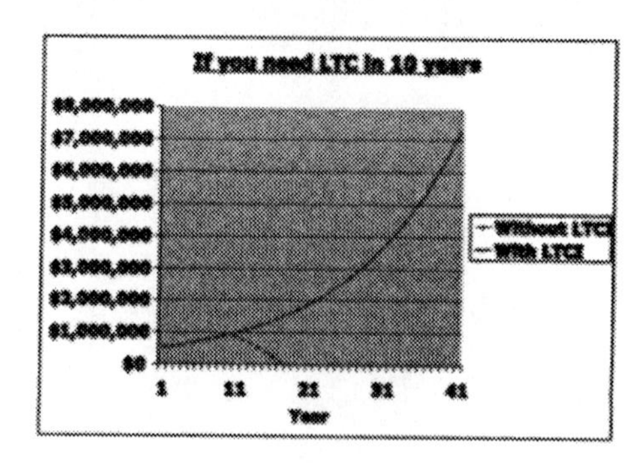

Printed with permission of Henrik Larsen, Advance Resources Marketing, Allston, Massachusetts.

Figure 3. Table and Graph Showing Long-Term Care Starting in Year 20

Year	Without LTCI	With LTCI
0	$500,000	$500,000
1	$535,000	$532,688
2	$572,450	$567,665
3	$612,522	$605,089
4	$655,398	$645,134
5	$701,276	$687,981
6	$750,365	$733,828
7	$802,891	$782,884
8	$859,093	$835,374
9	$919,230	$891,539
10	$983,576	$951,635
11	$1,052,426	$1,015,937
12	$1,126,096	$1,084,741
13	$1,204,923	$1,158,361
14	$1,289,267	$1,237,135
15	$1,379,516	$1,321,422
16	$1,476,082	$1,411,610
17	$1,579,408	$1,508,111
18	$1,689,968	$1,611,367
19	$1,808,264	$1,721,851
20	$1,702,413	$1,842,381
21	$1,577,532	$1,971,347
22	$1,431,706	$2,109,342
23	$1,262,860	$2,256,996
24	$1,068,742	$2,414,985
25	$846,909	$2,584,034
26	$594,716	$2,764,917
27	$309,295	$2,958,461
28	$0	$3,165,553
29	$0	$3,387,142
30	$0	$3,624,242
31	$0	$3,877,939
32	$0	$4,149,394
33	$0	$4,439,852
34	$0	$4,750,641
35	$0	$5,083,186
36	$0	$5,438,009
37	$0	$5,819,740
38	$0	$6,227,122
39	$0	$6,663,020
40	$0	$7,129,432

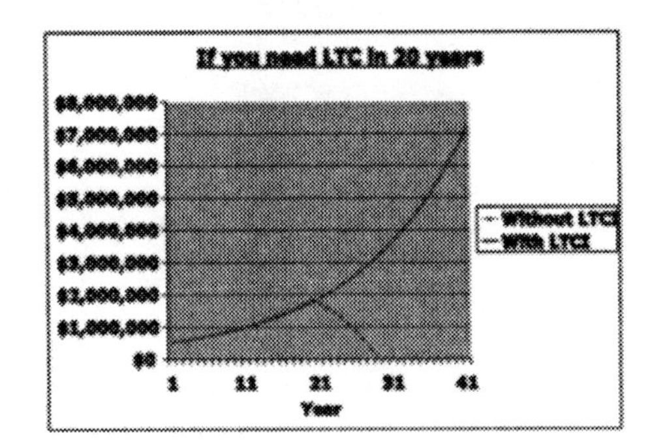

Printed with permission of Henrik Larsen, Advance Resources Marketing, Allston, Massachusetts.

Figure 4. Table and Graph Showing Long-Term Care Starting in Year 30

Year	Without LTCI	With LTCI
0	$500,000	$500,000
1	$535,000	$532,688
2	$572,450	$567,665
3	$612,522	$605,089
4	$655,398	$645,134
5	$701,276	$687,981
6	$750,365	$733,828
7	$802,891	$782,884
8	$859,093	$835,374
9	$919,230	$891,539
10	$983,576	$951,635
11	$1,052,426	$1,015,937
12	$1,126,096	$1,084,741
13	$1,204,923	$1,158,361
14	$1,289,267	$1,237,135
15	$1,379,516	$1,321,422
16	$1,476,082	$1,411,610
17	$1,579,408	$1,508,111
18	$1,689,966	$1,611,367
19	$1,808,264	$1,721,851
20	$1,934,842	$1,840,069
21	$2,070,281	$1,966,562
22	$2,215,201	$2,101,909
23	$2,370,265	$2,246,731
24	$2,536,183	$2,401,691
25	$2,713,716	$2,567,497
26	$2,903,676	$2,744,910
27	$3,106,934	$2,934,742
28	$3,324,419	$3,137,862
29	$3,557,129	$3,355,201
30	$3,427,525	$3,590,065
31	$3,269,920	$3,841,369
32	$3,081,405	$4,110,265
33	$2,858,824	$4,397,984
34	$2,598,749	$4,705,843
35	$2,297,458	$5,035,252
36	$1,950,917	$5,387,719
37	$1,554,750	$5,764,860
38	$1,104,215	$6,168,400
39	$594,174	$6,600,188
40	$19,063	$7,062,201

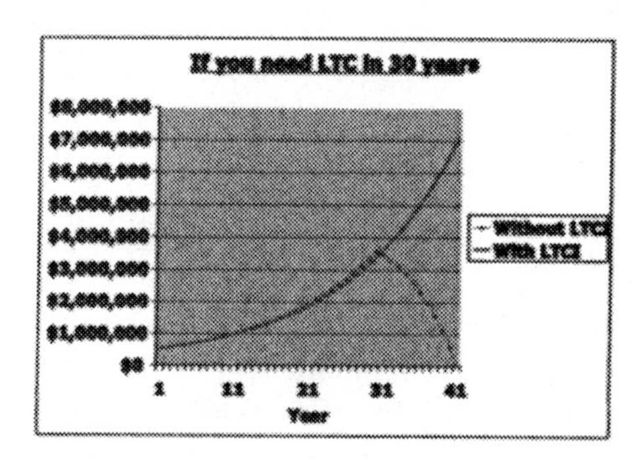

Printed with permission of Henrik Larsen, Advance Resources Marketing, Allston, Massachusetts.

Figure 2 shows the scenario if this person requires long-term care starting in year 10 and pays for it (1) from his investment account or (2) through the insurance policy. The asset would have grown to $919,230 at the end of year 9, but the cost of care would have increased from $80,000 per year now to $122,760 in year 10. By withdrawing from assets, he would run out of money in the 16th year. By using the insurance, the assets would grow to over $7 million.

Figures 3 and 4 illustrate the same scenario except that long-term care begins in year 20 and year 30 as opposed to year 10.

§ 15.6 Who Purchases Long-Term Care Insurance?

The typical purchasers of long term care insurance are couples concerned about the costs of long-term care and how those costs could affect them and their families. They do not want to be dependent on their children, they want to leave an inheritance to their survivors, and they do not ever want to be on Medicaid.

The average age of people purchasing long-term care policies has decreased dramatically in the past few years. The average age of those purchasing partnership long-term care policies in Connecticut in 2001 was 59. The average age will continue to drop as more employers make long-term care insurance available to employees.

Another important factor are the baby boomers. They are now in their 50s; their parents are in their 70s and 80s. The baby boomers themselves are beginning to experience the effect of long-term care costs for their parents and are purchasing coverage for themselves to spare their own children. In some cases, affluent baby boomers are purchasing coverage for their parents.

§ 15.7 The Long-Term Care Insurance Policy

The first question people ask about a long-term care insurance policy is, what does it cost? The answer is, it depends. It depends on a number of factors, including a proposed insured's age and health, the policy choices he or she makes, and optional increases in coverage (riders) that may be added to the basic policy.

Long-term care insurance premiums can be paid annually, semiannually, quarterly, or monthly. Most monthly premiums are paid via automatic deductions from checking accounts or from payroll deduction plans.

Annual premiums are usually the most cost-effective means of paying premiums because companies tend to charge fees when they have to handle premiums more than once a year. Some companies have found, however, that fewer people drop their policies when they have automatic deductions. Therefore, they give discounts for automatic monthly payments.

Premiums vary by age. The younger one is when one takes out a policy, the lower the premium. Premiums are designed to remain level for the lifetime of the policy, but all insurers reserve the right to increase premiums in the future. They cannot raise premiums on an individual's policy; they have to raise premiums on all policies of the same class in the state.

To get a rate increase, the insurance carrier has to petition the insurance department of the state and justify the premium increase it wants. A great deal is involved and it is not an easy process in most states. Companies must prove that their original assumptions were inadequate and that claims beyond their expectations, earnings below their actuarial calculations, or other factors warrant a rate increase.

§ 15.8 Policy Choices

The six basic choices affecting the cost of a comprehensive long-term care insurance policy are: 1. the nursing home maximum daily benefit; 2. the home health care maximum daily benefit; 3. the maximum lifetime benefit; 4. the elimination (waiting) period; 5. the inflation protection option; and 6. the rate classification.

§ 15.8[a] The Nursing Home Maximum Daily Benefit

A prospective client can select a daily benefit from $50 per day to $400 per day with most companies. The decision is usually based on the average cost for nursing home care in the client's home state. Costs vary widely; they are lower in the southern states and highest in the northeast. The average cost in Connecticut in 2001 was $232 per day, or $84,600 per year. The average cost in some southern states is less than half of that amount.

§ 15.8[b] The Home Health Care Maximum Daily Benefit

Most companies offer an insured a choice based on the nursing home benefit chosen. The choices are typically 50 percent, 75 percent, or 100 percent of the nursing home benefit.

§ 15.8[c] The Maximum Lifetime Benefit

This is defined in one of two ways: (1) as a dollar amount or (2) as a number of years. The dollar amount can start at $50,000 and can go as high as $1 million. Defined as a number of years, the benefit typically starts at 2 years and 3-, 4-, 5-, or 6-year benefit periods are offered. In both cases a lifetime (unlimited) benefit period is also available.

§ 15.8[d] The Elimination (Waiting) Period

This is the period of time between the day long-term care services are first provided and the day benefits begin to be paid. It is similar to a deductible. The insured pays up to the period chosen and then the policy takes over the payments. The longer the elimination period, the lower the premium. Clients can choose from 0-, 20-, 30-, 60-, 90-, or 100-day elimination periods. Some states offer 180- and 365-day elimination periods. A number of companies allow insureds to choose one elimination period for nursing home care and another for home health care.

§ 15.8[e] The Inflation Protection Options

The three inflation options typically available are no inflation; five percent simple inflation; and five percent compound inflation.

1. *No inflation.* The maximum daily benefit and the maximum lifetime benefit selected will remain level for the life of the contract. (Some companies offer a guaranteed purchase option every few years whereby an insured can increase coverage without evidence of insurability. Such purchases, however, will be at the insured's then attained age.)
2. *Five percent simple inflation.* The *initial maximum daily benefit* will increase by 5 percent each year.
3. *Five percent compound inflation.* The *maximum daily benefit each year* will be increase by 5 percent, compounded annually.

§ 15.8[f] The Rate Classification

Every insured is placed in a rate class. Rate classes are defined differently from company to company. Preferred Plus (or Preferred) is usually the lowest premium classification. Other common classifications are Standard, Select, or Smoker. An *individual* may be placed in a class based on his or her medical history, the medication currently being taken, and/or whether he or she is a smoker. *Couples* are almost always offered discounts ranging from ten percent to 25 percent, the rationale being that one partner will usually provide services to the other—possibly reducing the insurance company's costs.

§ 15.9 Key Provisions in Long-Term Care Insurance Policies

§ 15.9[a] How To Qualify for Benefits

Most policies being sold today are "tax qualified"; that is, they adhere to standards set by the Federal Government. One of the standards states that to receive benefits an insured must be chronically ill and that there be a written plan of care prepared by a licensed health care practitioner (usually the insured's doctor). These two items are common to all tax-qualified policies. Beyond these, standards may differ from company to company.

A *chronically ill individual* is a person who has been certified, in the twelve months prior to applying for benefits, by a licensed health care practitioner as being unable to perform, without substantial assistance from another individual, at least two of the six activities of daily living (ADLs) for at least 90 days due to a loss of functional capacity, or who requires substantial supervision to protect himself or herself from threats to health and safety due to severe cognitive impairment.

The ADLs are typically bathing, dressing, continence, toileting, transferring, and eating. Benefits will not be paid until the insured requires substantial assistance with at least two of the ADLs. It is always a prudent idea to request an outline of coverage and/or a specimen policy from the agent or the insurance company.

§ 15.10 Care Coordination Services

Most companies, in their required plan of care, require that services be coordinated through licensed agencies that develop, implement, and monitor the plan of care. This requirement can be of great help to families under stress to determine the appropriate level of care and where to get it.

§ 15.11 Methods of Payment

Insurance companies pay benefits via reimbursement or indemnity. Under the reimbursement method, the insurance company pays the provider of services up to the maximum daily benefit for the covered services provided. With indemnity, the insurance company pays the maximum daily benefit to the insured regardless of the cost of the services provided. (Indemnity benefits are sometimes paid directly tothe nursing home rather than to the insured.)

Reimbursement is the more common practice. It relieves families of the burden of tracking expenses and paying bills. Insurance companies favor it because they only pay for actual expenses incurred.

Indemnity does have its place. It allows an insured receiving services to pay immediate family members for their assistance. Many contracts specifically exclude immediate family members from being reimbursed.

§ 15.12 Alternate Plan of Care

Most companies will consider paying for another form of (alternate) care that may not be specifically covered by the policy but could be considered more appropriate for an insured's condition (e.g., alteration of a residence to accommodate a wheelchair or the purchase of special medical equipment are two possibilities). Such alternate care must be agreed upon by the insured, the licensed health care practitioner, and the insurance company before being provided.

§ 15.13 Home Health Care

Most people prefer to remain at home when they need assistance with the activities of daily living and most of the long-term care insurance benefits being paid by insurance companies are for home care. Because home care is usually provided less than seven days per week (often only once or twice a week), it is important to understand how the elimination period integrates with home care and how benefits are calculated—daily, weekly, or monthly.

§ 15.3[a] Elimination Period and Home Health Care

Many insurance companies define the elimination period for home health care as days of service, not calendar days. Therefore, an insured with a 90-

day elimination period receiving services only once a week would not begin receiving benefits under the policy until 90 weeks had passed. Some companies are now applying the elimination period only to nursing home benefits and paying benefits from the first day for home health care.

§ 15.3[b] Daily, Weekly, and Monthly Home Health Care Benefits

A *daily* benefit is that the maximum amount selected that will be paid for a day (e.g., $200). A *weekly* benefit is the daily benefit multiplied by seven (e.g., $1,400). A *monthly* is the daily benefit multiplied by 30 (e.g., $6,000).

If an insured has a maximum daily benefit of $200 and receives care twice a week at a cost of $800 per day ($1,600 per week), the insured would have to pay $600 out of pocket for each day of care ($1,200 per week).

Under the same scenario, the company pays a weekly benefit of $1,400. The insurance company would pay $700 per day ($1,400 per week), and the insured would have to pay $200 out of pocket.

On a monthly basis the company would have $6,000 in benefits available. Therefore, $800 four times a month would be fully covered since it amounts to $3,200.

The way in which companies pay benefits is very important.

As the choice of health care benefits can result in a wide disparity as to the out-of-pocket expenses for which the insured would be responsible, individuals should consult with a long-term care specialist before purchasing a policy.

§ 15.14 Summary

Long-term care insurance is a relatively new product. It was introduced in the mid-1970s and did not really take hold until 1997. Very few legal, financial, and insurance professionals are completely familiar with it. Purchasers should with an elder care attorney and/or insurance professionals certified in long-term care holding the CLTC designation; they are on the cutting edge of this industry.

---

1. National Alliance for Caregiving/AARP (1997), Caregiving in the U.S.: Findings from a National Study, Washington, D.C.

2. Medical Assistance Expenditures as of June 30, 1986; June 30, 1996; and June 30,2001, State of Connecticut, Office of Policy and Management.

3. HR 831, March 1, 2001, introduced by Rep. Nancy Johnson of Connecticcut; S 627, March 27, 2001, introduced by Senator Charles Grassley of Iowa.

4. Proposed Bill No. 5142, Sate of Connecticut General Assembly, introduced by Rep. Googins, 31st District.

INDEX

[*References are to section numbers.*]

G

H

Q

R

Printed in the United States
34980LVS00002B/105

9 781587 982323